Lecture Notes in Computer Science 6837

Commenced Publication in 1973
Founding and Former Series Editors:
Gerhard Goos, Juris Hartmanis, and Jan van Leeuwen

AF856297

Reggie Kwan Joseph Fong
Lam-for Kwok Jeanne Lam (Eds.)

Hybrid Learning

4th International Conference, ICHL 2011
Hong Kong, China, August 10-12, 2011
Proceedings

Springer

Volume Editors

Reggie Kwan
Caritas Institute of Higher Education
18 Chui Ling Road, Tseung Kwan O, Hong Kong, China
E-mail: rkwan@cihe.edu.hk

Joseph Fong
City University of Hong Kong, Department of Computer Science
83 Tat Chee Avenue, Kowloon Tong, Hong Kong, China
E-mail: csjfong@cityu.edu.hk

Lam-for Kwok
City University of Hong Kong, Department of Computer Science
83 Tat Chee Avenue, Kowloon Tong, Hong Kong, China
E-mail: cslfkwok@cityu.edu.hk

Jeanne Lam
The University of Hong Kong, Centre for Cyber Learning
School of Professional and Continuing Education
Hong Kong, China
E-mail: jeanne.lam@hkuspace.hku.hk

ISSN 0302-9743
e-ISSN 1611-3349
ISBN 978-3-642-22762-2
ISBN 978-3-642-22763-9 (eBook)
DOI 10.1007/978-3-642-22763-9
Springer Heidelberg Dordrecht London New York

Library of Congress Control Number: 2011932558

CR Subject Classification (1998): F.1.2, I.2.6, K.3-4, I.6, D.2.2, J.1

LNCS Sublibrary: SL 1 – Theoretical Computer Science and General Issues

Typesetting: Camera-ready by author, data conversion by Scientific Publishing Services, Chennai, India

Printed on acid-free paper

Springer is part of Springer Science+Business Media (www.springer.com)

Preface

Welcome to the 4th International Conference on Hybrid Learning (ICHL 2011). After spending ICHL 2010 at the Beijing Normal University and ICHL 2009 at University of Macau, we are back to Hong Kong with our new host, The University of Hong Kong's School of Professional and Continuing Education (HKU SPACE).

"Hybrid learning" is undoubtedly the new frontier in education as neither virtual nor physical resources alone can provide the best teaching and learning environment. Technology is finally advanced enough that information or learning materials can be accessed immediately anywhere and anytime. Hybrid learning provides a great way forward for educators who are interested in helping students to learn without blindly using of technology for technology's sake. We could ultimately create learning experiences to compensate for the shortcomings of, or at least to complement, conventional face-to-face teaching. We are thrilled that it has become mainstream and many models with educational underpinnings have emerged.

Many parties made ICHL 2011 a success. We would like to take this opportunity to thank: (a) the Organizing Committee; (b) the Program Committee; (c) the organizers; (d) all participants; (e) sponsors; and (f) all supporters.

August 2011

Reggie Kwan
Joseph Fong
Lam-for Kwok
Jeanne Lam

Organization

Organizing Committee

Honorary Chairs	Reggie Kwan (Caritas Institute of Higher Education) Enoch Young (The University of Hong Kong) Bebo White (Stanford University)
Conference Chairs	Philip Tsang (Caritas Institute of Higher Education) Joseph Fong (City University of Hong Kong) Jeanne Lam (The University of Hong Kong)
Program Chairs	Philips F.L. Wang (Caritas Institute of Higher Education) Simon K.S. Cheung (The Open University of Hong Kong)
Organization Chair	Janny Ng (The University of Hong Kong)
Financial Chair	Titus Lo (Caritas Institute of Higher Education) L.F. Kwok (City University of Hong Kong)
Local Arrangements Chair	Kennis Yan (The University of Hong Kong)
Registration Chair	Jonathan Diu (The Chinese University of Hong Kong)
Publication Chair	Siu Cheung Kong (The Hong Kong Institute of Education)
Publicity Chair	Norris Lau (The University of Hong Kong)
Academic Liaison Chairs	Will W. K. Ma (Hong Kong Shue Yan University)
Activities Chairs	Oliver Au (The Open University of Hong Kong) Kenneth Wong (Caritas Institute of Higher Education)

Steering Committee

Joseph Fong	City University of Hong Kong
Victor Lee	Chinese University of Hong Kong
Reggie Kwan	Caritas Institute of Higher Education
Ronghuai Huang	Beijing Normal University
Liming Zhang	University of Macau

International Program Committee

Oliver Au	The Open University of Hong Kong, Hong Kong, China
Vic Callaghan	Essex University, UK
F.T. Chan	HKU School of Professional and Continuing Education, Hong Kong, China
Kan-Kan Chan	University of Macau, Macau, China
Keith Chan	The Hong Kong Polytechnic University, Hong Kong, China
Simon Cheung	The Open University of Hong Kong, Hong Kong, China
S.L. Chung	The Open University of Hong Kong, Hong Kong, China
GiulianaDettori	Istituto di Tecnologie Didattiche del CNR, Italy
Cheng-GuiDuan	HKU School of Professional and Continuing Education, Hong Kong, China
Peter Duffy	The Hong Kong Polytechnic University, Hong Kong, China
Joseph Fong	City University of Hong Kong, Hong Kong, China
Bob Fox	The University of Hong Kong, Hong Kong, China
Wenge Guo	Peking University, China
Wolfgang Halang	Fernuniversität Hagen, Germany
Owen Hall Jr.	Pepperdine University, USA
Raquel Hijon	Universidad Rey Juan Carlos, Spain
Cordula Hunold	Goethe-Institut Peking, China
Jianjun Hou	Peking University, China
Le Jun	Guangdong Radio and TV University, China
Alexander Kling	Goethe-Institut Peking, China
Frances Kling	Goethe-Institut Peking, China
Siu-Cheung Kong	The Hong Kong Institute of Education, Hong Kong, China
Jeanne Lam	HKU School of Professional and Continuing Education, Hong Kong, China
Rebecca Launer	Goethe-Insitut Germany, Germany
John Lee	The Hong Kong Polytechnic University, Hong Kong, China
Yan Li	Zhejiang University, China
Yanyan Li	Beijing Normal University, China

Yi Li	Nanjing University, China
Will Ma	Hong Kong Shue Yan University, Hong Kong, China
Dennis Mcleod	University of Southern California, USA
Diana Perez-Marin	Universidad Rey Juan Carlos, Spain
Junjie Shang	Peking University, China
Stefanie Sieber	University of Bamberg, Germany
Liana Stanescu	University of Craiova, Romania
Stefanie Trausan-Matu	University of Bucharest, Romania
Minjuan Wang	San Diego State University, USA
Philips F.L. Wang	Caritas Institute of Higher Education, Hong Kong, China
Harrison Yang	State University of New York, USA
W.L. Yeung	Lingnan University, Hong Kong, China
K.S. Yuen	The Open University of Hong Kong, Hong Kong, China
Jiping Zhang	East China Normal University, China
Liming Zhang	University of Macau, Macau, China

Organizers

School of Professional and Continuing Education, The University of Hong Kong

City University of Hong Kong

Caritas Institute of Higher Education

The Hong Kong Institute of Education

School of Continuing and Professional Studies, The Chinese University of Hong Kong

Sponsors

International Hybrid Learning Society

The Open University of Hong Kong

Caritas Bianchi College of Careers

Hong Kong Pei Hua Education Foundation

K.C. Wong Education Foundation

Table of Contents

Keynote

Practices in Borderless Education

Pedagogical Issues and Practice

Organizational Frameworks for Hybrid Learning

Experiences in Hybrid Learning

Computer Supported Collaborative Learning

Interactive Hybrid Learning Systems

The Best of Both Worlds: Effective Hybrid Learning Designs in Higher Education in Hong Kong

Carmel McNaught

Director and Professor of Learning Enhancement
Centre for Learning Enhancement And Research (CLEAR)
The Chinese University of Hong Kong
carmel.mcnaught@cuhk.edu.hk
http://www.cuhk.edu.hk/clear/people/Carmel.html

Abstract. Higher education in Hong Kong is undergoing significant changes with the advent of a normative four-year undergraduate curriculum in 2012. The change from a three-year to a four-year curriculum has been made in order to assist students develop a broad set of capabilities. There is therefore an emphasis on designing learning environments that facilitate capability development as well as traditional knowledge acquisition. In Hong Kong there are a number of barriers to the development of effective hybrid learning designs that will be discussed. However, good examples exist and this paper will comment on a number of initiatives occurring in Hong Kong universities where learning technologies have been integrated into face-to-face teaching contexts in ways that facilitate desired student learning outcomes; the examples chosen will focus on the use of English language, a key area of learning need in Hong Kong.

1 Background and Context

The University Grants Committee (UGC) of Hong Kong is responsible for advising the Government of Hong Kong on the development and funding needs of higher-education institutions (HEIs) in Hong Kong. There are eight UGC-funded HEIs, seven of which have university status [1]. Higher education in Hong Kong is undergoing significant changes with the advent of a normative four-year undergraduate curriculum in 2012. The change from a three-year to a four-year curriculum has been made in order to assist students develop a broad set of capabilities. The extra year is for broadening; the curriculum components that have been added are language, General Education, experiential learning, capstones, etc. This new university curriculum will be the culmination of the educational reform throughput when the first graduates from the new Secondary 6 curriculum reach Hong Kong's university system [2]. A detailed account of the Hong Kong education-reform movement, with a focus on higher education, is in [3].

Outcomes-based approaches (OBAs) to teaching and learning (T&L) have received increasing attention in Hong Kong since 2005 when the UGC announced that OBA would be the 'new' direction for higher education in Hong Kong.

R. Kwan et al. (Eds.): ICHL 2011, LNCS 6837, pp. 1–9, 2011.

There are two contrasting views as to what constitutes learning and what appropriate learning outcomes might be. There are academic teachers who think of learning as reproducing knowledge and others who think of learning as a process in which understanding is constructed by the student with the assistance of the teacher (e.g. [4]). Among academics in the field of education, this is often called the instructivist/ constructivist paradigmatic divide. How well do these two different approaches to learning serve the purpose of education, especially if we take a lifelong view of learning? What are those essential skills and capacities that students ought to be developing in the course of their education in the 21st century? Having to cope with an uncertain future that calls for flexibility, adaptability and sound intellectual capabilities. It has been argued that 'directed instruction' may be useful in many specific situations but our ultimate goals in education are 'constructivist' [5].

Hong Kong universities are elite institutions; only about 18% of school-leavers can gain a university place. The school system, despite the current reforms, is still examination-dominated and competitive. Educational practice is conservative with respect to the use of technology for T&L. In both schools and universities, we have examples of innovative and educationally effective uses of technology but the mainstream use is in an adjunct mode which is information-based. Acceptance of educational innovations is often uncertain, particularly in Hong Kong, where issues of face [6] ensure a generally polite but risk-adverse society. For example, evidence from eLearning activity logs of the Learning Management Systems at CUHK indicates that the majority of eLearning activities used at CUHK are information-based [7]; this study contrasted two sets of log data from two consecutive academic years (2007–2008 versus 2008–2009). Results revealed an increase in the adoption of simple eLearning strategies (such as uploading notes and PowerPoints) but the adoption of complex strategies which encouraged interactions among students (such as structured forums, online role plays, quizzes, progressive case analyses) actually decreased over the two years. Even teachers who have adopted Web 2.0 and social-media technologies in their T&L have concerns about being adequately rewarded and supported in their attempts at innovation [8]. Further, in Hong Kong, many teachers are reluctant to become engaged in creating and sharing learning objects with others [9].

2 Hybrid Learning Designs

There are several terms used for the combination of technology-based learning activities with face-to-face ones. In this paper 'blended' or 'hybrid' learning designs will be used to designate a *purposeful* design for a unit of student work – which could vary in size from a single lesson to a module or course to an entire programme – where learning technologies are used for *separate* aspects of students' designed activities to those designed for face-to-face activities which do not involve technology. In other words, in a hybrid design, the technology component is not a duplication of what occurs in conventional classes; it is an integral part of the students' learning experience, and engagement in the technology-supported activities are needed in order for students to gain most from the unit of work.

Often, the term 'hybrid learning' is used for any combination of technology-based and face-to-face learning activities, for example, supplying additional notes to supplement class teaching. The use of the web for such adjunct purposes is now almost ubiquitous and is not considered to be hybrid learning in this paper. Students often ask for notes and PowerPoints slides to be uploaded on course websites (see for example a meta-analysis across 70 eLearning projects in Hong Kong [10]). Students' requests for more digital information is partly due to the heavy information-oriented examination system they have grown accustomed to and partly to a shrewd assessment that, even in a university system that seeks to support deeper learning, the 'quick fix' still works. However, our evidence in Hong Kong universities is that students understand that interactions that lead to constructive dialogue are more beneficial to learning than being provided with access to information alone. They are aware of what digital experiences are most conducive to effective learning [11]. Students appreciate the diversity of the functionality of technology but are cautious about changing old habits, especially if this might impact on their grades. However, interestingly, the more experience students have with eLearning, the more positive they appear to be towards the use of technology for learning [12, 13].

The technology component in a hybrid learning design need not be large. But it does need to be considered by the teacher as an essential part of students' learning experience. One example that might make this clear is the use of audience-response systems or 'clickers'. These systems have been used in several disciplines in many countries (e.g. [14, 15]) with usually positive results. Our own experience in the Faculty of Science at The Chinese University of Hong Kong (CUHK) has been positive and enabled passive large lectures to have interactive and interesting sections [16]. It is a minor component of course design but is a genuine example of a hybrid learning design.

So, the setting for the examples in this paper is an elite, conservative higher-education system where face-to-face teaching is predominant, and where there is a minority of innovators who engage in hybrid learning.

2.1 Teachers' Intentions in Hybrid Learning Designs

In a recent study of learning design, 20 teachers in a number of universities in Hong Kong, who used web-based technology in ways that fit our definition of what constitutes a hybrid learning design, participated. All of the teachers achieved good assessment outcomes and all were rated highly by their students as being effective teachers. The four-category classification of learning designs framed by an Australian team [17, 18] was adapted as shown in Tab.1.

An expert review of all 20 learning designs was conducted using interviews and examination of the course websites [19]; 78 instances of learning activities that appeared to be integral to the learning design of the course were recorded across the 20 cases. However, of these 78 instances, 51 were rule-based, 7 were incident-based, 13 were strategy-based and 7 were role-based. Even with these effective teachers, there is still limited use of highly immersive learning designs where students experience and explore authentic professional situations and problems. As noted above, this is not surprising in our context.

Table 1. Learning design intentions (adapted from [19])

Design intention	Description
Rule focus	The web is intended to enhance the teaching and explanation of knowledge and concepts.
Incident focus	The web is intended to display well-defined real cases and scenarios. Discussion is on the incident and understanding its context.
Strategy focus	The web is intended to support students in learning how to handle ill-defined realistic problems, cases and scenarios in the field of study. Discussion is on appropriateness of treatment, and/or alternative treatments. Here, the focus is on the development of useful learning processes.
Role focus	The web is intended to support students in playing the role of a professional in the field of study. Discussion relates to ill-defined real cases and scenarios in the field, and the different strategies used in different professional roles. A strong focus on immersion in authentic real-life situations.

3 English Language: A Key Area of Learning Need in Hong Kong

In Hong Kong in 2005 there was a report on medium of instruction for secondary schools [20]. The existence of a predominance of Chinese-medium instruction was confirmed, with an acknowledgement that English-medium secondary schools should be provided to allow diversity of choice for families. In practice, the English-medium secondary schools form an important elite group in Hong Kong education. Hong Kong has a banded system for secondary schools: Bands 1 to 3 with Band 1 being the most prestigious and most academic. All English-medium secondary schools in Hong Kong are in Band 1. There are, of course, also some highly prestigious Chinese-medium secondary schools. The allocation of places for secondary schools has long been a fraught process and, while measures have been taken to improve equity and fairness, basically the same processes continue. The competition for places in certain schools is fierce and the stress on students and their families is problematic. Language has, unfortunately, become a divisive selection strategy and all discussions about language in education in Hong Kong have socio-political overtones.

The medium-of-instruction policy in schools has had a dramatic follow-on effect in HEIs. All universities, except CUHK, claim to be English-medium. However, in reality, all are bilingual and the standard of English in Hong Kong is widely noted to be a significant educational challenge [21]. With this in mind, it is not surprising that motivating and engaging students is a pre-requisite for improving language skills.

The following four sections explore four examples of hybrid learning designs to support students' English-language skills.

3.1 Use of Mobile Learning in English Courses

SMS (short message service) has been use quite widely in educational institutions. The majority of the uses, however, are for administrative issues rather than for T&L. In Hong Kong, SMS is a robust, reliable and secure system. Messages are nearly always sent to the targeted recipients; safe and accurate delivery of messages can be assumed. As SMS is technologically and functionally very simple and is congruent with the principle that successful uptake of learning strategies is more likely in the situation when "learning activities can integrate into our lives in an unobtrusive fashion" [22:13].

In an effective hybrid learning design, students at CUHK were sent simple but interesting conversation questions each lunch-time during the semester [23]. The messages were timed to arrive when students were likely to be gathered in groups for lunch. Students did not need to reply and so did not incur any cost; the questions were just triggers for discussion, though follow-up discussions happened in class. The evaluation of this strategy was that it was fun and engaging, and did actually mean that students spoke English, albeit for a short time, outside class. Simple hybrid learning designs can be effective.

3.2 Use of ePortfolios in English Teaching

In Hong Kong there is a growing use of ePortfolios to support cumulative reflection and enhancement of language skills. In one ongoing project on English language learning at Lingnan University (a liberal arts university) in Hong Kong considerable resources have been committed to changing the course design using an OBA, and trialing of the ePortfolio Mahara, followed by full implementation of the system for all first-year undergraduate students and their English teachers [24]. The 18-month initiative was monitored by two surveys and a number of focus groups; outcomes point to a complex relationship between pedagogy, staff development and student expectations. While the project has had some degree of success thus far, there were both positive and negative impacts on student learning and motivation. Teachers who were confident with the technical aspects of the ePortfolio believed that the system saved them time and work, and were enthusiastic about the system with their students. However, about 50% of the student cohort reported not seeing any particular educational benefit and regarded the exercises with Mahara as an undesirable chore; they particularly complained about being asked to self-study. While there is no correlational evidence at this point in time between the teachers' and students' attitudes, the project does exemplify that hybrid learning designs using unfamiliar technology require careful induction of both teachers and students.

3.4 Use of Forums for Assessment Activities

One main consequence of the OBA 'movement' in Hong Kong has been a great deal of attention on assessment strategies. Diversity in assessment strategies is growing; articulation of learning outcomes is now a routine part of programme and course design, and alignment between these learning outcomes and assessment is built into both policy and practice in Hong Kong universities. However, the 'missing link' in the chain is that eLearning has not been built into the programme and course design process and is seen as an after-thought, largely for administrative convenience [25].

However, there are some notable exceptions. A few years ago, the eLearning research team at CUHK carried out a study of 13 online discussion forums (involving 1280 students) where, in each case, the forum was a key component of the course and teachers expected students to contribute. The courses involved in the study were in a number of universities in Hong Kong and ranged across a wide number of discipline areas [26]. The forums were classified into structured (usually involving an assessment component) or free (though course-related and not social in nature); and teacher-centred or student-centred according to the learning designs used to prepare the tasks and the style of online interactions. Evaluation data came from surveys, focus groups and an analysis of the quality of the responses posted in each forum using the SOLO Taxonomy [27, 28]. Findings are that structured forums generally have a higher quantity and quality of postings than free forums, and that student-centred ones also tend to be more effective than teacher-centred ones in encouraging quality online discussion. Further, the study identified three key factors that tend to affect forum success – ease of use, clear facilitation and motivation to engage. The facilitative role of the teacher was confirmed.

However, in another similar study of eight active forums [29] where students participated quite actively in the forums and contributed substantive ideas, the analysis did not indicate that these positive learning outcomes were correlated with the course level, course subject area, class size, forum nature, or degree of teachers' participation in the forum, suggesting that asynchronous online discussion might be a useful tool for various T&L styles and for various course designs.

These studies provided empirical data across multiple online forum experiences to better inform the pedagogy of using online forums. Indeed, our top-ten list for effective forums was based largely on these studies [30]. As newer technologies emerge, there is no need to discard well-tested and robust existing technologies.

3.5 Use of Social Media for Student Production of Learning Artefacts

The final example to be noted is the relatively recent use of social media in universities in Hong Kong. As noted early, teachers in Hong Kong are risk-averse and strategies that might be adopted elsewhere are not necessarily popular here [31]. In a recent study of 13 teachers who developed hybrid learning designs involving social media, six of the designs involved students in the production of learning artefacts, and five of the teachers in these courses were interviewed; (other designs involved teacher-generated resources or the use of existing social media as T&L resources) [8]. In line with the comments about constructivism earlier in the paper, it is particularly interesting to see if the new media really can support the development of important skills and capabilities, especially an orientation for independent learning and the ability to use language to describe one's own learning.

While this is a very small sample, it was clear to the research team that the teachers who involved student production in their learning designs appeared to be more satisfied with the potential of social media than teachers who invested a great deal of time themselves in sourcing and developing social-media artefacts. We do not have evaluation evidence on student learning outcomes at this stage, and this is clearly an important emerging area of research in hybrid learning designs.

4 The Future for Hybrid Learning Designs in Hong Kong

In Hong Kong we can find many examples of excellent practice in hybrid learning designs but the 'mainstream majority' [32] is yet to be attained. There are two main challenges facing hybrid learning in Hong Kong. One is the loose terminology surround the whole area of learning design. Hybrid learning does not occur just because a course has an adjunct website. I took care to emphasize the synergy and mutual reinforcement that exists between the immediacy and normal comfort of face-to-face interactions and the affordances that technology can provide. In the centre of Fig. 1 there is a model for curriculum alignment [33] that is actually part of the documents for CUHK's T&L policy and eLearning Strategy. Around the normal elements of curriculum are the affordances the technology can provide when designing learning environments. Appropriate hybrid learning designs will evolve as it becomes normal practice to ask the question "In what way can technology add to students' learning experience in this unit of work?" Good hybrid learning designs evolve when technology is seen as a normal and very useful set of tools that is part of course and programme design right from the outset.

The other challenge relates to the cautiousness of Hong Kong teachers. More than in other cultures, teachers need incentives in order to be prepared to try something new, to take a step into the unknown. At CUHK, we are revising our personnel policies and developing guidelines to assist teachers in articulating a teaching portfolio. Teachers need to be rewarded for the work they do in developing and implementing learning designs.

One very positive factor is that teachers in Hong Kong take teaching very seriously. They care about their students and set high standards in many aspects of teaching. We may not yet have achieved the majority of teachers understanding and appreciating the nuances of the potentials of hybrid learning, but we have made some good progress.

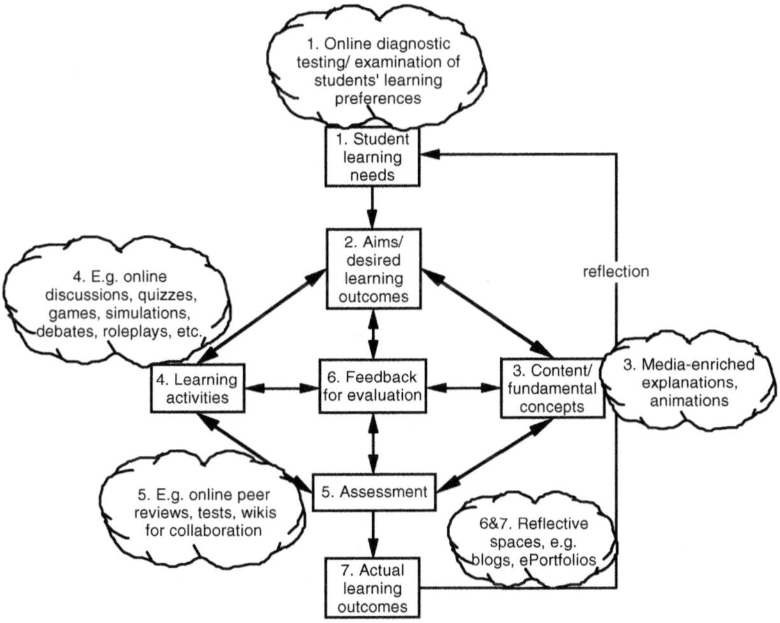

Fig. 1. Affordances of technology that can be used in hybrid learning designs

References

1. UGC-funded Institutions,
http://www.ugc.edu.hk/eng/ugc/site/fund_inst.htm
2. UGC "3+3+4" Group,
http://www.ugc.edu.hk/eng/ugc/about/term/334g.htm
3. McNaught, C.: The Role of Educational Technology in Educational Reform in Hong Kong: A Focus on the Higher-education Sector. In: Proceedings of 2011 KSET International Conference, pp. 176–190. Korea Society of Educational Technology, Seoul (2011)
4. Trigwell, K., Prosser, M., Taylor, P.: Qualitative Differences in Approaches to Teaching First Year University Science. Higher Education 27, 75–84 (1994)
5. McNaught, C., Storey, C., Leung, S.: Embedding Information Literacy into the Curriculum: A Case Study of Existing Practice and Future Possibilities at a Hong Kong University. Journal of Library and Information Science 30(1), 5–13 (2004)
6. Bond, M.H.: Beyond the Chinese Face. Insights from Psychology. Oxford University Press, Oxford (1991)
7. Lam, P., Lo, J., Yeung, A., McNaught, C.: Examining Diffusion and Sustainability of E-learning Strategies through Weblog Data. International Journal of E-Adoption 2(3), 39–52 (2010)
8. McNaught, C., Lam, P., Kwok, M., Ho, E.: Building Institutional Capacity for the Use of Social Media. In: White, B., King, I., Tsang, P. (eds.) Social-media Tools and Platforms in Learning Environments: Present and Future. Springer, Dordrecht (in press)
9. McNaught, C., Lam, P., Cheng, K.-F., Kennedy, D.M., Mohan, J.B.: Challenges in Employing Complex ELearning Strategies in Campus-based Universities. International Journal of Technology Enhanced Learning 1(4), 266–285 (2009)
10. Lam, P., McNaught, C., Cheng, K.-F.: Pragmatic Meta-analytic Studies: Learning the Lessons from Naturalistic Evaluations of Multiple Cases. ALT-J 16(2), 61–79 (2008)
11. Kember, D., McNaught, C., Chong, F.C.Y., Lam, P., Cheng, K.F.: Understanding the Ways in which Design Features of Educational Websites Impact upon Student Learning Outcomes in Blended Learning Environments. Computers & Education 55, 1183–1192 (2010)
12. Lam, P., Lee, J., Chan, M., McNaught, C.: ELearning Needs among Students who Lead a Digital Life in Nearly Every Aspect Except Learning. In: Cordeiro, J., Shishkov, B., Verbraeck, A., Helfert, M. (eds.) 2nd International Conference on Computer Supported Education, CSEDU 2010, pp. 268–275. Valencia, Spain (2010)
13. Lam, P., Lee, J., Chan, M., McNaught, C.: Students' Use of ELearning Strategies and Their Perceptions of ELearning Usefulness. In: Barton, S.-M., Hedberg, J., Suzuki, K. (eds.) Global Learn Asia Pacific 2011, pp. 1379–1388. AACE, Chesapeake (2011)
14. Caldwell, J.E.: Clickers in the Large Classroom: Current Research and Best-practice Tips. Life Sciences Education 6(1), 9–20 (2007)
15. Carnaghan, C., Webb, A.: Investigating the Effects of Group Response Systems on Student Satisfaction, Learning and Engagement in Accounting Education. Issues in Accounting Education 22(3), 391–409 (2007)
16. Centre for Promoting Science Education, Faculty of Science, The Chinese University of Hong Kong.: Using Clickers to Enhance Teaching and Learning: Pilot Case Studies in Science Programmes, http://www.cuhk.edu.hk/sci/clicker/
17. Oliver, R., Harper, B., Hedberg, J., Wills, S., Agostinho, S.: Formalising the Description of Learning Designs. In: Goody, A., Herrington, J., Northcote, M. (eds.) Annual International Conference of the Higher Education Research and Development Society of Australasia, HERDSA, vol. 25, pp. 496–504. ACT, Jamison (2002)

18. Agostinho, S., Bennett, S., Lockyer, L., Harper, B.: Developing a Learning Object Metadata Application Profile Based on LOM Suitable for the Australian Higher Education Context. Australasian Journal of Educational Technology 20(2), 191–208 (2004)
19. McNaught, C., Lam, P., Cheng, K.F.: Using Expert Reviews to Enhance Learning Designs. In: Lockyer, L., Bennett, S., Agostinho, S., Harper, B. (eds.) Handbook of Research on Learning Design and Learning Objects: Issues, Applications and Technologies, pp. 243–262. Information Science Publishing, Hershey (2009)
20. Hong Kong Education and Manpower Bureau: Medium of Instruction for Secondary Schools and Secondary School places Allocation (2005), http://www.edb.gov.hk/FileManager/En/Content_1914/moisspa%20booklet%20dec%202005_eng.pdf
21. Braine, G., McNaught, C.: Adaptation of the 'Writing Across Curriculum' Model to the Hong Kong Context. In: Liu, J. (ed.) English Language Teaching in China: New Approaches, Perspectives and Standards, pp. 311–328. Continuum International Publishing Ltd., London (2007)
22. Lee, M.J.W.: Getting a Move on with Mobile Learning. Training and Development in Australia 32(4), 8–13 (2005)
23. Clarke, P., Keing, C., Lam, P., McNaught, C.: Using SMSs to Engage Students in Language Learning. In: Weippl, E.R., Luca, J. (eds.) ED-MEDIA 2008, pp. 6132–6141. AACE, Chesapeake (2008)
24. Kennedy, D.M., Shirley, C.: Innovative Curriculum Design: Using EPortfolios to Change Practice and Process. In: Barton, S.-M., Hedberg, J., Suzuki, K. (eds.) Global Learn Asia Pacific 2011, pp. 409–416. AACE, Chesapeake (2011)
25. McNaught, C.: Tensions in Student Preferences for E-learning. University World News 161 (2011), http://www.universityworldnews.com/article.php?story=20110305091334889
26. McNaught, C., Cheng, K.F., Lam, P.: Developing Evidence-based Criteria for the Design and Use of Online Forums in Higher Education in Hong Kong. In: Lambropoulos, N., Zaphiris, P. (eds.) User-centered Design of Online Learning Communities, pp. 161–184. Idea Group Inc., Hershey (2006)
27. Biggs, J.: What the Student Does: Teaching for Enhanced Learning. Higher Education Research & Development 18(1), 57–75 (1999)
28. Biggs, J.B., Collis, K.F.: Evaluating the Quality of Learning: The SOLO Taxonomy (Structure of the Observed Learning Outcome). Academic Press, New York (1982)
29. Lam, P., Cheng, K.F., McNaught, C.: Asynchronous Online Discussion: Empirical Evidence on Quantity and Quality. In: Richards, G., Kommers, P. (eds.) ED-MEDIA 2005, pp. 3209–3215. AACE, Norfolk (2005)
30. ELearning Service, The Chinese University of Hong Kong. 10 Things to Do to Populate your Course Forums, http://www.cuhk.edu.hk/eLearning/resources/topten.htm#102
31. McNaught, C., Lam, P., Chan, E., Yuen, S., Ho, E.: The Challenges of Innovation: A Case Study with Implementing a Lecture-recording System in a University in Hong Kong. Journal of the NUS Teaching Academy (JNUSTA) (in press)
32. Rogers, E.M.: Diffusion of Innovations, 5th edn. Free Press, New York (2003)
33. Biggs, J.B.: Teaching for Quality Learning at University: What the Student Does, 2nd edn. Society for Research into Higher Education, and Open University Press, Buckingham, UK (2003)

Communicating across Cultures in the Classroom Using an Online 3D Virtual World

Theodor Wyeld

Flinders University, Australia
theodor.wyeld@flinders.edu.au

Abstract. The Information and Communication Technology (ICT) industry is inherently a global industry. As such, it requires workers to collaborate across timezones and different cultures. There is little scope for undergraduates of ICT to directly experience this sort of cross-cultural environment whilst studying. The project outlined in this paper describes the need to introduce students to cross-cultural experiences in a work environment and how this was achieved using an online collaborative 3D virtual world. Students from 3 geographically distant institutions collaborated in the online construction of a 3D Tower of Babel. How they went about this and their inventive methods for overcoming cross-cultural communication difficulties is discussed. This paper forms the basis for a keynote talk at ICHL2011.

Keywords: cross-culture, 3D virtual world, online collaboration.

1 Introduction

Information and Communication Technology (ICT) graduates need to be ready to work in collaborative, multicultural, international teams. This requires cross-cultural understandings with their co-collaborators exposing them to different approaches to the same task. It is difficult to simulate this in the classroom. This paper discusses a case study of a remote collaboration project with ICT students across three continents, timezones, and cultures. The remote collaboration project was conducted using a suite of tools, central of which was a 3D virtual world – ActiveWorlds. The benefits of this project were that students could work in teams collaborating across time zones on a single project complimenting each other's skills and learning about new ways to work and learn in a global environment. This fostered deep understandings of alternative meanings to everyday occurrences and work practices. The project involved students across three cooperating institutions: The University of Queensland (Australia); the National Yunlin University of Science and Technology (Taiwan); and, the Norwegian University of Science and Technology Trondheim (Norway). It builds on previous exercises conducted by the author (see Wyeld et al, 2005 - 2010). The cross-cultural understandings engendered by this project demonstrate the validity of the tools and teaching methods used [1].

R. Kwan et al. (Eds.): ICHL 2011, LNCS 6837, pp. 10–16, 2011.

2 Cross-Cultural Exchange in the Classroom

While being open to cultural difference (recognising, tolerating, adapting to and/or adopting an alternative cultural practice) is increasingly a necessary core attribute for ICT graduates it is seldom addressed in any depth, let alone actively practiced, in the classroom. Hence, when setting up cross-cultural exercises the teacher cannot assume students will receive it with the same enthusiasm they may do for other types of exercises. Indeed, students' pre-existing cultural practices can play a large role in how explicit cross-cultural exercises are received by students in the classroom environment. Therefore, to achieve the goal of cross-cultural learning the diversity of learners and their ways of learning needs to be accommodated. This can be achieved by employing 'strategies and techniques to facilitate, optimise and ensure equal participation and achievement of learning outcomes for all students' [2].

Achieving desired learning outcomes for students involves a process in which knowledge is created through transformative experiences. These transformative experiences can occur when working with technology and the ways it supports (or does not support) cross-cultural exchanges [3, 4]. Hence, for students to experience transformative experiences by collaborative learning in a multicultural team environment, a process of acculturation to new ways of knowing the 'other' needs to be facilitated. Through this process, students will become part of a knowledge community which they create through their cultural exchanges [5]. But, for this to be effective teachers have to act as learning facilitators rather than simply content providers. This is achieved by creating a meaningful real-world learning experience. In the context of a cross-cultural collaboration project, this means a project with real collaborators across different time zones and on different continents.

A meaningful real-world learning experience helps motivate students to engage in their own learning. A key factor in this motivation is the addressing of explicit and implicit meaning in the tasks they are undertaking [6]. Meaning in their work includes: meaningfulness of directions; relevance of learning tasks; and, level and comprehensibility of learning tasks [7]. For example, many students do not know how to recognise their own cross-cultural understandings. This needs to be made explicit. Differences in first language is an obvious cross-cultural difficulty students need to overcome. This affects their styles of communication.

In most collaborative activities, activity is directed towards a tool which is mediated by cultural artefacts – tokens of exchange: text, sketches, models etc – and socialised within a culture of practice [8, 9, 10]. Called 'work activity' in the field of Computer Supported Cooperative Work (CSCW), it is often used as the basic unit for analysing a cooperative work situation [11]. Hence, what constitutes a work activity needs to be understood in order to design efficient cooperative technologies [10].

Community is a central component of work activities. In an educational context, this community is a learning community. A learning community can be thought of as a community of practice where a shared history of learning occurs. In this learning community, students will experience a number of phases of development: belonging, control, and interdependence [12]. They experience this as they move along learning and participation trajectories. In order to perform activities and proceed through the phases successfully, and to negotiate roles and division of labour, it is crucial to provide effective group communication. Communication structures within the group are important as indicators of the group's power structure [13]. The students in this project demonstrated each of these phases and group structures.

3 The Project

In 2006 a group of 99 students from three different universities – Australia, Norway, and Taiwan – worked collaboratively on the construction of a virtual *Tower of Babel* in the 3D ActiveWorlds (AWs) programme. Based on the *Tower of Babel* parable, a series of complex social interactions were observed.

There were 9 groups of 11 students each (6 Australian, 4 Norwegian and 1 Taiwanese). Each group of 6 Multi-Media Technology students from the University of Queensland (Australia) collaborated with at least 1 Master of Computational Design student from the National Yuntech University of Science and Technology (Taiwan) and 4 Computer Science students from NTNU (Norway) in the online 3D ActiveWorlds virtual world.

Student groups were required to collaborate on construction of a *Tower of Babel.* This involved the manipulation of building blocks, managed through the simple 3D ActiveWorlds interface and all communications necessary for its design. A number of practice constructions preceded the final construction. In the final online building performance, towers were constructed from scratch in a one hour time limit per group (3 groups constructed at the same time, hence total time for all groups was 3 hours).

Each group included a team leader allocated by the lecturer. Initial contact with international group members was by email. This initial contact was used to organise times for all team members to be available online to discuss organisational issues such as tower designs, task allocation, and practice building. Explicit tasks were allocated to Australian, Norwegian and Taiwanese members by the teachers. Norwegian team members were allocated the task of choosing 20 different building blocks to use in the final tower design. Australian team members were required to direct the building of towers using the allocated blocks. Taiwanese students added animated content banners to the towers. While group leaders were assigned by the teachers, all other decisions were the domain of the individual groups to negotiate amongst themselves.

4 Modes of Communication

The different modes of communication the students chose highlights their inventive methods for communicating with each other: face-to-face, online chat, email, MSN, sketches, blog, ActiveWorlds, and videoconference. They used these to overcome language and technical barriers to share information. Working with cultural difference, they used these methods in dealing with participants who had English as a second language (ESL). They used different approaches to the same task, shared skills, and in so doing, overcame much of their social shyness due to cultural differences. However, various difficulties in communicating particular concepts could be identified. One way of overcoming communicating difficult concepts was the use of a basic computer programming language. This was due to its rigid syntax, regardless of the author's native language.

At a local level, team members walked over to each others' screens and made suggestions face-to-face. Their verbal communication in the lab allowed them to sort out problems without the restriction of a chat interface. The nuances of face-to-face communication allowed for tacit understandings (in [14] terms) not supported by chat alone. But, this form of communication also meant that their remote partners were not always informed of what was being communicated. Hence, the more salient points in their verbal conversations was communicated via text (in the AWs chat window, online chat, MSN etc). Email communication was also used. As an asynchronous information exchange platform it overcame the time difference between the different country time-zones. While initial contact was instigated by the various group leaders, all participants were required to exchange project information with at least one remote partner. Account names and arranged times (in each time zone) were often exchanged by email for setting up MSN chat conferences. MSN proved to be an effective medium for information exchanging, socialising, and project management. Conferences in MSN included representatives from each country at the same time allowing decision-making to proceed without the delays involved in email exchange alone. When online at the same time, despite time-zone differences, participants took the opportunity to 'bulk' communicate to achieve quick responses and results using MSN for chat and email to transfer files. A blog was set up. Sketches of proposed tower designs were exchanged. In the AWs environment itself the need to communicate textually was lessened by the visual stimulus and the ability to see the other's actions in real-time. The AWs environment was often visited at random times by most participants. In turn, this meant that participants came to rely on serendipitous meetings in the AWs environment when other forms of communication (email, MSN) were not eliciting the desired response. Those students who successfully made videoconference contact reported this as also a very worthwhile component of the exercise. As an ice-breaking exercise, the videoconference allowed participants to get know each other at a more intimate level than what the chat text alone offered. In turn, this led to closer cooperation on project tasks between those members who had used the videoconference tool.

After students from the different countries identified the particular traits in their remote counterparts' behaviour they took this into account in their communication strategies. For example, the Australians concluded that working with the Taiwanese was preferable because they seemed to have more in common (on completion, some students have continued friendships struck up during the online exercise). The Australians obliged by spending time discussing personal issues. According to the Australian students, the Norwegians appeared to ignore requests to meet in AWs until the last moment. The Taiwanese, by contrast, were almost always in AWs when the Australians checked. This suggested that the Taiwanese had a different, more engaged, culture with the technology in general, and were more agreeable in negotiating roles.

Developing trust between members of a team and across teams was an important element of cooperation (as identified by [7 & 15]). For the Australians, the Taiwanese were better at eliciting personal responses than the Norwegians. For the Norwegians, communicating with the Taiwanese students was opposite to that of the Australians – the Norwegians did not report spending as much time discussing personal issues with the Taiwanese as the Australians did. The different cultural approaches to communication was not always identified by the parties concerned in time to make the necessary adjustments for a more cooperative working environment. While the Australians reported that the Norwegians did not seem to respond to their emails in a timely manner, the Norwegians reported being confused by the sheer number of unsolicited emails sent by the Australians.

Self-reflection on cultural difference was an important outcome for the students. For example, students talked about how their own experience of using a second language helped them understand the other's ESL. A native Chinese speaker, for example, in an Australian group, could use their native language as a go-between. The other group members found this strategy was useful for overcoming the irritation of having to explain things many times over. More generally, once one member of a remote team understood some piece of pertinent information, this was very quickly relayed to all of the remote team members. If this came from a remote ESL member then the local member, for whom it was their native language, could translate for the rest of the group. This introduced a new role for foreign students at the local level. This meant they got to know their peers better, and internal cross-cultural exchanges also occurred.

There were conflicts. Most of them were centred on communication misunderstandings, control and leadership. These tended to occur during the construction phase, such as some participants deleting parts of other participants' work. This conflict within the AWs environment was resolved by intervention from the teachers and students alike, also from within the AWs environment.

Despite a few minor conflicts, most students in this exercise experienced cultural transformations, both with the technology and the different language skills and approach to a common task. This led to deeper understandings about the other cultures they encountered and their own interactions with local members.

Some students were Initially apprehensive about working with other students from abroad. Other students had prior-experiences they brought to the exercise, such as a prior history of 'talking' (text-chatting) to their friends online. On completion of the project, a number of students commented that interaction with their leader and the other members of the groups, both locally and remotely, was the most important and fulfilling aspect of the team work.

Students claimed, while, for them, the object of their communicating was information, over time, the back-and-forth exchanges, and social banter, constituted a community of sorts for them. This community evolved its own culture as a subset or hybrid of the participating cultures. Within this new hybrid culture, roles and divisions of labour emerged predicated on the identified skills of the individual contributors or members of that community.

The object of their communications – information – was transferred in a number of novel and culturally mediated ways. There were the more familiar emails, chat, file transfer, bulletin boards, and videoconferencing, but, building in the 3D virtual world proved to be the most effective method for communicating information pertinent to the task. This suggests the 3D virtual world was an effective form of communication that overcame cultural and language-based differences, albeit in less tangible ways than text messages alone. It was also an effective method for achieving the more pragmatic goals of the exercise. Although a less easily defined form of community formation, the fact that students could rely on serendipitously 'bumping into someone' in the AWs environment at any time inculcated them in a collective community activity for which most agreed was useful. After all, it was only through these community-formed social engagements that they were able to exchange information, derive meanings, and ascertain the different skill levels of their partners. In turn, this led to allocation of specific tasks and a strategic approach to completing the project, despite cultural and language differences in interpretation of the information available to each member.

5 Conclusion

ICT graduates are increasingly required to work in multi-cultural teams in the industry. The case study reported here describes a pedagogical exercise whereby ICT students from three different institutions, continents, timezones, and first languages, collaborated on a single project using various technologies, central of which was a 3D virtual world. It was found that they used novel methods for overcoming cross-cultural differences. This augers well for the continued use of 3D virtual worlds as a tool where notions of cross-cultural exchange can be investigated. Technology and language were identified as the greatest barriers to the process of communication. Yet, the fact that the students were able to complete the task within the allocated timeframe suggests that, despite their cultural differences, they were able to overcome most difficulties and communicate using some common protocols and rules of behaviour.

Besides the technical and language difficulties, three core issues emerged from this study that should be taken into account in any subsequent study: notions of identity, skill indicators; and, leadership:

1. As a self-organising strategy, each group member appended their avatar name with a country of origin sign or icon (Aust, Norg, TW). In future, participants should be free to customise their avatars, thus establishing an independent cultural identity within their group and across groups.
2. Skill indicators emerged through the exercise itself. It was noted by some that the different cohorts presented with different skills (Taiwanese: programmers, Norwegians: builders, Australians: designers). This formed a complimentary collection of skills that was shared across all the members of a group. Internal skill registers were established whereby tasks could be assigned by the team leader according to individual suitability for specific tasks. In future, this part of the exercise should be formalised up front so that group leaders are in a better position to allocate specific tasks according to skill early on leaving more time for task completion and socialisation.
3. Leadership proved to be critical to the success or otherwise of a group's performance in the exercise. With leadership comes trust and control. These were also key attributes of a student's sense of satisfaction with the exercise. Leadership needs to be more closely monitored in order to create an efficient group environment.

References

1. Wyeld, T.G.: Working with Cultural Differences: A Case Study in Multicultural Teamwork using a 3DCVE. In: Edvardsen, F., Kulle, H. (eds.) Educational Games: Design, Learning and Applications. Nova Science Pub Inc., Bombay (2010)
2. Latu, S., Young, A.: Teaching ICT to Pacific Island Background Students. In: Lister, R., Young, A. (eds.) Proceedings of the Sixth Australasian Computing Education Conference (ACE 2004), Dunedin, NZ. Conferences in Research and Practice in Information Technology, vol. 30 (2004)
3. Knowles, M.S.: Educational Materials Catalog: From Teacher to Facilitator of Learning. Follett Publishing Co., (1981)
4. Kolb, D.A.: Experimental Learning. Prentice – Hall, Englewood Cliffs (1984)
5. Leidner, D., Jarvenpaa, S.: The Use of Information Technology to Enhance Management School Education: A Theoretical View. MIS Quarterly (September 1995)
6. Seifert, T.: Understanding Student Motivation. Educational Research 46, 137–149 (2004)
7. Clear, T., Kassabova, D.: Motivational Patterns in Virtual Team Collaboration. In: Young, A., Tolhurst, D. (eds.) Proceedings of Australasian Computing Education Conference 2005, Conferences in Research and Practice in Information Technology, Newcastle, Australia, vol. 42 (2005)
8. Vygotsky, L.S.: Mind in Society. Harvard University Press, Cambridge (1978)
9. Engestrom, Y.: Learning by Expanding: An Activity-Theoretical Approach to Developmental Research. Orienta-Konsultit, Helsinki (1987)
10. Bardram, J.E.: Plans as Situated Action: An Activity Theory Approach to Workflow Systems. In: Proceedings of ECSCW 1997, Lancaster, UK, September 7-11, pp. 17–24. Kluwer Academic Publishers, The Netherlands (1997)
11. Kuutti, K.: Information Systems, Cooperative Work and Active Subjects: The Activity-Theoretical Perspective. Ph.D. Thesis, Research Papers Series A 23, Department of Information Processing Science. University of Oulu, Finland (1994)
12. Schutz, W.: Firo: A three-dimensional theory of interpersonal behavior. Holt, Rinehart, and Winston, New York (1958)
13. Cartwright, D., Zander, A.: Group Dynamics: Research and Theory. Harpercollins College Div., New York (1968)
14. Heath, C., Luff, P.: Convergent Activities: Line Control and passenger Information on the London Underground. In: Engestrom, Y., Middleton, D. (eds.) Cognition and Communication at Work, pp. 96–129. Cambridge University Press, USA (1996)
15. Jarvenpaa, S., Leidner, D.: Communication and Trust in Global Virtual Teams. Journal of Computer Mediated Communication 3 (1998)

Integrated Cooperation between Universities Exemplary for the Teacher Education in Rhineland-Palatinate, Germany

Eva Kleß and Anke Pfeiffer

Universität Koblenz-Landau, Germany
kless@uni-landau.de, apfeiff@uni-koblenz.de

Abstract. Since 2007 the German „Network educational science" has offered the students of five universities (Kaiserslautern, Koblenz-Landau, Mainz and Trier) in the area of Rhineland-Palatinate the opportunity to study educational science. In addition to campus-based events the students also have access to online courses at the partner universities in the federal state. The main goal of the network is the professional exchange and mutual recognition of selected courses. In order to achieve maximum benefits for all participants qualitative and quantitative minimum requirements have been arranged to ensure the quality of teaching. This article provides information on the educational policy background, presents the collaborative arrangements between the participating universities and reflects the exchange in university life on the basis of the hybrid (blended learning) course "Media-Education-Online".

Keywords: cooperation, universities, education.

1 Introduction

The Bologna Process offered the opportunity to restructure the European university education. The aim was on the one hand the establishment of a graduated degree courses system with the Bachelor and Master degrees and on the other hand an expected improvement of teacher education. Within the scope of this reshaping, the Federal State of Rhineland-Palatinate took advantage of this opportunity to develop a comprehensive reformation of the education for teachers.

In the Federal Republic of Germany the educational policy, whose system includes schools and universities, is realized by the German federal states and not by the national government. For the comprehensive teacher training reform in the Federal State of Rhineland-Palatinate first curricular standards for all subjects of the education for the teaching profession were developed in particular teams. The content consisted of basic subject- as well as a job-related competence [1].

Before the Bologna Process was initiated the students had studied their two main subjects and one educational accompanying subject. Now – after the reform – the educational subject is becoming more important than before. The new teaching curriculum henceforth contains the two teaching subjects as well as the educational science, which includes the sciences of pedagogy, sociology and psychology. The

R. Kwan et al. (Eds.): ICHL 2011, LNCS 6837, pp. 17–29, 2011.

problem of the universities in the Federal State of Rhineland-Palatinate (and in all other federal states in Germany) was that the subject matter not only was enlarged as regards content but also the focus of the courses was clearly orientated toward the competences, yet with similar resources. A development of a flexible proposal for the courses in all three modules was necessary.

The following article provides an overview on how the difficulties of the restructures of the education system were described with the aid of the project "Network educational science", supported by the Ministry. It will describe the project with its problems and approaches as well as the advantage for students and lectures. Also the workload and the resources of universities will be explained. Next to the introduction of the project, a concrete example with the help of the seminar "Media education Online" shall explain how the conversion looks in detail. The aim of the article is to demonstrate how the cooperation between universities is not only possible but also successful.

2 A Project to Network the Teacher Education

At the beginning of 2007 the Ministry of Education, Science, Youth and Culture in Rhineland-Palatinate [1] benefit these new challenges to start a state-wide project to support the universities in their restructuring process. The Ministry fosters and finances the project "Network educational science". All universities of Rhineland-Palatinate (Kaiserslautern, Koblenz-Landau, Mainz and Trier) united for this project.

The intended strategy was that all universities are confronted with the same problems and challenges: if they networked together a synergetic effect would be possible. The aim was to strengthen the universities in Rhineland-Palatinate by using common resources of educational science. The project was running for three years (2007-2010). The idea behind it was that after this period of time the project would be formed into a controlled operation in which the tested types of cooperation between the universities would be a standard to all universities in Rhineland-Palatinate [2].

Each of the university positions received one scientific assistant for the project's period of three years. The area of responsibility lied in the coordination of the project at the respective campus and the realization of evaluation and consultation. The "Virtual Campus Rhineland-Palatinate" (VCRP) supported the five locations with this coordination. Every university made a contribution to one (or more) blended-leaning courses with only few phases of attendance and put the blended-learning course into the common pool. At first the courses were tested on the own campus and gradually extended to the other locations afterward. In the winter term 2007/2008 a state-wide interexchange commenced. The exchange program contained educational lectures and seminars, such as

- General pedagogy (lecture; research provided by Kaiserslautern)
- Heterogeneity as a requirement of educational processes (seminar; research provided by Koblenz-Landau, campus Koblenz)
- Creation of a learning environment in school and lessons (lecture; research provided by Koblenz-Landau, campus Landau)

- Interaction and communication as a basal element of teaching and education (seminar; research provided by Mainz)
- Socialization, development and education (lecture; research provided by Trier)
- Learning programs in school lessons (seminar; research provided by Koblenz-Landau, campus Landau) and
- "Media education online" (seminar; research provided by Koblenz-Landau, campus Koblenz).

The scientific assistants develop a prototype of exchange of the courses. Each university analyzes which subjects are needed. On the one hand each university is the supplier of courses and on the other hand it is the recipient of classes of other universities. There are different assignments for suppliers and recipients of those courses [2].

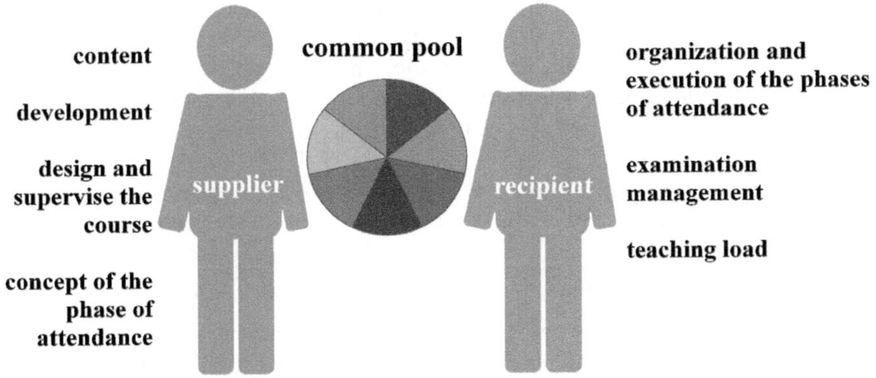

Fig. 1. Exchanges of the courses between the universities

Looking at it in detail, all universities put their blended-leaning courses into a common pool. Every university takes some of their own offered courses of the pool. As a countermove the university contributes blended-leaning courses of the own campus.

- The supplier determines the content. He or she develops, designs and supervises the course, no matter whether there are students from the own university or from other cooperating universities. The lecturer designs and develops the conception of the phases of attendance.
- The recipients are accountable for the organization and execution of the phases of attendance (e.g. inductions and closing sessions) and the examination management of the own students.

The supplier has got a higher workload and responsibility, not only for his or her own students but also for those from other universities in his or her course. In the role of the recipient the lecturer has less responsibility as regards content and organization.

The aim is to figure out a good balance between offerings and taking off courses. One possibility was that a lecturer offers one seminar for the pool and takes out a seminar and a lecture for his or her students. "The supply and acceptance of courses in the network are charged to the teaching load with the same semester periods per week" [3; p. 211].

3 Problem Areas and Attempts at a Solution

There already exist binding legal arrangements between universities about a mutual acceptance of the course achievements or academic achievements. Yet it is by no means a foregone conclusion. The new common curricular standards of the universities (since the beginning of the Bologna Process) have also facilitated the assurance of this recognition. This steady basis is an advantage for the students since they can use several blended-leaning lectures of other universities in Rhineland-Palatinate (next to the range of courses offered on the own campus).

Next to the formal performance the project needs to obtain the acceptance of the courses by students as well as lecturers. One important experience was that the lecturers had more reserves and resistances to the project than the students. In order to confront these reserves the project partners informed the lecturers about the expected advantages which would be the result of their own participation in the project. In Table 1 the benefits on behalf of the students and lecturers are presented.

Table 1. Advantages of the project "network educational science" for lecturers and students [4]

The benefit for students	The benefit for lecturers
• More flexible timetable • Avoiding overlaps in time between courses • Adherence to a certain number of semesters needed to complete a course • More course alternatives • Exchange with students of other universities • Project-orientated learning in small units • More individual responsibility • Increase in the quality of studies	• Course acceptance from partners by complete consideration of the own teaching load • exchange of experience between lecturers • putting a course to the test in all universities in the state • access to content and course conceptions of other lecturers • increase of the quality of courses

The acceptance of the course offer has been continually enhanced since the beginning of the exchange in 2007/2008 (see figure 2). The reason for this was the uncomplicated treatment of the students. There were no differences of the application between courses of the own university or other universities in Rhineland-Palatinate for the students because they applied for the same online university calendar of the "Virtual Campus Rhineland-Palatinate" (VCRP) [5]. The blended-leaning courses take place on the learning platform "Blackboard". In the introductory session on the own campus the students receive all necessary information regarding the semester process. The additional presence terms in the form of workshops, trainings or presentations of results also took place on the own campus [6].

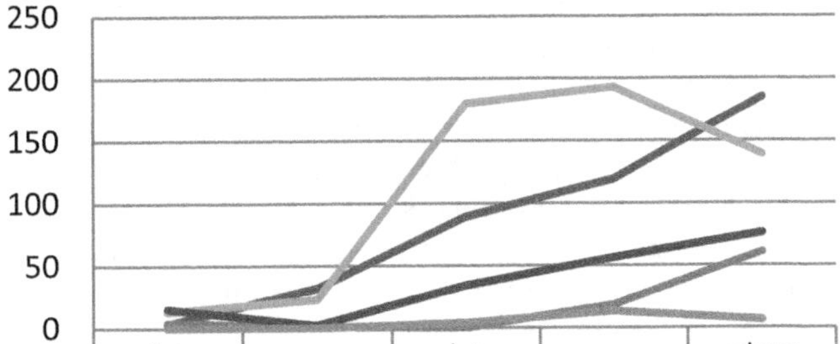

	winter term 2007/08	summer term 2008	winter term 2008/09	summer term 2009	winter term 2009/10
University Landau	3	32	89	119	185
University Kaiserslautern	13	23	180	193	139
University Trier	4	1	0	18	61
University Koblenz	15	2	34	56	76
University Mainz	0	0	4	13	6

Fig. 2. The increase of students between winter term 2007/2008 and winter term 2009/2010 at different universities

At every end of the term the students reply to an online-survey and give a distinguished feedback to the lecturers and the course design. The students give insight into their subjectively learning success of the learning process in coherence to the competitions of educational science and qualification aims. For example: 68% of the interviewees of a didactic course said that they now know how to plan ahead a lesson step by step with the help of a planning schedule.

This is an expansion of the improvements for prospective courses and it increases the acceptance of the whole project. In the summer term 2009, 546 students were interviewed on their participation in the "network educational science" project blended-learning about their extension of professional competence. In comparison with other surveys [7] the students succeeded well in acquiring professional competences.

Nevertheless, this shows that the courses of educational science must be improved: The offered blended-learning courses allow numerous possibilities to go into the learning content and give enough support but the students reported back that this learning process is not the optimum. In spite of varying courses with assignments, controversies, exercises, tutorials and reflections the students desire more learning support. The two-thirds majority wants more intensive feedback from the lecturers regarding their learning progress. Courses with peer-assessment methods were evaluated better than courses without peer-assessment methods (see the following chapter "The example Media-Education-Online"). In conclusion it could be declared that assessment is important for the students' learning processes, although it is not absolutely important who it comes from.

4 Workload and Resources

Indeed, the universities in the state have very similar contents of teaching and aims of qualification; however every university rates courses differently. For that it is important to design the courses as flexible as possible [8]. The amount of the needed credit points can vary depending on the respective university.

In order to solve the problems of the different workloads the project partners developed a system based upon points for every course. For instance, a student usually needs 100 course points to successfully finish a course. He or she needs two credit points for one class but the desired course from another university requires three credit points. The lecturers can come to the arrangement that the student doesn't need 100 but only 66 course-points to complete the class. It is the duty of the lecturer to regulate the amount of points a student receives for certain assignments. The benefit lies in the students' freedom to make a choice on how to obtain the course-points. Therefore the students learn to improve their personal responsibility for their learning process. The course-point-system also ensures the greatest possible transparency.

By offering the courses for more students (also from other universities in the state) an increasing support becomes necessary; also assistance for the lecturers who supply courses to other universities increases. They must look for solutions, which on the one hand allow an individual responsibility and on the other hand meet the raised number of participants.

For that fact a different peer-assessment-procedure got tested. Within the scope of a course the students need to write a comment on an article for their fellow students. The comment must be composed on the basis of specific criteria. The peer-assessment supports the ability of assessment in their future teaching profession. The convenient side-effect is an increased communication and activity on the platform, which should not be underestimated.

The presence terms which were offered at each university are limited to a minimum. The frequency of the presence dates in one term is dependent on the subject of the course, in average between one and three dates. The important presence dates are usually the introductory lesson and closing session, yet occasionally a few dates in the middle of the term are also substantial.

5 Extensions of the Content and Competences

In addition to the content and organizational charge and the outcome for teaching new methods are necessary to adapt to the statewide exchange. Right from the start the project partners integrated innovative didactic concepts into the range of the courses [5]. The lecturers, for instance, use class videos, case scenarios, e-portfolios, self guided assignments and peer-assessments. In the following passages one course and its learning methods will be described in detail.

5.1 The Example "Media-Education-Online"

"Media-Education-Online" is one of the blended-learning seminars in the common pool. The seminar is especially designed for the project. All students of the associate universities that offer the subject education science, have the opportunity to participate in the seminar "Media-Education-Online".

At the University of Koblenz-Landau, campus Koblenz the course was established on the following competence profile:

- Students are able to reflect their own use of media
- They are able to use media appropriate to the teaching objectives
- They can assess media design and impact
- They know the rules of media communication and media didactics and are able to use them accordingly.

The blended learning seminar "Media Education-Online" can be allocated since the winter semester 2007/2008 as part of the network project in the Rhineland-Palatinate universities. One aim for the students of the Seminar is to develop their own media-project. Three presence terms - one at the beginning, one in the middle and one at the end of the semester - are obligatory. An important focal point is the introductory session because the students get to know the content, the course activity and the organization of the teamwork there. The experience of the last semester showed that adequate knowledge of the course assembly increases the chance to achieve success. The presence term in the middle is used to support the students' work process and the presentation of results at the end is used to reflect the projects and the work flow during the semester. The online parts are supported by the learning management system (LMS) "Blackboard", because this LMS is available to all associates.

Before the students begin with their media project, they need to acquire basic information in media-pedagogy. Besides the classical teaching material like research literature, they can choose whether they will use audio-expert-interviews or video-tasks from the assignment pool. So the students have got different processing possibilities and this way several sensory channels are stimulated [9]. All tasks implement a combination of theoretical principles with practical examples.

Another major part of the course is the peer-assessment. On the basis of established criteria the students have to comment on the text and the media results of their fellow students. Thereby two aims are pursued: Firstly, the peer-assessment leads to an intensive feedback, supports and stimulates the individual learning process of the fellow students. Secondly, the student teachers intensively learn to give constructive feedback regarding an assessment and improve their ability to judge and acquire competences which they need in their future teaching profession [10].

5.2 Theoretical Conditions

As already mentioned the self-study is associated with the emergence of the workload-concept. The orientation toward the workload displays a change of perspective from teaching to learning and requires the teachers to reconsider their didactic and methodological concepts [11]. That change demands a high degree of autonomy and organizational skills from the students, while the teachers are confronted with a shift of paradigm at the same time, which leads them away from mere input and instruction to output, so that the focus will be put upon competencies and results. Especially virtual learning environments seem to be particularly suitable for the requested self-directed learning processes. Among other things this includes a stronger emphasis on reflection, regular feedback and the negotiability of time saving [12].

Self-directed learning processes cannot be implemented without preconditions. Therefore the orientation lesson in the course "Media Education-Online" prepares the students for the approach of a new self-directed learning experience and furthermore it offers the opportunity to explore and to experiment media-education in many ways.

The construct of self-determined learning processes can take different forms and profiles. The proportion of self- and external control during the learning process depends on the choices the learner is given by the lecturer. Therefore various dimensions must be discussed [13] and [14]:

- determination of learning-duration, -tempo and -pause (temporal structure)
- frequency of assistance
- determination of the learning place and the point in time
- provision of learning objectives respectively learning content

Self-regulated learning does not only mean that the learning process takes place without any assistance since external and instructional learning may also be present. Learners should be given a latitude for own decisions during self-determined learning processes [15]. The students' own learning process and their own knowledge construction should be accompanied by helpful instructions that are provided by the lecturer. In this context [16] designates six institutional elements that can support self-directed learning (see table 2).

Table 2. On recommendation of Dietrich [16 p. 129] and the conversion into the seminar "Media-Education-Online"

Recommendation for self-directed learning processes [16]	"Media-Education-Online" implementation
• providing necessary learning resources, such as media and tools	• providing specialized literature, self-study tests, videos, media library (Podcasts, Blogs, and Wikis) etc.
• proposals in which students can determine the objectives, content and learning paths	• students can select the main focus of the seminar, whether they prefer media-education or media-didactics amongst others
• offers that allow temporal and local flexibility	• the engaged LMS supports flexibility
• supporting services such as technical and content, process and personal counseling	• contacts in all named belongings are available to the students; lecturers make the agreement to be an duty at least once every 24 hours
• modulated courses should consider already acquired skills and allow students to gain specific examination	• students have the opportunity to study the offers according to their already acquired skills

The larger ability of self-directed learning simultaneously emphasizes a shift of responsibility for the learning process and with this a general transfer of responsibility [17]. Teachers should have confidence in the learning process and its results; it is not the time for skepticism and not the search for weaknesses and mistakes but faith in the ability of the learner [18]. These demands change on the behalf of the lecturer. His challenge is to support the learning process individually and to develop exercises, which challenge the students. Learning is rather a mutual process of development than the teaching of already prefabricated pieces of knowledge. This extract of self-determined learning shows the basic assumptions for the development of the course "Media-Education-Online". The following section shows basic aspects of the implementation.

5.3 Methodical Aspects

Communication: On the LMS Blackboard the communication tools contain e-mails, chats and forums on learning. In addition to face-to-face seminars, the students are always able to ask questions, demand responses or discuss items with the lecturer. Therefore they can use the regular consultation hour of the supervising lecturer of their university, the virtual consultation or the chat on the platform. Among the essentials there are clear activities and constant communication – these are definitely aspects of successful blended-learning-seminars.

Flexible Timing: Overall, the seminar can be studied by the participants in space and time flexibly. In particular, the modular structure, associated with their orientation toward competence, the high proportion of self-study and the introduction of curricular standards require an adjustment of the educational scientific events. For example, at the beginning of the semester the students receive a timetable and they are free to plan their semester weeks and their workload. Students, which have personal difficulties with this kind of free timing, can use an optimum scale that is recommended by the lecturer. With the use of blended learning scenarios flexible training courses arise. That also enables students with family or job commitments to study and gain a degree. With the flexible course management the associated universities take account of the teaching-learning culture change.

Evaluation: In the last six semesters approximately 300 students from the five partner universities attended the course successfully. An evaluation was based on a competence-orientated standardized questionnaire and a seminar-based student's interview. In the summer semester 2010 72 students successfully completed the course "Media-Education-Online". From these 72 students 34 belonged to the internal staff (students who were employed in courses on the own campus) and 44 to the external staff (Students who were employed in courses of partner universities).

Extract of results:

- Essential exercises were based on group work. Hence the teamwork was decisive for the successful attendance of the Seminar.

- Some students estimated the peer-assessment critically, because
    - they do not want to assess fellow students,
    - they think the estimation process is in most of the cases far too good and
    - they do not feel competent for the assessment of their fellow students.
- Nearly all students enjoyed working on their own media project.

Altogether the evaluation results provided an informative basis to optimize the course in the next semesters.

6 Consequences and Experiences

The achievement of the state-wide courses is clearly displayed by the drop-out proportion. It hardly visualizes differences between internal and external staff [2]. For example, in the summer term 2009 1047 Students applied for project courses (see figure 3). 646 students were employed on the own campus and 401 students were employed in courses of partner universities. Altogether 904 students brought their course to a successful termination (569 internal and 335 external students).

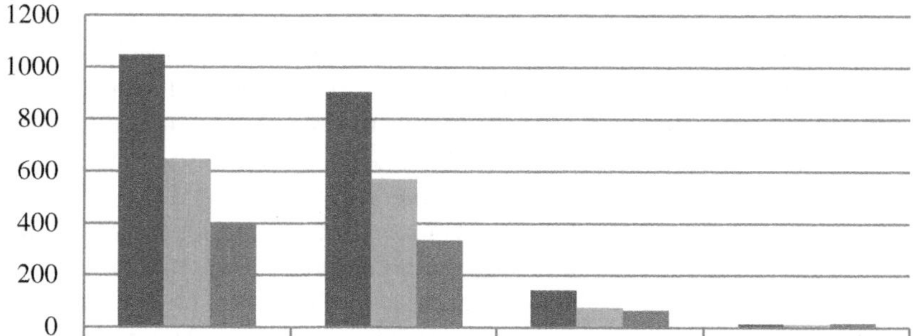

	Registration	Successful participation	Dropout	Dropout %
complete	1047	904	143	14
internal	646	569	77	12
external	401	335	66	16

Fig. 3. Dropouts in summer term 2009

The dropout proportion is at about 14% altogether. If one differentiates between internal and external students, it is shown that the dropout proportion of the external ones is a little higher with 16% than the dropout proportions of the internal students. The average drop-out proportion in German universities is close to 20% but in the subject education it only is at 9% [19]. In total the drop-out proportion of the project can be described as acceptable. The achievement of the project arises with the continuous inclination of the number of participants. One important cause is the intensive networking inside the departments of universities [2].

Next to the students also the lecturers, who were the recipients of the project courses, would be interviewed after the end of the term. In comparison to regular courses at the universities the lecturers noted a considerable exoneration from the decrease of the "network educational science" courses. Thereby the lecturers had more resources to support the students with an intensive assistance, for example.

In particular lecturers who had less experience in teaching evaluated the project courses as useful and inspiring ("It was a successful entrance for me to teach and a good entrance in the topic of E-Learning, too"). They don't teach alone but with a partner teacher who had the responsibility of the course content, course development and who supervised the course (see above: exchanges of the courses between the universities). On the level of the cooperation between the project partners an annual SWOT-analysis[1] demonstrates that the advantage of the project is predominant. The particulate teaching exchange had been described as highly positive. It came to an exchange of expert competences, concepts and materials. The participation of the project was an advantage [4].

7 Perspectives

At the end of the term of the project "network educational science" in February 2010 eight flexible and usable courses in three modules altogether were available to the students in Rhineland-Palatinate. A cooperation agreement between the partner universities and the Ministry of Education, Science, Youth and Culture arrange the continuation of the exchange. It is interesting that the students promptly accept the seminars and lecturers of the project when they see advantages by learning on the ground and time independent. Lecturers use the project when they are open for E-Learning elements, new E-Learning methods and cooperative work. The project shows that it has a lot of benefits for lecturers and students, too. The project "network educational science" was one of the first state-wide cooperative universities projects in Germany. It needs more openness and courage for change to bring more projects like this into being.

References

1. Ministerium für Bildung, Wirtschaft, Jugend und Kultur. Curriculare Standards der Studienfächer im lehramtsbezogenen Bachelor und Masterstudiengängen, `http://www.mbwjk.rlp.de/bildung/schuldienst-und-lehrerberuf/reform-der-lehrerinnen-und-lehrerausbildung/curriculare-standards/`
2. Bauer, P., Bogner, C., Kleß, E., Menzer, C., Pfeiffer, A., Thielen, T.: Ressourcen nutzen - Möglichkeiten erweitern: Interuniversitäre Kooperation im Netzwerk Bildungswissenschaften. Zeitschrift für Hochschulentwicklung 5, H. 1 (2010)

[1] The SWOT-analysis is a strategic planning method used to evaluate the Strengths, Weaknesses, Opportunities and Threats involved in a project.

3. Kleß, E.: Educational Cooperation between Universities in the Network Education Science. In: Pérez-Bustamante, G., Phusavat, K., Ferreira, F. (eds.) Proceedings of the IASK Conference on Teaching and Learning 2010, pp. 210–214. IASK (2010)
4. Menzer, C., Faber, K.: Lernen wo, wann, wie und mit wem ich möchte. Die Ermöglichung flexiblen Lernens im Netzwerk Bildungswissenschaft. In: Apostopoulos, N. (ed.) Grundfragen Multimedialen Lehrens und Lernens. E-Kooperation und E-Praxis, Waxmann, Münster, pp. 166–180 (2010)
5. Kleß, E.: Self-Guided Assignment as a New Way of Learning during Study. In: Munoz, M., Ferreira, F. (eds.) Proceedings of the IASK International Conference Teaching and Learning, pp. 412–416. IASK (2009)
6. Arnold, R., Faber, K., Hemsing, S., Menzer, C.: Der Virtuelle Campus Rheinland-Pfalz - im Zentrum hochschulübergreifender Netzwerke in Rheinland-Pfalz. In: Bremer, C. (ed.) Landesinitiativen für E-Learning an deutschen Hochschulen, Waxmann, Münster, pp. 123–136 (2010)
7. Thiel, F., Veit, S., Blüthmann, I., Lepa, S.: Ergebnisse der Befragung der Studierenden in den Bachelorstudiengängen an der Freien Universität Berlin im Sommersemster (2008), http://www.fu-berlin.de/praesidium/qm/bachelorbefragung/Bachelorbefragung_2008.pdf
8. Bogner, C., Menzer, C., Pätzold, H.: Standards umsetzen Hochschulübergreifende Kooperation im Zeichen curricularer Standards. In: Zauchner, S. (ed.) Offener Bildungsraum Hochschule. Freiheiten und Notwendigkeiten. 13. Europäische Jahrestagung der Gesellschaft für Medien in der Wissenschaft (GMW 2008), Waxmann, Münster, pp. 264–274 (2008)
9. Bremer, C.: Online Lernen leicht gemacht! Leitfaden für die Planung und Gestaltung von virtuellen Hochschulveranstaltungen, http://www.bremer.cx/paper13/artikelraabe_bremer03.pdf
10. Bostock, S.: Student Peer Assessment. Keele University, http://www.keele.ac.uk/depts/aa/landt/lt/docs/bostock_peer_assessment.htm
11. Wildt, J.: The Shift from Teaching to Learning – Thesen zum Wandel der Lernkultur in modularisierten Studienstrukturen. In: Ehlert, H., Welbers, U. (eds.) Qualitätssicherung und Studienreform. Strategie- und Programmentwicklung für Fachbereiche und Hochschulen im Rahmen von Zielvereinbarungen am Beispiel der Heinrich-Heine-Universität Düsseldorf, pp. 168–178. Grupello-Verlag, Düsseldorf (2004)
12. Grotlüschen, A.: Begründungslogik virtuellen Lernens. In: Faulstich, P. (ed.) Expansives Lernen, Schneider, Baltmannsweiler, pp. 196–208 (2004)
13. Friedrich, H.F.: Selbstgesteuertes Lernen – sechs Fragen, sechs Antworten, http://www.learn-line.nrw.de/angebote/selma/medio/grundlegendes/vortraegeaufsaetze/friedrich/friedrich.pdf
14. Kraft, S.: Wenn viele vom Gleichen sprechen...Annäherungen an die Thematik Selbstgesteuertes Lernen. In: Kraft, S. (ed.) Selbstgesteuertes Lernen, Schneider, Baltmannsweiler, pp. 16–30 (2002)
15. Reinmann, G., Mandl, H.: Unterrichten und Lernumgebungen gestalten. In: Krapp, A., Weidenmann, B. (eds.) Pädagogische Psychologie. Ein Lehrbuch, Beltz PVU, Weinheim, pp. 613–658 (2006)
16. Dietrich, S.: Die Rolle der Institution beim selbstgesteuerten Lernen. In: Faulstich, P., Gnahs, D., Seidel, S., Bayer, M. (eds.) Praxishandbuch selbstbestimmtes Lernen, Juventa, Weinheim, pp. 121–136 (2002)

17. Pätzold, H. (eds.) Verantwortungsdidaktik. Zum didaktischen Ort der Verantwortung in Erwachsenenbildung und Weiterbildung (Grundlagen der Berufs- und Erwachsenenbildung). Schneider, Baltmannsweiler (2008)
18. Risse, E.: Umgang mit Heterogenität – auch im Gymnasium. In: Boller, S., Rosowski, E., Stroot, T. (eds.) Heterogenität in Schule und Unterricht: Handlungsansätze zum pädagogischen Umgang mit Vielfalt, Beltz, Weinheim, pp. 118–127 (2007)
19. Heublein, U., Hutzsch, C., Schreiber, J., Sommer, D., Besuch, G.: Ursachen des Studienabbruchs in Bachelor- und in herkömmlichen Studiengängen Ergebnisse einer bundesweiten Befragung von Exmatrikulierten des Studienjahres. Projektbericht. HIS Hochschul-Informations-System GmbH (2007/2008), http://www.his.de/pdf/21/studienabbruch_ursachen.pdf

A Methodology for Integrating Traditional Classroom Learning with Contemporary Online Learning

Kanishka Bedi

U21Global Graduate School, 88B, Level Three, Amoy Street,
Singapore, 069907
kbedi@u21global.edu.sg

Abstract. Traditional classroom learning and contemporary online learning represent two distinct paradigms of learning, though one of them has existed for centuries while the other is a recent phenomenon. Critics argue about the merits and demerits of both types of pedagogies; however it appears that a 'blend' of both offers an avenue for bringing together 'the best of both worlds.' Traditional institutions have often grappled with achieving the right blend and have experimented in their own ways for inducting online component in conventional classroom learning, which happens to be their forte. In this paper, a methodology to integrate traditional classroom learning with online learning as a unified system has been proposed. The ten step methodology is simple yet effective in highlighting the pitfalls in the integration process and suggesting mitigation measures thereof.

Keywords: Methodology, Traditional, Classroom, Face-to-face, Contemporary, Online, Learning, Hybrid, Blended.

1 Introduction

Traditional classroom learning has predominantly been the medium of instruction for centuries. During the early 1990s, proliferation of computer technology resulted in the evolution of computer-based training (CBT). The ensuing years witnessed establishment of organizational intranets and sharing of information between organizational units. It was the advent of the Internet during the mid-90s that brought about a major revolution in the world. During the next decade, the World Wide Web (www) had spread like 'wild fire' all across the globe. This period witnessed the emergence of web-based learning, which was soon rechristened as "online" learning.

The USA has been the front-runner in achieving rapid growth rate in online enrollments, so much so that in 2010, it experienced a whopping 21 percent growth rate compared to the 2 percent growth in overall higher education student population [1]. Most institutions in the US now offer hybrid or online programs and the rest are seriously considering doing so soonest possible. However, the rest of the world is yet to catch up with this growth rate being experienced currently in the US. It is clear that traditional institutions would gradually experiment with online technology and pedagogy by way of creating "hybrid" or "blended" programs. This integration of

R. Kwan et al. (Eds.): ICHL 2011, LNCS 6837, pp. 30–39, 2011.

traditional classroom learning with contemporary online learning will provide them the comfort of understanding the nuances of the new ways of learning.

The gradual adaption of online learning into traditional ways has its merits; however the biggest challenge is to ensure "seamless" integration such that the students get the 'best of both worlds.' This is easier said than done, as many institutions have tasted failure in their vein to quickly 'blend' the two radically different pedagogical domains and create a hybrid program. Their lack of experience and understanding of the online system of the hybrid left them grappling with the determination of the 'right blend', while faculty and students alike were left bewildered with a new yet incomplete experience.

Several previous studies have attempted to bridge this gap in literature about the right methodology [2, 3, 4] to device a unified system of integrating traditional classroom learning with state-of-the-art online learning. However, in this study, the author utilizes his practical experience of creating several hybrid programs [5] in devising a simple yet effective methodology.

2 The Methodology

The methodology proposed for blending the traditional face-to-face learning with modern online learning as a unified system comprises of ten distinct steps as shown in fig. 1. A cursory examination of this diagram may suggest as if the methodology can be used for creating purely online programs as well. However, as we would discover in ensuing discussion, the traditional face-to-face learning provides subtle "glue" in binding together the two diverse ways of learning.

2.1 Step 1: Feasibility Study

The first step in the proposed methodology is conducting due diligence in integrating traditional classroom learning with contemporary online learning. In other words, a feasibility study should be meticulously performed in order to establish that blending traditional classroom learning with online learning would result in better achievement of program learning objectives, higher student satisfaction, and increased program outreach.

Inclusion of online component often results in increased program outreach by virtue of the program becoming more accessible to working professionals, people residing in distant areas from the main campus, and housewives unable to attend a purely traditional campus-based program. A fair assessment of potential student population to be addressed by a proposed hybrid program allows the planners to realistically ascertain the student volumes and plan for required resources accordingly. Exploratory studies utilizing focus group interviews can be helpful here.

Surveys of existing students in other programs may throw useful insights on student expectations and often help in deciding the proportion of blending. However, if the students surveyed have never experienced any form of online learning before, their opinion on blending may not be well-informed.

Learning objectives of the new program should be carefully developed, while deciding on which ones can be better addressed by online pedagogy and which ones through traditional classroom method. For example, a learning objective like "develop ability to make extempore speech" can be better achieved in a traditional face-to-face setting. Similarly, another learning objective "Critically compare the cultural attributes of managers in different global geographies" would lend itself to be attained in a more suitable way in online format extending to globally dispersed student base.

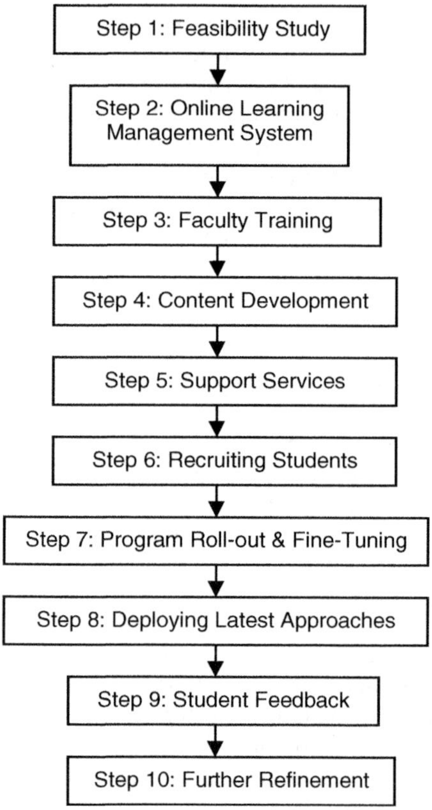

Fig. 1. Steps in integrating traditional classroom learning with contemporary online learning

Last but not the least, a candid assessment of the internal resources of the institution should be made. The capital investment required for including the online component, inclination of the existing faculty to develop online teaching skills, induction of new faculty exclusively to teach hybrid courses, creating online teaching infrastructure like the learning management system (LMS), etc., should be estimated prudently while making suitable provisions for possible exigencies.

2.2 Step 2: Online Learning Management System

Introduction of an online learning management system (LMS) is the next step for including the online component in traditional classroom learning. The idea here is to familiarize the students with fundamental online technologies, starting with features like online submission of assignments, viewing of professor announcements, sharing of PowerPoint slides, professor feedback on assignments, learner's grade book, and of course, the discussion board for discussion on case studies, relevant articles and key issues pertaining to the course of study. Choice of a good LMS usually hinges around:

- *Ease of deployment:* LMSs that require long deployment and configuration time hinder quick inclusion of online component in traditional classroom learning. Thus, off-the-shelf LMSs that have been tried and tested by several other institutions are preferable.
- *Features:* A variety of tools offered in an LMS allow institutions to pick and choose the ones that can fit more closely to their blending requirements. For example, an institution looking for retaining the face-to-face teaching may not be interested in synchronous lecture delivery tools that are in-built into some LMSs. Institutions should consider the LMSs that supports e-library functions such that all the academic resources contained in modern research databases may be provided to the students.
- *Reliability and Scalability:* It is expected that an LMS would be up and running at all times without frequent disruption in accessibility. Similarly, the LMS should be scalable to accommodate increasingly large numbers of students over a period of time.
- *User Friendly:* The tools and features of the LMS should be easy to use and learn. This allows for quick integration of online with traditional learning, as the need for training faculty and students on the LMS is greatly reduced.
- *Look and Feel:* It is imperative that the LMS should ooze out a distinct appeal commensurate with the ethos of the institution. The color scheme used, emblems inserted, and the overall layout of the LMS should be attractive enough and symbolic of the institution.

Several arguments are often made by experts for/ against open-source LMSs like Moodle as well as commercial LMSs like Blackboard/ WebCT. However, the choice of the LMS is dependent upon the feasibility study recommended in the previous step, which includes an assessment of institutional resources, target student population, and the student service quality to be achieved. External service providers with hosted platform service option may also be considered, as it may result into significant cost savings while kick-starting platform services.

2.3 Step 3: Faculty Training

The role of faculty in creating a hybrid programme is pivotal to its success. The key challenge is that the faculty members in most traditional institutions are "hard-wired" to teach in a face-to-face setting. An overt resistance from faculty to adapt to online teaching is not uncommon. In such a situation, invariably somebody needs to champion the cause of online learning and the benefits it brings about when blended with traditional learning.

One way of conditioning the mindset of faculty members towards online teaching is to design a faculty training program (FTP) that is immersive in nature. That means, faculty members should be provided the experience of an online classroom as if they were the students. Such training should be facilitated by a seasoned online professor, who can mentor, guide and coach the teaching staff while arousing their interest in online teaching.

Involving such trained faculty members in the design of the blended program can be conducive to its eventual success. Some of the faculty may even be involved in the next stage of content development of the hybrid program. Such creative endeavors often serve as a catalyst to easier acceptability of online component amongst faculty.

If in-house faculty has never experienced online teaching before, it would be a good idea to involve adjuncts having vast experience in teaching online at other institutions. This approach has the additional benefit of such experienced adjuncts sharing best practices in online education. However, two different professors teaching the face-to-face and online components in a hybrid program may have its challenges in seamless integration. Therefore, the preferred option should be to have the same professor facilitate both face-to-face and the online portions of the program.

2.4 Step 4: Content Development

As discussed in Step1, program learning objectives that can be addressed more suitably through online and face-to-face learning should be identified. If a particular learning objective can be taken care of equally well by online and face-to-face teaching, it is better to assign it to the online component of the hybrid program to allow for more flexibility and convenience on part of students.

At the outset, the overarching objectives for online content development should be set so as to make sure that the content is:

- *Engaging* – the online courseware is highly interactive
- *Meaningful* – the learning outcomes associated with each topic are clearly delineated
- *Authentic* – the course content is thoroughly grounded in reality

In contrast to the traditional face-to-face delivery, online content development process is highly resource intensive. This is especially so keeping in view that it would be recycled for several cohorts of the program without substantial modifications. In many instances, the content is developed in modular form such that the same modules can be used across several programs. Thus, overall investment in developing the online component in a hybrid course can be amortized across batches and other programs.

The process of online content development is more or less standardized across many institutions. It requires great coordination and cooperation between the subject matter expert (SME) and the learning design (LD) team to make the content highly engaging and interactive. After receiving the manuscript from the SME, the LD team prepares a Learning Object (LO) Matrix by highlighting the topics to be covered and the duration of each LO, any queries for the SME, etc. The LO Matrix is sent for approval by the SME, who answers the queries of the LD team and makes suggestions for any possible improvements in the matrix before approval. Upon receiving the approval from the SME, the LD team prepares the storyboards for each learning object and sends them across for approval to the SME. The SME meticulously reviews the storyboards, while making appropriate corrections/ modifications before granting the approval. The LD team then creates the LOs by including multimedia, images, animations, narration, etc. The LOs are then sent to the SME for final suggestions and approval.

As mentioned earlier, it is preferable that the SME of online component in the hybrid program is the professor facilitating the program (both online as well as F2F). However, it is not necessary, and the services of outside experts can be taken if in-house experts are not available, are facing acute time crunch, or have less inclination to undertake such a content development project.

There are several service providers globally, who provide LD expertise to institutions. It is a worthwhile option to explore, if an institution does not want to invest heavily into in-house staff for this purpose. It can be a cost effective option too, as many such service providers have facilities in low-cost nations, and hence charge competitively for their services.

Last but not the least, rights management is another area that should be prudently taken into consideration. International copyright laws are stringent and ignorance about them may badly tarnish an institution's image amongst academic community as well as public at large. Therefore, due permissions should be taken from various sources, if a part of content like images, figures, tables, etc. are required to be included in the online content.

2.5 Step 5: Support Services

It is essential in a hybrid program to provide additional support to the faculty as well as students, especially in the online component. Such support can at times be crucial in easing out the workload on part of faculty, while ensuring high student retention rate. Support services are typically of four types:

- *Student services*: This support staff helps in setting up the online classes, like procuring the case studies from sources like HBSP, ECCH, etc., configuring the assignment submission deadlines in the LMS, making opening announcements in the online class, organizing the discussion board through proper sequence of discussion topics as per the study schedule, and promptly responding to queries from the students as the first point of contact. Such staff is usually called program advisor or executive.
- *Dedicated IT help desk*: Technical issues are not uncommon when online component is introduced in a hybrid program. Technical problems faced by students and faculty may range from simple login issues to bigger LMS-related problems. It is therefore necessary to have a dedicated IT help desk, which may in an ideal scenario provide a 24x7 support to the learners. In order to track the service level of such staff, a ticket is issued as soon as a complaint is received and the number of hours taken to resolve the issue is recorded. Such data helps in enhancing the services further.
- *E-Library support:* In most instances, traditional institutions have created electronic libraries in addition to their physical library facility. Bringing in the online component in a traditional face-to-face program makes it even more important to provide e-library facilities to the students. However, at times, the students and faculty need support to locate the right resources for their assignments/ research. Thus, support staff can be of great help here.

- *Student orientation program:* The online component in the hybrid program requires hands-on experience for the students in navigating through the LMS, in using its various tools, and more importantly, in getting accustomed to the online pedagogy and its fundamentals. A student orientation program (SOP) should be designed in the LMS and should be made compulsory for students to complete successfully before embarking upon the main program.

2.6 Step 6: Recruiting Students

This step may seem out of place for some institutions that enjoy huge brand image by virtue of being into existence for several decades (or centuries in some cases) and having strived hard to provide quality education. However, this step may be crucial for newer institutions entering the hybrid education space. Traditional institutions are more accustomed to advertising about their new programs and expecting the students to visit their campus for more information. The student counselors at the campus help the potential students in choosing the right program as per their aspirations.

For achieving better student outreach for hybrid programs, the approach required may be different. In this case, the student population being targeted may include working professionals, housewives, people at geographically distant locations, etc. The online component allows such people to undertake academic programs from their respective locations and travel occasionally to the physical campus for attending face-to-face classes. Reaching out to this set of population may require special recruitment staff that is trained to make open house presentations, personally visit corporate houses, and may even visit homes to meet housewives interested in pursuing a hybrid program. Institutions, therefore, should be prepared to invest resources in this unique aspect of student outreach for hybrid programs.

2.7 Step 7: Program Roll-Out and Fine-Tuning

The pilot program is always a learning experience and it may require fine-tuning during its implementation. As discussed earlier, a student orientation program (SOP) is imperative before the students may undertake the main hybrid program. For a hybrid program, this SOP should be conducted in a face-to-face setting at the physical campus to 'break the ice' between the students and the faculty. The program director should preferably conduct the SOP herself, with support from other faculty colleagues.

During the program, face-to-face interactions provide an ideal avenue for students to clarify their doubts with faculty on the online content, discussions, and assignments. It is also an ideal time to conduct student 'interim' feedback surveys for better understanding their concerns and making mid-course corrections in the program accordingly.

2.8 Step 8: Deploying Latest Approaches

Depending upon the duration of the hybrid program, if all goes well with the initial part of the program, deployment of latest approaches to the online component may be considered. If the program duration is short, the latest approaches may be introduced during the subsequent cycles of the program. The pros and cons of each of the approaches should be carefully weighed before considering their application in the program. Some of these approaches are as under:

- *Digital Storytelling*: Digital storytelling can be used as a powerful tool for student and faculty introduction [6] at the commencement of a hybrid program as well as a contemporary assignment reporting medium [7]. Commonly available software like Microsoft PowerPoint can be utilized for this purpose by including images, background music, and narration to create a multimedia experience for the audience. File compression software allow uploading of such media-rich files on to the LMS. The face-to-face orientation of the program should be ideally used to provide hands-on training to the students in the creation of digital stories.
- *Wiki:* Wiki is a collaboration tool that has been successfully used in online component of hybrid programs, wherein student teams have worked together on projects based upon their real experiences. Akin to the world's biggest encyclopedia "Wikipedia", Wiki allows creation of knowledge objects by students that not only benefit students in the same cohort, but also in subsequent batches [8]. The 'history' tool in Wiki allows comparison of previous versions of content and the moderator can opt to delete unacceptable contributions by fellow students. The dynamic nature of such content on the Wiki keeps it up to date and captures key developments on the topic in most recent times. The face-to-face orientation is the ideal time to provide hands-on experience to the students on using the simple 'tags' in Wiki.
- *Open Book Open Web (OBOW) Examination:* Based upon constructivist pedagogy, OBOW examination provides an authentic context to the students to allow them to think as a consultant and to recommend ways for resolving a managerial problem. Use of images, hyperlinks leading to websites and videos, and imagery creates a scenario that is close to reality [9]. To ensure that the students do not get lost in the maze of information, a guide to task is included to encourage the students for referring to their notes, textbook, online content and the e-library. At the same time, the task is so unstructured that straight forward answers to it cannot be found on the Internet or other sources. Such unique format of examination has been well appreciated by faculty and students alike in hybrid programs.

2.9 Step 9: Student Feedback

At the culmination of a hybrid program, a comprehensive student survey should be designed and executed to seek their feedback. Typically, two separate surveys should be conducted – one focusing exclusively on the performance of the faculty and the other covering the program content/ pedagogy. Online survey tools like QuestBack or Survey Monkey are quite useful in creation, online execution, automated data collection, and report generation. Rare insights about the preferences of the students about the proportion of blending, areas of improvement, key challenges, and ways of overcoming them are gained through such surveys.

2.10 Step 10: Further Refinement

The feedback of the students received in the earlier step should be carefully analyzed. A dispassionate view of some of their recommendations allows the faculty to better understand their perspective. Often, students comment about the frequency of face-to-face sessions, their duration, and dates. At times, some of their suggestions may be absolutely contradictory to each other. If the need be, further discussion should be carried out with students to understand their views while explaining the constraints faced by the institution in not being able to accept all the recommendations.

The main objective here is to make sure that the teething troubles experienced in the pilot cohort do not occur in the next offering of the program.

3 Conclusion and Recommendation

Traditional institutions have been successfully delivering education in the conventional face-to-face format since times immemorial. Only in recent times, they are witnessing emergence of new technologies and pedagogy in relation to online learning. Their initial reaction, in most instances, to such developments was that of ignorance. However, the success of hybrid programs by combining the face-to-face learning with online learning in the West prompted such institutions to rethink their stand. The challenge faced by them is that they neither have expertise nor resources to kick-start hybrid programs. The faculty, in many cases, is reluctant to imbibe online teaching skills, thus adding to the ado surrounding hybrid programs.

In this conceptual paper, an integrated methodology for combining traditional face-to-face learning with contemporary online learning is proposed. The ten step methodology provides guidance to traditional institutions in gradually increasing their student outreach by way of creating hybrid programs that are more conducive to the requirements of working professionals, housewives, and people located at distant locations from the institution's campus.

The key recommendation here is to look at outsourcing options wherever a traditional institution does not have adequate resources, capability or intent. There are service providers available today that have amassed invaluable experience in serving the hybrid learning needs of various institutions globally. They have the ability to help traditional institutions kick-start hybrid programs while saving substantially on resources and time. However, institutions should prudently choose such service providers, keeping in view their unique requirements.

References

1. Allen, I.E., Seaman, J.: Class Differences: Online Education in the United States. Babson Survey Research Group, USA (2010)
2. Olapiriyakul, K., Scher, J.M.: A Guide to Establishing Hybrid Learning Courses: Employing Information Technology to Create a New Learning Experience and a Case Study. Internet and Higher Education 9, 287–301 (2006)
3. Stubbs, M., Martin, I., Endlar, L.: The "Structuration" of Blended Learning: Putting Holistic Design Principles into Practice. British Journal of Educational Technology 37(2), 163–175 (2006)

4. Derntl, M., Motschnig-Pitrik, R.: The Role of Structure, Patterns, and People in Blended Learning. Internet and Higher Education 8, 111–130 (2005)
5. Bedi, K.: Experiences of Hybrid Corporate Training Programmes at an Online Academic Institution. In: Fong, J., Kwan, R., Wang, F.L. (eds.) ICHL 2008. LNCS, vol. 5169, pp. 271–282. Springer, Heidelberg (2008)
6. Williams, J.B., Bedi, K., Goldberg, M.A.: The Impact of Digital Storytelling on Social Agency: Early Experience at an Online University. In: Third International Conference on Educational Technology, Singapore (September 7-8, 2006)
7. Williams, J.B., Bedi, K.: Using Digital Storytelling as an Assessment Instrument: Preliminary Findings at an Online University. In: 11th Computer Assisted Assessment Conference, July 10-11. Loughborough University, U.K (2007)
8. Bedi, K.: Innovations in Defining, Designing and Delivering Online Corporate Training Programmes: A Case Study. In: First E-Learning Excellence Forum, Dubai, UAE (January 14-17, 2008)
9. Williams, J.B., Wong, A.: The Efficacy of the Final Examination: A Comparative Study of Closed-Book, Invigilated Exams and Open-Book, Open-Web Exams. British Journal of Educational Technology 40(2), 227–236 (2009)

A Case Study on Design of Teacher Peer-Coaching Activities Supported by a Web 2.0 Community

Shuang Li, Hongtao Sun, and Xun Zheng

School of Educational Technology, Beijing Normal University,
19 Xinjiekouwai Street, Beijing, P.R. China
lsbnu@163.com, sunhtao@gmail.com, zhengxxls@gmail.com

Abstract. Recently, increased attention has been paid to the concept of the community of practice (CoP), which is seen as a valuable and sustainable way for teacher professional development. Peer coaching is always regarded as an effective way to build communities of teachers in that teachers enhance their expertise by sharing, learning from each other, and collaborating. Peer coaching supported by web 2.0 technology provides new opportunities for teacher professional development and building of CoP. And the great success of Social Network Services, such as Facebook, has shed a light on the importance of relationship building in community development. This paper presents a case study on the design of teachers' online peer coaching activities supported by a Web 2.0 community to enhance CoP building. Relation and knowledge flow are defined as a unit of activity design. The paper reports the theoretical framework and results of activity design, the implementation and evaluation of the activities and useful reflections.

Keywords: Peer coaching, Teacher professional development, Community of practice, Web2.0.

1 Introduction

The literature on teacher professional development suggested that teacher learning is always mediated through dialogues in their own practice with their peers and other teachers [1]. Compared with intensive training provided by experts, characterized by horizontal sharing, interaction and grounded in teachers' situations will be more suitable professional development ways for teachers. Among them, community of practice (CoP) and peer coaching has recently received increased attention.

Communities of practice are groups of people who share a concern or a passion for something they do and learn how to do it better as they interact regularly [14]. Members of CoPs are practitioners. In CoP, people develop a shared repertoire of resources and a shared practice, and build relationships that enable them to learn from each other. Wenger pointed out that CoPs attach great importance on social participation and shared identity through engaging in the community's activities, and provide useful means for capturing and constructing individual and collective practical knowledge for teaching [14]. Besides, CoPs can provide teachers with a

R. Kwan et al. (Eds.): ICHL 2011, LNCS 6837, pp. 40–50, 2011.

more economic and effective approach for supporting teacher individualized and sustainable learning and development.

Peer coaching is a valuable professional development strategy in that teachers enhance their expertise by sharing aspects of teaching with peers, observing each other's teaching, providing feedback, pooling their experiences, and being mentored by an experienced peer [7]. In peer coaching, teachers share in conversations, reflect on and refine their practice. Their relationship is built on confidentiality and trust in a non-threatening environment in which they learn and grow up together. The literature on peer coaching showed that teachers can be improved through kinds of peer coaching activities, which provide teachers with opportunities for experimentation, observation, reflection, the exchange of professional ideas, and shared problem solving [19][2][8]. Given that peer coaching contributes to a shared practice, construction of collective practical knowledge and positive relationship building among teachers, it is always regarded as an effective way to build communities of teachers [13]. Nevertheless, how to design peer coaching activities to improve teacher's expertise and building of teacher CoP have not yet to be described in detail in the literature.

Online professional development provides participants with web-based learning opportunities, including online activities, workshops, resources, and online collaboration with peers [3]. It is worthwhile to note that both CoPs and peer coaching activities began to embrace Web 2.0 technologies developed recently. Web 2.0 technologies can support and facilitate peer coaching among teachers who distributed at different schools or areas, and provide a powerful technology environment for building CoPs. So, we believe that peer coaching activities supported by Web 2.0 can break the barriers of space and time, facilitate mutual assistance and collaboration among teachers, and promote the construction of a wider community of teachers' practice.

Based on this idea, in May 2008, Research Center of Distance Education (RCDE) of Beijing Normal University launched the *Experimental Study on Web-Based 'Peer coaching' Teacher Professional Developmental Model*, funded by the Ford Foundation of United States. The purpose of the project is to explore how peer coaching supported by Web 2.0 technologies could enhance teacher professional competency and contribute to build teacher CoP. This paper reports the findings of the project.

The project team built a peer coaching teacher CoP named Libazhuang with Web2.0 technology and chose Learner-centered teaching method as a theme for this experimental study. A teacher training program on "Learner-centered" teaching method was developed by the project team, which including five days intensive training and sixteen months online activities grounded in teachers' own situations supported by peer coaching. The action research activity consisted of kinds of peer coaching sub-activities supported by the Libazhuang community, some of which were compulsory for training program, some were optional. It was worth noting that all peer coaching activities were also open to members of the Libazhuang community. Both peer coaching activities and Web 2.0 community discussed in this paper is drawn from this project.

2 Basic of Activity Design

In order to build a teacher CoP and improve teachers' professional competency of "learner centered" teaching, we analyzed Cops from the perspectives of knowledge and relationships and designed peer coaching activities.

Cops are social and technical ecologies in which knowledge is retained and created [14]. Among different kinds of explanations of knowledge sharing and creation, the SECI mode was widely accepted in the field of knowledge management, which interprets knowledge sharing and creation as a spiraling process, shown in Fig.1 [11].

Lin used SECI model to explain knowledge flows in online teachers' community [5]. They suggest that special effort should be made to help knowledge flows from Socialization to Externalization and Externalization to Combination.

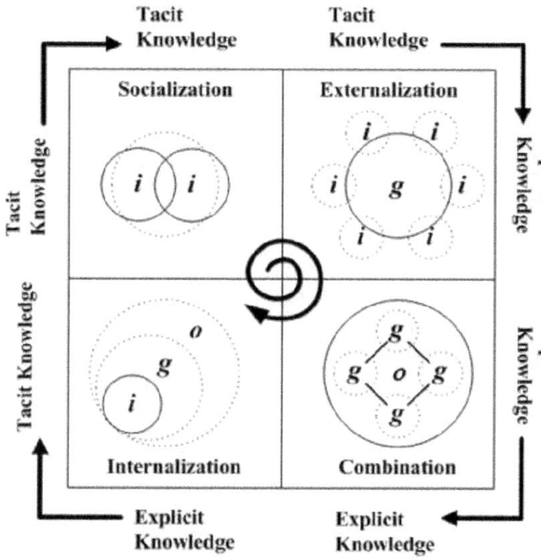

Fig. 1. SECI Knowledge Model

The SECI model inspires us in two important ways. Firstly, the knowledge sharing and creation among individuals, groups and the whole community can be explained as different levels of knowledge construction. The four stages of SECI are consistent with knowledge constructions. In the whole process, individuals, groups and the whole community construct their knowledge accordingly. The original knowledge may come from some individuals, while others construct their own knowledge by interacting with them. Individuals with common interests form various kinds of groups, which enhance the interaction among group members. In groups more knowledge is likely to be shared and created. And this knowledge can be shared to other groups and form community knowledge.

Secondly, relationship influences knowledge sharing and creation greatly. With the support of new web 2.0 technology and design pattern of Social Network Service

(SNS), different kinds of relationships could be built in CoPs. These relationships change the way of interaction in CoPs. And, in turn, the sharing and creation process of knowledge could be different. In the SECI model, all the stages can benefit from tighter relationships.

With these two understandings, we believe that relationship building could enhance knowledge sharing and creation, and consequently accelerate CoPs building. There are many ways to categorize relationships. In the literature, different types of peer coaching are analyzed. Robbins suggested that three kinds of peer coaching, which are instruction between experienced and less-experienced teachers, two or more colleagues working together around their teaching, and a pair or a team of teachers co-planning a lesson or curriculum unit [12]. The role of coach or mentor is emphasized in literatures [6]. Hennissen used expert coaching and reciprocal coaching to describe different types of peer coaching. While expert coaching occurs when teachers with more advanced expertise provide assistance to other teachers, reciprocal coaching refers to peers with similar experience and knowledge mentoring each other [4]. Peer coaching relationships often include teachers with different experiences. Various kinds of groups with different size from two to many are formed to achieve professional goals.

Besides, the success of Social Networking Services (SNS), such as Facebook, attracts our attention to the social ties among teachers in community. Literature shows two of the three purposes for Facebook usage are build social relations and help work (The other is daily activity) [10]. The social ties formed in community can enhance online interaction.

Based on the literature review and activities observation in the Libazhuang community, we defined five different relationships in the Libazhuang community, which were Follow, Help, Consult, Instruction and Collaboration. Basically, they are transformed from loose to close, simple to complex. These relationships reveal different kinds of peer coaching.

Follow refers to basic relationship when teachers get to know each other. Teacher starts their social interactions just like becoming "Friends" in Facebook. Help refers to a low level peer coaching happens occasionally, such as teachers ask questions in forum and give comments to other teachers' blog. Consult refers to a deeper and more constant peer coaching among teachers when they get together in community discuss some topics for getting deeper understanding or finding a solution. Instruction refers to specific mentor-ship. In Instruction relationships, there could be mentors and mentees. One mentor can instruct several mentees. Collaboration refers to long and complex cooperation among several teachers. When several teachers worked in community together to compose one lesson plan or design an action research, their relationship is Collaboration.

Relationships mentioned above are the framework of peer coaching of the Libazhuang community. With the analysis to knowledge sharing and relationships in CoPs, we designed activities to build these relationships and enhance online peer coaching. In the following description, we analyze activities, relationships and knowledge. The list of activities in the Libazhuang community is shown in Table1.

Table 1. List of activities in the Libazhuang community

Name	Compulsory/ optional
Friends Introduction	Compulsory
Action Researches	Compulsory
Micro-blog	Optional
Question and answer	Compulsory
"Learning Science" reading seminars	Optional
Expert studio	Optional
Online mentorship	Optional
Achievements competition	Optional
Instructional design co-editing	Optional
Instructional strategies co-constructing	Compulsory

3 The Web 2.0 community for Online Activities

With Web2.0 technologies, the Libazhuang community was designed and developed by the project team to support online peer coaching activities and CoP building. This Libazhuang community uses Social Networking Services (SNS) as its main structure. Benefitting from its user-centered nature, the Web 2.0 community provides more supports for socialization, externalization, combination, internalization of knowledge in CoPs.

Web2.0 modules in the community include Friends, Blog, Wiki, Sharing, Question, Forum, Repository, Group, Online mentorship, and Expert studio, which will facilitate building of various relationships among teachers and support online behaviors necessary for kinds of peer coaching activities, such as reflection, sharing, discussion, instruction, collaboration.

"Friends" is designed as a tool for a teacher to easily establish personal connections via "Friends" with other teachers in the community. When teachers become "Friends", the community keeps them updated with their friends' online activities, e.g. publishing a blog, editing a wiki, answering a question, etc. As a result, a wider social network would be built in the community.

In Blog, in addition to a basic web log, a micro-blog is also provided for the activities about reflection and presentation in socialization and internalization. Question is a module enables teachers to ask other questions for the activities about help and consulting. With Sharing, participants can share articles, videos, questions, and other type of resources. Teachers can establish groups according to their interests, and group members have more ways to collaborate with each other for the activities about externalization in groups. User-generated content repository is designed for teachers to upload their teaching plans and multimedia resources, which is the separation with other educational resources websites in China. Online mentorship and Expert studio are design for the corresponding activities. Wiki allows participants to add content, as on an Internet forum, but also allows anyone to edit the content [9], which is an evidence of the activities about collaboration and combination.

4 Peer Coaching Activity Design

Peer coaching activities in the Libazhuang community was designed to enhance CoPs in the project. According to how to facilitate the knowledge construction in individual, groups and the community, the participants' main activities were divided into three categories, individual activities, group activities and community activities.

As the relationships mentioned above start from Follow, we designed activities to build basic social connection among teachers, such as Friends introduction. After teachers got to know each other, activities like Micro-blog and Question and Answer gave teachers' opportunities to exchange ideas they met in their daily work to help each other. After social connections were built and fundamental interactions started, more complex activities like "Learning Science" reading seminars were organized to arouse deeper interaction among teachers. After the establishment of social ties and low level peer coaching relationships, Expert studio and Online mentorship started to build consult and instruction relationships. The most complex activities, such as Instructional design co-editing and Instructional strategies co-constructing, were organized to facilitate collaboration. We also designed Action research activities that last the whole process of online activities. In Action research, different level of relationships can be found.

In designing these activities, we not only attempt to build Peer coaching relationships step by step, but also intend to extend knowledge flows from individual to other individuals, groups and, finally, the whole community.

4.1 Individual Activities

The activity, Friends introduction, was organized in order to construct the basis of help, consulting, instruction and collaboration in the Libazhuang community. Most participants took this activity as soon as they sign up the community. In this activity, participants invited at least one friend in real world to sign up the community and introduced the friend through a blog post, including his or her interest and teaching stories. According to the introductions, participants followed more friends, the peers who have similar levels of experience, for further consultation and collaboration.

Borrowed the idea of twitter, the activity, Reflection in micro-blog, was designed to participants to reflect their teaching in several words. In this activity, first of all, as twitter and other micro-blogs, the content was appropriated in a shorted length but as soon as possible, which increased the opportunities for reflection on practice and teaching. Secondly, participants recorded their daily experiences through blog posts, tagging some words like "micro-blog", to distinguish from other blog posts. Then the most active participants were reward in the community.

Peers were needed to solve problems in teaching, working and researching. The activity, Question and answer, was organized for participants to seek helps. Considering the participants had many ill-structured problems in their teaching, such as how to use the "learner-centered" instructional strategies in class, participants were encouraged to summarize and refine their problems by communication and discussion. Then they invited someone who they considered could answer the question. Both the friends that participants had followed with and the experts not known are candidates. To get more answers, several strategies were used, such as encouraging participants to answer the questions their friends asked or they were familiar with. Finally, the best answer was summarized and the appreciation was given for help.

In these activities, participants' friend circles were extended while socializing and externalizing their knowledge. Fundamental interactions began. Further collaborations, such as instructional design co-editing in the wiki, were based in the relationship both the f2f training and these activities built up, which earned more opportunities to the knowledge construction in groups and in the community.

4.2 Group Activities

After social connection was built, the community required some activities (externalization, discussion, consulting and instruction) to facilitate participants to construct their knowledge with peers, which evidenced the knowledge's externalization in groups.

Reading seminar helped participants to build a peer-coaching group where they exchanged and shared their mind in one topic. "Learning Science" was a theory book demanded by participants. In the reading seminar activity, each participant read a part of the book and recoded reviews though blog posts. In an appointed time, participants discussed important issues of Learning Science by instant message tools. During the discussion, one of the participants took the responsibility to explain this book's idea, and others contributed their minds to the summary. After online discussion, the group posted their whole idea to the community to share and discuss.

In community of practice, expert teachers could lead other participants in their action researches and educational theory learning, which might promote their professional development. Some topics the participants interested were formulated in workshops, which supported their action researches powerfully. The activity of expert workshop could be divided into some tasks as following: experts' invitation for the participants who were good at specialized themes or special subject, expert workshop, experts lecture through videoconference online, and specialized theme Researches organized by experts which might promote participants' action research.

The value of mentorship in peer coaching as a form of continuing professional development for experienced faculty was largely recognized. In the Libazhuang community, online mentorships aimed at providing an online platform for mutual assistance for participants' ongoing development. This activity could be divided into some steps as following: mentors and apprentices' application, mentorships formulation, achievements demonstration and further instruction & collaboration. According to the subjects and grades they taught, mentorships were formed up, which continued in further activities, such as instructional design co-editing and action researches.

These activities broke the region limitation existed in the traditional peer coaching activities, providing more professional advice and guidance to the participants' researches and practice. Shared practice and knowledge were developed in the group rather than individual in these activities, which was the next step of the knowledge's socialization. It made the knowledge flowing from individual to groups in the community.

4.3 Community Activities

Knowledge construction in the Libazhuang community required participants in different groups to collaborate in the community, which took place in some activities about cooperation, collaboration, and combination.

In the activity, Instructional strategies co-constructing, participants followed two steps to complete joint construction in remote: strategy's pages creation which was partly completed during the five days intensive training in the project, and strategies' reviewing in collaborating to the extended content, more examples and reflections.

In the activities, pedagogical results contest, the recourses and results were required to share in the community. Participants uploaded the results they got in any activities, including articles, documents, videos, audios, PPTs and other files to Repository in the community. According to a given standard, participants scored for the recourses and results and voted for those regarded as valuable.

These activities provided the evidences that collaborative knowledge construction took place in the community, formulating a series of beneficial recourses and results for the community. The community's knowledge was built up in the cooperation and collaboration.

4.4 Action Research Activities

Action research activities based on teachers' daily practice were a main thread of the whole online activities. The task required participants to design and implement a "learner-centered" class (including instructional design, teaching video records, and teaching reflection) according to the project.

In the Libazhuang community, all of the online activities were designed to facilitate the participants in completing the action research, which provided useful scaffolds for the participants. To ensure each task's completion of the task, it was divided into a series of easy-to-follow sub-activities, what participants took part in, which gradually developed their action research with the help of peer participants: conversation for exploring the problems faced in teaching, making research plans, action researches based on the practice of their teaching, results demonstration by blog posts, wikis, videos, and topics in BBS, and evaluation & conclusion. In every task of action research, participants were encouraged to communicate with peers in the community. Useful scaffolds were given in other activities in the community, such as participants could make up the research plans easier by taking part in the expert workshops.

In action research, knowledge took the circle of socialization (posting blog and micro-blogs, following the experts), externalization (asking question, discussing in IM or BBS, commenting to blogs, sharing resources in groups, instructing in mentorship workshop), combination (planning the blueprint of research, editing wikis, co-editing blog) and internalization (acting the research, finishing the achievements) to. All kinds of relationships were required in this main thread of the whole online activities.

5 Implementation and Evaluation of Peer Coaching Activities

The training program was delivered in two Chinese districts in August 2009, Tianhe district of Guangzhou in Guangdong Province, and Wuhou district of Chengdu in Sicuan Province. Peer coaching activities had been launched following face-to-face training since September 2009, and lasted sixteen months. More than 120 participants, including subject teachers, school principals and local teaching researchers, took part in activities formally. In addition, other teachers of the Libazhuang community were also free to participate in these activities. By now, all peer coaching activities have been finished and comprehensive investigation and evaluation of the activities is still on-going, but initial results and observations collected during the process of activities give cause for optimism as to the prospect of achieving our goals.

On one hand, it was found that participants' professional competency on "learner centered" teaching were improved though peer coaching. Before activities, most participants had no idea of how to use "learner centered" teaching method into their class effectively even though they had received some relevant knowledge during face to face training. However, in reviewing the teaching plans submitted by participants at the end of the activities, three notable improvements were found compared with those submitted before the training. More work had been done on learner analysis when the participants designed their lessons, including analyzing learning characteristics, learners' background and interests, previous relevant knowledge and skills, and differences between learners. In addition, the design of objectives, content and strategies reflected the analysis of learning outcomes. Finally, there was an obvious shift about the focus of design from teaching activities to learning activities.

In Libazhuang community, participants generated 1603 blogs, 368 wiki entries, and 305 resources. This user-generated content covers 9 subjects in K12 education. Participants' deeper understand of learner-centered instruction are evident in this content. For example, they have started to think more about students' diversity. Teacher Liu wrote in his blog, "I start to think from students' perspective. When preparing a class, I consider more students' knowledge level and individual difference. " In addition, they are trying to give students more time to express their ideas. Teacher Lu wrote, "My understanding of teacher's role changed greatly. In every class, I give students more opportunities to ask questions and response to others' answers. I want to give back their right to learn."

On the other hand, a teacher CoP was gradually coming into be at least in terms of the following three aspects. Firstly, different kinds of ties among teachers are established in the Libazhuang community by various online behaviors in peer coaching activities, such as adding friends, commenting on other's blog, building mentorship, responding to questions, attending groups and expert workshop, co-writing blog. At the time of writing, 278 teachers have community friends, 22% of them have more than five friends. Average number of friends per teacher is 5, and maximum is up to 48; 855 blogs received comments and 115 questions brought up by teaches got feedbacks; 940 teachers attended groups and there are 79 groups built in the community. Average number of teachers per group is 11, and maximum is up to 132; there are 11 pairs of mentors and apprentices and 7 workshops; 31 co-writing blogs were established by teachers, the average number of teachers per co-writing blog is 8. According to above initial results, a wider teacher social network was established in the community, which provides more new opportunities for peer coaching and a foundation for building of CoP.

Secondly, some evidences informed us that culture of mutual assistance and learning is forming in the Libazhuang community and most participants had sense of belonging to the Libazhuang. Teachers learned to learn from each other through peer coaching. More and more teachers went to the community spontaneously seeking for help, getting suggestions, discussing questions, and finding collaborators. Teacher Lu wrote in his blog," I am surprised that so many teachers in Libazhuang can still keep writing their blogs and responding to questions though they are so busy." Teacher Zeng wrote," When I opened my blog tonight, I found there were three new comments on my blog. I was deeply touched by these few words in the comments. I want to say thank you to these three teachers and also to the Libazhuang."

Furthermore, participants became more ready to be giving and assisting other teachers in the community after benefiting from peer coaching. This change can be reflected by rising responding rate of questions in the community. Teacher Chen, a participant of mentorship activity, wrote, "Many thanks to my mentor. I hope to give some return to him and 'Libazhuang' by attending this activity." Teacher Li wrote, " I am happy we got a new member to join us, which encourage us to do our best to establish this virtual space of preparing for class provided by Libazhuang."

At last, through peer coaching in some activities, such as pedagogical results contest and co-writing blogs, both collective knowledge of a group and knowledge of an individual teacher were encouraged and facilitated to be externalized in the community which would provide a foundation for combination of knowledge in the whole community. Among all activities, instructional strategies co-constructing in Wiki was specially designed for combination and building of knowledge on "learner centered" instructional strategies in the whole community. Besides, it was worth noting that the community environment could record most user-generated content including reflection, discuss and creation, which provides a possibility for new combination of knowledge in the whole community in future.

6 Conclusions and Reflections

This case study on the design of peer coaching activities in a Web 2.0 community environment for building a teacher CoP has shown that well-designed peer coaching activities certainly contribute to build CoP which can provide both individual teacher and teacher groups with sustainable and effective supports for professional development. It seems to be crucially important to analyze the key features of CoP and requirements of teacher professional development before activity design. The relation for peer coaching appears to be the one that connect CoP, peer coaching and professional development. Building various relationships among teachers and facilitating knowledge transform from individual to groups and then to the community have been the focus of our peer coaching activity design, which was demonstrated preliminarily effective in this case study.

Secondly, the web2.0 technologies with a number of emerging social web services indeed facilitated relationships building and the knowledge construction in the community. The evidences of peer coaching were found in the modules of Wiki, Sharing, Question, Group, Online mentorship, and Expert workshop. With the teacher social network built through peer coaching in the community, the activities promoted the knowledge flow, which powerfully demonstrated that web2.0 technologies can support joint construction and CoP building.

Thirdly, some experiences are summarized from the design and implementation of all the online activities. We found that teachers' motivation is important to the success of online activities. Activities should be grounded in teachers' practice to increase their motivation. In addition, full consideration should be taken to the heavy workload of school teachers. Time pressure could lead to failure of online activities. Finally, multiple participations could benefit online interaction in CoPs. The Libazhuang community members include novice teachers, experienced teachers, school administrators and teaching research staffs. Various types of members improve dynamics in community.

Acknowledgments. The work presented in this paper is supported by a Ford Foundation Program award to the RCDE of Beijing Normal University. The authors would like to thank Prof. Chen, the director of this project, for her support to this paper, the support staff members of RCDE for their hard work and efforts. Meanwhile we would like to thank educational officers and participants in the two experimental areas: Tianhe district in Guangzhou, Guangdong Province, China and Wuhou district in Chengdu, Sichuan Province, China.

References

1. Avalos, B.: Teacher professional development in Teaching and Teacher Education over ten years. Teaching and Teacher Education 27, 10–20 (2011)
2. Bergen, T., Engelen, A., Derksen, K.: The quality of coaching in relation to the professional development of teachers. Teaching and Teacher Education 24, 97–114 (2006)
3. Chen, Y., Chen, N.S., Tsai, C.C.: The use of online synchronous discussion for web-based professional development for teachers. Computers & Education 53(4), 115 (2009)
4. Hennissen, P., Crasborn, F., Brouwer, N., Korthagen, F., Bergen, T.: Mapping mentor teachers' roles in mentoring dialogues. Educational Research Review 3(2), 168–186 (2008)
5. Lin, F., Lin, S., Huang, T.: Knowledge sharing and creation in a teachers' professional virtual community. Computers & Education 50(3), 742–756 (2008)
6. Lu, H.: Research on peer coaching in preservice teacher education - A review of literature. Teaching and Teacher Education 26(4), 748–753 (2010)
7. Joyce, B., Shower, B.: The evolution of peer coaching. Educational Leadership 53(6), 12–16 (1996)
8. Joyce, B., Showers, B.: Student achievement through staff development, 3rd edn. ASCD, Alexandria (2002)
9. Parslow, G.R.: Commentary: Wiki: The fast way to collaborative authoring. Biochemistry and Molecular Biology Education 5, 371–371 (2005)
10. Mazman, S.G., Usluel, Y.K.: Modeling educational usage of Facebook. Computers & Education 55(2), 444–453 (2010)
11. Nonaka, I., Takeuchi, H.: The knowledge-creating company: How Japanese companies create the dynamics of innovation? Oxford University Press, New York (1995)
12. Robbins, P.: How to plan and implement a peer coaching. ASCD, Alexandria (1991)
13. Russo, A.: A School-based coaching, `http://hepg.org/hel/article/269`
14. Wenger, E.: Communities of practice: learning, meaning, and identity. Cambridge University Press, Cambridge (1998)
15. Zwart, R.C., Wubbels, T., Bolhuis, S., Bergen, T.C.M.: Teacher learning through reciprocal peer coaching: an analysis of activity sequences. Teaching and Teacher Education 24(4), 982–1002 (2008)

Evidence-Based Educational Practices and a Theoretical Framework for Hybrid Learning

Jayshiro Tashiro[1,2,3], Patrick C.K. Hung[1,2], and Miguel Vargas Martin[1,4]

[1] University of Ontario Institute of Technology
Oshawa, Ontario, Canada L1H 7K4
[2] BeaconWall Limited
Hong Kong Science and Technology Park
[3] Wolfsong Informatics LLC
Tucson, Arizona, USA 85718
[4] PHractal Partnership
Oshawa, Ontario, Canada LIH 7K4

Abstract. Reviews of literature on hybrid learning reveal a general lack of theoretical coherence in the evolving instructional methods and materials as well as in the delivery modalities of courses designed as hybrid learning environments. In this paper, we first examine six critical barriers to development of evidence-based frameworks for how and why to build hybrid teaching-learning-assessment environments. Secondly, we review some of the implications for developing a theoretical framework for studying hybrid learning. Finally, we propose a Transtheoretical Model for Hybrid Learning that is substantially derived from ecosystem theory.

Keywords: theory of hybrid learning, evidence-based learning, e-learning, e-teaching, learning assessment, learning management systems.

1 Introduction

Despite an aggressive movement toward increased use of hybrid and totally online courses at all levels of education and training, there is still a lack of evidence-based frameworks for educational and training methods, materials, and delivery modalities that have a strong research base for optimizing the learning of diverse students at any academic or training level. The lack of evidence-based frameworks for hybrid learning results from the complexity of studying and implementing such frameworks as well as from absence of coherent theoretical framework that might guide systematic studies of the enormous complexity inherent in hybrid learning. Six profound deficiencies are particularly difficult barriers to overcome.

A first deficiency is a critical set of knowledge gaps related to educational environments and their effectiveness. These gaps emerged from a review of a large and diverse research literature [1,2]. The US National Research Council [3,4] offered a streamlined list of critical issues in developing expertise and these remain hallmarks of what educational methods and materials should provide (see also a more recent and extensive review by the American Association for the Advancement of Science [5] and Federation of American Scientists [6]). The National Research Council list can

R. Kwan et al. (Eds.): ICHL 2011, LNCS 6837, pp. 51–72, 2011.

be revised into questions that any set of instructional materials should address in order to improve higher order reasoning: (1) How do instructional materials enhance disposition to learn? (2) How do the materials provide multiple paths for learning? (3) How does an instructional package help students overcome limitations of prior knowledge? (4) When and how do the educational materials provide practice and feedback? (5) Can the instructional materials help students develop an ability to transfer knowledge acquired by extending knowledge and skills beyond the contexts in which they were gained? (6) How will the instructional package incorporate the role of social context? (7) How and why will the instructional methods and materials address cultural norms and student beliefs? Yet, the vast majority of instructional methods and materials do not satisfactorily address all of these questions.

Tashiro, Hung, and Vargas Martin [1] studied the critical issues outlined by the US National Research Council. A more recent literature review identified critical gaps in our knowledge, some identified in the National Research Council analysis, but others not identified. We found 10 gaps in knowledge about how educational materials "really work" to change an individual's learning outcomes and willingness as well as ability to sustain behaviours related to learning [1,2]: (1) How does an educational environment impact disposition to engage in a learning process? (2) What are the relationships between the level of realism in an educational environment and learning outcomes? (3) How do you define the threshold of experience within an educational environment that leads to measurable learning outcomes? (4) What are the knowledge domains being developed during learning? (5) In which knowledge domains is learning being retained and how stable is the retention? (6) What is the disposition to act on the knowledge gained during work within an educational environment? (7) How well can the knowledge be transferred? (8) What learning outcomes (conceptual and performance competencies) are developed during the learning process while working within an educational environment? (9) How are misconceptions developed during and sustained after working within an educational environment? (10) How do teacher-student and student-student social networks or e-communities impact learning? Without rigorous studies that help bridge these ten gaps, we simply cannot make generalized claims about the efficacy of hybrid learning.

A second deficiency is inherent in our lack of understanding about an individual's idiosyncratic response to a situated learning experience, particularly if the learning experience varies in time and space (e.g., when there are face-to-face interactions compartmentalized in a classroom interspersed with anytime-anywhere Web-based activities that have different types of faculty-student and student-student interactions). This second deficiency relates directly to a third deficiency, namely that individual students or trainees have patterns of cognition, motivation, and behavioral intention that manifest even when the situated learning experience is not temporally and spatially heterogeneous. In short, there is tremendous complexity in the emergence of interactions between the temporal variability of both the environment in which education is delivered and of the individual student's or trainee's engagement within the educational process. Evidence-based practices in education have been difficult to implement because of the multivariate nature of such emergence complexities between individual patterns of learning and the multivariate nature of teaching-learning-assessment environments created within educational or training setting for any particular suite of curricular objectives.

A fourth deficiency arises because current educational methods and materials, nested within any delivery modality, do not provide solutions to the first three deficiencies in ways that allow measurement of at least two kinds of learning outcomes, conceptual competencies and performance competencies. Here, we are using conceptual competencies as a thorough understanding of a knowledge and/or skills domain. Often conceptual competencies are further elaborated as: (1) competencies in which a person can describe how and why to use the knowledge or skill in different but appropriate contexts (generativity); and (2) competencies in which a person can describe how to use the knowledge or skill in situations that are unfamiliar (robustness). In contrast, performance competencies are those competencies in which knowledge is acted on as an expression of a variety of behaviors and decisions or skills that are implemented in the real world or some very close simulation of the real world [1,2,7].

Not unrelated to the first four deficiencies discussed above, within educational environments (broadly defined) cognition and learning will be shaped by the situated encounters in that environment, which are dynamic and strongly influenced by social contexts as well as by a diverse array of other elements reflective of the student's or trainee's prior knowledge, intrinsic motivation, extrinsic motivation, comfort within the social milieu of the educational environment and its deliver modality, disposition to engage in effortful cognitive endeavor, behavioural intentions to continue working within suites of articulated learning activities, learning resources, learning assessments, and access to as well as use of feedback provided within the educational environment. Furthermore, effective teaching-learning strategies require students or trainees to develop cognitive processes that lead to stable knowledge domains, with metacognitive pattern recognition capabilities that are critical to knowledge transfer and minimization of misconceptions. In regard to the fourth deficiency, current educational environments are often weak in authentic learning outcomes assessments in which students' and trainees' conceptual and performance competencies can be measured automatically and with detailed diagnostic feedback providing meaningful guidance for students to improve their learning. Importantly, the advances in social learning environments and social networking may introduce more complexity as they become integrated into learning and training environments in the following ways: (1) focusing on students; (2) personalizing learning; (3) discovering experts; (4) distributing authorship; (5) liberating knowledge; (6) roaming and learning; and (7) creating accountability. Such integration opens new opportunities for building teaching-learning-assessment environments that may enhance competency development, but also must be studied for their efficacy.

A fifth deficiency arises as students and trainees engage in educational activities or training. There must be adequate sampling of what they learn, what learning they retain, and what learning they can transfer into real-world problem-solving. Interestingly, educators are now realizing more completely the extreme importance of assessing spatial and temporal heterogeneity of the critical educational outcome variables that are supposed to measure an individual student's or group of students' conceptual and performance competencies.

A sixth deficiency arises because even if the prior five deficiencies could be overcome, individual faculty members and trainers do not agree on a singular theory of cognition or a theory of behavioral change. Consequently, a diversity of instructional designs emerge within a general failure to provide educational methods and materials that have the flexibility to accommodate any theory of cognition and any theory of behavioral change because. Certainly, it is clear that each theory or theory combination would have particular types of educational activities and learning assessments as well as particular types and arrangements of educational scaffolding to support a learner within learning environments.

Educational methods and materials have tried to couple learning activities to learning outcomes assessments using knowledge-based computerized mentoring systems, data mining applications, and other analytical systems to measure what has been learned, the stability of the learning, and students' and trainees' abilities to transfer the learning to real-world activities. However, these efforts have generally failed to adequately sample at any one time, let alone across time series in order to provide sufficient information to portray the likely impacts of educational methods and materials on the development of, the stability of, and the retention and knowledge transfer capabilities of students and trainees (as measured by both conceptual and performance competencies). Furthermore, current educational practices seldom allow the flexibility to customize teaching-learning-assessment environments in ways that would accommodate different theories of cognition or behavioral change resulting from educational interventions.

The six deficiencies discussed above, individually and in combination, contribute to a general failure to collect sufficient and high quality data on educational methods and materials, wherein the interpretation of such data can enhance the management of educational and training interventions and allow moving sensibly towards educational methods and materials empirically founded on evidence-based learning. Thus, using extant educational environments and practices, we usually cannot analyze the trajectories of critical variables that shape the educational outcomes and likelihood of knowledge transfer and knowledge translation, the stability of such knowledge, and the subsequent enhancement of such knowledge as the theory and praxis of education and training are advanced. We argue strongly that these six deficiencies point to the need for a theoretical framework that drives development of evidence-based educational practices for hybrid courses.

2 Exploring Translations from Theory to Praxis – Implications for Developing Theories of Hybrid Learning

2.1 What Is a Hybrid Course?

During the past decade we have looked for a theoretical framework, examining dominant theories of cognition and behavioral change [1,2,7]. As we began compiling examples of hybrid courses, we discovered a very diverse array of combinations in percentages of face-to-face classroom environment and online components that together constitute a "hybrid" or "blended" suite of learning environments for a course. Initially, we found no satisfactory evidence-based taxonomies for courses delivered totally or partially online.

Our own work had revealed three themes: quality of face-to-face classroom interactivity (faculty-student as well as student-student), quality of online interactivity (again, faculty-student and student-student), and complementarities of the classroom and online instructional design. For example, in Table 1, and using these three themes, we show a few of the many types of courses we observed. However, the proportion of face-to-face classroom and online components could vary considerably. We also realized that our nascent taxonomy had to account for course subtypes based on the duration and intent of interactions among faculty and students as well as among students and students, which varied considerably across courses in both the face-to-face and online course components. This was true at our university and can be observed across universities and colleges. We therefore added a subtype of hybrid courses that could account for time spent in face-to-face and online components.

Course difficulty emerged as another course subtype during our study of hybrid course types. Studying different courses we found some courses require, on average, more student time engaged in course work. Simple measures include: (1) time spent within the online component, and (2) the number of assignments multiplied by the time per assignment. Obviously, poor usability of the online component could increase both time in the online component and difficulty of completing assignments, but even for courses with high usability in online components, there can still be levels of difficulty associated with an instructor's demands on a student or the relative difficulty of course content (e.g., from beginning to advanced courses).

Figure 1 shows a diagrammatic representation of these two course subtypes within a course defined by the three themes of quality of classroom interactivity, quality of online interactivity, and complementarities of the classroom and online instructional design. Certainly, some would argue that these two subtypes actually represent fourth and fifth themes that disaggregate hybrid course types.

Of course, from the beginning of hybrid and online courses, there was a growing concern about not forcing a "sage on the stage" type of teaching into an online format. There also was evidence of growing concerns about understanding how instructional design evolved within the rapidly evolving educational technologies. Importantly, from 2000-2011 there has been an increasing appearance of articles focused on cognitive approaches to instructional design for multimedia learning [9] and a body of work by Mayer and colleagues arguing for a cognitive theory of multimedia learning as well as instructional multimedia methods and materials that had an evidence-based foundation [10]. Increasingly, articles coupling cognitive science and instructional design began appearing in the literature early in the development of Web-based education.

An interesting paper by Rudak and Sidor presented an intriguing taxonomy for what they called "e-courses" [11]. These researchers critiqued earlier taxonomies, proposed a new taxonomy, and experimentally studied the likelihood of course types in the proposed taxonomy. Their taxonomy drove course type disaggregation by examining relationships between faculty, content, and students, which allowed them to derive three themes: course organization, communications among participants in the educational process, and course structure. In this taxonomy, course organization referred to relative percentages and intent of lectures, discussions, work in small groups, demonstrations, presentations, laboratory and other embedded learning activities, learning resources (text, images, hyperlinks), and learning assessment and feedback within face-to-face and online course components. Rudak and Sidor defined communication as one-alone (e.g., self reflection), one-to-one (student to student, faculty to student), one-to-many (faculty to students or a student presentation to others), and many to many (group presentations and discussions of various types, both synchronous and asynchronous).

Table 1. Examples of different combinations of in-class and online components in hybrid learning environments. Note that the five types listed are only a few of the many different combinations.

Course Type	Face-to-Face Interactivity	Online Interactivity	Complementarities of Classroom and Online Components
Type 1	Low – Instructor lectures with little discussion.	Low – Online learning activities are reading and images with no simulations or interactive learning objects.	Low – Lecture material is reiterated within online component.
Type 2	Low – Instructor lectures with little discussion.	Medium – Online learning activities include reading and images with some relevant simulations or interactive learning objects.	Low – Lecture material is reiterated within online component.
Type 3	Medium – Instructor lectures with some discussion and directed use of online learning activities and learning resources.	High – Online learning activities include reading and images with relevant simulations and learning objects that are highly interactive and reinforce content and skills areas covered by face-to-face and online reading and images.	Medium – Lecture material is reiterated within online component but extended and consolidated by relevant simulations and learning objects.
Type 4	High – Instructor facilitates students' engagement with content and skills, using classroom time to engage students in online components with discussion and clarification of intended use of online course learning activities and learning resources.	High – Online learning activities include reading and images with relevant simulations and learning objects that are highly interactive and reinforce content and skills areas covered by face-to-face and online reading and images.	Medium – Lecture material is reiterated within online component but extended and consolidated by relevant simulations and learning objects.
Type 5	High – Instructor facilitates students' engagement with content and skills, using classroom time to engage students in online components with discussion and clarification of intended use of online course learning activities and learning resources.	High – Online learning activities include reading and images with relevant simulations and learning objects that are highly interactive and reinforce content and skills areas covered by face-to-face and online reading and images.	High –Online component is designed to use face-to-face component as point of departure into content and images that are in turn coupled to relevant simulations and learning objects.

However, the Rudak-Sidor taxonomy extended these communication modalities to quality of interactions, for example: (1) self teaching – students working mostly alone; (2) peer communication – student to student communication; (3) course of open tasks – individualized faculty to student communication; (4) consultation – student to student or teacher to student; (5) teacher's instructions – provision of additional information or learning resources without direct interaction from either side; and (6) full communication – the course includes all or multiple forms of communication (with social networks).

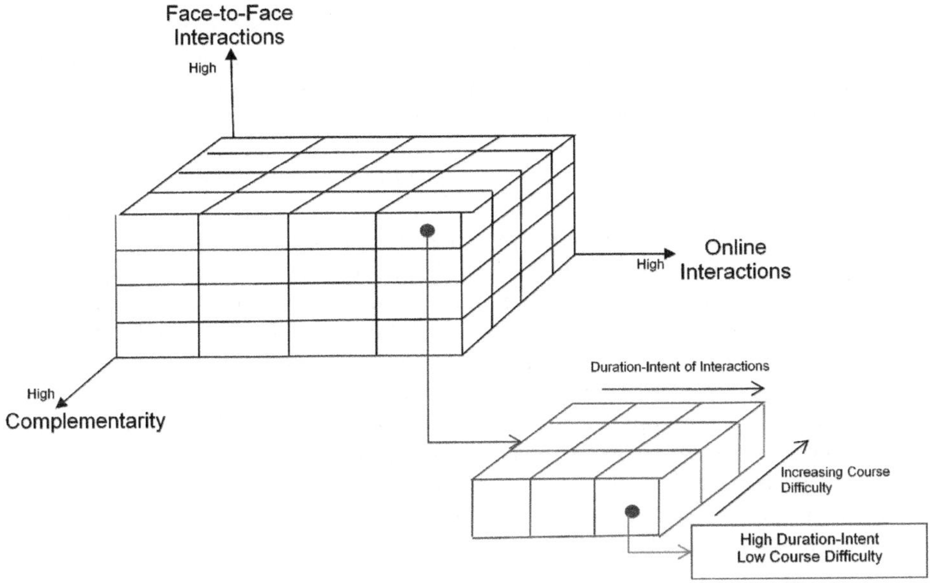

Fig. 1. An early model for classifying hybrid course types and subtypes

We revised the Rudak-Sidor taxonomy to focus on hybrid courses. We also focused on courses with "full communication" as the communication modality since most currently used learning management systems have the capacity for multiple modalities of communication among students and students with faculty members. Based on the literature and our own work [1,2] we added additional disaggregating themes. Table 2 shows a taxonomy for hybrid courses with full communication capacities. Course types based on organization are disaggregated by the relative proportion of face-to-face and online course elements. To simplify, we used Low Percentage (≤ 35%), Medium Percentage (36-70%), and High Percentage (>70%) for the face-to-face course elements. We further disaggregated course organization by degree of complementarities of the face-to-face and online course components.

For course structure, we revised the Rudak-Sidor taxonomy to include: (1) Complete Release – all materials of all course elements are available from the start and remain accessible throughout the course duration; (2) Time Hierarchical Release – with course materials released on a time schedule and without requirement for demonstration of student mastery to move through course materials; (3) Topic Hierarchy without Mastery – course elements are released to students by topic-subject area cluster but without condition of their mastery of prior topic-subject cluster; (4) Topic Hierarch with mastery – course elements are released by course topic-subject area cluster (defined by the faculty member) and with the condition of mastery of the prior topic-subject cluster. We then added an additional disaggregating variable suite related to the degree of educational scaffolding provided for each course structure. To simplify somewhat, we used the terms "Guided" to mean high levels of scaffolding and "Unguided" to mean no or little educational scaffolding related to the course structure and how to move through that structure. Table 2 shows this taxonomy as a {6 x 8} matrix of cells, each cell representing a type of hybrid course.

In Table 2, the cell labeled "A" represents hybrid courses that have a low percentage of faculty face-to-face components (so mostly online), with the face-to-face and online course elements integrated and complementary, with course materials released at the start of the course and available throughout the course, and with guidance provided to the student by scaffolding on how to proceed through the course. The cell labeled "B" represents hybrid courses that have a medium percentage of faculty face-to-face components (more balanced face-to-face and online elements), with the face-to-face and online course elements not very well designed to be complementary, with course materials released on a timed schedule not necessarily correlated with topic-subject clusters, and with little guidance provided to the student by scaffolding that would facilitate how to proceed through the course. As a third example, the cell labeled "C" represents hybrid courses that have a high percentage of faculty face-to-face components (thus, small proportion of online), with the face-to-face and online course elements integrated and complementary, with course materials released by topic-subject cluster on the condition of student mastery of prior topic-subject clusters, and with guidance provided to the student by scaffolding that would facilitate how to proceed through the course.

Table 2. Hybrid course taxonomy derived from the Rudak-Sidor taxonomy (C = Complementary, NC = Not Complementary, G = Guided by Scaffolding, U = Unguided by Scaffolding)

		Course Structure							
		Complete Release		Time Hierarchy		Topic Hierarchy		Topic Hierarchy with Mastery	
Face-to-Face		G	U	G	U	G	U	G	U
Low (≤35%)	C	A							
	NC								
Medium (36-70%)	C								
	NC				B				
High (>70%)	C							C	
	NC								

We have found courses that fit the requirements of each cell of the taxonomy shown in Table 2. Obviously, conditions of lack of complementarities in face-to-face and online components would not usually be good course design. Furthermore, courses that were "Unguided" in amount of scaffolding provided would not necessarily be good instructional design. Of course our point throughout this paper is that we need better empirical bases for what course designs "really work" to improve learning as defined by conceptual and performance competencies.

2.2 What Really Works in Hybrid Learning

Over a decade ago, Tashiro and Rowland [12] published a challenge to educators and researchers, posing the confounded questions of "What really works in instructional approaches and materials, for whom, when, why, and with what outcomes?" Indeed, by 1994-1995 the US National Center for Education Statistics (NCES) noted that 33% of colleges and universities had some type of online courses, and by 2000-2001 NCES reported 56% of post-secondary institutions were offering what was then called distance courses [13-16]. Hybrid learning (in some countries called "blended learning") was thought to provide a judicious and complementary meshing of educational components by combining online and face-to-face instructor mediated classroom experiences. However, evidence could not be generalized. With our revised Rudak-Sidor taxonomy, we could better assign hybrid courses to course types.

Since 2005, hybrid courses for undergraduates, graduate students, professional development, and corporate training have become even more common. We began to focus on instructional designs related to blended learning for three groups: (a) pre-professional healthcare students (e.g., nursing and medical students, medical laboratory technologists, respiratory therapists, physical therapists, and so on); (b) healthcare providers; and (3) individuals receiving healthcare services (patients with chronic illness, patients recently discharged from acute care settings, individuals in nursing homes, and community health as well as health promotion educational outreach). As our work in this area deepened, we became increasingly concerned that instructional design should be shaped by theories of cognition as well as theories of behaviour change.

Patel and colleagues [7] examined how cognition could be shaped by the situated encounters in educational environments designed for healthcare student and practitioner training. These researchers argued that such environments are dynamic and strongly influenced by social contexts and by a diverse array of other elements in the setting, such as technology as well as temporal and spatial heterogeneity in a educational simulation or game environment. We adapted Patel's framework to health sciences education and re-examined possible cognitive frameworks for serious game design that could become part of evidence-based hybrid courses [1,2]. Patel's work led us to ask what would happen if different combinations of Aesthetics, Mechanics, and Dynamics in a Web-based learning object (e.g., a images, animations, simulations, or serious games) led to different types of reasoning, and if so, what might be the results of such reasoning. This was a critical concern for training healthcare students who would soon become healthcare providers and make life-death decisions with patients. Note, please, that herein we are using the terms from the literature on gaming: (1) Aesthetics denotes the sense of the fictional world created by graphics and sound; (2) Mechanics denotes the underlying programming that provides fictional interactions within the virtual setting; and (3) Dynamics is a term used to capture the potential interactions possible in a game and the emergence of the end user's engagement within such interactions. We had to struggle with how and why Aesthetics, Mechanics, and Dynamics could shape learning and development of cognitive processes leading to patterns of students' reasoning.

Some research examined how very sophisticated virtual world might be valuable to examine differences between cognitive theories and their projected educational strategies for more individualistic structured learning (e.g., strategies based on the adaptive character of thought or on the cognitive load theories) or for what educators call constructivist learning (e.g., strategies based on the cognitive flexibility theory or the situated learning theories) [1,2,7]. Yet, for healthcare students and practitioners a startling realization was that behavioural intentions to act on what was learned and actual acting on what had been learned during clinical care required us to examine how and why theories of behavioural change ought to be integrated along with theories of cognition into instructional design of hybrid courses. For patient education or for more generalized health promotion education, such integration of cognitive and behavioural theories would also be important. We extended this idea of combining cognitive and behaviour change theories to all educational environments because eventually all students are required to act on what they know, at least to some extent.

The knowledge gaps identified earlier remain barriers to instructional design for effective hybrid courses and had not been mapped into the numerous theoretical frameworks for cognition or behaviour change. The gaps were an *a posteriori* discovery from reviews by of a very extensive literature. [1]. Our research began mapping the gaps to theoretical frameworks in order to see if any encapsulated the gaps within a coherent interpretative framework that also would help us understand an individual's motivation to learn a content or skill area, what the individual learned (including misconceptions) when engaged within hybrid learning courses, the retention of their knowledge and ability to transfer that knowledge, their motivation to act, their behavioral shifts, in applying knowledge, any misconceptions that were evident in such behavioral shifts, and overall impact of social networking or e-communities.

However, there is no consensus theory of cognition. We could argue from the literature, that there are many theories of cognition and several theories seem very promising in application to studies of hybrid learning (e..g., cognitive load, cognitive theory of multimedia, character of thought, cognitive flexibility and situated learning theories). Analogously, there is no consensus theory of behaviour change and, furthermore, behaviour change theories tend to cluster into individual, social, and ecological levels of perspective [17]. For example, the Transtheoretical Model of Change is more individually focused [18], while DiMatteo and DiNicola offer the Information Motivation Strategy Model that provides a framework that could accommodate multiple theories and allowed across-theory comparison [19]. Fishbein and colleagues reviewed leading theories of behaviour change in order to identify overlapping variables that might explain most of the variance in behaviour change [20]. Interestingly, an e-Health Behaviour Management Model has emerged , combining two models of behaviour [21], and Baranowski and colleagues argued that even with technology constraints, e-Health behaviour change programs based on theory are more likely to be successful [22, 23]. Yet, no current literature that we know of has examined the 10 knowledge gaps from the perspective of exploring instructional design, the human-computer interface, active/passive interactions as well as impacts on individuals' motivation to engage, with confounding related to realism of the digital educational environments as well as willingness to stay engaged to achieve some threshold necessary for retention, subsequent transfer of knowledge gained, and the demonstration of learning outcomes (conceptual competencies) and behavioural shifts (performance competencies).

As we mentioned above, we have tried to clarify what we do not know about "what really works" in hybrid learning and the barriers we face to development of evidence-based practices for hybrid learning course designs. Certainly, in health sciences education, our research has focused on the possibility of health sciences students developing misconceptions that could have deadly consequences if these students became healthcare providers and engaged in patient care. Ongoing studies of simulation and serious game environments for hybrid learning left us with uncertainties about what is being learned in such environments, how learning actually progresses, and what opportunities there are for students to engage in and follow tangents to the educational objectives, which may lead to the development of misconceptions. Again, we emphatically note that non-hybrid methods and materials of education are certainly not free of the potential to lead students to develop misconceptions. However, as hybrid courses become more ubiquitous we actually have an opportunity to shift education to a more evidence-based framework and to be more thoughtful about and critical of educational methods and materials.

3 A Transtheoretical Model of Hybrid Learning

3.1 A Promising Framework from Ecosystems Research

Hybrid learning courses have an enormous diversity of blending combinations, but all have some classroom or face-to-face component and some online component. In many hybrid learning environments, the classroom and the online components have coherent instructional design within and across the online and classroom or face-to-face experiences. Ideally, the instructional methods, materials, and delivery modality have been selected to optimize learning and are based on some evidence that the teaching-learning activities, the learning resources, and the learning assessment sensibly complement each other so that the emergent course "really works" to meet the educational objectives outlined for the respective student or trainee audience. While few instructors engage in rigorous self-study of their courses' development, implementation, and outcomes, most faculty members and trainers do attend to how and why to design their course to meet programmatic, curricular, and students' needs. And, fairly regular program, curricular, and course evaluations by a department or instructional unit provide some objective analysis of effectiveness as gauged by student outcomes and accreditation reviews. Consequently, most of what the average faculty member believe "really works" in educational practice for hybrid courses is fairly anecdotal and/or weak in data as well as lacking in rigorous research design. To be fair, faculty members are not generally trained in the complex relationships between cognitive and behavioural sciences and instructional design.

In order to develop a transtheoretical model for hybrid learning, we first developed a taxonomy of hybrid courses, as discussed above. The {6x8} matrix of course types

(Table 2) allowed us to examine key elements that must be explained by any theoretical framework. Almost two decades ago, we began examining theory and research in ecology to see if we might gain insight into the "ecosystems" and dynamics of academic institutions [24]. This early work began to mature when we reviewed an interesting ecological theoretical framework, which was developed by very well respected researchers in the ecological sciences [25,26]. Holling, Gunderson, and colleagues looked broadly and deeply into how a theory of adaptive change could be developed [26], which they called Panarchy. As their work matured, a particularly interesting facet of theory development focused on dimensions of organization and behaviour in natural ecosystems and in social systems. This critical and detailed analysis revealed an "adaptive cycle" theoretical framework that could be sensibly applied to natural ecosystems as well as social systems. Review a broad spectrum of work from ecology and the social sciences, Holling and Gunderson argued that there appear to be three fundamental clusters of factors that shape dynamics within ecosystems, social agencies, and people:

Potential.— the potential for change defined the range of change options that were possible for a particular system.

Connectedness.— the degree of connectedness provided a capacity for a system's internal controlling variables to interact with each other and reflects sensitivity to external variables and variation in external variables.

Resilience.— the resilience of a system was defined as the capacity for vulnerability to unpredictable perturbations.

In simple terms, Potential is the measure of ability for a system or subsystem to achieve desired outcomes. Connectedness is a measure of collaboration among members of subsystems as well as articulation of subsystems in service of the system. Resilience is a measure of ability of subsystems or the system as a whole to recover from crises or setbacks, as well as manage complex transformations of the system in general or the subsystem in particular. Tashiro and colleagues [27] have provided examples of how to determine values for a system or subsystem for each of these dimensions.

These three clusters of factors could each be reduced to a dimension, and values on that dimension calculated from the variables that individually were part of the dimension value but together represented a position along the respective dimension. This reduction to three-dimensional space allowed a diagrammatic representation of an adaptive cycle as shown in Figure 2 below. Furthermore, the three dimensions define a volume that has regions defined as $\boldsymbol{K}$, $\boldsymbol{\Omega}$, $\boldsymbol{\alpha}$, and $\boldsymbol{r}$. These different regions of an Adaptive Cycle have very specific characteristics, and they each represent different combinations of values for Potential, Connectedness, and Resilience within the three-dimensional space. The following descriptions provide an overview of the four regions of the adaptive cycle as well as two transitional loops in the cycle.

K.— The ***K*** region is more typically one in which variability is controlled, with increasing efficiency, streamlined operations, and improving connections within a system. Potential and Connectedness are high while Resilience is decreased.

Ω.— As Connectedness leads to rigidity, accumulated resources can be released from controlled and sequestered compartments or subsystems. Connections within the system become weakened and feedback regulatory controls can become weakened. The organization or some of its units may be collapsing in this region.

α.— This is a region typified by reorganization that can lead to subsequent growth and resource accumulation. Resilience and Potential is generally high, while Connectedness is low. This region has the most uncertainty.

r.— In the ***r*** region, there is considerable external variability impacting a system. Resilience is relatively high, while Potential and Connectedness are low.

Ω to ***α***.— This transition from one region to another, often called the "backloop," can be seen as a sudden and often dramatic increase in uncertainty, with many chaotic elements. Gunderson and Holling [25,26] point out that long period of relatively predictable behavior and periods of chaos can lead to systems probing and even reaching tests of their limits.

r to ***K***.— The transition from ***r*** to ***K***, called the "front loop" of the adaptive cycle, is typified by a period in which short-term predictability increases. Resources are accumulated and connections with in the system increase and so increase efficiency.

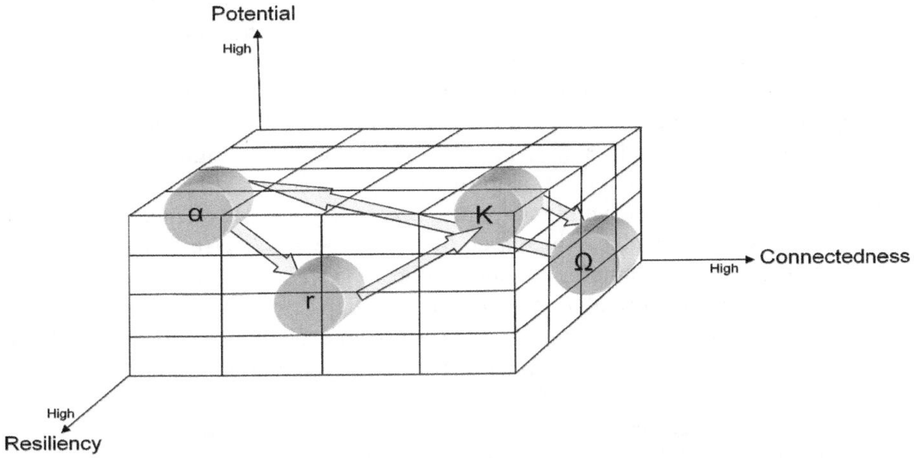

Fig. 2. The three-dimensional space of an Adaptive Cycle

3.2 Studying Hybrid Learning within an Adaptive Cycle

Translating a hybrid learning environment into a social system, and consistent with the Panarchy theoretical framework, we defined Potential as the measure of ability for a hybrid learning system or subsystem to achieve desired learning outcomes. Connectedness was then defined as a measure of collaboration among faculty members in service of a particular department or curricular framework, which we argue has to include: (1) connections of faculty to IT services providing an online delivery modality; and (2) connections of faculty to content experts and instructional designers. Resilience was defined as a measure of ability of the hybrid learning system as a whole to recover from: (1) crises or setbacks (server crashes, IT problems of other kinds, and so on); (2) IT services' implementing upgrades; (3) fairly regular and sometimes complex issues related to maintaining integrity of a learning management system (LMS); and (4) replacing an existing LMS or some of its components. A particular value of the Adaptive Cycle was its scalability, so that a "hybrid learning system" could be a course, a set of courses within a curriculum, a curriculum or academic program, a department, or a larger academic or training unit such as a college, university, professional development program, and so on.

We then used Gedanken experiments to define different types of hybrid learning systems or subsystems and began to map them onto Adaptive Cycles. Our method was to examine in detail the {6x8} taxonomy of hybrid course types and study each type in the context of the Adaptive Cycle. This process allowed us to study what variables could be measured to define Potential, Connectedness, and Resilience. In addition, we analyzed what would be optimal for a hybrid learning system. Again, examining the idea of scalability, if the hybrid learning system was a university-wide LMS, then subsystems could be faculty or departmental instances of the university-wide system, while courses in a faculty or department could be sub-sub-systems of the larger university-wide hybrid learning system. These studies followed a similar type of analysis for using Panarchy to probe the complexity of healthcare systems and data-drive decision making within such systems, so our work was guided by these earlier efforts as well as by a patent (spending) for software engines that could actually create any hybrid course type in our taxonomy and then measure positions for each course within any three-dimensional Adaptive Cycle volume [27,28].

In brief, we discovered that the ***K*** region of the Adaptive Cycle is most probably the region of optimization for a hybrid learning system because that is the region reflective of high Potential, High Connectivity, and relatively high Resilience. In the ***K*** regions variability is controlled, with increasing efficiency, streamlined operations, and improving connections within a system. The reason that Resilience is "relatively" high is that as Connectedness increases there can be rigidity in a system that can reduce Resilience. For example, in both healthcare systems and in academic systems, there can be increasing articulations within a unit, department, or faculty that leads to decreased articulations across units, departments, and faculties. This "silo" effect is well documented as a problem in interprofessional care and across-unit articulations in healthcare systems and is often seen in lack of collaboration and increased competition for limited resources among academic departments and faculties [28].

In any case, the Adaptive Cycle framework of Panarchy provides an interesting theoretical model for studying the complexity of hybrid learning systems, again across the levels of scale from individual courses to university-level hybrid learning initiatives. Of course, human systems differ from ecological systems in that they are developed within a frame of consciousness and this consciousness contains processes for foresight, planning, and modification based on system feedback. Usually, humans strive to keep their systems in the ***K*** region of the Adaptive Cycle, or at least work to move their systems towards the ***K*** region. Certainly, many, if not most, human systems go through periods of collapse ($\boldsymbol{\Omega}$,), reorganization ($\boldsymbol{\alpha}$), growing though external variability ($\boldsymbol{r}$), and achieving some level of consolidation, efficiency, and productivity (***K***). However, even when in the ***K*** region faculty and administrators of academic institutions (and other human systems) seldom have sufficient data to know what set of conditions exist at any moment in time, let alone through time. That is, decision makers of academic institutions do not generally know if, and why, they are in the ***K*** region.

In studies of hybrid learning systems, we explored our taxonomy of course types to delineate data collection processes and sampling strategies that would allow us to move toward evidence-based practices in developing, implementing, and evaluating hybrid learning courses. Our research led to an approach for data collection and analysis framework that meshed with the interpretive framework of the Adaptive Cycle. With advances in software architecture for knowledge systems as well improved and automated data mining, we could increase sampling and develop strong analytical frameworks. The major problem was collecting data that related to the three dimensions of the Adaptive Cycle – Potential, Connectedness, and Resilience. These types of conceptual dimensions had not been well developed very broadly outside of ecology.

Tashiro and colleagues [27,28] solved the problem of measuring Potential, Connectedness, and Resilience within healthcare systems by working with experts in hospital management to come up with data domains routinely collected by health care systems and their respective subsystems. These data domains were then evaluated in terms of their contributions to Potential, Connectedness, and Resilience and mapped to these dimension areas. In simple terms, the data domains were reduced to a set of variables for each dimension, that is, a set of variables for Potential, a set for Connectedness, and a set for Resilience. The variables for each dimension were combined into a single composite variable for the respective dimension. Data could be collected at any time for each variable related to a particular dimension and a composite variable could be created. Therefore, at any time, the data from multiple variables for a dimension could be combined to yield a single composite variable for that dimension and a single value for that composite variable could be calculated. The three composite variables (one for each dimension) would give us the three coordinates of a point that represented the location of a system, subsystem, or cluster of subsystems at a particular time in the three dimensional space defined by Potential, Connectedness, and Resilience. This location would represent a set of conditions defined by the variable values at a particular moment in time.

The authors of this paper followed an analogous approach to delineating meaningful variable clusters for each of the Adaptive Cycle dimensions in the context of hybrid learning. We then explored how conditions change through time for different examples of developing and implementing hybrid learning within educational setting, analyzing implications for each course type in the {6x8} course type taxonomy matrix. These types of explorations were essentially *Gedanken* experiments [1,2,29] in which we changed conditions for a hypothetical educational setting and analyzed how these changes in conditions would alter calculations of the composite variables for Potential, Connectedness, and Resilience. This was done by looking at consecutive times over a week or a month, and, for each time interval, imposing different but realistic changes in conditions from the previous time. Each time was examined to see what location within the Adaptive Cycle would result from the change in working conditions of the various hybrid course types.

For the moment, suppose we follow faculty member from a Health Sciences department who is developing and implementing two courses in the health informatics curriculum. This condition would allow us to control the effects of spatial heterogeneity (i.e., the work is based in the Health Sciences department and so dedicated to a single academic unit). Even so, for this single faculty member as a subsystem there would be temporal variability. For example, a faculty member in a tenure-track line has research, teaching, and service responsibilities. Even with the best of planning, the time dedicated to these responsibilities will fluctuate during a semester or over an academic year. These fluctuations can lead to reallocation of work load. Reallocation represents a temporal perturbation to the processes of the health informatics course development and implementation.

Therefore, for one type of *Gedanken* experiment, some conditions that change through time were imposed, with the faculty member facing the choice of working longer hours to maintain momentum in implementing the health informatics courses or keeping the same workload and reducing time spent on the health informatics courses. We added to this set of conditions a breakdown in communication between the IT services groups maintaining the online course components and the faculty member developing the informatics courses. For example, we could model the perturbation that key features in the learning management capacities were not communicated to the faculty member. In this type of Gedanken experiment, we could explore how course development proceeded through various reallocations of workload and without sufficient input from the IT services group managing the learning management system providing the instances for the courses being developed.

To be more specific, the reallocation of workload and breakdown of communication with IT services could decrease the value of Connectedness. The reduced effectiveness of the faculty member could result in increased stress among the Health Sciences faculty who are depending on curricular integrity in which the health informatics courses were critical to a curriculum sequence that needed to be in place prior to the next semester. Increased stress among Health Sciences faculty could weaken the unit, and reduce their Resilience to managing the curricular modification that was intended to incorporate the health informatics courses.

Oddly enough, the Gedanken experiments described above was very close to what actually emerged as a problem in Health Sciences at our university, except that an additional perturbation occurred when the Dean suddenly decided to resigned and leave at the end of the academic year. Our point is that the scenarios of the Gedanken experiments were very realistic and provided a way to examine the viability of Panarchy and Adaptive Cycles as a theoretical framework understanding the complexity of developing, implementing, and evaluating hybrid learning systems.

Using this health informatics course development and implementation Gedanken experiment, we looked at four consecutive times, each a month apart. For each time, we focused on each health informatics course as a subsystem of the Health Sciences department. For each subsystem, and at each time, we modeled composite variable values for Potential, Connectedness, and Resilience. At each time, as conditions changed, the composite variables values would change. As a result the location representing the changed conditions would change within the three dimensional space of the Adaptive Cycle. In terms of the Adaptive Cycle, perturbations could reduce Connectedness among the informatics instructor and other faculty members, while ineffectiveness could reduce Resilience. Poor learning outcomes and decreased student satisfaction could reduce Potential. Obviously, there are some perturbations that could increase Connectedness, Resilience, and Potential. We diagrammatically show this temporal sequence in Figure 3, which reveals "moments" in an ongoing course implementation. One set of conditions exists within T_1, when the faculty member starts an informatics course at the beginning of a term. The conditions at that point of time result in values for Potential (P_1), Connectedness (C_1), and Resilience (R_1), and so the coordinates (P_1, C_1, R_1) which can be plotted for time T_1 in the three-dimensional space of Potential, Connectedness, and Resilience.

As a starting point, let us assume that these conditions represent a position within the ***K*** region of the Adaptive Cycle. Following this particular informatics course through one month we arrive at T_2, following for yet another month, we arrive at T_3, and after another month, we are at T_4. These times represent a series of sampling times following time T_1, and during each month a number of conditions change. In Figure 3, we have plotted the changes in conditions from T_1 through the subsequent time intervals to T_4. Figure 3 shows the new locations in the Adaptive Cycle, each of which represents the set of conditions for the respective time. Maybe the changes in conditions moved the faculty member from one location in the ***K*** region to another location within ***K*** as shown in Figure 3. However, maybe the changes moved the team to a more chaotic position closer to the ***Ω*** region.

If we based curricular development decisions for hybrid learning courses only on what was discovered at time T_4, we would not pick up the changes and the implications of change through the subsequent time series of T_1-T_4, when workload shifts and breakdowns in communications were destructuring effective course implementation and as students' learning outcomes, satisfaction, and engagement with course activities may have changed. If we could more continuously collect and analyze data for each moment of time and examine the conditions that establish values for Potential, Connectedness, and Resilience, we would be able to identify any conditions that have changed and so are contributing to a shift from the original state of the health informatics course at T_1.

In this example, we were looking at only at one faculty member as a subsystem of Health Sciences who is implementing two courses and treating each course as a sub-subsystem in a Health Sciences department. However, treating the Health Sciences department as a system, we could choose to look at any level or unit within that system. On the other hand, we could have looked at the Health Sciences department as a sub-unit of the university. At any level of scale, we could still calculate a composite variable value for Potential, Connectedness, and Resilience at any time. Certainly, we have simplified how you get one variable from many variables for a dimension, and how you get one variable value from many variable values for the respective dimension. However, the point is that mathematically this process is well defined, as long as the variables mapped to a particular dimension are valid and reliable estimators for that dimension [27]. In Figure 4, we show a simplified representation of how a composite variable value along a dimension is conceptualized, and also how three coordinates can then be derived in order to find a point within the three-dimensional space of the Adaptive Cycle volume, one coordinate for each dimensions – Potential, Connectedness, and Resilience.

Certainly, the orthogonal nature of the three dimensions in the Adaptive Cycle can be challenged. In particular, as variables are chosen for each dimension and validated, careful examination of correlations among variables in different dimensions would have to be pursued. While tedious, this is not a difficult problem to solve, and even if there was perceived value in treating the three dimensions as non-orthogonal, a vector solution could be developed and studied to determine validity and value as an interpretative framework for hybrid learning.

Importantly, the theoretical framework afforded by the Adaptive Cycle could be placed within a research framework and the estimators of Potential, Connectedness, and Resilience studied to determine validity and reliability of variables for any scale of hybrid learning course development. Therefore, we continued to develop the Adaptive Cycle as a theoretical framework for studying hybrid learning. We argue that the capacity to plot the location of a system or its subsystems within the Adaptive Cycle allow us to conceptualize and operationalize how to intervene adaptively in development, implementation, and evaluation of hybrid learning environments.

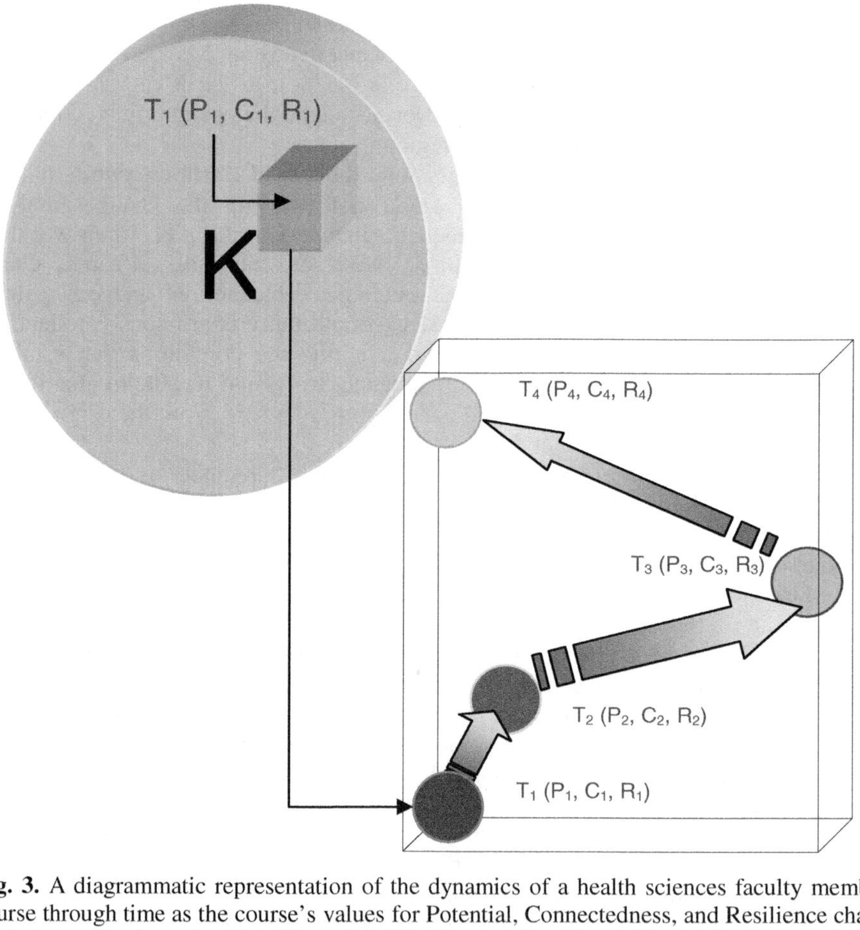

Fig. 3. A diagrammatic representation of the dynamics of a health sciences faculty member's course through time as the course's values for Potential, Connectedness, and Resilience change. An intervention just after time T_3 could shift the conditions in which the faculty member had been working within during development of health informatics courses, resulting in a dramatic trajectory change (e.g. LMS problems).

3.3 A Transtheoretical Approach

We argue that currently there is no consensus single theory of cognition or behaviour change that has sufficient theoretical foundations for understanding the complexities of "what really works" in hybrid learning, for whom, when, how, and with what outcomes. We also argue that the Adaptive Cycle for ecological and social systems is a theoretical framework that can substantially advance our understanding of hybrid learning. Finally, we argue that the Adaptive Cycle can provide a transtheoretical approach. This last argument is based on our studies of health education and health promotion research; however, we believe the Adaptive Cycle may offer a more complete theoretical approach.

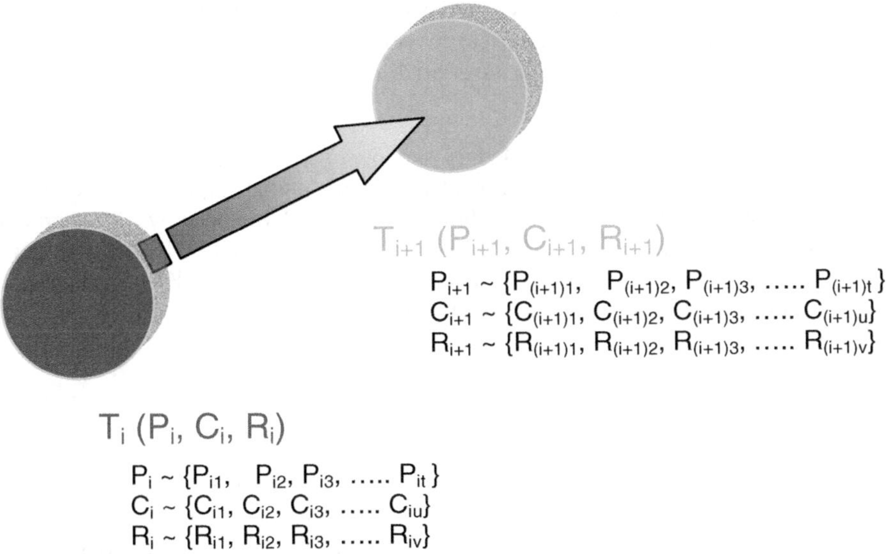

Fig. 4. At some time T_i, an estimate of the value on the dimension of Potential (P_i) is calculated from multiple variables P_{i1}, P_{i2}, P_{i3} through P_{it}. Analogously, a value along the Connectedness dimension (C_i) and along the Resilience dimension (R_i) also can be calculated as composite variables at time T_i. At some later point in time T_{i+1}, a new set of values can be calculated for Potential, Connectedness, and Resilience, providing another set of coordinates identifying the point in Adaptive Cycle space for the system at T_{i+1}.

4 Conclusions

Based on our work studying healthcare systems, we believe the Adaptive Cycle framework provides a transtheoretical approach and offers the flexibility to incorporate theories of cognition and theories of behaviour [7,17-23,30-32). In fact, the Adaptive Cycles may provide one of the best conceptual and operational frameworks for across-theory comparisons. A point within the three dimensions of Adaptive Cycle space represents coordinates of Potential, Connectedness, and Resilience at some time. Each coordinate represents a composite variable value that has been calculated from variable clusters related to the respective dimensions. We feel that the dimension of Potential is most likely to contain variables related to cognition and behaviour change for individual students and groups of students. Consequently, variables for cognition could be selected to capture any single theory of cognition. Analogously, variables for behaviour could be selected to capture any single theory of behaviour change. This means that single theories of cognition or single theories of behaviour change could be studied, or combinations of theories could be studied to see which variables were most predictive of learning and behaviour related to educational objectives for a hybrid course (e.g., combinations of cognitive theories or combinations of behaviour change theories or combinations of cognition and behaviour change theories). Importantly, the {6x8} matrix of our hybrid course taxonomy provided a starting point or the development of a theoretical framework for hybrid learning. This framework evolved into the use of the Adaptive Cycle of Panarchy for a transtheoretical model to develop new software engines that could be used to study hybrid learning. Such engines are the focus of our ongoing research.

Acknowledgments. Tashiro acknowledges support of a grant from HealthForceOntario that funded research on the development of the initial simulations to improve interprofessional education and care. Tashiro and Vargas Martin acknowledge support of a grant from the Social Sciences and Humanities Research Council of Canada (SSHRC) to develop models of tracking users' choices within simulations. Hung acknowledges support from the Natural Sciences and Engineering Research Council of Canada (NSERC).

References

1. Tashiro, J., Hung, P.C.K., Vargas Martin, M.: ROAD-MAP for Educational Simulations and Serious Games. In: Tsang, P., Cheung, S.K.S., Lee, C.S.K., Huang, R. (eds.) Hybrid Learning – Proceedings of The Third International Conference ICHL, Beijing China, pp. 186–204 (August 2010)
2. Garcia-Ruiz, M.A., Tashiro, J., Kapralos, B., Vargas Martin, M.: Crouching Tangents, Hidden Danger: Assessing Development of Dangerous Misconceptions Within Serious Games For Healthcare Education. In: Hai-Jew, S. (ed.) Virtual Immersive and 3D Learning Spaces: Emerging Technologies and Trends, pp. 269–306. IGI Global, Hershey (2011)
3. National Research Council: How People Learn: Brain, Mind, Experience, and School. National Academy Press, Washington (2000)
4. National Research Council: How Students Learn: History, Mathematics, and Science in the Classroom. National Academy Press, Washington (2005)
5. American Association for the Advancement of Science: Invention and Impact: Building Excellence in Undergraduate Science, Technology, Engineering and Mathematics (STEM) education. American Association for the Advancement of Science, Washington, DC (2004)
6. Federation of American Scientists: Summit on Educational Games – Harnessing the power of Video Games for Learning. Federation of American Scientists, Washington, DC (2006)

7. Patel, V.L., Yoskowitz, N.A., Arocha, J.F., Shortliffe, E.H.: Cognitive and learning sciences in biomedical and health instructional design: A Review with Lessons for Biomedical Informatics Education. Journal of Biomedical Informatics 42, 176–197 (2009)
8. Tashiro, J.: Ethical Analysis of Publisher and Faculty Roles in Building and Using Electronic Educational Products. Journal of Electronic Commerce in Organizations 7(1), 1–17 (2009)
9. Sorden, S.D.: A Cognitive Approach to Instructional Design for Multimedia Learning. Informing Science Journal 8, 263–279 (2005)
10. Mayer, R.E., Fennell, S., Farmer, L., Campbell, J.: A Personalization Effect in Multimedia Learning: Students Learn Better When Words Are in Conversational Style Rather Than Formal Style. Journal of Educational Psychology 96(2), 389–395 (2004)
11. Rudak, L., Sidor, D.: Taxonomy of E-courses. In: Islander, M., Kapila, V., Karim, M.A. (eds.) Technological Developments in Education and Automation, pp. 275–280. Springer Science and Budiness Media, New York (2010)
12. Tashiro, J.S., Rowland, P.: McD.: What Works: Empirical approaches to restructuring courses in biology and environmental sciences. In: McNeal, A., D'Avanzo, C. (eds.) Student Active Science – Models of Innovation in College Science Teaching, pp. 163–187. Harcourt, Brace, & Company, New York (1997)
13. Young, J.R.: Hybrid Teaching Seeks to End the Divide Between Traditional and Online Instruction. Chronicle of Higher Education 48(28), A33 (2002)
14. National Center for Education Statistics, Distance Education in Higher Education Institutions (NCES 98-062) (October 1997), `http://nces.ed.gov/pubsearch/pubsinfo.asp?pubid=98062`
15. National Center for Education Statistics, Distance Education at Degree-Granting Postsecondary Institutions, 2000-2001 (NCES 2003-017) (July 2003), `http://nces.ed.gov/pubs2003/2003017.pdf`
16. Wolfe, C.R. (ed.): Learning and Teaching on the World Wide Web, pp. 1–2. Academic Press, San Diego (2000)
17. Martin, L., Haskard-Zolnierek, K., DiMatteo, M.R.: Health Behavior Change and Treatment Adherence: Evidence-based Guidelines for Improving Healthcare. Oxford University Press, New York (2010)
18. Prochaska, J.O., Redding, C.A., Evers, K.E.: The Transtheoretical Model and stages of change. In: Glanz, K., Rimer, B., Viswanath, K. (eds.) Health Behavior and Health Education, pp. 97–121. Jossey-Bass, San Francisco (2008)
19. DiMatteo, M.R., DiNicola, D.: Achieving Patient Compliance. Pergamon Press, New York (1982)
20. Fishbein, M., Hennessey, M., Kamb, M., Bolan, G., Hoxworth, T., Latesta, M., et al.: Using Intervention Therapy to Model Factors Influencing Behavior Change: Project RESPECT. Evaluation and Health Professions 24(4), 363–384 (2001)
21. Bensley, R., Mercer, N., Brusk, J., Underhile, R., Rivas, J., Anderson, J., et al.: The e-Health Behavior Management Model: A Stage-based Approach to Behavior Change and Management. Preventing Chronic Disease 1(4), A14 (2004)
22. Baranowski, T., Cullen, K., Nicklas, T., Thompson, D. & Baranowski, J.: Are Current Health Behavioral Change Models Helpful in Guiding Prevention of Weight Gain Efforts? Obesity Research (Suppl.), 23S–43S (2003)
23. Leventhal, H., Halm, E., Horowitz, C., Leventhal, E., Ozakinci, G.: Living with chronic Illness: A Contextualized, Self-Regulation Approach. In: Sutton, S., Baum, A., Johnston, M. (eds.) Handbook of Health Psychology, pp. 159–194. Sage Publications, London (2004)

24. Sullins, E., Hernandez, D., Fuller, C., Tashiro, J.: Predicting who will major in a science discipline: Expectancy-value theory as part of an ecological model for studying academic communities. Journal of Research in Science Teaching 32, 99–119 (1995)
25. Westley, F., Carpenter, S.R., Brock, W.A., Holling, C.S., Gunderson, L.H.: In: Gunderson, L.H., Holling, C.S. (eds.) Panarchy – Understanding transformations in human and natural systems, pp. 103–119. Island Press, Washington, DC (2002)
26. Gunderson, L.H., Holling, C.S.: Panarchy – Understanding transformations in human and natural systems. Island Press, Washington, DC (2002)
27. Tashiro, J., Tashiro, R., Alvarado-Yule, J.: Adaptive Intervention and Management for Health Care Systems. U.S. Patent (pending) No. 60/938,682. U.S. Patent and Trademark Office, Washington, DC (2008)
28. Johnson, K., Tashiro, J.: Interprofessional Care and Health Care Complexity: Factors Shaping Human Resources Effectiveness in Health Information Management. In: Kabene, S.M. (ed.) Human Resources in Healthcare, Health Informatics and Healthcare Systems, pp. 250–280. IGI Global, Hershey (2011)
29. Tashiro, J. Dunlap, D.: The Impact of Realism on Learning Engagement in Educational Games. Association of Computing Machinery Digital Library 978-1-59593-943-2/07/011, pp. 113–120 (2008)
30. Kahan, B., Groulx, D., Wong, J.P.-W.: The Interactive Domain Model Approach to Best Practices in Health Promotion. In: DiClemente, R., Crosby, R., Kegler, M. (eds.) Health Promotion Practice and Research, pp. 511–534. Jossey-Bass, San Francisco (2009)
31. Tan, J., Hung, P., Dohan, M., Trojer, T., Farwick, M., Tashiro, J.: Gateway to Quality Living for the Elderly: Charting an Innovative Approach to Evidence-based E-Health Technologies For Serving the Chronically Ill. In: Proceedings of the 13th IEEE International Conference on Computational Science and Engineering (CSE 2010), Hong Kong, China (December 11-13, 2010)
32. Vargas Martin, M., Hung, P.C.K., Tashiro, J.: Method for Competency Assessment of Healthcare Students and Practitioners. U.S. Patent (pending) No. 61/162,597. U.S. Patent and Trademark Office, Washington, DC (2009)

E-instructor for Online Learning

Li Zheng, Yushan Li, Jun Xu, Xinyu Zhang, and Lei Xu

Computer Science & Technology Department, Tsinghua University, Beijing, 100084, China
zhengli@tsinghua.edu.cn,
{lyshan05,xujun603,xlxlx9}@gmail.com,
zxy@cic.tsinghuaedu.cn

Abstract. Most traditional learning systems only provide users learning resources, but can not support user executing personalized and collaborative learning plans, and that makes online learning lacking communication and guidance compared with traditional learning. E-instructor is proposed to narrow the gap between traditional learning and online learning, it supports making personalized and collaborative learning design besides providing learning resources. This paper analyses traditional learning systems, brings up what an e-instructor should have, then discusses the supporting environments for an e-instructor, finally this paper proposes a service oriented and layered architecture design for e-learning systems and gives a sample implementation.

Keywords: E-instructor, learning design, e-learning.

1 Introduction

Learning, an activity throughout everyone's life, means acquiring knowledge, mastering method, developing potential creative ability. Learning process also includes understanding new knowledge, imitating and practicing, and creative attempting. Instructor teacher usually play important roles in the whole learning process.

Teacher used to leading in the teaching process in traditional classroom teaching, and students learning with teacher's guide. Now learning activities are no longer limited to classrooms anymore, but also can go with the help of information technology and network environment. However, most of these learning activities are self-study, and students rarely get help from teachers. This can be reflected in lacking guidance in selecting learning resources, making learning plan without personalized instruction, lacking answers for questions on time and monitoring in learning activities, lacking collaborative learning environment with teacher's organize and guide, and lacking evaluation for learning effect.

This paper discusses E-instructor under network learning environment, includes E-instructor's effect, requisite supporting environment and design and implementation of an E-instructor system.

R. Kwan et al. (Eds.): ICHL 2011, LNCS 6837, pp. 73–82, 2011.

2 Functions of E-instructors

2.1 Providing Learning Resources

Learning resources are learning activities' basis. In traditional teaching activities, teachers provide limited learning resources, which have more clearly objectives, but this isn't propitious for students' expansion and creative thinking. As network is used widespread today, there are many ways to get learning resources, and that is very good for learners, as they can use rich learning resources, but this can bring another problem: users often don't know what to do when facing so many learning resources, even lost learning target in rich resources. So, the first thing to do for an useful network learning environment is helping learner select learning resource, this is an E-instructor's basic function. E-instructor should be built on learning resource system with considerable scale, and this learning resource system isn't just a collection of learning resources, but also handles resources with carefully filtering, scientific classification and effective indexing. With learning resource system, e-instructor can conduct learner searching, selecting and organizing learning content based on learner's personalized learning target.

2.2 Making Learning Plans

Making scientific and reasonable learning plans is an important prerequisite for effective learning activities. In traditional learning activities, teachers make one unified learning plan for the whole students in one class and carry out as collective teaching. Such teaching pattern will usually ignore students' individual learning needs and limit the development of students' individual characteristics. In network environment students' study are no longer limited to specified time or place. Network can make study available at any time and place, so we can make one personalized learning plan for individual students. E-instructor should guide students to make a suitable learning plan and change with the execution of the plan in an interactive way.

2.3 Guiding Learning Activities

In learning process, learners will certainly have sorts of difficulties and doubts. In traditional teaching, teachers provide face-to-face teachers' guide for learning activities. This is one of the great strengths of traditional teaching pattern, but in information society the great majorities of part time learners have no time or condition to take part in face-to-face guide with the quickening pace of work and life. As a result in network learning environment it is extremely important to provide timely and personalized guide for students. E-instructor should help students get answered in a convenient way anytime and instructions at suitable time.

2.4 Guiding Collaborative Learning

Learning activities are not only processes for acquiring knowledge but also for learners to communicate and cooperate together. In modern society, any significant achievement is a result of collaborative work. Successful education can help learners acquire new knowledge and learn to communicate and cooperate together. The traditional learning process groups learners as a team and team members will divide work and cooperate together to accomplish assignment.But in network learning environment learners are difficult to cooperate face-to-face with the limitation of distance and time. Network learning environment can provide a modern way to communicate and cooperate together, e-instructor can make full use of this technology and organize learners to work together. For Example the on-line forum is a important way for on-line learners to collaborate with others. Most forums only manage the posts so that it is difficult to reuse partners' content. E-instructor can organize the useful contents in a structured way on the basis of the structure of knowledge in course and produce new structured learning contents which will be added to the learning bank and be the basic resource of building new course and learning plan. As a result, every learner makes contribution and the growth of the resource bank is a virtuous and order circle of growth.

2.5 Evaluating Learning Effect

In learning processes, learners can test the degrees of knowledge by timely evaluation. In network learning environment, we could make use of hypermedia as often as possible and finally achieve automatic evaluation for example, creating test quizzes automatically from quiz bank and on-line competition. At the same time we can make some particular rules from the learning time, learning mark and curve of memory to teach and test the important and difficult points over and over and make a suitable plan with learners' study ability according to study marks. Learning evaluation can revise learners' plan and avoid errors through learning process without delay.

3 E-instructor's Supporting Environments

3.1 Sharable Learning Contents

One of the most important things for e-instructor is providing and displaying learning resources, learning resource is the basis for learning activities, so learning resource management is a requirement supporting environment for e-instructor, and it mainly includes learning object management and content packaging (CP).

Learning object management includes adding, deleting, modifying, searching and viewing learning resources. Learning object management system also has to support learning object metadata (LOM) standard description for learning resource's exchange and use between different platforms. With LOM tool, it is easy to generate the smallest reusable unit in e-learning systems—learning object.

Content packaging defines a uniform data model, which makes learning resources can be organized and hierarchical, this new "packaged" learning resource (this calls learning content) can be copied, exchanged, bought, executed and used independently, and can be used in a new package. Content packaging improves learning resources' interoperability and the efficiency for generating learning resources.

Fig. 1 shows the functions that a learning resource management system should have.

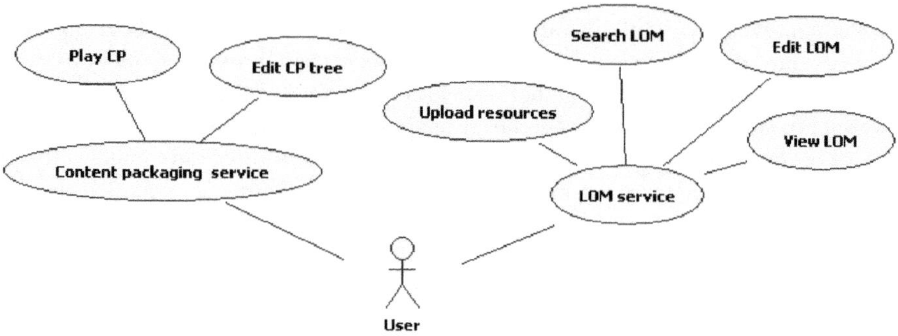

Fig. 1. Requirement analysis for a learning resource management system

In a e-instructor system, learning resource and content packaging can be used more than one time, different user can reference learning resource and content in different ways, but when system is used to display and search, it will use the same learning object database and content packaging database, the system design is shown as Fig. 2.

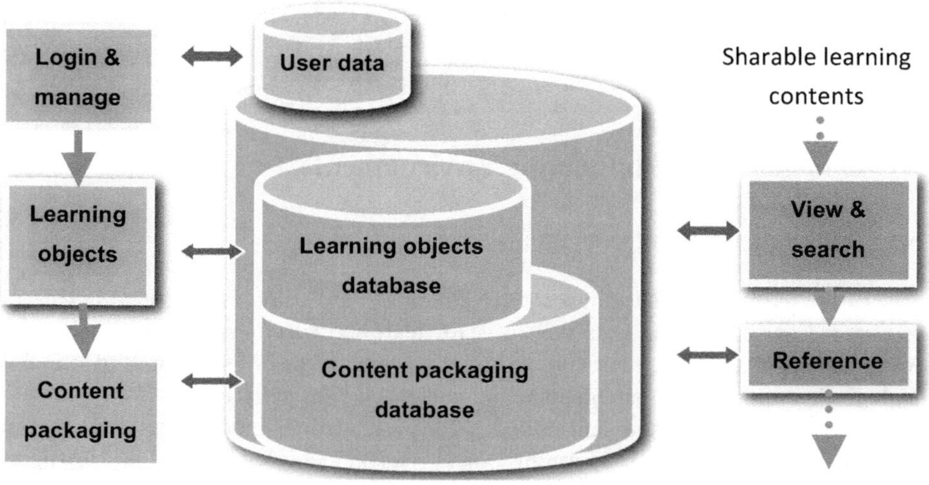

Fig. 2. Sharable learning contents

From Fig. 2, we can see that user can login learning resource system, manage learning resource and edit LOM info and content packaging tree. Besides, learning resource management system provides search, view and reference interfaces, which can be used by upper layer.

3.2 Scalable Learning Design

In a perfect learning system, user can not only manage and share resources, but also can learn, discuss and ask questions in it. This needs learning system manage learning designs, the learning design here can not just view slides, post in forums and so on, but also can learn collaboratively, edit personalized learning designs, role games and so on. Collaborative learning and personalized learning are the main things for e-instructor systems.

In learning design platforms, what is important is that how to provide a learner first environment. Because we believe that if learners can join the process of creating, improving and evaluating learning design, not only learners' learning enthusiasm would be greatly increased, but also teacher can optimize learning design base on learners' requirements, which can achieve best learning effect. Learning design systems improve learning effect by collaborative and personalized learning.

Collaborative learning means dividing learners by groups and completing one learning activity together. For learning designs that support collaborative learning is mainly composed of attending role, groups, information flow between different jobs. Compared with traditional e-learning, collaborative learning brings the concept of roles, and learners' enthusiasm can be greatly improved by assigning them roles. And in the collaborative learning process, group member can supervise each other to make sure that everyone input enough energy in learning activity.

Personalized learning is to satisfy personalized requirements from different person or group, which can improve participant's learning effect. Users might have the

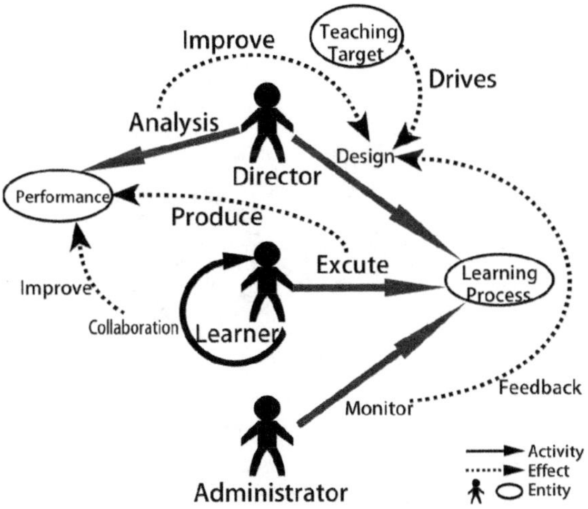

Fig. 3. Learning design system concept model

following requirements when learning: asking questions about unclear learning content, pointing out wrong places in slides, provide learning experience about some learning content and so on. Although some e-learning systems can satisfy these needs, but they all need user to leave from learning interface, which breaks user's learning activity. If these functions can be integrated in the learning page, user's learning would not be interrupted and also other users from this activity can see the what the user do and be encouraged to do this.

In the concept model, most important data is learning process, it is produced by director's design activity, it is supported by electronic learning resources and service system. When user executes learning design, it will generate every learner's processing data, some reflect learning performance. The data of the whole performance and learning process can improve learning process's design.

3.3 Knowledge Building Environment

One significant difference between online learning and traditional learning is user can view rich online learning resource, but with so many resources, e-instructor need to let user find the best resources, which can avoid user wasting time on finding resources. For learning forums, we bring out knowledge building environment, which means learning forums have public knowledge repository, when users contribute their resource or knowledge, administrator can bring them into public knowledge repository. When bringing into the repository, administrator has to organize knowledge by knowledge system, which can make learning forum's learning system is organized and let user find knowledge easily.

There are two types for users' contribution: learning resources and learning experiences, when bringing them into public knowledge repository, administrators have to organize them by content packaging, and some learning resources have to provide LOM description, these needs to call interfaces provided by learning resource system. The whole process can be shown as Fig. 4.

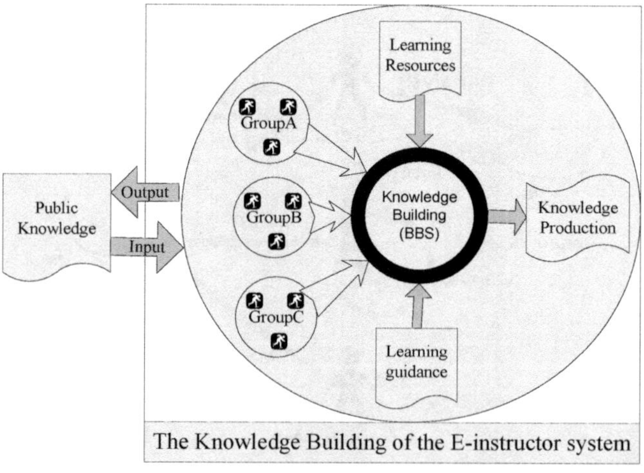

Fig. 4. Process of Community Knowledge Building in the E-instructor [1]

Fig. 4 presents the community's knowledge building process in E-instructor. At the beginning, members in the community acquire public knowledge which is organized by the knowledge hierarchy; with the instructions of learning guidance, individuals and groups construct interactive activities (email, forum, etc.) to add, edit, integrate public knowledge, and finally generate new constructed public knowledge. Learning tools (Individual Exhibition Room and Group Exhibition Room) presents such Knowledge Production; members in Knowledge building Community now come to a new round of Knowledge building. In this construction process, learners are able to positively construct new knowledge, rather than negatively receive in the former time.

4 The Design and Implementation of an E-instructor System

4.1 E-instructor's System Design

E-instructor can be an independent system, but also can be a part of a larger learning system, so we need to make it not only could be exist independently, but also easily integrated. The whole platform's architecture is layered and service oriented, as shown in Fig. 5, the dotted lines between services present call relation.

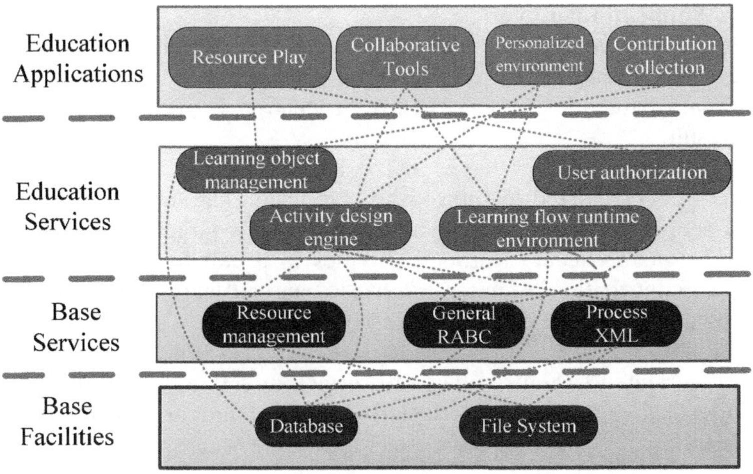

Fig. 5. The architecture of E-instructor system

From the above architecture, to ensure the efficiency and feasibility, it allows call different layers. For example, learning design activity may call database service from base facilities layer and XML service from base service layer. There are database and file system in base facilities, these services provide standard data access service; from base service layer, services' definitions belong to e-learning domain, they are explained as below:

Base service layer

These services are not limited to specific domains, they're selected for upper specific education services and more specific in management objects than base facilities, but they're still useful for most information systems.

XML processing service provides general XML accessing, storage and searching service for LOM and learning design services in upper layer; RBAC provides general role management function, which authorizes participant and provides runtime supporting for designing and run learning activities; resource management abstracts storage service from base facilities, it provides general accessing and searching functions for resources.

Education service layer

The objects managed by services from this layer are all e-learning concept entities, which are based on various requirements from e-learning and abstracted differently from target objects. These services provide data and logic support for front services.

LOM service provide standardized accessing and searching for resources, it has natural connect with learning design; participants authorization and accredit manage user in e-learning systems, it is the first step interaction between user and system, including user's login, role assignment, authority identification and so on; learning design engine is used for maintaining various entities and their relationships in learning design, to ensure correct functions and logics for learning design.

Education Applications Layer

This layer is a bridge for user and system modules, which displays entities from e-learning systems in a proper way, guides users operating correctly and collects users' interactive data, calls relevant services from education service layer and notifies user operation result.

Learning design editor's target users are learning activities' designers and participants in personalized learning, who can design learning activities in different levels and scope; collaborative activity environment's target users are participants, which can let them execute learning activities in a collaborative way and provide feedback and contribution; monitoring service can call learning activities services to analyzed data base on learning director and administrator's need, then display in visualized ways.

In service-oriented systems, either call service or service return results, they both need data exchange. In service-oriented designs, there are mainly two ways to exchange data.

1) Web Service and its description language WSDL, this service uses XML as data exchange format, and provides a method of packaged service including registration, discovery, call and the combination. Since XML has poor support in HTML application environment, this method is not friendly to JavaScript, and could only obtain native support form high version Flash.
2) the way HTTP request +JSON, it applies JSON as data exchange format, high efficiency, which obtain good support in JavaScript and Flash, more practical, but lacks unified service description method, and when used alone could only through specific technical documents coordination.

From the above analysis, we find that Web Service form is more suitable loosely coupled systems, but JSON is more suitable for tightly coupled systems. We have proposed that the above two call means should be provided at the same time to a set of interfaces of one service. Since JOSN lacks unified service description method, we have adopted WSDL to describe HTTP request +JSON service. Compared with Web Service, except the different access points, other attributes (operation name and parameters) are all the same.

4.2 An E-instructor's Implementation

Base on the designed architecture above, we implement an e-instructor system in J2EE technology. Fig. 6 shows a student's learning plan after login.

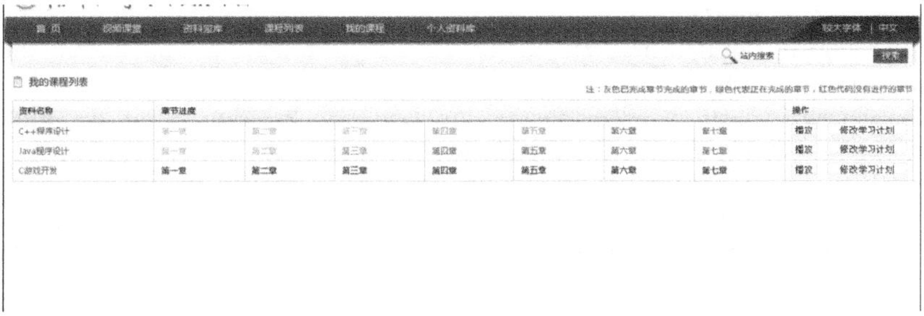

Fig. 6. A student's learning plan

After login, students can what they're learning, and also can change learning plan personalized. Fig. 7 shows a student's learning activity, learner can view slides on the web.

Fig. 7. Executing a learning activity

Students can also view all the courses and add course to their own learning plans. Course usually recommend user a learning plan, after adding to their plans, they can modify the recommended learning plan.

5 Conclusion and Future Work

E-instructor can narrow the gap between online and classroom learning by supporting personalized and collaborative learning, learners can bring out questions to teachers in this system. For the e-instructor's system design, we propose an open and service oriented architecture.

Future works will focus on enriching the e-instructor's architecture with more service and facilitating the application of it with the joint effort of merchants and institutes.

References

1. Zhang, Xinyu, NianLong, L., Chen, S.: The knowledge building of the eco-classroom. In: ITNG 2009, pp. 1100–1103 (2009)
2. Hasegawa, S., Ochimizu, K.: A Learning Management System based on the Life Cycle Management Model of e-Learning Courseware. In: Proceedings of the Fifth IEEE International Conference on Advanced Learning Technologies (ICALT 2005) (2005)
3. Dan Burdescu, D., Mihăescu, M.C., Ionaşcu, C.M., Logofătu, B.: Support System for e-Learning Environment Based on Learning Activities and Processes. In: Fourth International Conference on Research Challenges in Information Science (RCIS 2010), May 19-21, pp. 37–42 (2010)
4. China E-learning Technology Standards Committee: Specification for Learning Object Metadata: Information Model, GB 21365-2008, `http://www.celtsc.org`
5. China E-learning Technology Standards Committee: Learning system architecture and service interface: Abstract framework and core interface (2010), `http://www.celtsc.org`
6. Zheng, L., Xu, L., Li, Y.: Application of E-Learning Standardization Technology. Advanced Learning (2009) ISBN 978-953-307-010-0; IN-TECH Company

Does Outcomes Based Teaching and Learning Make a Difference in Students' Learning Approach?

Xiaoyan Wang, Yelin Su, Stephen Cheung, Eva Wong, Theresa Kwong, and Keng T. Tan

Centre for Holistic Teaching and Learning
Hong Kong Baptist University
Kowloon Tong, Hong Kong
wangxi38@hkbu.edu.hk

Abstract. This paper investigates whether instructors' adoption of outcomes based teaching and learning (OBTL) has any impact on university students' deep learning approach, which is highly correlated with students' learning outcomes. A multi-method model with a combination of qualitative and quantitative design was adopted, using document analysis, interviews, and survey. The analysis of covariance (ANCOVA) results suggested that regardless individual differences, students would adjust their learning approaches and study behaviors in response to the classroom teaching and learning environment. Students in more "OBTL courses" were more likely to adopt deep learning approaches in their study of a particular course.

Keywords: OBTL, Student Learning Approach, Student Learning Experience.

1 Introduction

Higher education in Hong Kong has been going through tremendous changes since Hong Kong's re-integration to the People's Republic of China in 1997. The education reforms have covered nearly every aspect of the entire education system -- academic structures, curricula, teaching and learning, assessments, and financing. One of the most profound moves was initiated by funding and monitoring agency of the tertiary sector -- the University Grants Committee, which recommended that Hong Kong's eight publicly funded tertiary institutions adopt an outcome based approach to student learning (OBASL) in order to provide a learner-centered educational experience for students.

The higher education community of Hong Kong has been hiring external consultants, conducting workshops and seminars and providing various resources to promote the implementation of OBASL. Despite these efforts, some academics have been resistant to the adoption of a unified pedagogical approach. Although successful experience of using OBASL was reported from other countries, such experiences were largely from K-12 education [1]. The Western Australian government's recent move to abandon most of its outcome based education (OBE) system for upper school [2] has further discouraged the university community in Hong Kong to adapt to the OBASL.

R. Kwan et al. (Eds.): ICHL 2011, LNCS 6837, pp. 83–94, 2011.

Previous studies on OBASL were largely perceptual and anecdotal and there is a lack of empirical data for the argument that the application of the OBASL approach would have any positive impact on students' learning approaches or would lead to enhanced students learning experiences. Our current study explores whether instructors' adoption of outcome based teaching and learning (OBTL), as the project is called in our institution, has any impact on university students' learning. The result of the study will help the higher education community in Hong Kong to make objective choices as to whether to embrace this paradigm shift to student-centred teaching and learning.

2 Literature Review

Outcomes based teaching and learning is a pedagogical approach that emphasizes the achievement of the pre-determined learning outcomes. It is concerned with curriculum design and tries to ensure that the course contents, delivery, activities, and assessments are all aligned to help facilitate students' achievement of specific intended learning outcomes [3]. OBTL corresponds closely to the outcome based education (OBE), which has its roots in the competency-based movement introduced in the late 60's and has been recognized as a model to restructure education, mostly at K-12 level. OBE focuses on measuring students' performances empirically irrespective of teaching styles, whereas OBTL is concerned with the process of teaching and learning: teaching is not a matter of knowledge transmission but of engaging students in active learning [4]. However, OBTL has been mistakenly regarded as OBE and been criticized by various scholars [2, 5].

One of the major underpinning concepts of OBTL is constructive alignment, which is derived from the principles of the constructivism in learning and the alignment in the design of teaching and assessments. Biggs and Tang [4] stated that instructors adopting constructive alignment shall clearly specify intended learning outcomes, design the learning activities that are appropriate for the tasks so that students could construct their knowledge and achieve the outcomes, and establish assessment criteria for giving feedback to the learners. According to Biggs and Tang [4], criterion-based -referencing for assessment is regarded as a major principle under the framework of OBTL.

OBTL, as a pedagogical approach, has been taken as an effective and pragmatic way of designing curricula, delivering teaching and documenting the results of students' learning [6]; it also has been criticized for imposing a rigid model and excessive demands on teachers in terms of specification of outcomes, assessment and record keeping [7]; restricting and inhibiting emergent learning outcomes [5]. OBTL has further been blamed for giving a false sense of accountability when assessment method was used inappropriately [2]. Very few empirical studies address whether OBTL has any impact on students' learning.

Despite the various criticism of OBTL, the aim of any pedagogical approach is to facilitate students to achieve learning outcomes, which are directly associated with both the teaching context and students' learning approaches. Schmeck [8] took learning approach as an unchangeable style regardless of immediate learning context and tasks, and Marton and Saljo [9] regarded it as entirely contextual and situational.

Other literature suggested students' learning approaches could be influenced by personal factors such as motivation, conceptions of learning, prior knowledge, ability [10], age and personality [11] as well as situational factors such as the teaching and learning environment. Biggs [11] proposed a "3P" model of teaching and learning (Figure 1) to depict how various presage factors (personal and situational factors) influenced the product – students learning through the "learning process complex" [11].

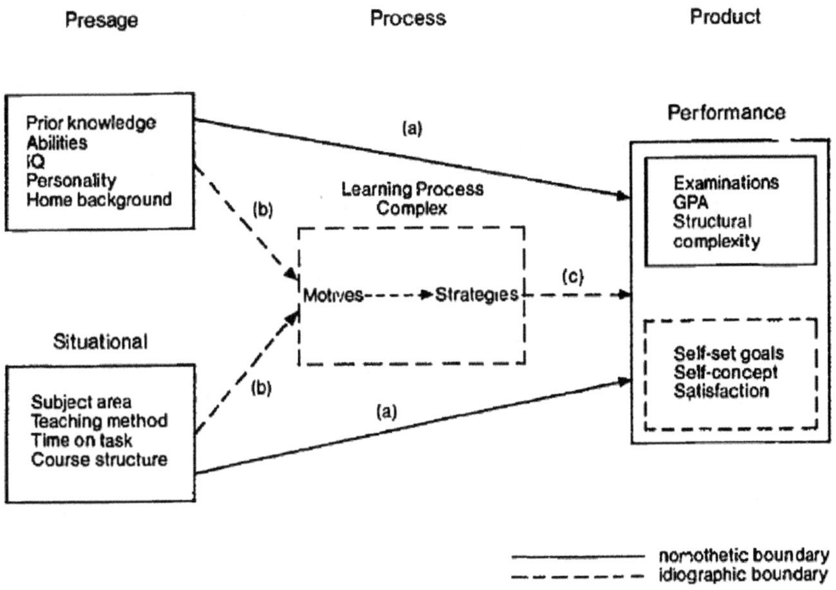

Fig. 1. "3P" model of teaching and learning [11]

The current study argues that there are two levels of students learning approach, the preferred learning approach and the situation-specific learning approach. Similar to the learning styles, the preferred learning approach is relatively stable and determined by the individual characteristics. The situation-specific learning approach or the "on-task approaches to learning" is relatively unstable as it is determined by how students modify their preferred approach to fit the requirements of the teaching context. Hence, irrespective of their underlying preferred learning approaches, students might adopt a surface or a deep learning approach in different contexts. A surface learning approach "arises from an intention to get the task out of the way with minimum trouble, while appearing to meet course requirements" [4], while a deep approach "arises from a felt need to engage the task appropriately and meaningfully, so the student tries to use the most appropriate cognitive activities for handing it" [4]. Therefore, a measure of students' on-task learning approaches could be indicators of the immediate teaching context.

Students' deep approach to studying is generally related to high levels of academic achievement [12] and relates well to meaningful learning [13]; For a deep approach, the quality of teaching, the clarity of goals and independence in learning are the foci of the attention, while for a surface approach, the nature of the assessment and workload demands are the foci of the attention [14]. According to Biggs and Tang [4], when the teaching and learning contexts feature OBTL, which includes an appropriate motivational context, a well-structured knowledge base, relevant learner activities, formative feedbacks, reflective practices and self-monitorings, students' surface learning approach will be reduced and a 'deeper' learning approach will be enhanced. However, they did not provide empirical data to support the hypothesis of OBTL and its impact on the change of students' learning approaches.

Balasorriya, Toohey, and Hughs [10] used the Revised Study Process Questionnaire (R-SPQ-2F), an instrument published by Biggs, Kember, and Leung in 2001, to examine 190 medical students' change of learning approach in a deep-engaging teaching context using three carefully designed course units. A key finding from this study was that the interaction of student factors and context factors was so complex that even the best designed educational context could lead to undesired or unexpected outcomes. For example, they found that those students whose preferred learning approach was surface did not approximate the deep approach as was predicted by Biggs. Although the three courses in the study were deemed as carefully designed and deep-engaging by the authors, such courses did not necessarily embody the features of OBTL, for example, it was not known whether the intended learning outcomes (ILOs), teaching and learning activities (TLAs) and assessment tasks (ATs) were constructively aligned. Therefore, such studies did not provide evidence as to whether OBTL has any impact on students' learning approaches.

3 Methodology

The current study explored the relationship between the implementation of the OBTL and its impact on students' learning approaches. Kember et al. [13] argued that students' deep learning approach was a more relevant and representative indicator to meaningful learning, and an increase of students' deep learning approach suggested that the educational programme encouraged higher quality of learning. Therefore, this study seeks to answer the research question whether the adoption of OBTL would encourage students to engage more in deep learning approach. The following is the hypothesis of this study:

- After taking courses, students in "more OBTL" courses would have higher deep approach scores than those in "less OBTL" courses.

This study consisted of two different sections. A multi-method model with a combination of qualitative and quantitative design was adopted. Section one examined whether and how much had the instructors adopted OBTL, therefore, we took a qualitative approach -- data were collected through document analysis and semi-structured interviews with instructors and students. Section two examined whether students' deep learning approach had significantly altered as a result of different stages (or degrees) of the OBTL implementation. Data in this section were collected through surveys.

Two academic programmes in a university in Hong Kong were invited to participate in the study. One programme (programme A) has adopted OBTL systematically for a few years due to the requirements of external accreditation. The other programme (programme B) was newly established and just started to adopt the OBTL approach in curriculum design and teaching practices in September of 2010. The assumption was that courses offered by programme A were "more OBTL" orientated than courses offered by programme B.

Instructors of three courses from programme A and four courses from programme B consented to join the study respectively. All participating courses were undergraduate level courses. There were 337 students enrolled in these 7 courses.

Data collection of section one (qualitative): Teaching and learning contexts in courses from programmes A and B.

To investigate the real classroom teaching and learning environment and to probe the degree of the constructive alignment (CA) in individual courses, course syllabi were collected for document analysis, and semi-structured interviews were carried out with the three instructors and 14 students from programme A and four instructors and 14 students from programme B. In the interviews with both students and instructors, participants were asked about their perspectives and experiences in whether, and how, course intended learning outcomes (CILOs), teaching and learning activities (TLAs) and assessment tasks (ATs) were constructively aligned, and whether and how classroom instructions, activities and assessments provided clear CILOs, facilitated the achievement of the CILOs, and effectively assessed the CILO. All interviews were tape-recorded, transcribed, and analyzed. The results of interviews from instructors and students for a particular course were triangulated to assess the degree of OBTL implementation.

Data collection of the second section (quantitative): Changes in students' learning approaches

To identify changes in students' learning approaches, Biggs et. al's [15] Revised Study Process Questionnaire (R-SPQ-2F) were administered to participating courses. Using the R-SPQ-2F, students' learning approaches were operationalized as "Deep Approach (DA)" and "Surface Approach (SA)" and calculated based on students' responses to the questionnaire. Scores from R-SPQ-2F could be used as an indicator of the teaching context as R-SPQ-2F was supposed to be administered in a pre-and post-test fashion to track variations in learning approaches before and after taking certain courses. The scores from the pre- R-SPQ-2F describes pre-existing individual differences since it measures students' preferred approach, and the scores from the post- R-SPQ-2F may be used to reveal the differences between teaching contexts among courses as it measures students' contextual approaches [15]. In the current study, students' pre- R-SPQ-2F served as a control variable since as a presage factor, students' preferred learning approach had significant bearings on students' learning outcomes, their contextual learning approach [15].

The R-SPQ-2F were administered both at the beginning (week 2 and 3 of the semester) and toward the end of the semester (week 11 and 12 of the semester). For the beginning-of-the-semester R-SPQ-2F (SPQ-1) administration, students were instructed to fill in the questionnaire based on their attitudes to, and ways of, learning in general, while for the toward- the-end-of the-semester R-SPQ-2F (SPQ-2) administration, they were requested to fill in the questionnaire according to their attitudes to, and ways of, learning in a particular course. 224 students chose to complete both pre- and post- SPQ questionnaires (Appendix 1).

4 Results

4.1 Degrees of OBTL Implementations of Programme A

It was assumed that courses from programme A were "more OBTL" than those from programme B. Document analysis on individual course syllabus and interviews were conducted to test the assumption.

The syllabi of three courses from programme A, contained clearly defined and articulated intended learning outcomes (ILOs). For example, all the three courses used appropriate action verbs such as analyze, apply, or synthesize, which represented the expected achievements of a higher cognitive level and signified "highly satisfactory outcomes" [4] in terms of the constructive alignment. Syllabi of all three courses from programme A also included diversified and engaging teaching and learning activities that mirrored the ILOs to activate the action verbs in ILOs. A wide range of TLAs were incorporated into the curricula, ranging from the traditional lectures, presentations, exercises, to more student centered TLAs such as case studies, field trips, and e-learning supported activities. As for the assessment, various assessment tasks were employed in the courses in a way it seemed, on paper at least, to not only evaluate the desired outcomes, but also to monitor students' progressions and to provide formative feedbacks. However, there were no specific assessment criteria provided in the documents.

Follow-up interviews with instructors and students respectively allowed insights into the real classroom practices. The following is an excerpt of the interview data from the interviews with three instructors from programme A, that helps to illustrate how OBTL was implemented.

"We make the learning outcomes, course expectations, and criteria very clear and transparent to students. "

"... we want to nurture students to become successful leaders in this field. The single objective and guiding principle is to design all the activities, exam, assignment and even extra-curricular activities to achieve this."

"I always tell them I am not an instructor. I am only a facilitator."

Instructor's claim of adopting OBTL in their teaching was further triangulated by interviews with 14 students.

"I think it's much clear about what we are going to learn, because our professor has told us in the first lesson. "

"The instructor always has interactions with his students; he always asks us many questions during lessons. And he will tell the weakness of our presentations."

"We have to visit a company, apply some of the knowledge and theory for a project. After finish the project, we are able to apply what we have learnt in the class and apply to the project."

Student interviews also revealed that there were various interactions between instructors and students. Data showed that various teaching and learning activities were applied to activate the course ILOs, prompt feedback to students were provided by instructors, diversified and continuous evaluation methods were applied in each course. However, both instructors and students acknowledged that assessment results were still norm-referenced to some extent in all courses. Given the application of norm-referenced assessment, we are inclined to conclude that the three courses from programme A were partially implementing OBTL both in documentation and classroom practices based on the analysis from course syllabi and interviews.

4.2 Degrees of OBTL Implementations of Programme B

The syllabi from the four courses of programme B revealed that the CILOs and course objectives were deeply intertwined together, for example, one course contained as many as 18 CILOs. Vague and low-level action verbs, such as "understand", "demonstrate" were used in describing the CILOs. Lectures were the major teaching and learning activities and tests were the only assessment method in some cases.

The following excerpt of interview data from the three instructors partially reflected their teaching philosophy and classroom environment.

"I don't make the learning outcome explicit to them. I don't let them know what my criteria are because I do not want them to be exam oriented. "

"I just taught them what I would like them to learn and they are supposed to learn whatever I taught."

"Teaching and learning activities include lectures or in-class assignments. I used exams a lot for evaluation."

Interviews with the 14 students further verified the instructors' teaching philosophy and provided insights in the teaching and learning environment.

"Even the instructor briefly explained learning outcomes in the first lesson, I did not quite understand."

"The instructor just delivers lecture, not diversified enough. There is a lack of interactions between instructors and students, and even among students."

"The instructor did not provide feedback to us about how well we did in our assignments. I was not very clear about how I was going to be."

"The exam focuses on one thing and the lecture on another."

From the analysis of the course syllabi, and interviews with students and instructors, we are inclined to conclude that programme B adopted "less OBTL" in comparison with programme A, given that CILOs were not very clearly articulated, the teaching and learning environment was teacher centered, and there was minimum student engagement in the teaching and learning activities with almost no feedbacks from the instructors. The courses also applied norm referenced assessment, which continued to be a policy of the university at the time of this study.

In view of the above analysis, it was reasonable to conclude that there were substantial differences in terms of the teaching and learning contexts and students' experiences. Therefore, it was justifiable to retain the assumption that courses from programme A were more outcome-based than those from programme B.

4.3 Students' Learning Approaches by Groups

Descriptive Statistics

Table 1. Distribution of Valid Survey Responses by Groups

Groups	Courses	Valid Responses
Programme A	Course A1	49
	Course A2	50
	Course A3	32
	Total	131
Programme B	Course B1	13
	Course B2	12
	Course B3	10
	Course B4	58
	Total	93

As displayed in Table 1 above, 131 students from programme A and 93 students from programme B completed both the SPQ-1 and the SPQ-2 questionnaire. A brief summary of their deep approach scores is shown in Table 2.

Table 2. Descriptive Statistics for Students' DA Scores by Groups

	More OBTL Courses (Programme A)			Less OBTL Courses (Programme B)		
	DA		*n*	DA		*n*
	M	*SD*		*M*	*SD*	
SPQ-1	32.00	5.43	131	31.51	5.23	93
SPQ-2	34.48	5.70		31.70	5.01	

Hypothesis Test

The research hypothesis was tested in an attempt to reveal the association between the various stages (or degrees) of the OBTL implementation and changes in students' learning approaches.

5 Differences in Students' Learning Approaches

The following hypothesis was tested to examine whether students in courses with different degrees of the OBTL implementation would adopt deep approach and surface approach differently in their studies.

- After taking courses, students in "more OBTL" courses will have higher deep approach scores than those in "less OBTL" courses.

Since the scores from the SPQ-1 represent pre-existing students' individual differences (students' preferred approach) and the scores from the SPQ-2 measure students' contextual approaches [15], an analysis of covariance (ANCOVA) at .05 probability level was conducted using students' deep learning approach (DA) scores in SPQ-2 as the dependent variable and their DA scores in SPQ-1 as the covariate.

Table 3. ANCOVA for Students' SPQ-2 Deep Approach

Source	*SS*	*df*	*MS*	*F*
SPQ-1 DA	1395.12	1	1395.12	60.98*
Group	309.42	1	309.42	13.53*
Error	4827.14	211	22.88	
Corrected Total	6595.10	213		

*p<.05

Table 3 above shows that with $F_{SPQ\text{-}1\ DA}$ (1,211) = 60.98, p<.05, the null hypothesis that there was no relationship between students' SPQ-1 DA scores and SPQ-2 DA scores was rejected. It suggested that student's DA scores in SPQ-2 were significantly influenced by their DA scores in SPQ-1 and hence was an appropriate covariate.

After adjusted by the covariate, students' DA scores in SPQ-1, with F_{Group} (1,211) = 13.53, p<.05, the null hypothesis that there was no difference in students' SPQ-2 DA scores between students in "more OBTL" courses and "less OBTL" courses was also rejected. The follow-up pairwise comparison as shown in Table 4 indicated that students in programme A courses had significant higher DA scores than students in programme B courses.

Table 4. Pairwise Comparison for Students' DA scores

Group	Estimated Marginal Means	Mean Differences (A-B)
More OBTL Courses (Programme A)	34.35[a]	2.44*
Less OBTL Courses (Programme B)	31.91[a]	-2.44*

a. Covariates appearing in the model are evaluated at the following values: Deep Approach SPQ1 = 31.73.

*p<.05

6 Discussions

The present study investigated whether the implementation of outcome based teaching and learning would encourage students to employ more deep learning approaches in their study. By comparing students' learning approaches in courses from two programmes with significant different degrees of the OBTL implementation using students' preferred learning approaches as the control variable, results of the current study showed that compared with students in "less OBTL" courses, students in more "OBTL courses" were more likely to adopt a deep learning approach in their study of a particular course. The results suggested that regardless their individual differences, students would adjust their learning approaches and study behaviors in response to the classroom teaching and learning environment, which corresponded to and provided empirical data for Biggs' "3P" model of teaching and learning.

The "3P" model [11] proposed that the course instructions or the so-called "learning process complex" [11], were the key to enhance the products of students' learning, such as students' GPA, satisfaction, and goals. Biggs [11] identified many factors that had significant direct or indirect impacts on students' learning experiences and academic performances. Biggs [15] called them as "presage factors" of students learning and categorized them into two groups, student factors which were the pre-existing students' individual characteristics such as prior knowledge, learning styles and cognitive skills, and the situational factor which was the teaching context such as the course objectives, assessments, and teaching methods. These factors affected students learning directly, indirectly, and through complicated interactions with each other. They also influenced students learning through impacting students' motives of learning and their strategies of learning [11]. From this perspective, applying the pedagogies promoting students' intrinsic motivation and deep learning strategies, could lead to more effective students' achievements of the desired learning outcomes.

7 Conclusions

Literature suggested that a more student-centered teaching and learning approach with challenging yet reachable desired learning outcomes, engaging teaching and learning activities, and timely constructive feedback would promote students' intrinsic motivation and sequentially their increased application of deep learning strategies or behaviors [16]. As these are key features of the OBTL, there is no wonder that in this study, courses with more OBTL implementation would lead to more deep learning approaches of students. In view of the course syllabi and interviews from two programmes, it was obvious that in this study, courses in programme A were more students-centered classes practising the well-known seven principals for good practices in undergraduate education by Chickering and Gamson [17]. In this sense, disregarding the different terminology used, the application of the OBTL is essentially the application of the good teaching practice.

8 Limitations and Implications

This study was based on Biggs' "3P" model which simplified the complicated relationships between various influential factors, personal and situational, into two intervening variables, students' motives and strategies as they were regarded as the manifesto of the products of the complex interactions of contributing factors. Hence, though with the differences in students' outcomes detected, it was hard to infer how much and how individual factors, in our case, the teaching and learning context, had contributed to students' achievements. Thus the results of the current study should be generalized with caution and further studies are warranted.

The study is intended to examine whether the adoption of OBTL exerts positive influences on students' learning approach so as to provide empirical evidence for the higher education community of Hong Kong to make an informed choice. Although scholars had criticized OBTL for imposing a rigid model and excessive demands on teachers, the result of this study suggested that the implementation of OBTL is associated with enhanced students' learning outcomes in terms of learning approaches. This result is consistent with Biggs' hypothesis that students' deep learning approach significantly increased in more OBTL oriented courses than otherwise. Therefore, the adoption of OBTL promotes the quality of learning and is a good practice of teaching.

References

1. Engelbrecht, J., Harding, A.: The Impact of the Transition to Outcomes-based Teaching on University Preparedness in Mathematics in South Africa. Mathematics Education Research Journal 20(2), 57–70 (2008)
2. Au, O., Kwan, R.: Experience on Outcome-Based Teaching and Learning. In: Wang, F.L., Fong, J., Zhang, L., Lee, V.S.K. (eds.) ICHL 2009. LNCS, vol. 5685, pp. 133–139. Springer, Heidelberg (2009)
3. Pang, M., Ho, T., Man, R.: Learning Approaches and Outcome Based Teaching and Learning: A Case Study in Hong Kong, China. Journal of Teaching in International Business 20, 106–122 (2009)
4. Biggs, J., Tang, C.: Teaching for Quality Learning at University: What the Students Does. McGraw-Hill company, NY (2007)
5. Rees, C.: The Problem with Outcomes-based Curricula in Medical Education: Insights from Educational Theory. Medical Education 38(6), 593–598 (2004)
6. Spady, W.G.: Organising for Results: the Basis of Authentic Restructuring and Reform. Educational Leadership 46, 4–8 (1988)
7. Harden, R.M.: Developments in Outcome-based Education. Med. Teacher 24, 117–120 (2002)
8. Schmeck, R. (ed.): Learning Strategies and Learning Styles. Plenum, NY (1988)
9. Marton, F., Saljo, R.: On Qualitative Differences in Learning-1: Outcome and Process. British Journal of Educational Psychology 46, 4–11 (1976)
10. Balasooriya, C., Toohey, S., Hughs, C.: The Cross-over Phenomenon: Unexpected Patterns of Change in Students' Approaches to Learning. Studies in Higher Education 34(7), 781–794 (2009)
11. Biggs, J.B.: Student Approaches to Learning and Studying. Australian Council for Educational Research, Melbourne (1987)
12. Entwistle, N.: Promoting Deep Learning through Teaching and Assessment: Conceptual Frameworks and Educational Context. In: TLRP Conference (2000)
13. Kember, D., Charlesworth, M., Davies, H., McKay, J., Storr, V.: Evaluating the Effectiveness of Educational Innovations: Using the Study Process Questionnaire to Show that Meaningful Learning Occurs. Studies in Educational Evaluation 23(2), 141–157 (1997)
14. Prosser, M., Trigwell, K.: Relations between Perceptions of the Teaching environment and approaches to teaching. British Journal of Educational Psychology 67(1), 25–35 (1997)
15. Biggs, J., Kember, D., Leung, D.Y.P.: The Revised Two-Factor Study Process Questionnaire: R-SPQ-2F. British Journal of Educational Psychology 71, 133–149 (2001)
16. Ames, C.: Classrooms: Goals, Structures, and Student Motivation. Journal of Educational Psychology 84(3), 261–271 (1992)
17. Chickering, A., Gamson, Z.: Seven Principles of Good Practice in Undergraduate Education. AAHE Bulletin 39, 3–7 (1987)

Appendix

Distribution of Students' Responses in SPQ-1 and SPQ-2

Programme /Courses	Programme A			Programme B				Total
	Course A1	CourseA2	Course A3	Course B1	Course B2	Course B3	Course B4	
SPQ1	62	53	59	104	34	15	10	337
SPQ2	32	49	50	58	13	12	10	224
% of Valid Responses	52.5%	83.1%	80.6%	43.0%	26.5%	66.7%	100.0%	66.5%

A Study of Relations between Students' CMC Behaviors and Perceived Effects of CMC on Learning for Incorporating CMC in Hybrid Learning

Aihua Wang[1] and Siu Cheung Kong[2]

[1] Department of Educational Technology, Graduate School of Education, Peking University, Beijing, China, 100871
ahwang@gse.pku.edu.cn
[2] Department of Mathematics and Information Technology, Hong Kong Institute of Education, Hong Kong, China
sckong@ied.edu.hk

Abstract. This study aimed to explore the relations between students' free, independent and voluntary CMC (Computer-Mediated Communication) behaviors and their perceived effects of CMC on learning. A research model focusing on five types of CMC behaviors and the perceived positive and negative effects of CMC on learning was built based on previous researches in this area. An online questionnaire survey was conducted with 163 university students in Beijing. This study found that it was common for students to make CMC by using instant messaging system, email and social network services. It also found that the students positively perceived the effects of CMC on learning. This study found that asynchronous CMC usage and private CMC usage correlated more strongly with the positive effects of CMC on learning. Based on the findings, this study made two recommendations for incorporating CMC into hybrid disciplinary learning in the academic context: designing collaborative learning activities; and choosing asynchronous CMC and private CMC as starters for collaborative learning.

Keywords: CMC (Computer-Mediated Communication), CMC behavior, effects on learning, hybrid learning, collaborative learning.

1 Introduction

The Internet plays a prime role for social interaction in the online era. People nowadays often use online communication tools such as instant messaging systems (IMS), email, chatrooms, newsgroups, etc. to keep in touch with family and friends and make daily sharing with others [1]. These activities are regarded as computer-mediated-communication (CMC).

CMC refers to the human process of interchanging idea and information through computer networks by using a wide range of technologies [2, 3]. Some researchers call CMC as online interaction, technological-mediated communication [4] and social media use [5]. The specific acts in CMC are referred as CMC behaviors. Examples of

R. Kwan et al. (Eds.): ICHL 2011, LNCS 6837, pp. 95–104, 2011.

CMC behaviors include chatting using IMS, sending messages to others by using email, posting information in a bulletin board system (BBS) forum, leaving messages in a blog, presenting profile about oneself in social network system (SNS), interacting with others when playing computer games, etc. CMC behaviors can be described in terms of CMC usage intensity and CMC genres. The usage intensity of CMC behaviors is indicated by the number of hours per day/week/month or usage intensity scale [6]. The usage genres of CMC behaviors are classified in two ways.

First, CMC behaviors can be divided into the synchronous and asynchronous types [7]. The synchronous CMC refers to the online communication that each communication process requires two or more people to interact through the Internet at a certain point of time. Examples include online communication using IMS, online chatroom and online game. The asynchronous CMC refers to the online communication that each communication process allows two or more people to interact through the Internet at different points of time. Examples include online communication using email, BBS forum, blog, micro blog and SNS.

Second, CMC behaviors can be divided into the public and private types. The public CMC refers to the online communication that the online access to communication contents is open to all Internet users. Examples include online communication using BBS forum, blog, micro blog, SNS and online chatroom. The private CMC refers to the online communication that the online access to communication contents is limited to few designated people through the Internet. Examples include online communication using IMS, email and online game.

Previous studies found that CMC has positive and negative effects on student learning. For the positive effects, researchers state that CMC can offer students more learning opportunities [8]. For example, education-based SNSs can be very effective in distance education courses as a technological tool for improving online communication among students in higher distance education courses [9]. Twitter can be used to encourage free-flowing just-in-time interactions among students, and these interactions can enhance the social presence of students in online courses [10]. IMS can be also used to support and coordinate school work [11]. For the negative effects, researchers state that the explosion to CMC may stunt students' language skills, because children may lose the ability to pick up on nonverbal cues when they rely only on written text [8]. In addition, the explosion to CMC may make students spend less time on learning and perform poorer in their study. For example, students who like to use IMS may spend less time on other activities, in particular study time, for more time for using IMS in daily life. The synchronous nature of IMS may affect students' focus on learning [11]. Students who like to use Facebook also spend less time on learning, and their learning achievements are poorer than the nonusers of Facebook [12, 13].

Students now are the largest group in the population of Chinese net citizens, and many students in China make CMC in daily life. It is potential for Chinese educators to incorporate CMC into students' hybrid learning process, but there is no research which investigates how students think about the influence of CMC behaviors on their learning. This study aimed to explore how students use CMC, how CMC usage influences learning, and how students' CMC behaviors relate to their perceived effects of CMC on learning.

2 Research Framework

This study investigated the relations between students' CMC behaviors and their perceived effects of CMC on learning for promoting CMC in student learning. Based on previous studies in this area, a research framework (see Fig. 1) was designed in this study to investigate how different types of students' CMC behaviors relate to their perceived effects of CMC on learning.

In this study, CMC was defined as an Internet activity of acquiring information or sharing feelings between human beings for influencing or understanding one another. The five target types of CMC behaviors were synchronous CMC, asynchronous CMC, public CMC, private CMC and CMC usage intensity. This study focused on CMC behaviors using eight types of CMC genres, namely IMS, email, SNS, BBS forum, blog, micro blog, chatroom and online game. The genres of IMS, chatroom and online game were classified into the synchronous CMC usage; the genres of email, SNS, BBS forum, blog and micro blog were classified into the asynchronous CMC usage; the genres of SNS, BBS forum, blog, micro blog and chatroom were classified into the public CMC usage; the genres of IMS, email and online game were classified into the private CMC usage.

This study classified the perceived effects of CMC on learning into two types: positive and negative. The positive effects relate to the gains in learning process and learning achievement when students make CMC in daily life. The negative effects relate to the losses in learning process and learning achievement when students make CMC in daily life.

There are two research questions in this study:

1) When the students freely, independently and voluntarily use the CMC, What are students' CMC behaviors and their perceived effects of CMC on learning?
2) What are the relations between students' CMC behaviors and their perceived effects of CMC on learning?

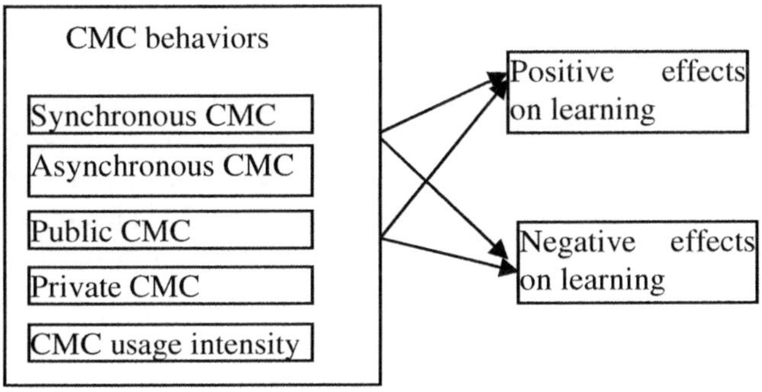

Fig. 1. Research framework of this study

3 Research Method

This study conducted an online survey in November and December 2010 to investigate students' CMC behaviors and their perceived effects of CMC on learning. A questionnaire consisted of three questions was used in the survey. The first question of the questionnaire was related to CMC genres, which asked students to indicate how frequently they used CMC genres in a 4-point Likert scale from 1 = "never" to 4 = "often".

The next question was related to CMC usage intensity, which was adapted from the Facebook usage intensity scale with reliability coefficient α of 0.83 [6]. The students were asked to indicate their level of agreement with each of the following six items in a 5-point Likert scale from 1 = "strongly disagree" to 5 = "strongly agree". In this study, the Cronbach's coefficient α for the scale was 0.76.

1) I make online communication every day.
2) I am proud when I tell other people that I make online communication.
3) Online communication is part of my daily activity.
4) I feel out of touch when I haven't logged onto the online communication platform for a while.
5) I feel I am part of the online community.
6) I will feel disappointed if the online communication platform which I use daily is shut down.

The last question was related to the perceived effects of CMC on learning. We developed five items for the positive effect scale and five items for the negative effect scale based on the literature review. The students were asked to indicate their level of agreement with each of the following ten items (the first five for the positive effect scale and the other five for the negative effect scale) in a 5-point Likert scale from 1 = "strongly disagree" to 5 = "strongly agree". In this study, the Cronbach's coefficient α for the positive effect scale and negative effect scale were 0.82 and 0.72 respectively.

1) Online communication offers me more learning opportunities.
2) Online communication improves my interaction with classmates and teachers.
3) Online communication broadens my knowledge scope.
4) Online communication promotes my collaboration with classmates in group learning.
5) Online communication offers me many useful learning materials.
6) Online communication stunts my development of language skills.
7) Online communication makes me spend less time on learning.
8) Online communication makes me perform poorly in learning.
9) Online communication makes me miss important learning opportunities.
10) Online communication makes me truant.

Through BBS forum or email in the universities, this study invited 171 university students in Beijing to take part in the online survey. A total of 163 students, about half were male (53%) and half were female (47%), were valid respondents who answered each question in questionnaire or left at most one item unanswered in one question, and gave answers to reversed items without contradiction with other items.

4 Results and Discussion

4.1 Students' CMC Behaviors and Perceived Effects of CMC on Learning

Table 1 shows students' use of CMC genres. From Table 1, the students used IMS, email and SNS in daily life most frequently. More than 90%, 80% and 60% of the students always used these three CMC genres respectively. Chatroom and online game were the CMC genres that students used least in daily life. Less than 10% of the students indicated that they always used these two CMC genres respectively.

Table 1. Students' use of CMC genres

CMC genres	Mean [1]	S.D.
Instant Messaging Systems (IMS)	3.90	0.37
Email	3.79	0.51
Social Network Services (SNS)	3.42	0.89
Bulletin Board Systems (BBS) Forum	3.04	0.91
Blog	2.38	0.98
Micro Blog	2.06	1.06
Chatroom	1.72	0.85
Online Game	1.64	0.84

Remark 1. 1 = never; 2 = rarely; 3 = sometimes; 4 = often.

From Table 2, most of the students indicated that they frequently made private CMC, as the highest mean-rating of the item "Private CMC". This is related to students' frequent use of IMS and email, which are the CMC genres for private CMC usage. In addition, most of the students indicated that they frequently made asynchronous CMC, as the high mean-rating of the item "Asynchronous CMC" shown in Table 2. This is related to students' frequent use of email, BBS and SNS, which are the CMC genres for asynchronous CMC usage.

Table 2. Students' CMC behaviors

CMC behaviors	Mean	S.D.
Synchronous CMC	2.42 [1]	0.46
Asynchronous CMC	2.94 [1]	0.54
Public CMC	2.52 [1]	0.55
Private CMC	3.11 [1]	0.35
CMC usage intensity	3.41 [2]	0.63

Remark 1. 1 = never; 2 = rarely; 3 = sometimes; 4 = often.

Remark 2. 1 = strongly disagree; 2 = disagree; 3 = neutral; 4 = agree; 5 = strongly agree.

From Table 3, most of the students thought CMC had positive effects on learning, as the high mean-rating of the item "Positive effects". This is because most students agreed with the items related to the positive effects on learning as shown in Table 4.

Table 3. Students' perceived effects of CMC on learning

Perceived effects of CMC on learning	Mean [1]	S.D.
Positive effects	3.95	0.48
Negative effects	2.56	0.63

Remark 1. 1 = strongly disagree; 2 = disagree; 3 = neutral; 4 = agree; 5 = strongly agree.

Table 4 further shows that the students perceived that CMC usage generally had a positive effect on promoting their learning. The mean-ratings of all items related to the positive effects of CMC on learning, including "Having many useful learning materials", "Broadening knowledge scope", "Having more learning opportunities", "Improving interaction with classmates and teachers" and "Promoting collaboration with classmates in group learning" are high. This means that the students agreed that they had gains in learning process and learning achievement when they make CMC in daily life. In contrast, the mean-ratings of all items related to the negative effects of CMC on learning, including "Spending less time on learning", "Missing important learning opportunities", "Performing poorly in learning", "Stunting development of language skills" and "Truanting" are relatively low. This means that the students generally disagreed that they had losses in learning process and learning achievement when they make CMC in daily life.

Table 4. Students' views on the positive and negative effects of CMC on learning

Perceived effects of CMC on learning	Mean [1]	S.D.
Having many useful learning materials	4.07	0.56
Broadening knowledge scope	4.01	0.63
Having more learning opportunities	3.93	0.63
Improving interaction with classmates and teachers	3.91	0.67
Promoting collaboration with classmates in group learning	3.86	0.67
Spending less time on learning	3.28	0.94
Missing important learning opportunities	2.42	0.86
Performing poorly in learning	2.39	0.84
Stunting development of language skills	2.36	0.83
Truanting	2.34	1.07

Remark 1. 1 = strongly disagree; 2 = disagree; 3 = neutral; 4 = agree; 5 = strongly agree.

4.2 Relations between Students' CMC Behaviors and Perceived Effects of CMC on Learning

Table 5 shows that the relations between the different types of CMC usage among students. This study found that the positive correlation between students' asynchronous CMC usage and synchronous CMC usage was statistically significant. This means that the more often the students made asynchronous CMC, the more often they also made synchronous CMC in daily life. For the relation between their public CMC usage and private CMC usage, this study also found that there was a positive correlation between students' use of these two types of CMC. The statistically significant result means that the more often the students made private CMC, the more often they also made public CMC in daily life.

Table 5. Relations between the different types of CMC usage among students

Pairs of CMC usage	Pearson coefficient
Asynchronous CMC usage & Synchronous CMC usage	0.21^{**}
Private CMC usage & Public CMC usage	0.33^{***}

$^{**}p < .01$, $^{***}p < .001$.

Table 6 shows that there were positive correlations between different types of CMC usage and the perceived positive effects of CMC on learning. The statistically significant results mean that the students thought that every type of CMC usage could be helpful for their learning. The positive correlation between CMC usage intensity and the perceived positive effects of CMC on learning is also statistically significant. This means that the more time the students spent on CMC, the more positive views they had on the effects of CMC on learning.

Table 6. Relations between students' CMC behaviors and perceived effects of CMC on learning

CMC behaviors	Positive effects	Negative effects
Synchronous CMC	0.20^{*}	0.10
Asynchronous CMC	0.25^{*}	-0.12
Public CMC	0.24^{*}	-0.07
Private CMC	0.27^{*}	-0.01
CMC usage intensity	0.34^{*}	0.10

$^{*}p < .05$ *(one-tail).*

A regression analysis was conducted to further explore how different CMC behaviors correlate with the perceived positive effects of CMC on learning (see Table 7). Table 7 shows that the influence of CMC usage intensity on students' perceived positive effects of CMC on learning is much more significant than the four types of CMC usage. This may be related to the frequent use of CMC for a wider usage of CMC. Students who frequently use CMC are familiar with the use of CMC in many aspects in daily life. The more frequently the students use CMC, the more likely the students apply CMC in learning. This reveals that students must be given enough time to explore and get familiar with the use of CMC in learning process.

From Table 7, the influence of asynchronous CMC usage on students' perceived positive effects of CMC on learning (standardized coefficient = 0.22, $p<.01$) is much more significant than that of synchronous CMC usage (standardized coefficient = 0.17, $p<.05$). This may be related to the characteristics of students' use of asynchronous CMC. For example, when students use synchronous CMC genres such as IMS and chatroom, the communication messages are temporary, instantaneous and fragmentary. Students may have not much time to deeply think about present messages and easily retrieve past messages. When students use asynchronous CMC genres such as BBS and blog, students can think more about the messages received for future posting. They can also retrieve past messages easily. Students may regard the characteristics of asynchronous CMC more helpful for their learning.

Table 7 also shows that the influence of private CMC usage on students' perceived positive effects of CMC on learning (standardized coefficient = 0.21, $p<.01$) is much more significant than that of public CMC usage (standardized coefficient = 0.17, $p<.05$). This may be related to the characteristics of students' use of private CMC. In the use of public CMC genres such as chatroom, students may mainly focus on sharing their daily life or interests. They seldom share learning materials, learning strategies or learning information with whom they are not familiar through public CMC. In contrast, students may often need to make private CMC with classmates to exchange what they have learned and discuss homework or projects. The characteristics of private CMC may be more helpful for student learning.

Table 7. Regression models of the relations between students' CMC behaviors and their perceived positive effects of CMC on learning

Model		Standardized coefficients	t
1	(Constant)		10.66^{***}
	Synchronous CMC	0.16	2.19^{*}
	CMC usage intensity	0.33	4.42^{***}
2	(Constant)		11.89^{***}
	Asynchronous CMC	0.15	1.86
	CMC usage intensity	0.29	3.73^{***}
3	(Constant)		13.06^{***}
	Public CMC	0.14	1.81
	CMC usage intensity	0.30	3.81^{***}
4	(Constant)		6.60^{***}
	Private CMC	0.21	2.89^{**}
	CMC usage intensity	0.31	4.19^{***}
5	(Constant)		11.83^{***}
	Synchronous CMC	0.15	1.97^{*}
	Asynchronous CMC	0.22	2.80^{**}
6	(Constant)		8.16^{***}
	Public CMC	0.17	2.14^{*}
	Private CMC	0.21	2.62^{**}

Note: the dependant variable is positive effects.

$^{*}p < .05$, $^{**}p < .01$, $^{***}p < .001$

4.3 Recommendations for Hybrid Disciplinary Learning Design in the Academic Context

Based on the above results, this study makes two recommendations for incorporating CMC into hybrid disciplinary learning in the academic context. First, since all types of CMC usage were perceived helpful for student learning, teachers should make effort to leverage CMC in students' learning process, such as asking students to make CMC for connecting to peers and learning materials. In educational settings, the usage of CMC for learning material acquisition and learning resource augmentation are potential to support students to build knowledge with additional information from different sources. To increase the effectiveness of CMC on student learning, students should be encouraged to make use of CMC for exchanging educational information on the learning topics with classmates or other people. This implies the need of learning activities which aim at information acquisition through CMC between students. In this regard, teachers who incorporate CMC in class are recommended to design collaborative learning activities which ask students to exchange information on target topics through CMC with classmates or other people who can help their learning.

Second, when incorporating CMC in students' hybrid learning process to enhance collaboration among students, teachers should consider arranging students who like to make asynchronous CMC and private CMC as starters of collaborative learning. From this study, students who used asynchronous CMC and private CMC more frequently tended to perceive the effects of CMC on learning more positively. In this regard, teachers should arrange students who like to make these two types of CMC in every student group and ask them to start collaborative learning activities. This helps to promote students who like to use other types of CMC to be more active in learning through peer encouragement.

5 Conclusion

This study conducted an online questionnaire survey with 163 university students in Beijing to explore the relations between students' CMC behaviors and their perceived effects of CMC on learning. The results show that students commonly used instant messaging systems, email and social network services for their CMC. The results also show that the students made asynchronous CMC and private CMC more. This study found that the students perceived positively the effects of CMC on learning.

In addition, this study had three findings on the relationship between students' CMC behaviors and their perceived effects of CMC on learning. First, all types of CMC were positively correlated with perceived positive effects of CMC on learning. Second, the more frequently the students made CMC, the more positive they perceived the effects of CMC on learning. Third, the asynchronous CMC usage and public CMC usage had more influence on students to positively perceive the effects of CMC on learning.

Based on the results in this study, two recommendations for incorporating CMC in hybrid disciplinary learning in the academic context are made. First, the teachers should design collaborative learning activities which ask students to exchange information on target topics through CMC with classmates or other people who can be helpful in their learning. Second, the teachers should choose asynchronous or private CMC, and encourage the students to spend some time on CMC for leveraging the advantages of CMC.

Further studies are needed to validate the results of this study, such as checking the logs of computer platforms and school records to triangulate the information received by the questionnaires and the students with the registered data. Also, further research could be considered to compare the results achieved by Chinese students with other nationality students to investigate possible differences and allow the generalization of the results achieved.

Acknowledgement. The authors would like to thank the Croucher Foundation for granting A. Wang a Chinese Visitorship in the Hong Kong Institute of Education for the collaborative research in this study.

References

1. McKenna, K.Y.A., Green, A.S., Gleason, M.E.J.: Relationship Formation on the Internet: What's the Big Attraction? Journal of Social Issues 58(1), 9–31 (2002)
2. Barnes, S.B.: Computer-Mediated Communication: Haman-to-Human Communication Across the Internet. Allyn and Bacon, Boston (2003)
3. Spitzberg, B.H.: Preliminary Development of a Model and Measure of Computer-Mediated Communication (CMC) Competence. Journal of Computer-Mediated Communication 11, 629–666 (2006)
4. Miller, M.D., Brunner, C.C.: Social Impact in Technologically-Mediated Communication: An Examination of Online Influence. Computers in Human Behavior 24, 2972–2991 (2008)
5. Correa, T., Hinsley, A.W., de Zúñiga, H.G.: Who Interacts on the Web? The Intersection of Users' Personality and Social Media Use. Computers in Human Behavior 26, 247–253 (2010)
6. Ellison, N.B., Steinfield, C., Lampe, C.: The Benefits of Facebook "Friends:" Social Capital and College Students' Use of Online Social Network Sites. Journal of Computer-Mediated Communication 23, 1143–1168 (2007)
7. Huang, S.: Internet Communication Structure of Juvenile Net Users. Journal of Lanzhou University (Social Science) 37(1), 70–78 (2009)
8. Conrath, K., Zeccola, J.: Does Social Networking Hurt Student Grades? American Teacher 94(2), 3 (2009)
9. Brady, K.P., Holcomb, L.B., Smith, B.V.: The Use of Alternative Social Networking Sites in Higher Educational Settings: A Case Study of the E-Learning Benefits of Ning in Education. Journal of Interactive Online Learning 9(2), 151–170 (2010)
10. Dunlap, J.C., Lowenthal, P.R.: Tweeting the Night Away: Using Twitter to Enhance Social Presence. Journal of Information Systems Education 20(2), 129–135 (2009)
11. Quan-Haase, A.: Instant Messaging on Campus: Use and Integration in University Students Everyday Communication. The Information Society 24, 105–115 (2008)
12. Young, J.R.: Facebook, Grades, and Media Hype. Chronicle of Higher Education 55(33), A13 (2009)
13. Kirschner, P.A., Karpinski, A.C.: Facebook and Academic Performance. Computers in Human Behavior 26, 1237–1245 (2010)

Hybrid Learning Meets Assessment for Learning: Facing the Misconceptions

Alice Lau and Haydn Blackey

Centre for Excellence in Learning and Teaching (CELT),
University of Glamorgan, United Kingdom, CF37 1DL
{amlau,hblackey}@glam.ac.uk

Abstract. This paper provides a case study of an institutional approach to assessment for learning and the role hybrid learning plays in the process. The paper reports on the successful implementation of assessment for learning at the University of Glamorgan, highlighting the importance of understanding the pedagogical underpinning of assessment for learning before being lured into the "wonders" of e-assessment in a hybrid learning context. A set of common misconceptions and illusions about the way e-assessment is seen as helping achieve assessment for learning is presented. An institutional wide project that has helped address these misconceptions and illusions is discussed, and by sharing this case study we hope to generate new thinking on the role of hybrid learning in developing not only assessment for learning but other learning and teaching strategies.

Keywords: Assessment for Learning, Blended Learning, Technology Enhanced Learning, e-assessment.

1 Introduction

Hybrid learning is increasingly prevalent in higher education given the potential benefits it can bring to the student learning experience [46]. This paper focuses on the role of hybrid learning in the context of assessment for learning in higher education. Assessment is seen as the key to student learning [7] [8] [9] [24] [31] [39] and a significant feature of the student learning experience because as Boud [7, p.35] states "Students can, with difficulty, escape from the effects of poor teaching, they cannot (by definition if they want to graduate) escape the effects of poor assessment." In the UK, the National Student Survey (NSS) has for consecutive years found assessment feedback as the least satisfactory areas for students across UK HEIs. With the potential benefits hybrid learning could bring, this paper aims to explore the current relationship between hybrid learning and the idea of assessment for learning. The paper will identify the misconceptions in assessment for learning, and how these are translated into the hybrid learning context. In this paper, the term e-assessment is used to describe the use of technologies in student assessment in a hybrid learning environment. Following the misconceptions in assessment for learning, illusions which can emerge in the implementation of e-assessment will be identified. The paper

R. Kwan et al. (Eds.): ICHL 2011, LNCS 6837, pp. 105–115, 2011.

will then illustrates how these misconceptions and illusions were addressed in the context of an institutional change project. We will conclude the paper by identifying concepts which emerged from practice and will inform future development of assessment for learning in a hybrid learning context.

2 Assessment for Learning in a Hybrid Learning Context

Assessment for learning has gained increased popularity since the research by Black and Wiliam [5] and is being taken up by the higher education sector as one of the keys to enhancing students' learning experience [50]. Much of the assessment literature argues that assessment has to move from 'assessment of learning' to 'assessment for learning', for example [5] [21] [47] [51]. Technology is seen as a key in supporting and adding value to assessment practice and therefore perceived to have a significant role in helping the drive towards assessment for learning [26] [27]. However, we would argue that although there is a growing body of evidence , such as [26] [27] [36], that indicate effective use of technological innovations in assessment, there are still many misconceptions in the use of technology in assessment for learning.

Assessment for learning is about "creating an environment that would foster student development in taking responsibility for evaluating, judging and improving their own performance by actively using a range of feedback" [1]. There are many principles from the literature that provide "to do" lists in order to achieve assessment for learning. While technology in many cases seems to be able to achieve this, many uses of technology for assessment remain at "surface" level. We would argue that this is due to the lack of understanding of assessment for learning.

As a result, core assessment-related activities may remain as an optional "add-on" to embed technologies, especially in the context of Welsh HEIs [22]. Many universities may provide facilities such as electronic coursework submission with plagiarism detection and publishing results online. Most of these are administrative tasks carried out by faculty administrators and have less engagement by the academic staff. The use of technologies to manage the assessment process is certainty a key part to students' assessment experience, however to truly achieve assessment for learning, we need to involve our staff to rethink the way they conduct their assessment and truly understand assessment for learning before they jump onto the e-assessment bandwagon.

There has long been research on the importance of assessment to learning and a plethora of assessment for learning principles e.g. [15] [18] [20] [37] [42]. There is also a rich literature which tends to focus either on design and development of the online assessment system and practices [10] [17]; or student/staff perception and experiences of e-assessment such as the use of audio feedback or online peer assessment [19] [32]. However, little radical change has happened in the assessment system [48]. There is little research that investigates the role technology has in an institutional wide move towards assessment for learning. This is important to the area of hybrid learning and e-assessment if they are to be embedded into the sector and contribute to bridging the gap between research that can often be seen as technical, e.g. CAA, to learning, teaching and assessment.

3 Misconceptions of Assessment for Learning Principles and Their Effect on Hybrid Learning Assessment

Assessment for learning is a contested term that is often seen as synonymous to formative assessment [5]. This understanding works well in the school sector where dialogues are enabled by the day to day interactions within the classroom. In higher education, Taras [49] argues, the situation is different. In higher education, formative assessment is often seen as practice assessment that does not contribute to any final mark, i.e. low-stake assessment. As a result, by seeing assessment for learning as synonymous to formative assessment in this case, it immediately lessens the perceived pedagogic acceptability of the idea. This misconception is often translated into e-assessment. As Ashton, Beevers and Thomas [2] state, compromises are often made in traditional assessment practice but rather than using e-assessment to address these compromises, what often happens is that these compromises are translated directly to e-assessment. This problem of direct translation is also what happened to assessment for learning. Rather than challenging our understanding of assessment for learning, this misunderstanding is translated to e-assessment. In our case, this misconception has resulted in the overwhelming response from academics that students would not complete the assessment when it does not contribute to the final mark. The initial take up of Question Mark Perception (QMP) and Blackboard online quizzes was therefore small, as they were seen by academics as mainly fulfilling a formative role only. In addition, by seeing assessment for learning as formative assessment alone, a dichotomy of summative and formative assessment is created. The idea of summative bad and formative good is prevalent in the literature of assessment for learning; this concept often creates tension in the uptake of formative assessment and assessment for learning, as lecturers feel that they have to move from one to another completely which is often seen as unrealistic. Lecturers when faced with time and resources pressure are also more likely to give up the formative element and hence less likely to consider e-assessment which is seen to be enhancing formative assessment.

Another misconception surrounding the idea of assessment for learning is that it is a tick-box exercise. There has been a surge in the number of assessment for learning principles in the higher education sector, for example, [20] [35] [37] [44] [52]. These principles highlight very similar ideas and are no doubt a key to changing assessment practice. The principles themselves are not the problem; issues very often arise from how these principles are implemented. The idea of assessment for learning, as mentioned earlier, is to create an environment that would support learners' engagement and ownership of their learning. These principles should therefore work together in harmony to create such an environment. However in many of the case studies arising from institutions that have implemented these principles in practice, only one or two principles were selected to be implemented. While this is understandable when many of the case studies are only focusing on a specific problematic area, i.e. feedback, this unintentionally conveyed the message that these principles can work in isolation. In addition, when these principles are viewed in isolation, the social constructivist idea that underpins assessment for learning is often missed. As a result, much of these principles become a tick-box administrative task.

4 Examples of Illusions Which Assume That E-assessment Helps Achieve Assessment for Learning

E-assessment is often presented in the literature with lists of its potential benefits [26] [27]. The literature emphasises the need for "skill and imagination" for these benefits to be realised. We would like to argue here that there is also a need for clear understanding of assessment for learning to underpin these practices. A number of issues created by such a lack of understanding mean the benefit such as the ability to provide speedy feedback, enhanced validity and clear and transparent assessment criteria could simply become an illusion.

One of the key advantages of e-assessment often highlighted in the literature is the ability to provide immediate or speedy feedback to students [26][38][40]. The reasoning behind this claim is that by providing feedback quickly, the feedback is more likely to have a positive effect on student learning by supporting rapid iteration [38]. While the speed of feedback is no doubt one of the key principles of assessment for learning, it is only one part of the feedback equation. In fact, we would like to argue that if e-assessment is to support assessment for learning, the focus on benefit needs to be moved from the ability to provide speedy feedback to the ability to enable dialogue. Assessment for learning as Pachler et al [38] states, "can be seen to be premised on high quality interactions, including questioning, listening, responding and reflecting, between teacher and learners, learners and learners as well as learners with themselves." The current focus on e-assessment to achieve assessment for learning is often about how tutors can provide feedback to students. It ranges from automatic responses for objective test questions to the arguably more advance free text feedback like those by Jordon and Mitchell [30]. While the development by Jordon and Mitchell [30] attempts to provide and imitate dialogues by providing multiple attempts for students to answer questions and increasingly detailed feedback, and claims to provide opportunity for self assessment and dialogue between tutors and students on its Virtual Learning Environment (VLE), its focus is still heavily on tutor controlled feedback and structured interactions. The danger here is that by highlighting the speed of feedback as the key advantage of e-assessment, it conveys a message that by simply offering speedy feedback, academics can claim that they have achieved assessment for learning even when poor practice still exist. For example, in our case, some lecturers have embraced the use of electronic marking but were translating poor feedback practice such as the use of 'final vocabulary' [41] online and speedy feedback is seen by some as speedy availability of marks to students on the VLE.

Assessment for learning as Black and Wiliam [6] asserts should account for what he describes as "moment of contingency" where learning occurs outside any pre-planned structure and arises out of dialogues either between tutors and student or students themselves. In addition, Sadler [45] argues, we need to rework current tutor and students interactions and shift the responsibility of feedback to equipping our students to take on more responsibilities at monitoring their own learning progress during their assessment. Carless et al. [11] also expresses similar ideas to develop sustainable feedback. The literature provides a new direction for e-assessment to redirect its perceived benefits of speedy feedback to its ability to enable dialogue and the opportunity for learners to take control. The emphasis here is to enable the dialogue between different stakeholders and create engagement. E-assessment provides much more opportunity for diverse forms of feedback that is often overlooked.

E-assessment is also seen to be able to enhance the validity of assessment systems and encourage deeper learning due to its ability to increase the range of what is assessed and create authentic assessment [26]. This is certainty the case with many clinical subjects such as Nursing where e-assessment are used to enhance the authenticity and validity of its assessment [25]. Authentic assessment is seen as a key to assessment for learning in particular with its ability to engage students in meaningful assessment. However, for many professional practices, the use of e-assessment often fails to achieve this promise [33]. Maharg and Owen [33] explain that this is because these e-assessment systems, such as simulation, often sit in isolation with the rest of the hybrid learning environment due to the current constraint on our use of VLEs. This created difficulties to the implementation of this form of assessment and often affected the buy-in from staff and students. As Hargreaves [23] suggests, the validity of e-assessment could be threatened if the learning condition is not supportive. In the case of e-assessment, the technical support for tutor and students are crucial. However, the support often only remains at system level, rather than as a cohesive learning experience that is embedded within many institutions' learning environment. Such isolation will also affect the crucial importance of dialogue that is essential for assessment for learning.

There is an argument for e-assessment to be more valid and authentic simply due to its use of a computer, this is based on the assumption that students are more familiar with the use of IT [40]. This is a dangerous claim as Clariana and Wallace [16] argue that just because the same questions are used in both computer-based and paper-based tests, we cannot expect equivalent measures of student learning will be produced taking into account the "test mode effect". This is an important consideration for many Higher Education Institutions with widening participation agenda, as our previous research [28] finds, many students in our institution taking e-learning courses are not necessarily comfortable with the use of technology and still require significant support.

The potential benefits of e-assessment also include its ability to easily share assessment information with students, in particular by sharing assessment criteria and learning outcomes on VLEs [3]. The importance of students' understanding what is expected of them and how the assessment would lead them to learning is another key principle in assessment for learning. This idea of alignment by Biggs [4] is seen as key to assessment for learning as it is important that students understand why they are being assessed and how the assessment can help learning. The idea is widely accepted and alignment is now a key theme in most assessment resources, textbooks and many assessment guidelines e.g. assessment resources from the Higher Education Academy. In our case, the majority of lecturers when asked why they assess their student the way they do, refer to the learning outcomes and express that all the learning outcomes are available to students via the VLE, Blackboard. It would seem that technology has helped the communication and enabled the students to see the learning outcomes. However, from our research with lecturers, it is clear that very often students do not necessary know the learning outcomes, and lecturers do not necessary see the importance for students knowing them. Furthermore, simply by putting learning outcomes on the VLE as a management requirement means that staff very often do it as an administrative task rather than understanding the true meaning of this action. This is no difference to putting the outcomes in the student handbook. The key which is to engage students in dialogue is still missing. Students often find the words and terminologies used in the subject difficult to understand and it would take time for students to understand and be engaged. Without engaging students in the discussions, alignment of learning outcomes to assessment is just another management exercise and technologies are used simply as a tool to speed up the process.

5 Addressing the Misconceptions and Illusions at the University - An Institution Wide Change to Assessment for Learning

Having identified that the illusions of e-assessment in practice are underpinned by the misconceptions about assessment for learning, the key step towards improving e-assessment in practice is therefore to resolve these misconceptions. To do this, the University adopted an institutional wide project focusing on challenging the current assumptions on assessment as a whole rather than only tackling the adoption of e-assessment. The University partnered with the Higher Education Academy in a change academy project. The project aimed to achieve complex institutional change in the area of assessment. The aim of the project was to improve the quality of student experience by putting assessment at the heart of students' learning. E-assessments is encouraged to support the process but only if assessment for learning can be achieved via its usage. The University has a strong history in hybrid learning, with established framework and strong record in using hybrid learning to initiate change. Many of these have been presented in this specific conference over the years [12][13][14]. Such a strong support background in hybrid learning has allowed the project team to really focus on how assessment for learning could work better with such strong hybrid learning background.

The project team involved staff from across the faculties and student representatives.

The team centred its effort to address the misconceptions surrounding assessment for learning with a combination of top down and bottom up approaches. As McCartan and Hare [34] assert, senior management support, along with staff development, central support services and funding opportunities are all key factors towards effective institutional change.

5.1 Addressing the Misconceptions

As stated earlier, one of the key misconceptions surrounding assessment for learning is the lack of consistent understanding of what the term means, which affects the perceived pedagogic acceptability of the concept. In order to create a common ground towards the implementation of assessment for learning and for e-assessment to have a clearer role, an institutional 'Assessment for Learning policy' was developed. The policy clarifies the idea that assessment for learning is more than formative assessment and provides a focal point to addressing the misconceptions and illusions across the University. The policy was developed in consultation with faculty staff across the University which generated much discussion around the idea of assessment for learning. These discussions did not only allow many of the misconceptions from different faculties to be raised and addressed, they also provided a sense of ownership, and therefore buy-in, from faculties in implementing the idea of assessment for learning. However, the policy can still be seen as a top down approach, and as Ruedel et al. [43] explain, top-down approaches "without sufficient support or pedagogically sound exemplars from well respected members of staff has the potential to promote resistance and slow development."

The project therefore collected a selection of good practices in assessment for learning across the University and created a "living" good practice guide with the guide growing as the project developed. Exemplars of good practice were collated from across all five faculties in order to provide a sense to staff that changes are not only desirable but possible. The guides were disseminated across the faculties to encourage discussion.

Staff development events including seminars and workshops were carried out to further promote the policy of assessment for learning and maintain discussion around the idea. Existing good practice in the use of e-assessment across the university were identified and academic staff were invited to deliver seminars about their practice highlighting how their e-assessment achieved assessment for learning. In order to highlight the importance of dialogue in assessment for learning, seminars including a student panel were used to share the student voice in order to generate a better understanding on students' perception and experience of assessment for learning.

The development of the assessment policy along with the good practice guides and staff development sessions promoted the idea of assessment for learning that included a supportive learning environment and are more than a tick box exercise. To further develop the idea, the project provided funding opportunities for staff within the faculties. This allowed them to put forward changes to their assessment practice within their modules, based on the principles of assessment for learning. These included the use of technology to support and enhance assessment. As Knight [31] states, effective assessment reform requires not only departmental and institutional action, but also actions from individual staff. Faculty representatives from the project sent out invites to all their staff to put forward expressions of interest to relook at their assessment practice. Funding was provided to staff that would like to be involved. Over 70 modules were submitted by staff to participate in this change process. A number of these proposals were looking at a course level change, involving academic staff from a department or team which enabled much dialogue and understanding between staff. Some of these changes will be looked at in the next section as examples of how the institution addressed the illusions.

5.2 Resolving the Illusions

The project team found that the key to addressing the feedback e-assessment illusion is to address the need for students to take more responsibility for their assessment and to encourage dialogue between tutors and students. Changes within the University included promoting the use of plagiarism detection tools as a learning tool for students rather than a policing tool alone. The use of the plagiarism tool as dialogue is especially useful as it is a topic that students and staff are equally concerned about. The originality reports generated from the plagiarism detection system provided to learners and tutors are being used by tutors to explore with students how they should reference or use quotations in their essay. The idea of dialogue is being developed further with the use of other e-assessment tools in particular the use of wikis and blogs in a number of subject disciplines. In addition, staff are also experimenting with the use of audio and video feedback which helps avoid the tendency to use final vocabulary in feedback. In one faculty, they have developed feedback leaflets with their students to explain what students can expect from the faculty in terms of feedback and the role students have to play. While this might be seen as outside the remit of e-assessment, it is discussions like these between staff and students that have helped resolve some of the illusions surrounding e-assessment and ensured that staff are aware of the students' positive reactions to the use of e-assessment tools.

The key to enhancing the validity of e-assessment, as highlighted earlier is the support to create an integrated hybrid learning and assessment environment. Rather than working only with faculty staff, the project worked closely with the university's technical team to integrate e-assessment usage to the existing VLE. The use of Question Mark Perception, Turnitin and Campus Pack are all integrated within Blackboard as part of GlamLearn, a single sign-on student portal to provide a supportive and consistent hybrid learning and assessment environment for students and staff. In addition, the funding opportunities have allowed staff to experiment with simulation tools and the uses of simulations are increasing with a focus on authentic assessment rather than a simple use of MCQ questions.

The use of enhanced hybrid learning and assessment tools has encouraged staff to reflect on the learning experience from a student focused perspective. As part of the staff development provided it has become clearer to staff that assessment criteria and learning outcomes which might be obvious and simple from their perspectives appear complex and challenging from a student perspective. The use of e-assessment tools prompts staff to think more imaginatively about the way they communicate the nature of assessment to their students. As part of the project the institution developed an online assessment diary which provides a clearer course overview of the assessment expectations, including criteria, learning outcomes, deadlines and feedback dates to students than the often isolated and inconsistent modular view. The assessment diary was developed by course team with administrative staff and students representatives to again encourage dialogue between stakeholders when developing an assessment for learning environment. This has resulted in a better understanding of assessment requirements not only from students but a better understanding amongst course team to the often private assessment design process.

6 Conclusions

The University's project has been cited by the Higher Education Academy and JISC as example of good practice on institutional wide changes that produced effective assessment practice in a hybrid learning environment [27] [50]. The project has resulted in improved student satisfaction, in one department for example, the NSS score for assessment and feedback in particular has improved significantly [29]. Some of the module leaders are already looking to cascade the changes they initiated to other modules across the institution, and creating synergies and dialogue between staff. The success of the project lies in its focus in generating and sustaining dialogues between all stakeholders across the University on e-assessment with a specific pedagogic focus – assessment for learning.

This paper has highlighted the importance of a clear pedagogic focus when implementing hybrid learning, and the need to identify any misconceptions and illusions often lurking under the high profile banners of institutional hybrid learning practice. The use of an institutional assessment for learning policy to create a focal point along with collaborations and involvement from across the institution is a vital step for the development of e-assessment in our hybrid environment. With a pedagogical focal point developed, good practice examples identified from within the institution along with staff development are all vital to instilling the possibility of any hybrid learning practice. Concrete support in the form of time and space via funding and development of a stable and supportive learning environment are needed to drive innovative ideas into reality. While this paper focused on assessment in a hybrid learning environment, the experiences from this institutional wide project should provide a different but important way to think about implementation of hybrid learning with pedagogy leading the change.

References

1. AfL, Cetl. (2005), `http://www.northumbria.ac.uk/sd/central/ar/academy/cetl_afl/`
2. Ashton, H., Beevers, C., Thomas, R.: Can e-assessment become mainstream? In: The 12th CAA Conference. Loughborough University, UK (2008), `http://www.caaconference.com/pastConferences/2008/proceedings/Ashton_H_Beevers_C_Thomas_R_final_formatted_f1.pdf`
3. Aubrey-Smith, F.: VLEs make assessment for learning safely social. In: NAACE (2009), `http://www.agent4change.net/policy/learning-platforms/352-vles-make-assessment-for-learning-a-social-affair.html`
4. Biggs, J.: Teaching for quality learning at university. Open University, Buckingham (1999)
5. Black, P., Wiliam, D.: Assessment and classroom learning. Assessment in Education 5(1), 7–74 (1998)
6. Black, P., Wiliam, D.: Developing the theory of formative assessment. Educational Assessment, Evaluation and Accountability 21(1), 5–31 (2009)
7. Boud, D.: Assessment and learning: contradictory or complimentary? In: Knight, P. (ed.) Assessment for Learning in Higher Education, pp. 35–48. Kogan Page/SEDA, London (1995)
8. Boud, D.: Sustainable Assessment: Rethinking assessment for the learning society. Studies in Continuing Education 22(2), 151–167 (2000)
9. Brown, S., Knight, P.: Assessing Learners in Higher Education. Kogan Page, London (1994)
10. CAA: Annual International CAA Conference Since 1997, Loughborough (2009)
11. Carless, D., Salter, D., Yang, M., Lam, J.: Developing sustainable feedback practices. Studies in Higher Education 36(1), 1–13 (2010)
12. Chew, E., Jones, N.: 'The E-Vangelist's plan of Action – Exemplars of the UK Universities' Strategies of Blended Learning. In: Wang, F.L., Fong, J., Zhang, L., Lee, V.S.K. (eds.) ICHL 2009. LNCS, vol. 5685, pp. 378–389. Springer, Heidelberg (2009)
13. Chew, E., Jones, N., Blackey, H.: Implementing Institutional Online Assessment – Addressing the Challenges. In: Tsang, P., Cheung, S.K.S., Lee, V.S.K., Huang, R. (eds.) ICHL 2010. LNCS, vol. 6248, pp. 453–464. Springer, Heidelberg (2010)

14. Chew, E., Jones N.: The Blended Learning Journey of the University of Glamorgan. In: International Conference of Hybrid Learning, Hong Kong (August 2011) (in press)
15. Chickering, A.W., Gamson, Z.F.: Seven Principles to Good Practice in Undergraudate Education. The Wingspread Journal 9(2) (1987)
16. Clariana, R.B., Wallace, P.: Paper-based versus computer-based assessment: key factors associated with the test mode effect. British Journal of Educational Technology 33(5), 593–602 (2002)
17. Crisp, V., Ward, C.: The development of a formative scenario-based computer assisted assessment tool in psychology for teachers: The PePCAA project. Computers & Education 50, 1509–1526 (2008)
18. Crooks, T.J.: The impact of classroom evaluation practices on students. Review of Educational Researcher 58, 438–481 (1988)
19. Davies, P.: Review and Reward within the Computerized Peer-Assessment of Essays. Assessment & Evaluation in Higher Education 34(3), 321–333 (2009)
20. Gibbs, G., Simpson, C.: Conditions under which Assessment Supports Students' Learning. Learning and Teaching in Higher Education 1, 3–31 (2004)
21. Gipps, C.: Beyond Testing Towards a Theory of Educational Assessment. Routledge, London (1994)
22. Gwella: Second Gwella Programme Meeting event, Gregynog Hall in Wales (2009), http://www.heacademy.ac.uk/events/detail/2009/second_gwella_meeting_nov09
23. Hargreaves, E.: The validity of collaborative assessment for learning. Assessment in Education 14(2), 185–199 (2007)
24. Harvey, L.: Quality Assessment in Higher Education: Collected Papers of the QHE Project. In: Quality, C.f.R.i. (ed.), Birmingham, UCE (1993)
25. Hutton, M., Coben, D., Hall, C., Rowe, D., Sabin, M., Weeks, K., Woolley, N.: Numeracy for nursing, report of a pilot study to compare outcomes of two practical simulation tools – An online medication dosage assessment and practical assessment in the style of objective structured clinical examination. Nurse Education Today 30(7), 608–614 (2010)
26. JISC: Effective Practice With E-Assessment: An Overview Of Technologies, Policies And Practice In Further And Higher Education (2007), http://www.jisc.ac.uk/media/documents/themes/elearning/effpraceassess.pdf
27. JISC: Effective Assessment in a Digital Age (2010), http://www.jisc.ac.uk/media/documents/programmes/elearning/digiassass_eada.pdf
28. Jones, N., Lau, M.S.A.: Blending learning: widening participation in higher education. Innovations in Education and Teaching International 47(4), 405–416 (2010)
29. Jones, C., Lau, A., Taylor, R.: Assessment Diaries: Responding to the Needs of Tutors and Students. LINK 25 Learning from Developments in Higher Education in Wales. The Higher Education Academy Hospitality, Leisure, Sport & Tourism Network (2010), http://www.heacademy.ac.uk/assets/hlst/documents/LINK_Newsletter/Link_25_wales.pdf
30. Jordan, S., Mitchell, T.: e-Assessment for learning? The potential of short-answer free-text questions with tailored feedback. British Journal of Educational Technology 40(2), 371–385 (2009)
31. Knight, P. (ed.): Assessment for Learning in Higher Education. Routledge, London (1995)
32. Lunt, T., Curran, J.: Are you listening please? The advantages of electronic audio feedback compared to written feedback. Assessment & Evaluation in Higher Education 35(7), 759–769 (2010)

33. Maharg, P., Owen, M.: Simulations, Learning and the Metaverse: Changing Cultures in Legal Education. UK Centre for Legal Education (2007), SSRN http://ssrn.com/abstract=999541
34. McCartan, A., Hare, C.: Effective institutional change: the impact of some strategic issues in the integrative use of IT in teaching and learning. ALT-J Research in Learning Technology 4, 21–28 (1996)
35. Mcdowell, L.: What is CETL AfL? (2005), http://www.northumbria.ac.uk/sd/central/ar/academy/cetl_afl/
36. Nicol, D.: Increasing success in first year courses: Assessment re-design, self-regulation and learning technologies. In: Markauskaite, L., Goodyear, P., Reimann, P. (eds.) The 23rd Annual Conference of the Australasian Society for Computers in Learning in Tertiary Education Who's Learning? Whose Technology?. The University of Sydney, Sydney (2006)
37. Nicol, D.: Principles of good assessment and feedback: Theory and practice. In: The REAP International Online Conference on Assessment Design for Learner Responsibility (2007)
38. Pachler, N., Mellar, H., Daly, C., Mor, Y., Wiliam, D., Laurillard, D.: Scoping a vision for formative e-assessment: a project report for JISC (2009), http://www.jisc.ac.uk/media/documents/projects/scopingfinalreport.pdf
39. Ramsden, P.: Learning to teach in Higher Education. Routledge, London (1992)
40. Ridgway, J., McCusker, S., Pead, D.: Literature Review of E-assessment. NESTA Futurelab, Bristol (2004)
41. Rorty, R.: Contingency, Irony and Solidarity. Cambridge University Press, Cambridge (1989)
42. Rowntree, D.: Assessing Students: How Shall We Know Them? Harper & Row, London (1977)
43. Ruedel, C., Whitelock, D., Mackenzie, D.: Key factors for effective organisation of e-assessment. In: The 11th International CAA conference Loughborough University (2007), http://oro.open.ac.uk/11951/1/CAA_2007_organisational_structures.pdf
44. Rust, C., O'Donovan, B., Price, M.: A social constructivist assessment process model: how the research literature shows us this could be best practice. Assessment and Evaluation in Higher Education 30(3), 231–240 (2005)
45. Sadler, R.: Phasing out feedback: towards making it redundant ASKe Public Lecture. Oxford Brookes University (2010)
46. Sharpe, R., Benfield, G., Roberts, G., Grancis, R.: The undergraduate experience of blended e-learning: a review of UK literature and practice. The Higher Education Academy (2006)
47. Shepard, L.A.: The Role of Assessment in a Learning Culture. Educational Researcher 29(4), 4–14 (2000)
48. Stobart, G.: Assessment fit-for-the-future. In: IAEA Annual Conference 2010, Bangkok, Thailand (2010)
49. Taras, M.: Assessment for learning: understanding theory to improve practice. Journal of Further and Higher Education 31(4), 363–371 (2007)
50. The Higher Education Academy, http://www.heacademy.ac.uk/resources/detail/ourwork/ipp/Issue3_Academywork
51. Torrance, H., Pryor, J.: Investigating Formative Assessment. Open University Press, Buckingham (1998)
52. National Student Union: NUS briefing Assessment Purposes and practice (2009), http://www.timeshighereducation.co.uk/story.asp?sectioncode=26&storycode=405152&c=2

Gender Differences of Knowledge Sharing in Online Learning Environment

Will Wai Kit Ma[1] and Allan Hoi Kau Yuen[2]

[1] Online Communication Research Centre, Department of Journalism & Communication, Hong Kong Shue Yan University, 10 Wai Tsui Crescent, North Point, Hong Kong SAR, P.R. China
wkma@hksyu.edu

[2] Faculty of Education, The University of Hong Kong, Pokfulam, Hong Kong SAR, P.R. China
hkyuen@hkucc.hku.hk

Abstract. Although online learning environments are perceived to facilitate knowledge sharing among individuals, various empirical studies find that participants do not log on frequently or are reluctant to share ideas with others. It is thus crucial for educators to understand when and how online knowledge sharing occurs. Prior model framework has been adapted to explore the motivational factors that drive knowledge sharing among individuals in online learning environments, esp. if there are any gender differences of online knowledge sharing. The hypothesized relationships between the identified motivational factors and online knowledge sharing behavior are then tested using a survey questionnaire administered to a sample of 333 undergraduate students. The results indicate that perceived attachment motivation (the need to form) and perceived relationship commitment (the need to main a relationship) are important determinants of online knowledge sharing. Further analysis on gender differences reveals that male participants rated the need to form relationships more highly than their female counterparts. Implications to ensure online learning environments to encourage knowledge sharing behavior are discussed.

Keywords: Gender differences, online knowledge sharing, perceived online attachment motivation, perceived online relationship commitment.

1 Introduction

The past decade or so has seen a rise in the adoption of web-based technologies for teaching and learning in higher education institutions. Previous studies have focused on how online learning environments can be designed to allow interactions among participants and to embed learning in social experiences, provide access to a wide range of resources, and support collaboration [1].

However, these benefits cannot be realized by design alone: they also require the active participation of individuals. Recent empirical studies have revealed low levels of participation and a reluctance to share knowledge in online learning environments [2] and studies of the motivational factors influencing participation in such

R. Kwan et al. (Eds.): ICHL 2011, LNCS 6837, pp. 116–128, 2011.

environments indicate that this issue remains unresolved [3-5]. More recent studies suggest that future research should consider "the wider social relations underpinning the relatively modest use of technology in higher education," [1].

In response to this suggestion, this study aims to explore the motivational factors that affect knowledge sharing among individuals, with a specific focus on how interpersonal relationships influence knowledge sharing in online learning environments. The study also uses a framework to identify whether there are any gender differences in online knowledge sharing behavior. The way in which the study extends previous research and provides an alternative perspective to explain knowledge sharing in online learning environments is discussed, with particular reference to the need for interpersonal relationships among online learners.

2 Literature Review

2.1 Knowledge Sharing and Online Learning Environments

In online learning environments, collaborative online learning and online learning communities are observed to be the two main modes of knowledge sharing.

In collaborative online learning, learners form small groups that work together to solve problems or complete common tasks, aided by communication tools provided by the online learning environment [6]. Collaborative online learning, especially when facilitated by online discussion forums, stimulates deep learning and a high level of motivation through joint efforts to solve problems [7]. Individuals contribute by sharing and interacting with peer learners to solve problems and complete tasks [8]. In contrast, individuals who are passive and feel alienated are reluctant to share, avoid their peers, and have low levels of participation in online learning activities [3].

In online learning communities, informal learning takes place when pools of peer learners help each other and offer both intellectual and interpersonal support [e.g., 9]. Online learning community members who have a strong sense of belonging are committed, communicate extensively with each other, are willing to offer help, and share learning experiences [10]. Online learning communities promote mutual support, as members help other members who are experiencing isolation, loneliness, or distress in learning online [11].

2.2 Perceived Online Attachment Motivation (POAM)

Several in-group studies provide explanations as to what makes individuals prepared to work together in small groups, even without additional rewards or specified conditions. For example, the discrimination of group identity has been identified through even simple and random categorizations of individuals into groups [12].

However, individuals may not always be accepted into a relationship, and may instead be ignored, excluded, or rejected by others. Ignored individuals feel bad and lose a sense of belonging, both in the physical world [13] and on the Internet [14]. These findings are consistent with the observations in online learning research of online participants who feel isolated or lonely [15].

Previous studies also reveal that relationships predict a sense of belonging [16], and that there is a direct link between a sense of belonging and academic outcomes [17]. Hence, interpersonal relationships have been widely applied to explain the sense of belonging and academic outcomes in various age groups and educational settings.

2.3 Perceived Online Relationship Commitment (PORC)

Prior studies suggest that commitment explains why an individual persists in a relationship [18], and why satisfying relationships may not be sustained whereas unsatisfying links can sometimes persist for decades [19]. Overall commitment depends on the investment that has been made in the relationship, among other factors, and is inversely related to the quality of alternatives [20].

There is ample support for the relationship between interpersonal relationships and observed behavior in collaborative online learning and online learning communities. For example, students report that availability or lack of time is an important factor determining whether or not they will contribute to online discussion forums [5]. Students also report that participation in online learning activities is a low priority in their learning activities, as they perceive online conversation to be of little value [2]. The maintenance of successful communities requires that individuals recognize the value of participation and invest time and effort.

2.4 Gender Differences in Knowledge Sharing

It has been suggested that there are gender differences in belief, attitude, and behavior in the formation and maintenance of relationships. Shaver and Buhrmester [21] argue that in general, males are less well suited to social life because of their tendency toward independence and their fear of social contact and relatedness.

Taking an alternative perspective, Cross and Madson [22] argue that there are significant gender differences in individual structures of the self, with men in the United States constructing and maintaining an independent self-construal and women constructing and maintaining an interdependent self-construal. Independent self-construal refers to representations of others who are separate from the self, whereas interdependent self-construal refers to others who are considered part of the self.

Extending this line of thought, Baumeister and Sommer [23] explore gender differences in terms of the size of the reference social spheres of belonging. They propose that men's behavior is directed toward the formation of relationships with others but in a broader social sphere, whereas women's sociality is focused on dyadic close relationships.

In the online learning context, Anderson and Haddad [24] find that female learners show greater social interdependence than male learners in online discussions, which leads to higher levels of perceived deep learning. They also find that females appear to express themselves more often in online than in face-to-face courses. Caspi et al. [25] examine participation in face-to-face versus web-based classroom discussions, and in comparing the actual participation ratio of men and women to the attendance (or login) ratio find that men speak much more than women in face-to-face discussions but that women post many more messages than men in web-based discussions.

3 Framework and Hypotheses Development

The following definitions would be used in the discussion of the relationships and hypotheses development in this study [26, 27].

Online knowledge sharing behavior (OKSB) is defined as "*the online communication of knowledge so that knowledge is learned and applied by an individual*"

Perceived online attachment motivation (POAM) is defined as "*the degree to which an individual believes that he or she can improve his or her social interaction and sense of communion with others on an online learning platform*"

Perceived online relationship commitment (PORC) is defined as "*the degree to which a learner tends to continue with an established relationship in an online learning environment*"

It is argued that the desire to form relationships is an important determinant of online knowledge sharing. If an individual perceives that an online learning environment is a good place to form relationships, then he or she will be motivated to approach and interact with other learners in that environment. He or she will also be more willing to engage in greater interaction with other members of the online learning community through various means, including small talk, certain forms of address, communicative norms, and self-disclosure. In online learning communities, all individuals share the common goal of learning, and thus sharing one's knowledge is a good way to develop relationships. However, if an individual perceives that an online learning environment is not a good place to form relationships, then he or she will choose not to spend time and effort in that environment. Both external factors, such as the functions of the online learning environment, and internal factors, such as the composition of learners in the environment, affect an individual's perception of an online learning environment. Perceived online attachment motivation (POAM) can thus be used to measure an individual's overall evaluation of an online learning environment. This argument leads to the hypothesis H1.

Second, it is argued that in a learning community, individuals establish relationships with other members. Sharing is a means of establishing close relationships, and can be viewed as a kind of social support and a form of prosocial behavior. In the process of maintaining established relationships, individual learners become more willing to share with other members of the online community. Knowledge sharing then comes to be viewed as a positive act that benefits the sharing parties. This argument leads to the hypothesis H2a.

Third, concern about belonging is a powerful factor shaping human thought and behavior. People often interpret situations and events in terms of their implications for their relationships with others, and think more deeply about interaction partners than about other people. Thus, both actual and potential bonds have a substantial effect on the way in which people think [28]. It is thus likely that an individual's perceived online attachment motivation is affected by his or her perceived online relationship commitment. Specifically, the greater the engagement of an individual in an online learning community, the greater his or her sense of belonging to that community. This gives rise to switching costs, in that the more that the individual contributes to the community, the higher the cost of switching to another, as the individual will be left with nothing once he or she leaves. Thus, an individual will have a stronger attachment to an online learning community when he or she is more committed to that community. This argument leads to the hypothesis H2b.

Fourth, previous studies reveal that there may be gender differences in perception, affect, and behavior with regard to interpersonal relationships. If such differences exist, then the online knowledge sharing of females and males should also be different. Based on the different social spheres of males and females [23], it is argued that if males have a larger sphere of belonging than females, then they will have a greater motivation than females to form new relationships with peer learners. This leads to the hypothesis H3.

However, although females have a smaller sphere of belonging than males, they are likely to spend more time and effort than males in maintaining established relationships. This leads to the hypothesis H4.

Therefore, four hypotheses are employed to examine the online knowledge sharing and the gender differences:

H1: *The perceived online attachment motivation of an individual regarding an online learning environment has a positive effect on his or her knowledge sharing behavior in that environment.*

H2a: *The perceived online relationship commitment of an individual to an online learning environment has a positive effect on his or her knowledge sharing behavior in that environment.*

H2b: *The perceived relationship commitment of an individual to an online learning environment has a positive effect on his or her perceived online attachment motivation regarding that environment.*

H3: *The perceived online attachment motivation of a male learner (versus a female learner) regarding an online learning environment has a stronger positive effect on his knowledge sharing behavior in that environment.*

H4: *The perceived online relationship commitment of a female learner (versus a male learner) to an online learning environment has a stronger positive effect on her knowledge sharing behavior in that environment.*

4 Methodology

Background: The subjects in this study were all undergraduate students using an online learning environment, "HKNews," to support their learning about news writing in the Department of Journalism and Communication of a local university in Hong Kong. HKNews is based on MediaWiki (www.wikipedia.org), and allows students to post news articles at any time and edit previously posted articles as often as they wish. The platform is open to all, and learners can read each other's articles. As of November 2009, there were 27,628 articles, 1,667 photos, 184,446 instances of article editing, and 2,435 registered users recorded in HKNews.

Subjects: Among the 389 journalism students in the department, 333 (83 men, 247 women, 3 gender unreported) took part, yielding a response rate of 85.60%. Of the

389 students, 152 were in Year 2, 122 were in Year 3, and 115 were in Year 4. The average age of the participants was 21.79 years. The proportion of respondents to the total number of students in each year was similar: in Year 2 it was 39.1%, in Year 3 31.5%, and in Year 4 29.4%. On average, the participants had been using HKNews for approximately two and a half years (mean = 2.56; SD = 0.708).

Table 1. Gender and course distribution of respondents in the sample

	Male	Female	Not reported
Year 2	30	99	1
Year 3	30	74	0
Year 4	23	74	2
Subtotal	83	247	3
Total (N)	333		

Data collection: Near the end of the semester, the investigator distributed a paper questionnaire in class for students to complete. The respondents were reminded that their cooperation was purely voluntary, and that they could stop at any time without penalty. They were also told that their participation would be appreciated, as it would provide valuable information for the improvement of the online learning environment. On average, the respondents took about 10 minutes to complete the survey questionnaire, and all completed it within 20 minutes. Upon collection of the completed questionnaires, the respondents were given a small gift of a highlighter costing HKD1.00 as a token of appreciation. The data collection process took two weeks to complete.

Measures: The questionnaire was divided into two parts. Part A solicited information about the demographic characteristics of the participants and their use of the online learning environment, including age, gender, year of study, years of experience and self-reported skill in using an online learning environment, self-reported subject knowledge in news writing, and the frequency and duration of their usage of the online learning environment. Part B included statements asking for their opinions about forming and maintaining relationships and knowledge sharing behavior. The scale for the constructs was developed based on previously validated instruments whereas wordings were revised to reflect the online learning context. The questionnaire was adapted from previous validated scale [26] and included five items about perceived online attachment motivation (POAM1 – POAM5), five items about perceived online relationship commitment (PORC1 – PORC5), and five items about online knowledge sharing behavior (OKSB1 – OKSB5). The full scale is presented in the Appendix. All of the question items were measured on a seven-point Likert scale ranging from 1 (strongly disagree) to 7 (strongly agree). Additional statements for another study were also included in the questionnaire. The statements were randomly arranged to reduce a potential ceiling or floor effect that might induce monotonous responses.

5 Findings

5.1 Descriptive Summary and Validity Testing of the Observed Variables

The descriptive statistics of the measurement items are listed in Table 2. The table shows that the respondents had generally positive perceptions toward of relationships in online learning environments. The mean values for POAM, PORC, and OKSB range between 3.54 and 3.98, 3.42 and 3.99, and 4.08 and 4.24, respectively.

Validity is the degree to which a measure accurately represents what it is supposed to represent, whereas reliability is the degree to which an observed variable measures the "true" value and is "error free"[29].

Cronbach's alpha is generally the most appropriate type of reliability measure for survey research that involves a range of possible answers for each item [30]. The Cronbach's alpha values for each of the constructs exceeded the suggested threshold value of 0.7 [31], with a range from 0.83 to 0.88. This indicates that the constructs were internally consistent.

The measurement model and constructs were assessed by confirmatory factor analysis using LISREL 8.5 and a sample correlation matrix for scale validation. The measured factor loadings of the construct items were all significant ($p<0.001$), which means that they were explained more by the hypothesized construct than by error [29](see Table 2).

Table 2. Descriptive statistics for the observed variables (N=333)

POAM	Mean / StdDev	Factor Loadings	PORC	Mean / StdDev	Factor Loadings	OKSB	Mean / StdDev	Factor Loadings
POAM1	3.54 (1.12)	0.59***	PORC1	3.78 (1.15)	0.80***	OKSB1	4.24 (1.15)	0.79***
POAM2	3.67 (1.07)	0.68***	PORC2	3.86 (1.17)	0..80***	OKSB2	4.11 (1.10)	0.72***
POAM3	3.76 (1.01)	0.83***	PORC3	3.49 (1.14)	0.76***	OKSB3	4.08 (1.05)	0.74***
POAM4	3.93 (1.01)	0.80***	PORC4	3.42 (1.17)	0.72***	OKSB4	4.19 (1.13)	0.76***
POAM5	3.98 (1.08)	0.74***	PORC5	3.99 (1.15)	0.69***	OKSB5	4.18 (1.11)	0.80***
Reliability Alpha	0.83			0.85			0.88	

5.2 Model Testing Results

The corresponding hypotheses were examined using structural equation modeling. The results of the model testing produced a list of goodness-of-fit indices, including a Root Mean Square Residue (RMR) of 0.038 (< 0.1), a Root Mean Square Error of Approximation (RMSEA) of 0.062 (< 0.1), and a Goodness of Fit Index (GFI) of 0.94. All of these and the other indices exceeded the suggested values, indicating that the model fit the data well [29] (see Table 3).

Table 3. Summary of the hypothesis testing results of overall model

Causal Paths	Path Coefficients	Hypothesis
POAM → OKSB	0.49***	H1: supported
PORC → OKSB	0.31**	H2a: supported
PORC → POAM	0.87***	H2b: supported
R^2: OKSB (0.54, in reduced form); POAM (0.76).		****p* < 0.001; ***p* < 0.01*.

5.3 Model Testing Results by Gender

It was hypothesized that the framework would fit the data for both gender groups, but that there would be significant differences in the estimated parameters or the means in explaining online knowledge sharing. Post hoc analysis was employed to test these hypotheses.

As noted, three of the respondents (3/333 = 0.9%) did not disclose their gender, and their records were thus removed from the dataset for this part of the analysis. The sample (N = 330) was then split into two subsamples, female (n = 247) and male (n = 83). The gender ratio was similar to the distribution of the whole Department of Journalism and Communication.

Structural equation modeling analysis of group differences was employed to test for the equality of the factor structures and to estimate the parameters for the relationships in the two gender groups [32]. The measurement factor structures were assumed to be the same for the two groups, but the coefficients for the hypothesized gender differences were estimated independently. The model testing results generated two solutions, one for each group (see Figure 2). The resulting global goodness-of-fit indices reflect the measure of fit for all of the models in all of the groups, and show only a mildly acceptable fit (chi-sq/df = 2.74; RMR = 0.081; GFI = 0.72). This is probably due to the small sample size in the male group (n = 83). Structural equation modeling requires a large sample size for analysis, and the chi-square test is very sensitive to sample size.

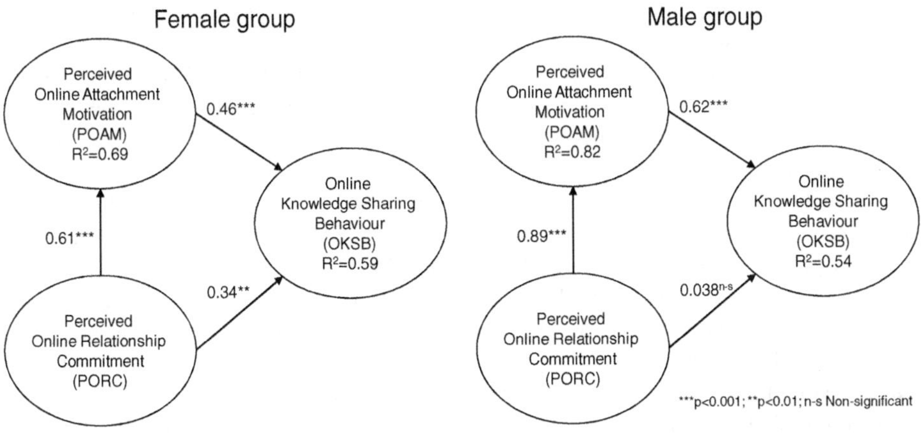

Fig. 1. Model testing for the gender groups

6 Discussions

6.1 Interpersonal Relationships and Online Knowledge Sharing

The first hypothesis posited a direct, positive, and significant relationship between perceived online attachment motivation (POAM) and online knowledge sharing behavior (OKSB). The data analysis revealed the existence of this relationship, and thus Hypothesis 1 is supported.

The second hypothesis posited a direct, positive, and significant relationship between perceived online relationship commitment (PORC) and online knowledge sharing behavior (OKSB). The findings confirm the existence of this relationship exists, and thus Hypothesis 2a is supported.

The third hypothesis posited a direct, positive, and significant relationship between perceived online attachment motivation (POAM) and perceived online relationship commitment (PORC). The findings indicate the existence of this relationship exists, and thus Hypothesis 2b is supported.

6.2 Gender Differences in Knowledge Sharing

The fourth hypothesis posited a direct, positive, and significant relationship between the perceived online attachment motivation (POAM) of learners and their online knowledge sharing behavior (OKSB), and that this relationship would be stronger for male than for female learners. The results reveal a positive significant effect for both genders, but the effect for the male learners is much greater than that of the female learners by nearly a third. Hence, Hypothesis 3 is supported.

Consistent with the results of previous studies [23], the findings of this study indicate a stronger desire among males than females to form relationships in online environments. Thus, male learners care more than female learners about whether an online learning environment supports relationship formation and offers a wider social sphere [23].

Both males and females evaluate an online learning environment to see whether it supports relationship formation. If they perceive that it does, then they will engage in a higher level of online knowledge sharing in that environment. The findings reveal that, regardless of gender, learners' evaluations of whether an online learning environment can meet their need to form relationships strongly predict their level of online knowledge sharing.

The fifth hypothesis posited a direct, positive, and significant relationship between the perceived online relationship commitment (PORC) of learners and their online knowledge sharing behavior (OKSB), and that this relationship would be stronger for female than for male learners. The results reveal that such a relationship exists for female learners, whereas for male learners the relationship is strong and significant but indirect, being mediated by perceived online attachment motivation (POAM). The direct path from perceived online relationship commitment (PORC) to online knowledge sharing behavior (OKSB) is non-significant, which means that perceived online attachment motivation (POAM) fully mediates the relationship between perceived online relationship commitment (PORC) and online knowledge sharing behavior (OKSB) among male learners. Thus, Hypothesis 4 is supported.

Consistent with the suggestion of previous work [23], the findings of this study indicate a stronger desire among female learners to maintain established relationships. The findings support the theory of the need to belong, but show that men and women place a different emphasis on belonging. Compared with females, males have a higher level of approach motivation to form new relationships with peers, whereas females have a greater need to both form and maintain relationships. Male and female learners thus use different strategies and have different criteria in the pursuit of belonging through interaction with peers in online learning environments.

Various implementation strategies could be applied to meet the different needs of female and male learners in online learning environments. For example, instructors could help individuals to form small voluntary study groups, which would allow female learners to engage in closer and more frequent interaction in smaller social circles. At the same time, instructors could establish an activity update list to organize and display input from all individuals. This would give learners the opportunity to find out more about what is going on in the wider social sphere and interact with a greater number of peers, which would cater to the needs of male learners.

6.3 Limitations and Future Research

This study has several limitations. First, the generalization of the findings depends on the wider application of the framework to different online learning domains, different learning disciplines, and different subjects. Out of convenience, the current study applied the instrument to a specific group. Future studies should apply the framework to validate the findings in different online learning contexts and subjects. Second, the small sample size of the male participants may have diminished the validity of the analysis results. Future studies should thus apply the framework to a larger data sample to validate the results. Third, this study adopted a self-reported measure of knowledge sharing behavior, rather than an objective measure, which may have resulted in self-reported bias and halo-effects. However, this measurement method is not without support [33], and it is appropriate to measure knowledge sharing by asking individuals whether it really occurs.

7 Conclusion

This study offers an alternative explanation of knowledge sharing in online learning environments. Previous studies provide empirical evidence of the importance of interpersonal relationships in explaining social interaction and knowledge sharing, but few studies have given details of the relevant mechanisms in online learning environments. The findings of this study provide significant insights that can be translated into practical strategies, especially in terms of the design and implementation of online learning environments to promote knowledge sharing.

References

1. Selwyn, N.: The use of computer technology in university teaching and learning: A critical perspective. Journal of Computer Assisted Learning 23, 83–94 (2007)
2. Carr, N., Chambers, D.P.: Teacher professional learning in an online community: The experiences of the National Quality Schooling Framework Pilot Project. Technology, Pedagogy and Education 15, 143–157 (2006)
3. Ng, K.-C.: Using e-mail to foster collaboration in distance education. Open Learning 16, 191–200 (2001)
4. Xie, K.U.I., Debacker, T.K., Ferguson, C.: Extending the traditional classroom through online discussion: The role of student motivation. Journal of Educational Computing Research 34, 67–89 (2006)
5. Cheung, W.S., Hew, K.F., Ling Ng, C.S.: Toward an understanding of why students contribute in asynchronous online discussions. Journal of Educational Computing Research 38, 29–50 (2008)
6. Hiltz, S.R., Coppola, N., Rotter, N., Turoff, M., Benbunan-Fich, R.: Measuring the importance of collaborative learning for the effectiveness of ALN: A multi-measure, multi-method approach. Journal of Asynchronous Learning Networks 4 (2000)
7. Moreno, L., Gonzalez, C., Castilla, I., Gonzalez, E., Sigut, J.: Applying a constructivist and collaborative methodological approach in engineering education. Computers & Education 49, 891–915 (2007)
8. Zhang, J., Scardamalia, M., Lamon, M., Messina, R., Reeve, R.: Socio-cognitive dynamics of knowledge building in the work of 9- and 10-years-olds. Educational Technology Research and Development 55, 117–145 (2007)
9. Moller, L.: Designing communities of learners for asynchronous distance education. Educational Technology, Research and Development 46, 115–122 (1998)
10. Thurston, A.: Building online learning communities. Technology, Pedagogy and Education 14, 353–369 (2005)
11. Rovai, A.P., Wighting, M.J.: Feelings of alienation and community among higher education students in a virtual classroom. The Internet and Higher Education 8, 97–110 (2005)
12. Tajfel, H., Billig, M.G., Bundy, R.F., Flament, C.: Social categorization and intergroup behaviour. European Journal of Social Psychology 1, 149–178 (1971)
13. Smith, A., Williams, K.D.: R U there? Ostracism by cell phone text messages. Group Dynamics: Theory, Research, & Practice 8, 291–301 (2004)
14. Williams, K.D., Cheung, C.K.T., Choi, W.: Cyberostracism: Effects of being ignored over the Internet. Journal of Personality & Social Psychology 79, 748–762 (2000)
15. Löfström, E., Nevgi, A.: From strategic planning to meaningful learning: Diverse perspectives on the development of web-based teaching and learning in higher education. British Journal of Educational Technology 38, 312–324 (2007)
16. Levett-Jones, T., Lathlean, J., Higgins, I., McMillan, M.: Staff - student relationships and their impact on nursing students belongingness and learning. Journal of Advanced Nursing 65, 316–324 (2009)
17. Furrer, C., Skinner, E.: Sense of relatedness as a factor in children's academic engagement and performance. Journal of Educational Psychology 95, 148–162 (2003)
18. Rusbult, C.E., Farrell, D.: A longitudinal test of the investment model: The impact on job satisfaction, job commitment, and turnover of variations in rewards, costs, alternatives, and investments. Journal of Applied Psychology 68, 429 (1983)

19. Rusbult, C.E.: Commitment in close relationships: The investment model. In: Peplau, L.A., Sears, D.O., Taylor, S.E., Freedman, J.L. (eds.) Readings in Social Psychology: Classic and Contemporary Contributions, pp. 147–157. Prentice-Hall, Englewood Cliffs (1988)
20. Rusbult, C.E., Martz, J.M., Agnew, C.R.: The investment model scale: Measuring commitment level, satisfaction level, quality of alternatives, and investment size. Personal Relationships 5, 357–391 (1998)
21. Shaver, P., Buhrmester, D.: Loneliness, sex-role orientation, and group life: A social needs perspective. In: Paulus, P. (ed.) Basic Group Processes, pp. 259–288. Springer, New York (1983)
22. Cross, S.E., Madson, L.: Models of the self: Self-construals and gender. Psychological Bulletin 122, 5–37 (1997)
23. Baumeister, R.F., Sommer, K.L.: What do men want? Gender differences and two spheres of belongingness: Comment on Cross and Madson. Psychological Bulletin 122(1997), 38–44 (1997)
24. Anderson, D.M., Haddad, C.J.: Gender, voice and learning in online course environments. Journal of Asynchronous Learning Networks 9 (2005)
25. Caspi, A., Chajut, E., Saporta, K.: Participation in class and in online discussions: Gender differences. Computers & Education 50, 718–724 (2008)
26. Ma, W.W.K., Yuen, A.H.K.: Understanding Online Knowledge Sharing: An Interpersonal Relationship Perspective. Computers & Education 56, 210–219 (2011)
27. Ma, W.W.K., Yuen, A.H.K.: Understanding online knowledge sharing: An exploratory theoretical framework. In: Tsang, P., Cheung, S.K.S., Lee, V.S.K., Huang, R. (eds.) ICHL 2010. LNCS, vol. 6248, pp. 239–248. Springer, Heidelberg (2010)
28. Baumeister, R.F., Leary, M.R.: The need to belong: Desire for interpersonal attachments as a fundamental human motivation. Psychological Bulletin 117, 497–529 (1995)
29. Hair, J.F., Black, B., Babin, B., Anderson, R.E., Tatham, R.L.: Multivariate Data Analysis. Pearson Prentice Hall, Upper Saddle River (2006)
30. McMillan, J.H., Schmacher, S.: Research in education: A conceptual introduction. HarperCollins Publishers, New York (1989)
31. Nunnally, J.C., Bernstein, I.H.: Psychometric theory. McGraw-Hill, New York (1994)
32. Jöreskog, K.G., Sörbom, D.: LISREL 8: Structural equation modeling with the SIMPLIS command language. Lawrence Erlbaum Associates, Hillsdale (1993)
33. Ko, D.-G., Kirsch, L.J., King, W.R.: Antecedents of knowledge transfer from consultants to clients in enterprise system implementations. MIS Quarterly 29, 59 (2005)

Appendix

Instrument Items (Adapted from [26])

Constructs	Items
Perceived Online Attachment Motivation (POAM)	1. If I feel unhappy or depressed in learning news writing, I usually try to be around other members using HKNews to make me feel better. 2. I usually have a great need to have other members using HKNews around me when I feel upset in learning news writing. 3. I often have a strong need to be around other HKNews users who are impressed with what I am like and what I do in news writing. 4. I mainly like to be around other HKNews users who think I am an important, exciting person when learning news writing. 5. I often have a strong desire to get other HKNews users around to notice me and appreciate what I am like when learning news writing.
Perceived Online Relationship Commitment (PORC)	1. I am committed to maintaining my relationships with other members using HKNews. 2. I want my relationships with other members using HKNews to last for a very long time. 3. I feel very strongly linked to my relationships with other members using HKNews. 4. I would feel very upset if my relationships with other members using HKNews were to end. 5. I tend to the long-term future of my relationships with other HKNews members.
Online Knowledge Sharing Behavior (OKSB)	1. The advice that I receive from other HKNews members has increased my understanding of news writing. 2. The advice that I receive from other HKNews members has increased my knowledge of news writing. 3. The advice that I receive from other HKNews members will allow me to complete similar news writing tasks more efficiently in the future. 4. The advice that I receive from other HKNews members will help me to improve the quality of similar news writing work in the future. 5. The advice that I receive from other HKNews members will allow me to conduct similar news writing tasks with greater independence in the future.

Hybrid Learning in Lifelong Learning Implementation

Jianjun Hou and Haidi Lu

School of Distance Learning, Peking University
Beijing 100871, China
houjj@pku.edu.cn, luhaidi@163.com

Abstract. This paper, starting out from the concept and practice of lifelong learning, explores hybrid learning model as an effective and efficient way to meet individual's lifelong learning needs. The study focuses on the concept and framework of lifelong hybrid learning. And practice of lifelong hybrid learning provided by colleges and universities is investigated.

Keywords: lifelong learning, hybrid learning, lifelong hybrid learning, colleges and universities.

1 Lifelong Learning

Lifelong learning has in recent years been an important concept in an individual's life. Lifelong learning occurs throughout life, which is a life-span endeavor by an individual with the aim of improving knowledge, skills and competences.

Lifelong learning is of public value rather than for just the individual good. For it brings about economic progress and development, and seeks to bring about personal development and fulfillment. Lifeling learning has become a fundamental element of many educational policy strategies aimed at achieving the goal of socio-economic development (EC, 2001) in many countries the world over.

Since the beginning of the 1990s China has expressed the concept of lifelong learning and learning society in many policy documents and showed supports for its development. On Sixteenth CPC National Congress which took place in Nov. 2002 and Seventeenth CPC National Congress, which took place in Oct. 2007, China made it clear that distance learning and continuing education will be promoted to make learning society in which every citizen is committed to learning and pursues lifelong learning.

What should be the effective and efficient lifelong learning? This paper explores a hybrid learning model for lifelong learning to gain the aim effectively and efficiently.

2 Lifelong Hybrid Learning

2.1 Lifelong Hybrid Learning Model

Lifelong learning takes place in formal, non-formal and informal learning situations. Individuals take diffident aims at achieving specific goals such as improving

R. Kwan et al. (Eds.): ICHL 2011, LNCS 6837, pp. 129–134, 2011.

knowledge, skills and competences. With the core of aim, the three components of formal, non-formal and informal learning are framed around the purpose of lifelong hybrid learning (Fig 1. Lifelong hybrid learning mode) .

Formal learning is planned learning with the aid of guiding institutions, and informal learning is planned learning by oneself. Informal learning takes unplanned. The lifelong hybrid learning model stresses on the interdependency and complex interconnection between three learning situations. It therefore should be a process of integrated continuous learning that goes throughout life.

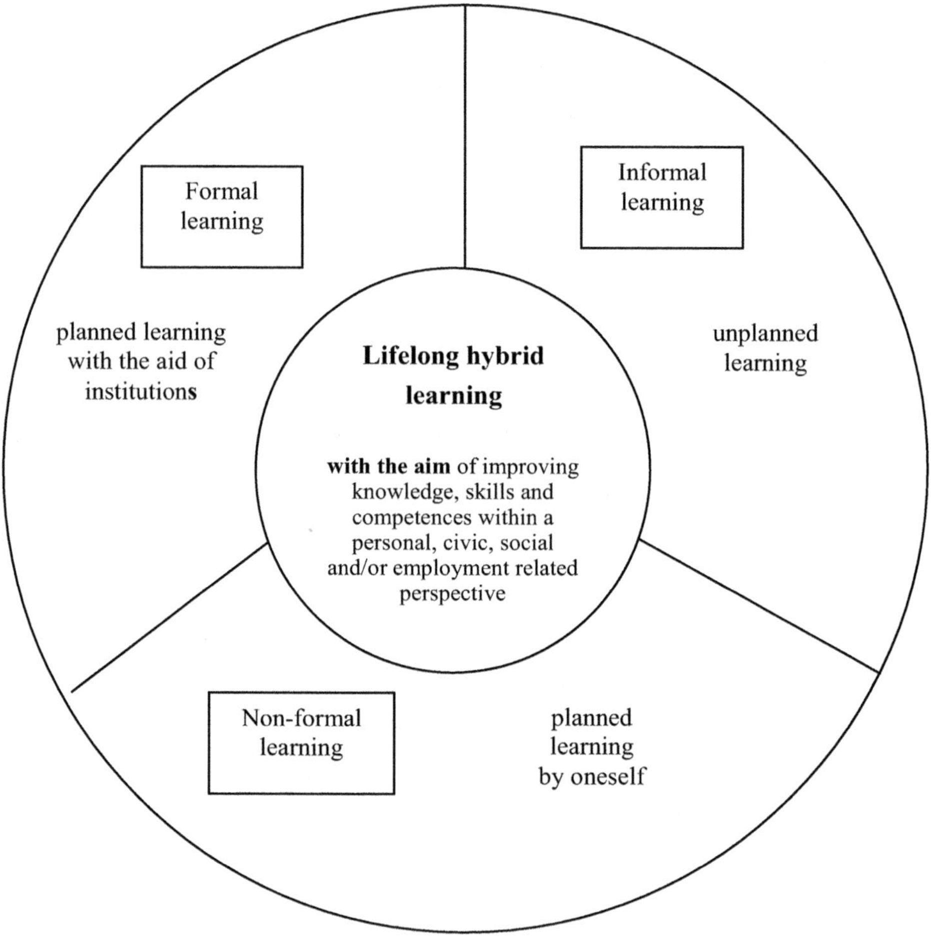

Fig. 1. Lifelong Hybrid Learning Model

2.2 Elements of Lifelong Hybrid Learning

Learners who engage in leaning play core roles of lifelong hybrid learning. Institutions provide educational resources and/or activities to make contribution to leaning models

(Fig 2. Elements of lifelong hybrid learning). Learners choose appropriate opportunities. In formal learning situation, individuals learn by the aid of institutions' educational resources and educational activities. In non-formal learning situation, individuals implement self-directed learning based on instructed materials and no educational activities. Learners perform informal learning by oneself without institutions' instructions of recourse and activities.

		Formal learning	**Non-formal learning**	**Informal learning**
Learners	**Learners' Engagement**	Instructed learning	Self-directed learning based on institutions' instructed materials	Self-directed Learning
Institutions	**Educational Resources**	YES	YES	NO
	Educational Activities	YES	NO	NO

Fig. 2. Elements of lifelong hybrid learning

3 Practice of Hybrid Learning Provided by Colleges and Universities

In the new era, China will build a complete lifelong education system with the focus on making education more equitable and with improving educational quality as the core, so that all the people can enjoy their rights to education, make progress and apply what they have learned to practice.

Putting this in the context of colleges and universities, lifelong learning is pursued to respond to the new realities and forces guiding the evolving information age and of learning society. In this context lifelong learning is viewed as involving all strategies that are put in place to created opportunities for people to learn throughout life. (Abdulai Abukari, 2005)

Colleges and universities serve as the main base of learning providers with advantages of a wide range of disciplines, good teachers, abundant resources and good atmosphere of study. They should play an important role to support the construction of modern national education system and lifelong education system. Services for lifelong learning have become the new mission of continuing higher education. Colleges and universities should take great measures to promote the development of higher education reform.

Lifelong learning makes an important link between teaching, research and society. Colleges and universities make full use of special features and advantages of university's disciplines and specialties; give priority to train talented people through many types of lifelong learning: training classes, special training, professional education, job training certificates, professional qualification training, visiting scholars, research studies and lifelong learning for diploma.

Education is a public good. Colleges and universities should open resources to the society and actively promote the sharing and services of lifelong learning (Fig.3 Roles of colleges and universities in lifelong leaning provision).

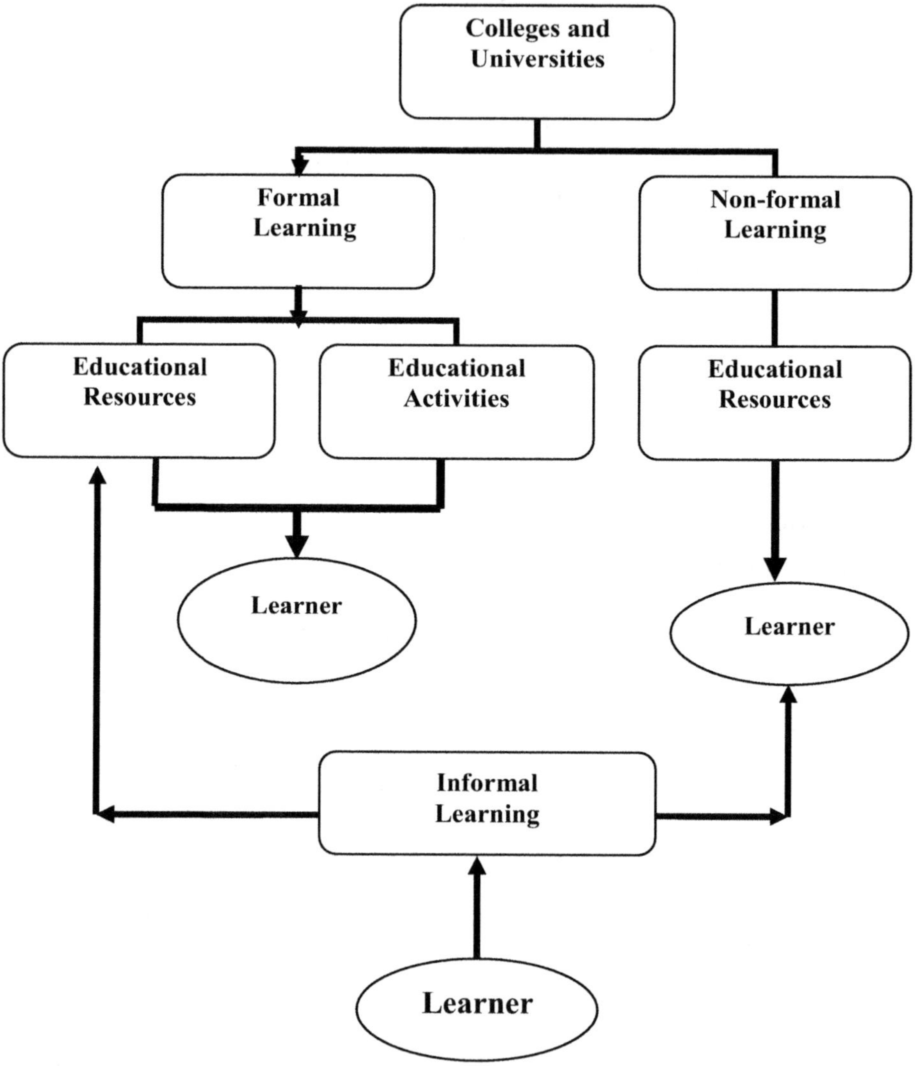

Fig. 3. Roles of colleges and universities in lifelong leaning provision

Colleges and universities should take measures to make lifelong learning effective and efficient:

- concentrate on educational resources and educational activity

- provide many types of learning routines: training classes, special training, professional education, job training certificates, professional qualification training, visiting scholars, research studies and continuing education for diploma
- coordinate the development of scale, structure, quality and efficiency
- follow the guidelines of active development, standardize management, deepen the content, quality improvement
- make positive, steady, healthy, high-quality development
- innovate lifelong learning and training content and methods
- establish lifelong learning quality management system and implement it
- manage and supervise quality standards for teacher appointment, courses development, teaching process,learning support services, faculty management, resources provision, technology support and management.
- put forward a system of learning and its supportive service, which facilitates the working people to enjoy the distance self-study and a life-long learning anytime and anywhere.
- improve quality and establish higher lifelong learning quality assurance system. Lifelong learning should meet the standards for personnel training improve the quality. Institutions study literacy competency standards for all kinds of talents and build personnel training objectives cored with quality, knowledge and ability.
- establish internal quality control mechanisms, implement quality audit and assessment, make continuous quality improvement
- establish quality assessment and monitoring mechanisms by school, students, teachers, businesses and the community together

4 Conclusions

Lifelong learning is also the cause of the whole society. Colleges and universities would further strengthen the cooperation with the community. Government departments, universities, research institutes, enterprises and social groups would cooperate with each other, participate in and coordinate the work under environment for healthy development of lifelong learning.

Acknowledgement. This paper is funded by Beijing Science of Education Eleventh Five-Year Planed Project (No. AJA09134), Year 2009.6 – 2011.6, titled by Study on Construction and Application of Network Education Resources for Beijing Learning City Construction.

References

1. China's Human Resources, Information Office of the State Council. The People's Republic of China, Beijing (September 2010)
2. Conceptualizing Lifelong Learning: a reflection on lifelong learning at Lund University (Sweden) and Middlesex University (UK) Abdulai Abukari. European Journal of Education. Dorchester-on-Thames vol. 40(2), p. 143, 13 pgs (June 2005)

3. Hunt, M.: The worldwide learning explosion at the local level: On structuring a broadened reality of lifelong learning from twelve learners perspectives. Journal of Continuing Higher Education 56, 38–48 (2008)
4. Congress. Lifelong Learning Accounts Act of 2007. U.S. Government Printing Office, Washington (2007), http://www.govtrack.us/congress/bill.xpd?bill=s110-26 (retrieved May 16, 2008)
5. European Commission. Lifelong Learning: the implications for the universities in the EU (2001)
6. Learning Outcomes Studies, http://depts.alverno.edu/ere/
7. No Longer Optional: Educating for Personal and Social Responsibility. In: AAC&U pre-meeting symposium, Assessing Ineffable Outcomes, Marcia Mentkowski, Alverno College (January 23, 2008), http://depts.alverno.edu/ere/
8. Tuijman, A., Bostrom, A.: Changing Notions of Lifelong Education and Lifelong Learning. International Review of Education 48(1/2), 93–110 (2002)
9. Green, A.: Lifelong Learning and the Learning Society: Different European Models and Organisation. In: Hodgson, A. (ed.) Policies, Politics and the Future of Lifelong Learning. Kogan Page, London (2000)
10. European Commission. Lifelong Learning: the implications for the universities in the EU (2001)
11. Costly, C.: The Boundaries and Frontiers of Work Based Knowledge. In: Portwood, D., Costly, C. (eds.) Work Based Learning and the University: New Perspectives and Practices, SEDA Paper (2000)

Applying Higher-Order Thinking in E-learning Design

Judy Huang

Associate Researcher, Director, Department of Research & Development
National Open University
172 Chung-Cheng Road, Lu Chow
24702 New Taipei City, Taiwan, R.O.C.
ht@mail.nou.edu.tw

Abstract. Learning is not only about knowledge acquiring but also about thinking skill gaining and polishing. Computer related learning was somehow limited to the capacity of technology for a long while and was often imputed by educators for its lower end learning such as information conveying or simply drill & practice. As the maturing of communication technology supporting hybrid learning which makes a good teaching-learning integration possible and anticipated, a better practice of teaching is expected without too much limitation from the technological tool itself. Higher-order thinking and learning is one of the main concerns about hybrid learning when coming into the instructional design and teaching strategy. This paper is a review on applying higher-order thinking skill into e-learning course for teachers of higher and adult learning institution.

Keywords: higher-order thinking, e-activities, blended e-learning design.

1 Introduction

Higher-order thinking is one of the leading competencies required in the 21st century which is known as an accelerative changing era than ever. To live better or even merely exist in this highly competitive world, individual needs to be not only knowledgeable but also possess the crucial ability; being able to think effectively and to make proper decision as well as creative in many way.

The most important mission of nowadays higher education institution is to nurture its students to be competitive. To teach processes of thinking skill that can be applied from a classroom situation to a wider range of real-life context is emphasized. As e-learning becoming an important way of teaching and learning, the effectiveness of technology on teaching higher-order thinking skill is widely discussed during the past decade. Along with the positive development of communication technology used in educational setting, a proper use of e-learning to foster higher-order thinking and learning is much more important issue in e-learning academic arena.

2 Higher Order Thinking and Learning in E-learning Context

As information scientist built the first platform for information exchange, practitioners have been making a great use of this creation to educational settings.

R. Kwan et al. (Eds.): ICHL 2011, LNCS 6837, pp. 135–145, 2011.

Information technology has been helping learning out toward a much more interactive environment than its old time. Somehow, e-learning became a necessary part in higher education institution without questions. Along the development of e-learning, researchers and practitioners in education area have been taking closer look at the educational application of information technology wondering if learning really happens within e-learning context. Questions are answered from different angles in many ways.

2.1 Could Higher-Order Thinking be Taught by Computer?

Technology in education setting is often questioned about its effectiveness of teaching and learning. Much of the argument was that teaching through technology does not guarantee learning. Unfortunately this argument is also sustained in classroom situation. Improper use of teaching strategy or assessment would timid away real learning. Wegerif conducted a quite thorough literature review in thinking skills, technology, and learning, He asked important question on is higher-order thinking teachable with technology. Wegerif's solid review led to a crucial conclusion that it is the moderators (instructors) who exercise properly make higher-order thinking and learning happens[4].

Yah (2011) conducted a research on the effectiveness of blended learning on a teacher training program during their professional development in creativity instruction; After a 17-week experimental instructional program on 44 pre-service teachers, significant result was found that training program designed in this study effectively improved pre-service teachers' professional knowledge and personal teaching efficacy in their teaching of creativity[8] Yah's study has shown that higher-order thinking and learning could be taught through a well arranged and guided blended learning,

2.2 The Spirit That Makes Higher-Order Thinking Happen in Blended E-learning

Is e-learning an effective way to foster higher-order learning? That is a questions often asked and answered by a variety of research. Wegerif's review of literature on the effectiveness of educational technology has somehow answered the question. According to Wegerif 's observation, computer as a tutor, computer as a mind-tool, computer as a support for learning conversations would lead to different level of effectiveness. Wegerif 's report reminds us that perhaps it is a wrong question to ask at all! The question should probably be: What is the proper way of using computer to assist learning?

Hybrid learning is one of the best paradigms of human education history. Hybrid learning integrates classroom and on-line learning and should be celebrated for its clever mixture of cocktail-like treatment Interaction on-&-off line is the spirit that makes learning effective.

3 Fostering Higher Order Thinking and Learning in Blended E-learning Context

3.1 The Design for Effective Higher-Order Thinking and Learning in Blended Learning Environment

According to Yah(2010), while learning in a blended learning environment, a proper mix use of learning mode and strategies contribute significantly to positive learning results. And guided practice, observational learning, group discussion, peer evaluation, and feedback by and through supportive learning platform are important mechanisms for higher-order thinking and learning [7]. These practical strategies have been widely implemented by on-line instructors and tutors in both synchronous and asynchronous interactive settings and have been proven to be effective. In another words, a proper design that blends face to face classroom and on-line activities well enough could enhance learning result, but core that makes these blended learning activities effective should lie the underlying substance of teaching itself.

3.2 Framework for Teaching Higher-Order Thinking

Wegerif summerized a common but essential element for teaching higher-order thinking through information and communication technology as follow[4]:

- Teaching a thinking vocabulary and giving learners an explicit explanation of the thinking skills that are to be learnt.
- Observing an expert performing the task
- Giving timely feedback on performance
- Direct support in the early stages of learning a task and then a gradual move towards self-regulation and autonomy
- The opportunity to articulate thinking strategies and discuss these with other learners
- The explicit demonstration of how thinking strategies acquired in one subject area can be used to solve problems of another area

Accordingly, the elements for teaching higher-order thinking could be abbreviated into six stages: thinking vocabulary, modeling, coaching, scaffolding & teacher-fading, reflection and transfer.

3.3 Stages for E-moderating and Higher-Order Thinking and Learning

The well-known e-moderating 5 stages model [2] by Gilly Salmon is widely apply to blended learning for years. Compared and combined with the Salmon's 5 stages e-Moderating, Practice could be clearly and easily conducted to enhance higher-order thinking and learning in e-learning settings as shown in figure 1.

According to Fig. 1, higher-order thinking and learning activities take place at stage 3 and above after learning group is ready for formal learning process. We could easily perceive from Figure 1 that the higher-order thinking and learning activities play an importance role in supporting the stage 3-5 e-moderating with intense and meaningful instructor-learner & learner-learner interactions.

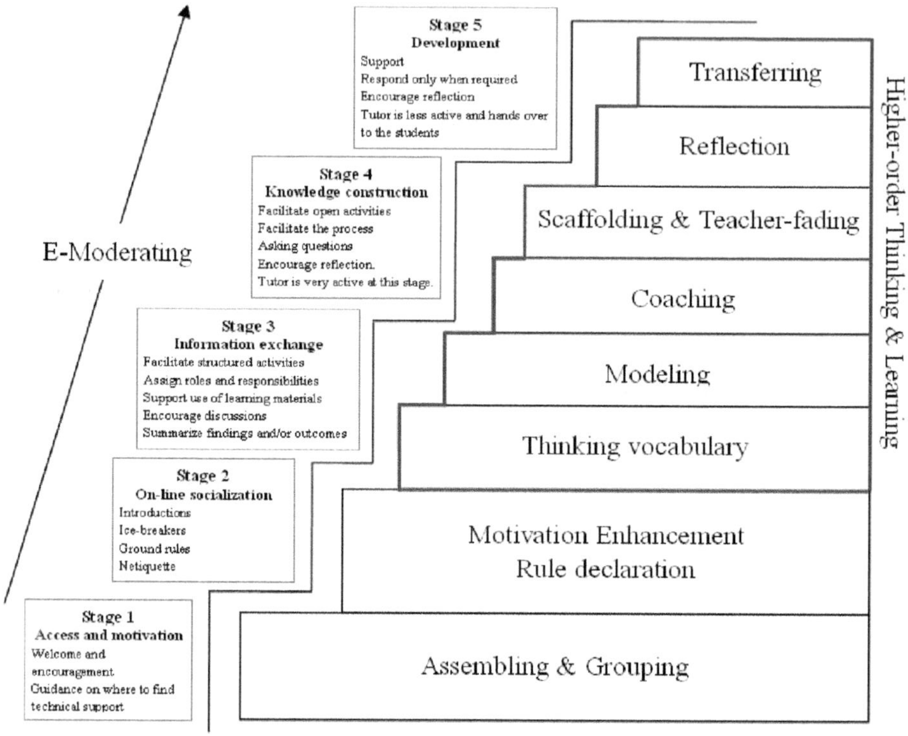

Fig. 1. Gilly Salmon's 5 stages e-Moderating and 6 stages of higher order thinking and learning activities

3.4 The Blended Design to Enhance Higher-Order Thinking and Learning

As stated above, the core for teaching higher-order thinking lies in the teaching strategies rather than the form of it. Yah(2002) coordinated from O'Tuel & Bullard of demonstrated three teaching approaches that are usually employed in teaching higher-order thinking skill, They are deductive approach, deductive approach and holistic approach [6]. Instructional design for blended learning is suggested with the three approach is shown table 1.

Table 1. Teaching strategies to implement higher-order thinking and learning.activities

6 stages for effective higher-order thinking	Deductive models (Direct instruction)	Inductive models (Inquiry approach)	Holistic Approach
Thinking vocabulary	◆Introducing the subject to be learnt ▲ digital content	◆Define the question to be answered ▲classroom teaching and discussion	◆Exploring disagreement and difference ▲classroom teaching and discussion

Table 1. (*continued*)

Modeling	◆Providing variety of examples ▲digital content	◆Providing example of a research project ▲digital content	◆Providing framework for discussion ▲classroom teaching and discussion
Coaching	◆Monitoring learning activity and providing feedback ▲ synchronous and asynchronous on-line forum ▲ individual guidance through e-mail or other digital form of communications	◆Set up hypothesis and goal ▲ synchronous and asynchronous on-line forum ▲ classroom discussion	◆expressing individual opinions ▲ synchronous and asynchronous on-line forum ▲ classroom discussion
Scaffolding & teacher-fading .	◆Apply thinking skill in other context ▲ individual or group face to face or on-line presentation	◆Collecting data ◆Discussion for a conclusion ▲ individual or group face to face or on-line presentation	◆Moderating investigate into information ◆Idea collection and finding Solutions ▲ synchronous and asynchronous on-line forum ▲ classroom discussion
Reflection	◆Providing opportunity for individual exercise ▲ individual project on-line sharing	◆ Review and retest ▲ individual project on-line sharing	◆Evaluating tentative conclusion ◆Refinement ▲ synchronous and asynchronous on-line forum ▲ classroom discussion
Transfer	◆Independent project ▲project & assessment	◆Generalization to new topics ▲project & assessment	◆Cooperative learning project ◆Group exercise

◆ Strategies used

▲ Blended e-learning format

4 Applying Higher Order Thinking and Learning Activity Design in Blended E-learning Context

Basically speaking, blended E-learning design could break into four major parts: digital content, on-line teaching and support, face to face instruction, and learning assessment. (see fig.2) These components is usually blended in every e-learning situation without questions. But the real concern is not about "what" but "how", especially when the learning goal is set upon higher order thinking and learning.

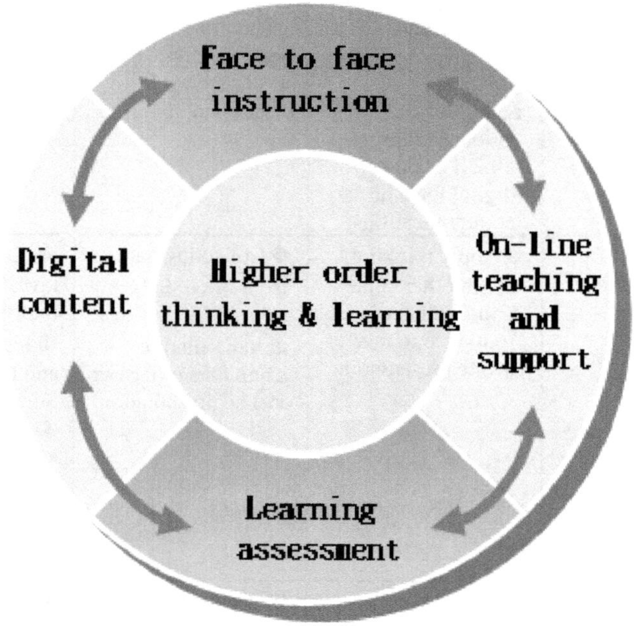

Fig. 2. Components of blended e-learning activities

4.1 A Shift from Classroom Teaching to Blended E-learning

It is indeed an uneasy task for a classroom teacher to dive into e-learning. Not only a certain number of e-technologies need to be conquered but also a smooth shift from classroom teaching to e-activities are needed which includes the preparation of e-content, e-teaching & learning activity design and implement, and a proper use of assessment & evaluation. Most beginner e-instructors is occupied with the format of e-learning rather than the effectiveness of teaching and learning, It is important to pay equal attention to what is learnt and how it is learnt, e-instructors need to step beyond the tool of teaching and learning.

According to Wegerif [4], the spirit of e-learning is not about technologies, but about teaching and learning. The what and how to teach higher order thinking is a challenge to both classroom instructor as well as e-learning instructor. Still more, the proper e-learning design is further challenge for e-learning instructor. We need to assist beginner instructor to make use of an array of teaching strategies for higher-order thinking in e-learning environment. An example of paradigm shift from classroom to e-learning is provided as the following;

When holistic approach (see table 1) is decided, instructor might want to use discussion method in classroom to guide learners to explore a topic. Basically, teaching tasks shall include [9],:

1. Motivating: to initiate a small opinion exchange among learners on the topic
2. Formal start: to disclose the topic and the research method to be used in the session.
3. Exploration: to support clarification through reading, field trip, film and other activities
4. Discussion: to discussion in large or small groups and temporary conclusion
5. Conclusion: Making final conclusion and review

Shifting to blended e-learning context, instructor needs to pay attention to proper design according both teaching method as well as technology used.

Table 2. A design example of higher-order thinking and learning in blended situation

Teaching Tasks	E-learning activity design	Activities
Motivating	▼ Starting a dialogue ▼ Encourage opinion expression or experience sharing	✓ A short essay or news could be posted online as a start of warm-up interactions.
Formal start	▼ Coordinate and close discussion ▼ Introducing class subject matter ▼ Assigning reading	✓ Instructor or on-line tutor assist class members to close-up the warm-up interaction. ✓ Give a short session on this-week-topic ✓ Remind weekly reading or homework ✓ Announce learning task for the following week
Exploration	▼ Field trip or film ▼ Reviewing reading assignment ▼ Panel discussion	✓ An actual trip to places or watch video that help subject matter learning ✓ Face to face or on-line discussion based on trip or film. ✓ Sharing thoughts and ideas among class member by either on-line forum or discussion room.
Discussion	▼ Collaborative learning	✓ Class member divided into group for discussion or project. Discussion could be on-line or face to face
Conclusion	▼ Class discussion and conclusion ▼ Final review	✓ Synchronous or face-to-face group report ✓ Comment from instructor ✓ Group report is asked to share on-line for other class members to review

4.2 Activities to Use for Higher-Order Thinking E-learning Design

Yang[1] listed an array of Synchronous and Asynchronous E-learning that could be adopted in blended e-learning situations. They are integrated in table 3.

Table 3. Activities for e-learning design

E-activity	Activity description
Lecture or E-lecture	A direct transfer from classroom instruction which could be used both in synchronous and asynchronous on-line teaching with subsidiary text & graphics. Lecture could be real-time or video taped. Discussion is be used following e-lecturing.
Public Teaching	To publicly answer or discuss questions raised by class members in on-line classroom. Questions are sent to instructors before class by e-mail or other electronic ways.
Structured Seminar	Assign topics in accordance with weekly learning-content. Class members share opinions under the guidance of instructor in on-line class. It is important that discussion topics must support the learning of weekly e-content.
Situated teaching	Description of a situation followed by an array of questions to class members. Individual is asked to provide opinions in group interaction.
Wheel Discussion	Class member who receive a "talking stick" has the right to express opinion on the class topic. Instructor would ask each one of the learners to speak just like taking turns upon a wheel. The spirit of wheel discussion is about each one of the learners should have a chance to speak in class.
Disclosure	Instructor collects ideas and thoughts upon certain topic individually through e-mails to avoid cross influence among class members. After a certain amount of time, instructor discloses thoughts from class members publicly (on-line or another way) for further discussion.
Bombard	Assign one of the class members to chair discussion and is responsible to answer all the questions raised by other class members. It is important that the activity is carried out at an asynchronous environment so that class members would have enough time to think and response.
Symposium	On-line symposium conducted by class instructor and invited content experts. Class members raise questions after a speech for further discussion.
Tutored Discussion	An instructor modeled an on-line class discussion on certain topic. Enough think-and-response time and proper guidance are important to quality of learning.
Q & A	Questions are answered by instructor on certain topics related to learning content either in synchronous or asynchronous setting. Questions and answers are edited into a FAQ for class members to review or trigger further interactions.

Table 3. (*continued*)

Cross Query	Each assigned member take the responsibility to answer questions from other members to clarify thoughts on certain topic. Members take turns to be the target person to answer questions raised by the next person.
Case Study Report	Case study is assigned to one of the class members who is responsible for a complete research project including data collection, analysis and class report (either on-line or face to face). Questions and queries are accept after report. Instructor takes the chair position to lead to a satisfying conclusion.
Subject topic review	Class members (in group or individually) assigned with specific topic in accordance with the different theme within the course content. The assigned member reports to the whole class and chair discussion.
Group Panel	Class members are divided into several groups, each group member carries out discussion through e-mails, on-line discussion room as well as face to face class interaction. Each group is responsible for a plenary discussion on which group members are to take questions from the whole class.
Debate	Class members are divided into two groups for formal on-line debates based on topics assigned which supports learning of the course theme. At the end of the debate, instructor takes chair for a final discussion
Role-playing	Different roles are taken by class members who are responsible for script on the assigned topic. After the role playing activity, class gets together for further discussion.
Community decision making	Discussion initiated by instructor or class member. After class discussion, final decision is made based on the result of votes. Community decision making is basically used in situations such as when a test is to be taken or whom to invite for a speech
Brainstorming	Members are free to express their thoughts and ideas under a certain topic. After a certain amount of time when ideas are collected, instructor starts a class discussion based on the collections of brainstorming. It is important that thoughts and ideas are to be given by keywords and short terms when post it on.
Answer or pass	Certain amount of questions are open to class member. Each member is to answer question raised by the instructor. Question unanswered is open again to others. Correct answers adds up credits accumulatively for final grades.
Collaborative Writing	Each member is responsible to respond upon other members writing of certain class topic. Individual member would be able to receive others opinions and reflect upon ones own point of view.
Meta analysis project	Individual is assigned a final report on what has been discussed through weeks of classes based on data and record collected from synchronous and asynchronous forum on LMS. The purpose of record analysis is to provide a chance for a final review and personal conclusion upon the class.

Table 4. A cross table for e-activities design for 6 stages of effective higher-order thinking and learning

6 stages for effective higher-order thinking	Deductive models (direct instruction)	Inductive models (Inquiry approach)	Holistic Approach
Thinking vocabulary	Lecture or E-lecture C, SE, AE	Situated teaching C, SE	Situated teaching C, SE
Modeling	Symposium C, SE	Disclosure AE	Structured Seminar C, SE
Coaching	Public Teaching C, SE Q & A C, SE Subject topic review C, SE Brainstorming C, SE, AE Answer or pass C, SE	Brainstorming C, SE, AE Answer or pass C, SE, AE	Subject topic review C, SE Disclosure C, SE Brainstorming C, SE, AE Role-playing C, SE Answer or pass C, SE
Scaffolding & teacher-fading	Debate C, SE Group Panel C, SE Tutored Discussion C, SE	Debate C, SE Cross Query C, SE Wheel Discussion C, SE Bombard C, SE Group Panel C, SE Tutored Discussion C, SE	Debate C, SE Cross Query C, SE Wheel Discussion C, SE Bombard C, SE Group Panel C, SE Tutored Discussion C, SE
Reflection	Wheel Discussion C, SE Cross Query C, SE	Wheel Discussion C, SE Cross Query C, SE	Wheel Discussion C, SE Cross Query C, SE
Transfer	Collaborative Writing AE Case Study Report C, SE Meta analysis project SE, AE	Collaborative Writing AE Case Study Report C, SE Meta analysis project SE, AE	Collaborative Writing AE Case Study Report C, SE Meta analysis project SE, AE

note: C: classroom activity
SE: Synchronous E-learning activity
AE: Asynchronous E-learning activity

4.3 Applications of E-activities into 6 Stages for Effective Higher-Order Thinking and Learning Design

It is important that the above e-activities are properly used to adopt higher order thinking and learning. E-activities arrangement into the 6 stages for effective higher-order thinking and learning is listed in table 4 for beginner instructor to consider:

5 Conclusion

As the Web 2.0 idea provided a good direction for learning, the concept of e-learning 2.0 helpfully provokes a new developmental goal for e-learning platform. A new generation of e-learning platform adopting collaborative note tool allowed learners to think together on-line which provides a sense of collaboration that brings more satisfactions.

As we know for a long while that learning within a distance mode with little interactions usually frustrate learners who would drop-out easily. When sense of progress from either positive interactions or knowledge and skill learnt would bring to the learner sense of satisfaction and enhance retention [3]. Thus, employing and designing higher-order thinking and learning activities properly means as much for the learner and institutions.

References

1. Yang, C.-S.: Theories and Activity Designs of the On-Line Instruction. Journal of Management and Information 11, 271–308 (2006)
2. Salmon, G.: E-moderating: The key to teaching and learning online. Kogan Page, London (2000)
3. Huang, T.J.: A research on Learner Retention and Learning Support. US-China Education Review, Inc. (January 2005)
4. Wegerif, R.W.: Literature review in thinking skills, technology, and learning. NESTA Futurelab, Bristol (2002)
5. Willis, D.: Critical thinking and the Internet. Wilfrid Laurier University, Ontario (2005)
6. Yeh, Y.C.: An analysis on the instructional design for higher-order thinking. Sun Yat-sen Journal of General Education 1, 75–101 (2002)
7. Yeh, Y.: Integrating collaborative PBL with blended learning to explore preservice teachers development of online learning communities. Teaching and Teacher Education 26, 1630–1640 (2010)
8. Yeh, Y., Huang, L., Yeh, Y.: Knowledge management in blended learning: Effects on professional development in creativity instruction. Computers & Education 56, 146–156 (2011)
9. 黃政傑主編 (民85)，多元化教學方法，台北：師大書苑

Trends of Open Educational Resources in Higher Education

Yueqing Yin and Lei Fan

Department of Educational Technology, Capital Normal University,
100048 Beijing, China
iamyyq0307@163.com, fanlei.cnu@gmail.com

Abstract. The purpose of Open Educational Resources movement is to provide open access to high quality digital learning materials, there is broad participation by universities, organizations and volunteers, and has gained a far-reaching influence on higher education. Meanwhile, the growth of Web2.0 has diversified forms as well as channels of learning content and accelerated the openness of this movement, so it is necessary to harness the reusability and quality of open resources. However, current applications and quality improvements are often separated from specific educational contexts. Therefore, it is a pressing task to carry practices around open educational resources, especially pay more attention to the sharing and collaboration in related learning environments, and the opening of pedagogical knowledge and teaching process, as well as learners' feedbacks and assessments, thus promoting the open educational resources to the open educational practices.

Keywords: open educational resources, higher education, Web2.0, open educational practices, pedagogical, learning environments.

1 Introduction

Since the beginning of 21st century, two big waves, informatization and globalization, have changed the way of people's living, working and studying with amazing pace, and led the education systems to a visualization, internationalization and personalization environment. Universities and colleges are facing more and more rigorous challenges, as well as opportunities to innovate. Open Educational Resources (OER) movement is one of the key strength to promote this transformation, which will have a profound and lasting influence on higher education's instructional resources, teaching and learning patterns and educational ideologies.

In this paper, we give a brief introduction of OER movement and its impact on teaching and learning, as well as opportunities brought by Web2.0 technologies and services. Then we focus on the reusability and quality of open learning resources, thus leading to the reality that the applications and quality assessments often separate from the educational contexts, therefore, it is urgent to strengthen the practice of open

R. Kwan et al. (Eds.): ICHL 2011, LNCS 6837, pp. 146–156, 2011.

educational resources. Following this, we discuss the raise of open educational practices (OEP), compared with OER, OEP will pay more attention to the sharing and collaboration in related learning environments, and the opening of pedagogical knowledge and teaching process, as well as learners' feedbacks and assessments. Finally, the paper is concluded, we then illustrate the increasing web applications may enrich OER.

2 Open Educational Resources Movement

Back to 1994, Wayne Hodgins raised the term "learning objects" which emphasis the reusage of learning content. In 1998, David Wiley coined the concept "open content", advocated that people should apply the philosophy of Free Software movement to content, especially to education, in order to create free and simple access to knowledge and information through collaboration and innovation. This idea became popular quickly. Following this, Stallman announced the GNU Free Documentation License (GNU FDL) in 2000. Creative Commons released its first set of copyright licenses free to the public in 2002. Meanwhile, Massachusetts Institute of Technology (MIT) announced plan of OpenCourseWare (OCW) and put all of its core curricula on the Internet for educators, students, and individual learners who can access freely. MIT's action inspired other universities around the world to launch similar projects, since then, the prelude to the Open Educational Resources movement was opened.

The term "Open Educational Resources" was first coined in July 2002 at the forum of the Impact of Open Courseware for Higher Education in Developing Countries which hosted by United Nations Educational, Scientific and Cultural Organization (UNESCO). Participants in the forum defined Open Educational Resources as: "technology-enabled, open provision of educational resources for consultation, use and adaptation by a community of users for non-commercial purposes". They are typically made freely available over the Web or the Internet. Their principal use is by teachers and educational institutions support course development, but they can also be used directly by students [1].

There are also many other successful projects in the movement, such as Open Courseware Consortium (http://www.ocwconsortium.org/), OpenContent (http://opencontent.org/), Internet Archive (http://www.archive.org/), MERLOT (http://www.merlot.org/), Connexions (http://cnx.org/) , OpenLearn (http://openlearn.open.ac.uk/), etc. These projects among others have been engaged with major libraries, including university libraries, made worthy efforts to digital learning materials and made them globally accessible.

The term OER covers a wide range of learning materials and free applications, from whole course materials to modules and segments, from open access journals to reference works, from textbooks, images to games, audios and videos available online. OER can also include course and learning management software, tools that enable users to create and design materials, and licenses for publishing digital resources. These tools allow users to adapt resources in accordance with their cultural, linguistic, curricular and pedagogical requirements [2]. Extensive collaboration and circulation is the kernel of the OER movement.

3 Impact of OER in Teaching and Learning

OER are raising the possibility of substantially changing the materials used in teaching and learning and the ways that they are created and organized. In the recent years, educational institutions have rushed to the wave of OER movement. Learning resources are no longer rare and scarce, but widely available and retrievable, which allow teachers and students to actively use, build upon, and share. Some advantages toward open educational resources include the following:

Cut Down the Cost of Subscription and Publication. Most universities and colleges annually pay large sums to subscribe scholarly journals, however, with the prices of scholarly articles have risen sharply over the past two decades, often forcing libraries to cancel subscriptions [3]. But open license like Creative Commons (CC) are free. In addition, open licenses can also help authors reserve their intellectual property, and enormously simplify the procedure of publication compared with traditional model.

Flexibility, Cost-effectiveness, Customizability. Most of open educational resources are customizable. Users can have free access to these materials, and can also modify, innovate, reuse them in specific contexts for any purpose, which will effectively cut down the preparing time. In the open context, learners are given greater control and are also asked to take more responsibility.

Promote the Changes and Shares. It is possible to freely search the full text of published articles to locate specific ideas, experimental results, and observations. It enables scientists, instructors, librarians and students to develop innovative ways to explore and use the world's treasury of scientific ideas and discoveries.

Continuous Improvement. Extensive collaboration ensures that educational materials keep improving. Supports from different institutions and organizations, along with volunteers, contribute freely to ensure the sustainable development of open educational resources. The huge collaborative network of the open educational community lowers the risk of discontinued service.

The main potential drawback of open educational resources is license issues. Increased awareness of copyright issues needs to be raised and discussed in higher education. Copyright issues are taken extraordinary seriously in higher education scenarios. Institutions should pay close heed and inform their faculty of the copyright policies. The development of Open educational resources has other potential disadvantages. In order to complete teaching plan, faculty members may lack dedication time to contribute the releasing of learning materials, this is a social barrier. Trust in OER available from others is another barrier for most learners. Insufficient pedagogical knowledge and guides may also make teachers depressed. All in all, to gain broader widespread acceptance, OER movement will still need to experience more tests.

4 New Face of Open Educational Resources: Web2.0

The term Web2.0 encompasses a set of technologies and practices that have redefined the Internet's user interface and radically changed the way people use the Internet [4]. We have seen a tremendous increase in the use of Web2.0 tools and services such as social networking sites, Weblogs, Wikis, video-and-audio sites, bookmarks sharing, discussion forums, etc. These new generations of web-based technologies empower learners to create and share content easily, as well as assist students in developing team working skills and online cooperation and communication skills, which will help them to easily fit into the work settings. Teachers all over the world encourage their students to get more involved in interactive web applications, to enhance social learning and communication in and outside the classroom.

Blogs are the most widely used Web2.0 tools. Many institutions have carried out blog teaching, through blogs publish course materials and organize discusses around certain topics. Using blogs can invite people to collaborate and bridge formal and informal studies.

Videocasting and podcasting have been adopted by many institutions to make content available to students. For example, some of the top flight universities, Stanford, Yale, Harvard, Oxford, and Princeton, already participated in Apple's iTunes University (iTunes U) program [5]. Students are able to download audio and video content directly from iTunes U to their iPad, iPhone or computer. Podcasting technologies have encouraged an increase in learner-generated content, enhancing learners' participation in digital education.

Meanwhile, iTunes has set the standard for mobile, free and online learning because of its user-friendliness of programs and reliable resources. Recently, LectureHall in MIT also joined in the mobile market, which provide to access to OpenCourseWare videos and related documents in a mobile-friendly form [6]. Mobility can allow learners to access to free learning resources in a pocket and enable learners post discussions and leave ratings and reviews of videos, audios and texts.

Media Sharing sites have emerged as another powerful vehicle for the learning community. We can put lab demonstrations on YouTube, reference images on Flickr, presentations on SlideShare. As social commentary usually accompany with Media Sharing sites, so we can share with peers and teachers to receive critical feedbacks. Through Media Sharing sites we can also find channels of Open University, Yale University and University of California etc., these institutions can help learners to acquire superior materials.

In addition, content can be integrated into services which deliver some type of information, that is so called mashups. A mashup is generally characteristic by presenting information without forcing the user to click through various screens and URLs [7]. Mashups is important to make existing data more useful. One of the important fashionable services is the Really Simple Syndication (RSS) feed mechanism which is a standard for content distribution and syndication. It can be used by learners or content providers to bring fresh, continuously updated information to their portals. RSS allow individual learners and study groups to select feeds on certain subjects, in order to provide them with relevant topics. The updated works may include blog entries, news headlines, podcasts and videocasts. Most of the open content repositories and Media Sharing sites support RSS feeds.

5 Enhance the Reusablity of OER

Since the raise of learning objects, the importance of reusing has been put on the agenda. In a broader sense, the term "reuse" refers to the adoption of the thing itself to better suit our situation. Many new technologies, instructional designers, learners want to absorb learning objects into their works, reasons may range from durability, flexibility, cost-effectiveness to customizability. Among them, cost-effectiveness may be the apt choice, especially for teachers, so that they can spend more time on preparing their class, and make more effort to see the issues students encounter with the materials and individual performance matters, however reusability is the driving force behind cost-effectiveness. In 2007, Wiley [8] broadened the meaning of reuse and described four methods to reuse the open content freely without restrictions:

1. Reuse – Use the work verbatim, just exactly as you found it
2. Revise – Alter or transform the work so that it better meets your needs
3. Remix – Combine the (verbatim or altered) work with other works to better meet your needs
4. Redistribute – Share the verbatim work, the reworked work, or the remixed work with others

This is known as "4Rs" model. For better put the four factors into effect, we may take the following considerations.

5.1 Modules and Collections

Learning resources should be able to breakdown and reassembled, that is instructional designers should be able to build small (relative to the size of an entire course) instructional components that can be reused a number of times in different learning contexts [9], thus promoting learning objects' reusing, revising, remixing and redistribution. Take Rice University's Connexions for example, in Connexions, all the learning resources are organized in small modules that are easily jointed into larger collections or courses. From an instructional standpoint each module is designed to be a relatively short, standalone learning resource - a chapter, a section within a chapter, a journal article, or a single lab experiment, to name a few examples [10]. Learners then can assemble and reassemble these modules to create a variety of customized web courses, textbooks, study guides and curricular. In Connexions, there are already 1044 collections which are composed of 17413 open reusable learning objects.

5.2 Technology and Metadata Standard

To improve information's compatibility and interoperability, facilitate the widespread adoption of learning materials, many content repositories follow the instructional technology standards, such as the Sharable Content Object Reference Model (SCORM), the Instructional Management Systems (IMS) etc. For example, MIT's metadata standard is compatible with SCORM, OpenLearn's moodle platform can support both SCORM and IMS. In order to achieve sharing and reusing among various audio and video resources, lots of Media Sharing sites are also favor of IMS. In addition, some systems, such as Connexions and OpenLearn, adopt light-weighted

XML, support developing and sharing XML authoring tools to facilitate the production of compatibility materials. XML is a metalanguage that allows users to define markup for their documents using tags, it is one of the standard for the representation of structured information on the web and supports machine processing of information, it can separate content and structure from formatting [11]. As one of the metadata standard, XML has been widely used on the Web.

5.3 Open License

In the process of reusing, we should also pay close attention to the legal issues of educational resources themselves. Every time the content is created and must be licensed under an open license. As the legal framework for OER movement, open license can provide material with potential to be reused in an educational setting.

Commonly used open licenses include the GNU Free Documentation License, the Open Publication License and the Creative Commons Licenses. Among these licenses, Creative Commons (CC) licenses are the most frequently employed. CC aims to build a distributed information commons by encouraging copyright owners to license of their material through open content licensing protocols and thereby promote better identification, negotiation and reutilization of content for the purposes of creativity and innovation [12]. Most of open content repositories are licensed under CC. In addition, properly licensed open educational resources can help users find content that they know they can use, customize, and reshare. Higher education institutions should foster their faculty members the awareness of the policy choices, such as license choices.

6 Improve the Quality of OER

Trust in OER available from others is a barrier for most learners. Critics have questioned how open learning resources can ensure the quality, while the resources is open to everyone and anyone can publish, edit and republish, but not all of the changes are good. However, there are already some possible solutions to evaluate the quality of OER. One is peer-review—the process academic researchers have used for centuries to certify research papers and books. MERLOT which has fifteen different discipline-based groups have been organized to provide such reviews. Another suggest by Connexions which called Lens, rather than makes a single pre-review accept or rejects decision regarding each learning module and collection, it allow third-party reviewers to edit the post-publication peer-review papers. Then users have the abilities to preferentially locate and view modules and collections that have been endorsed by third parties through the Lens they trust to obtain evaluations of the available OER [13].

Most recently, Rice University's Connexions joint hands with the Institute of Electrical and Electronics Engineers Signal Process Society (IEEE-SPS), released a set of open educational resources on signal processing. The high-quality resources are also peer-reviewed and available for free on the Connexions IEEE-SPS portal [14]. This is the first time that authority organizations collaborate with open projects, which has made a further effort to the quality of open content.

However, learning materials in different languages and teaching contexts may show different performances and qualities. In these existing cases, learners and teachers are separated from the educational context of practice. It is simply overlooked that quality is not fixed and stable characteristic of an educational resource, but that educational quality is only established in the situation where a resource is employed in a specific context through a specific learner, or teacher [15]. In order to support high quality application of OER, it is necessary to open up the variety practices and activities of OER, as well as share the effective methods and experiences of using OER.

7 From Open Educational Resources to Open Educational Practices

The development of OER has showed far-reaching influences on higher education. More recently, the trend is to include "practices". In 2007, the Open e-Learning Content Observatory Services (OLCOS) project which as a Transversal Action under the European eLearning Programme emphasized the need to foster open practices of teaching and learning that are informed by a competency-based educational framework [16]. The static learning materials will have little effect on equipping instructors, students and faculties with the knowledge and skills to establish themselves in the knowledge economy and society. In fact, open education is not limited to just open educational resources. It also draws upon open technologies that facilitate collaborative, flexible learning and the open sharing of teaching practices that empower educators to benefit from the best ideas of their colleagues. It may also grow to include new approaches to assessment, accreditation and collaborative learning [17].

According to Williams etc., who contend that we should acknowledge the potential of content, that is to open up educational processes, which we are calling Open Pedagogy (OP) enabled by the Web2.0 technologies that are set to play the more transformational role in the collaborations between students and lectures [18].

The concept of OP coincides with Conole's “Open Educational Practices (OEP)”. Conole suggest that OEP are the set of activities and support around the creation, use and repurposing of Open Educational Resources. It also includes the contextual settings within which these practices occur [19]. Moreover, the two years Open Educational Quality Initiative (OPAL) also moves beyond the issue of access to OER, focus on innovation and quality through OEP. In OPAL, OEP aim to improve the quality of using OER, promote innovate pedagogical models, and empower learners as co-producers on their life long learning path [20].

In a sense, OEP means using tools and technologies (especially Web2.0) to put OER into practice by creating educational activities, interactions and feedbacks around the learning materials. In the process, sharing and collaboration as well as openness in pedagogical is important. Compared to OER, OEP will focus more on learners' learning experiences rather than content, learners should be assisted in developing cognitive strategies and learn to monitor one's own level of understanding [21] in open learning environment, the role of teachers should shift from resources producers to tutors who lead students to gain more learning experiences.

7.1 Harness the Co-creation and Collaboration

The creation and use of open educational resources strengthen the point that learning as a collaborative social activity and shows the potential for making new and customizable learning materials available on the Internet. In this sense, the practice is a kind of collaborative practice.

In the actual production of OER, we need a laboratory (virtual or reality) to best practices for co-creation and the growth of communities of practice. OpenLearn project in Open Universities is involved in such studies. OpenLearn is based on Moodle, which is an open source course management system and extensible collaboration learning environment. LabSpace in OpenLearn has customized and developed some interactive modules in Moodle, in order to support learners and study groups to practice and share learning materials. In Labspace, users can not only communicate with others in the form of learning club and learning journal, but also use various tools which support distance education to download/upload learning materials and exchange notes. Moreover, some collaborative learning tools such as video conferencing tools, experimental knowledge mapping tools and instant messaging tools can help support peer-to-peer interaction. In addition, we also need Web2.0 technologies and services to reinforce learners' social communications and collaborations. Web2.0 can help to construct a widget-based learning environment, for example, embedding tags of YouTube, SlideShare, Facebook or Twitters into open content repositories, so that provide learners with a wider range of OER to choose from, and also enhance the building of communities around open content. When learners participate fully in the socially suited practices of a community, learning is a process of becoming part of a community of practice [22]. Collaboration which based on community is the characteristic of this era, and that would be a great loss if the OER community fails to seize the opportunity.

7.2 Emphasis the Pedagogical Knowledge and Design

Content separated from its contexts is difficult to adopt and employ without some understanding of the pedagogical. The final report of the digital resource study project in Berkeley point out that, for faculties, the foremost reason for not using digital resources was that they did not support faculty's teaching approaches [23]. In fact, many of faculty members have a general (even rich) knowledge of teaching methods, they are the most interested in pouring into these experiences to certain domains they teach. Therefore, leading and training teachers to touch the web to find, analyze, and customize online materials for class will benefit redesign of a course.

In order to solve these problems, MERLOT program at California State University inspired its faculties to provide pedagogical knowledge in their content areas through professional and scholarly collaborations with their disciplinary and institutional colleagues. Pedagogical knowledge may cover the knowledge of discipline content, this expertise is suited in specific disciplines and topics and both supplements and instantiates more generic pedagogical knowledge. What MERLOT has carried mainly include: member comments, learning assignments, author snapshots and peer reviews [24].

After adding pedagogical knowledge to the learning resources, the next step is to enhance the leading of educational contexts. Because almost all of the users (low or advanced level) will face the challenges when integrating a new learning object into their designs, so that, for a certain topics, we should guide learners to a specific related research result. The direct way is to provide a link to research result and community scholarship, which however must guarantee the openness of linked resources. Another feasible way may strengthen the relevance of learning resources, digital collections will assist a lot. Digital collections can range from teaching writing and research collections developed by well-known institutional entities to collections developed by individuals. Collections should emphasize the interrelations of segment resources, so as to guide learners to master the mainline of content quickly. However, different resources may have different contexts, to build high quality of collections is in need of efficacy and interoperability tools for collecting, constructing and managing multitude of available resources.

Pedagogical design is a complex process, so it must be more pertinent. Recognizing and analyzing the teaching style and the differences of disciplines is important.

7.3 Feedbacks and Assessments

OEP is carried out in open learning architecture. The open environment will place more attention to learners' reaction and self-cognition ability. In this process, feedbacks and assessments are essential, for they can impact or modify students' future actions and the teachers' teaching plan. Carnegie Mellon University's Open Learning Initiative (OLI) has engaged in such practices. OLI use appropriate pedagogical techniques and human-computer interface technologies, taking full advantage of the capabilities of digital materials to collect learners' real-time interactive data, and then utilize these data to build continuous assessments, feedbacks, and supports (called feedback loops), these feedbacks information will finally return to students, instructors and courses designers [25]. Learners can learn more efficiently and effectively when they are provided with feedbacks to help them monitor their own understanding levels. Also, according to the performance of their students, teachers can alter the strategy of their teaching. All of the courses in OLI are from Open Courseware Consortium. However, only a few courses are open to free learners, most of the curricula must be of teacher's participation. But the work at OLI provides a clearer view of OER's long-term potential and the utility of digital media in general, particularly for improved assessment and feedback [26].

In order to capture, extract and evaluate useful information for the repurposing of OER, Open University and Carnegie Mellon University launched the three years project OLnet [27]. The workshop takes pedagogical patterns, web2.0 sharing and discussion tools, and some learning design tools into consideration. The implementation of OEP will provide OER with a good quality framework, but it still need time, effort and potentially even policy and equipment to make it work well.

8 Conclusion

Under the background of education globalization, universities and colleges have opportunities to integrate many of open ways to change their operations, teachings and researches, while open educational resources is one of the key role to promote this transform. We should continue to harness the openness of open educational resources in teaching and learning, enhance the reusability and quality of learning materials. Moreover, it is pressing to reinforce practices around open content in educational contexts, lay stress on pedagogical, transform to open educational practices, thus constructing a better learning environment through sharing and collaboration.

In addition, the increasing web applications may provide OER with more novel ways to use knowledge. For example, Semantic web, which can help to build domain ontology, thus enhancing the relations of knowledge and giving learners a better guide to the body of knowledge in certain domains , so that structure a more personalized learning space.

References

1. United Nations Educational, Scientific, and Cultural Organization, http://www.unesco.org/education/news_en/080702_free_edu_ress.shtml
2. D'antoni, S., Savage, C.: Open Educational Resources. The United Nations Educational, Scientific and Cultural Organization 30 (2009)
3. Nguyen, T.: Science Commons: Open Doors and Open Minds: What Faculty Authors Can Do to Ensure Access to Their Work through Their Institution. SPARC and Science Commons 1 (2008)
4. ClickZ Network, http://www.clickz.com/showPage.html?page=3625146
5. Apple iTunes University, http://www.apple.com/education/itunes-u/what-is.html
6. Enhancing Education, http://ccnmtl.columbia.edu/enhanced/primers/media_channels_open_educational_resources.html
7. Feiler, J.: How to Do Everything with Web2.0 Mashups. The McGraw-Hill Companies, New York (2008)
8. OpenContent, http://opencontent.org/blog/archives/355
9. Wiley, D.A.: The Instructional Use of Learning Objects. Association for Instructional Technology and the Association for Educational Communications and Technology, Bloomington (2002)
10. Connexions, http://cnx.org/aboutus/overview/content_type
11. Antoniou, G., van Harmelen, F.: A Semantic Web Primer, 2nd edn. The MIT press, London (2008)
12. Organization for Economic Co-operation and Development: Giving Knowledge for Free: The Emergence of Open Educational Resources, 76. OECD Publishing (2007)
13. Iiyoshi, T., Vijay Kumar, M.S.: Opening Up Education: The Collective Advancement of Education through Open Technology, Open Content, and Open Knowledge. The MIT Press, London (2008)
14. Rice University, http://www.media.rice.edu/media/NewsBot.asp?MODE=VIEW&ID=15110
15. International Council for Open and Distance Education, http://www.icde.org/filestore/Resources/OPAL/Openeducational practice-approachingadefinitionforanewconcept.pdf

16. Geser, G.: Salzburg Research: Open educational practices and resources: OLCOS Roadmap 2012. Open eLearning Content Observatory Services 12 (2007)
17. The Cape Town Open Education Declaration, http://www.capetowndeclaration.org/read-the-declaration
18. Hodgkinson-Williams, C., Gray, E.: Degrees of Openness: The Emergence of Open Educational Resources at the University of Cape Town. International Journal of Education and Development using Information and Communication Technology 75 (2009)
19. E-learning innovation: research, evaluation, practice and policy, http://e4innovation.com/?p=373
20. Open Educational Quality Initiative, http://oer-quality.org/
21. Commission on Behavioral and Social Sciences and Education National Research Council: How People Learn: Brain, Mind, Experience, and School. National Academy Press, Washington (2003)
22. Lave, J., Wenger, E.: Situated Learning: Legitimate peripheral participation. Cambridge University Press, Cambridge (1991)
23. Harley, D., Henke, J., Lawrence, S.: Use and Users of Digital Resources. Center for Studies in Higher Education, Berkeley (2006)
24. Carey, T., Hanley, G.L.: Extending the Impact of Open Educational Resources through Alignment with Pedagogical Content Knowledge and Institutional Strategy: Lessons Learned from the MERLOT Community Experience. pp. 183–186. The MIT Press, Cambridge (2008)
25. Zhiting, Z., Ping, Y.: Research and Analysis on Typical OER Projects. E-education Research 71 (2009)
26. The Committee for Economic Development Digital Connections Council: Harnessing Openness to Improve Research, Teaching and Learning in Higher Education. Committee for Economic Development, Washington (2009)
27. Open Learning Network, http://olnet.org/node/112

The Blended Learning Journey of the University of Glamorgan

Norah Jones, Esyin Chew, and Haydn Blackey

Centre for Excellence in Learning and Teaching (CELT),
University of Glamorgan, United Kingdom, CF37 1DL
{echew,njones2,hblackey}@glam.ac.uk

Abstract. This paper provides a case study of an institutional journey of enhancing learning and teaching with technology as a catalyst of change. The paper considers one such set of institutional efforts to generate change – at many levels, including pedagogic change – through technology. Such institutional activities have enhanced learning and teaching experiences this is supported by both internal and external evidence. The summary of the journey are drawn from the institutional efforts: (1) Challenge: enhancement than embedding; (2) Celebrate the focus: Pedagogy than technology; (3) Change: student experience-driven change.

Keywords: Blended Learning, Technology Enhanced Learning, Institutional Framework.

1 Introduction

Technology is widely seen as central to the transformation of Higher Education Institutions (HEIs) providing opportunities to enhance traditional modes of teaching and learning. Many, universities in the UK and beyond have adopted deliberative strategies that are intended to develop and promote pedagogic technologies. There has been much effort made to identify the "best way" of introducing technology into higher education (Garrison and Anderson, 2003, Sharpe et al., 2006). This is a major issue for HEIs across the UK as they have sought to manage technological developments and their implications for teaching and learning. A number have embraced these developments, actively developing a strategic process for managing planned changes around them. Nonetheless Oliver and Dempster (2003, pp. 144) conclude "there appears no ready model – no single, clearly successful path – that ensures e-learning will be embedded".

The paper considers one such set of institutional efforts to generate change – at many levels, including pedagogic change – through technology. The University of Glamorgan's central focus is on the complexities and tensions involved in this enterprise in a UK HEI that sought as a matter of policy to enhance technology in teaching and learning. The key argument is that technology is a dynamic and nebulous entity, and it is not the sole focus in the change process but acts as a catalyst for change in Glamorgan's context. Indeed it has been argued that a complete

R. Kwan et al. (Eds.): ICHL 2011, LNCS 6837, pp. 157–166, 2011.

e-learning process may be a disruptive, rather than a sustaining, technology (Connolly et al 2006, drawing on Christensen's analysis (2000)). Hence this generates uncertainties preventing any easy mode of implementation. Hence there is a complex, incremental mode of change taking place, in which technological developments mesh with other change pressures and the intended and unintended consequences of action – managerial and non-managerial – play out in unpredictable ways.

2 Institutional Journey at Glamorgan

The case-study HEI is a large modern university located in an area of economic deprivation. Its location is such that securing the requisite number of students is a continuing challenge. In part the motivation to move into blended learning reflects a marketing effort, as well as the views of senior management about the use of technology to support the students' experience. In addition, senior management sought to capitalise on experience and expertise gained as a result of a successful EU bid to develop a range of business-related degrees which would be made available across Wales using web-based technologies, as well as a number of Further Education Colleges.

The University of Glamorgan (UoG) initiated a large-scale 6 millions e-learning project (2002-2005) – E-College Wales (ECW) - with funding from the European Union. The results indicated that the most effective delivery method online is a blended delivery model and in 2005 the university made a commitment to adopt blended learning across the institution and its delivery partners. The objectives were to (1) provide the learning environment where all students are commonly experience technology aided delivery and assessment within their regular programmes of study, and (2) enable academics to enhance their teaching experiences by undertaking training, design and development in the use of technology (including collaborative and social networking technology). Thus a three-year project was funded to embed blended learning across the work of all Faculties. A multi-disciplinary team including the Centre for Excellence in Learning and Teaching (CELT) which consisted of the Blended Learning Team and an e-Support Team who both provide advice and support on the blended learning practice and development, was established.

The Benchmarking Exercise in 2006-2007 was the institutional initiatives that aimed to improving the University current exercise by learning from others. The University's senior management team have committed to enhancing learning, teaching and assessment, and as part of this a benchmarking project at the University showed that Technology-Enhanced Learning (TEL) is integral to the University's learning, teaching and assessment landscape and is a vital adjunct to its face-to-face delivery of learning. The University has chosen to build on the Blended Learning Project by continuing its enhancement initiatives and focusing more explicitly on putting assessment at the heart of learning (Jones, 2009) and online assessment as a central aim of future TEL developments.

Gwella is a cross institutional authority for enhancing learning and teaching through technology for Higher Education in Wales. It funded all universities in Wales for TEL agenda. After ECW, Blended Learning Project and Benchmarking Exercise, Gwella is the next TEL drive for the University of Glamorgan. In light of the University's pedagogically-led TEL initiatives, the following Gwella targets have been drawn up in line with the University's Learning, Teaching and Assessment Strategy 2007-12 and HEFCW's TEL Strategy. Gwella enhancement activities in 2008 to 2010 are focused on a number of key development areas for the institution, i.e.:

1. Embedding assessment policy (2010) throughout the University by promoting and raising awareness of online submission and assessment, by providing training and support in its use for 30% of academic staff in 08/09, and a further 50% of academic staff in 09/10.
2. Developing the use of social networking software to support and strengthen the online learning experience for Glamorgan students.
3. Enhancing the already established Good Practice Website, providing examples based on online assessment developments to share good practice across the institution.
4. Continuing the TEL seminar series to share good practice in the University with colleagues from the Welsh HE and Further Education sector.

Along with the educational ethos for a centralised support team supporting TEL, seven evidence-based 'Good Practice' guides, have been realised to support these key developments and strategies (Chew, Jones and Blackey, 2010).

3 Key Enhancement: The 3Cs Framework

3.1 Change: Enchancement Than Embedding

TEL-embedded policy and "Technology-enhanced learning" as standard have been introduced across the University Strategy, Learning and Teaching Strategy, Research Strategy and ICT Strategy. Such consistent message and support are prioritised by senior management. These efforts are not merely meant to embed technolgy in learning and teaching but to enhance student learning and teaching through technology. For example, a personalised Student Portal, Glamlife (2009) has been developed with enhanced student-focussed facilities built into it. The student engagement and voices for supporting student learning enhancement in the digital world has been recognised by the JISC Study of how UK FE and HE institutions are supporting effective learners in a digital age (SLiDA, 2010). For example, online submission and self-assessment for learning through Turnitin on GlamLearn have enhanced both home and international student experiences. Richer and prompter assessment feedback is provided to students via GradeMark and audio feedback (Chew et al., 2009; 2010). Further details can be found from SLiDA wiki (2010) and Turn it in or Turn it off project (2010). Figure 1 shows the milestones for an institutional initiatives in the past three years:

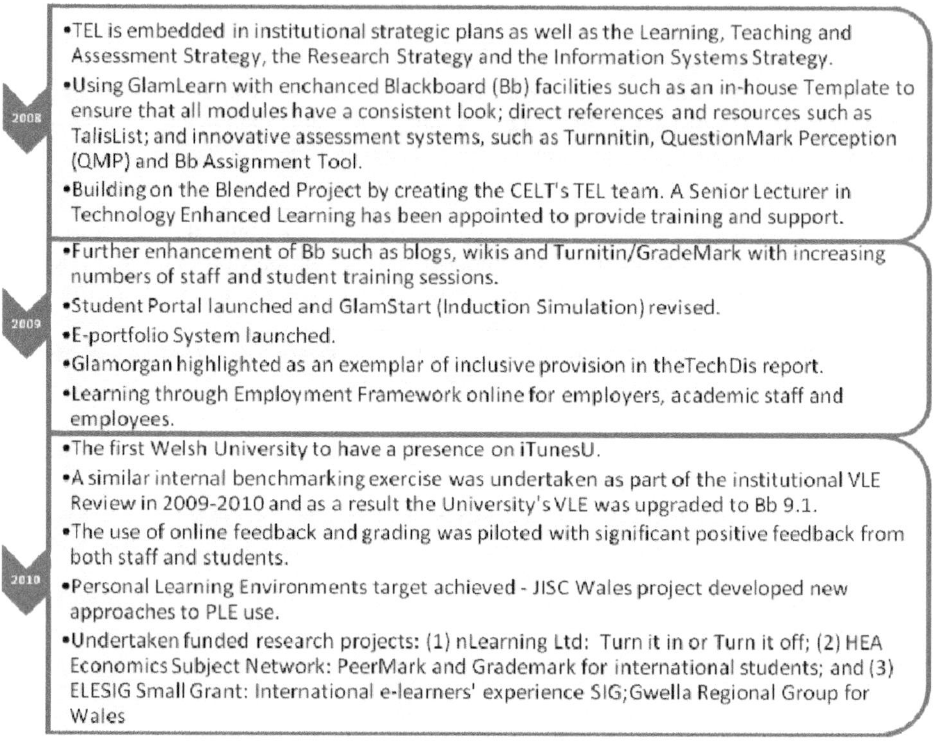

Fig. 1. Institutional Milestones and Achievements for Technology Enchance Learning

The development of the assessment diary has helped the assessment burden to be more evenly distributed throughout the academic year. This has been disseminated across the UK HEIs through the JISC Effective Assessment in a Digital Age case studies (JISC, 2010). In addition, all students have access and support to an e-portfolio as well as web 2.0 technologies such as wikis and blogs on GlamLearn to enrich their learning experience. Online Reading Lists (TalisList) with embedded direct links to resources are now available for 80% of modules. Interactive simulation game for new students, GlamStart (2010), is an innovative approach to student induction which was well-received and received UCISA Award of Excellence (2008). Learning through iTunesU (2010) and publishing Glamorgan students' work on iTunesU. Alongside with the Gwella initiatives, more than 64 TEL related student training sessions, with more than 2000 participants, have been delivered directly by the TEL team.

Staff teaching and assessment experiences at Glamorgan have also been enhacned. A variety of tools introduced to staff have been perceived as "extensions of educators" (Chew And Price, 2010), i.e. wikis, pods, Turnitin, GradeMark and the Bb Assignment tool. More than 90 staff technology training sessions, with about 600 participants, have been delivered. Also, about 20-30 staff per month were supported by the TEL team in 121 sessions. There are monthly meetings with faculty Champions, Bb Administrators and Heads of Learning and Teaching. As a result of these measures more than 80% of all University staff were supported by Gwella activities, directly or indirectly, from 2008 to 2010. The University also developed and delivered complete online programmes. For example, an online education programme for NHS Health Care Assistants and an MSc in Sustainable Business Risk Management.

Being the first Welsh University to have a presence on, and in the use of iTunesU to display student work, the Glamorgan iTunesU site has attracted 1 million visitors, averaging 13,087 downloads per week. A social software Policy document and associated guidance has been developed for the institution and institutional commitment has been secured for the implementation of Campus Pack to add web 2.0 enabled tools into all courses. Data from Learning Objects, the hosting company for Campus Pack, shows that from July to December 2010 there has been an increase in engagement in both course and e-portfolio based web 2.0 tools.

The enthusiastic and widespread take-up of Turnitin/GradeMark, QMP and CampusPack are highlighted as a particularly pleasing aspect of the institution's enhancement activities. For example Turnitin, with 33,187 total submissions, and QMP, with 71,242 assessment attempts have become popular. The online assessment project has exceeded its targets, with 100% online submission of assessments (where applicable) being the standard using either Turnitin or the Bb Assignment tool. Also all modules are now using Online Module Evaluation through QMP. The University's Good Practice website has been further developed with the addition of new tools, an online assessment wiki (2009) and a wiki with advice and further information on Turnitin and GradeMark (2010). The Turnitin wiki and GradeMark (2010) wiki has attracted 4097 absolute visitors from more than 50 countries between June 2009 and Jan 2011. As a result of Gwella initiatives, institutional efforts for the online submission and assessment agenda have greatly increased the engagement of both staff and students for TEL. Turnitin usage for example has increased more than four times, see Figure 2:

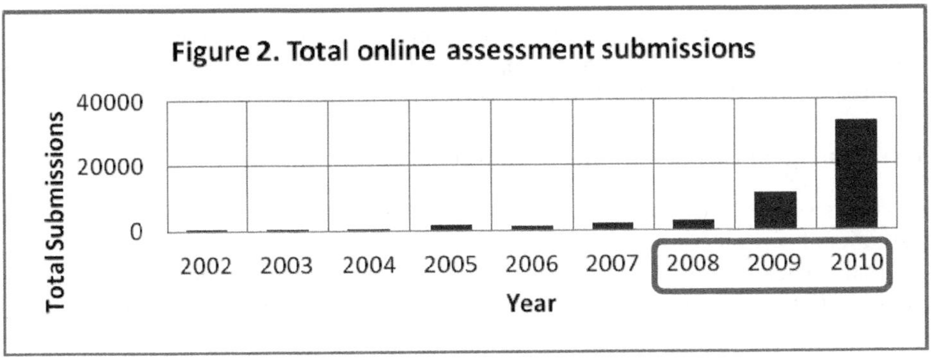

Fig. 2. Total Submissions for Turnitin

3.2 Celebrate the Focus: Pedagogy Than Technology

The new technologies have the potential to be both helpful and harmful. The problem is complicated further if technologies were introduced in higher education. Higher education is changing and change is unplanned and unpredictable, but emerges from responses by people in the organisation to issues as they come up. Lecturers and learning technologist cannot merely geared by all sorts of e-learning technologies but left behind the pedagogy. Instead, quick responses and reasonably understanding of pedagogy and student experiences are required. The heart of the TEL agenda lays the need for a deep understanding of the trends and pedagogy, only through that understanding can emerge initial interest and passion (Chew, Jones and Turner, 2008). The University has a pedagogical-led TEL policy which has asserted that the learning and teaching experience remain the fundamental foundation for any technology embedded to the classroom.

> "It's very exciting because the University was taking the opportunity **not just to change in technology enhancement but to change the learning and teaching,** and using technology as the trojan horse…get people thinking about it, and get them to start talking about all of the ways they do learning and teaching" ~Principal Lecturer (Faculty of Humanities and Social Sciences)

The annual Excellence in Learning and Teaching Awards (ELTA) encourage and boost efforts in the innovative redesign and transformation of pedagogically and technologically-focussed teaching, learning and assessment. It is not all about the advancement in technology but all about the change in learning and teaching. Pedagogical-focused staff and student training are delivered and pedagogical-focused one-to-one-support are provided. There are many positive experiences have been gathered in the Turn it in or Turn it off project (2010). For example,

> "I think I have given more feedback than I probably would have done in a paper method with a pencil…before, I would probably put a tick to indicate it is on the right track…putting comments through Turnitin GradeMark obviously gave more feedback!" ~Senior Lecturer (Education)

> "Much better for interpreting feedback. Symbols are placed in the relevant part of my essay...they could be used to improve my next assignment...I am now actually reading the feedback" ~Student (Business)

3.3 Change: Student Experience Driven Change

All the five key developments (see section 3) have been achieved through the institutional Gwella enhancement evidenced by Glamorgan students, staff and external bodies (i.e. SLiDA project and JISC e-learning evaluation programme case studies, 2010) as discussed. There are also increasing discussion and debates across the faculties about the technical limitations and support, good practices, consistencies and readiness of both staff and students for TEL. This will be a continuing discourse and challenges in years to come. However, Glamorgan academics are overcoming these challenges by realising for themselves the student-driven benefits of their increased use of TEL (Chew and Price, 2010). Such commitment to enhance student learning and assessment experiences, added to some individuals' persistency and patience towards technological constraints has given rise to enhanced performance. Within the seven evidence-based 'Good Practice' for implementing TEL, student experienced-driven change has been recognised as the most effective and powerful practice (Chew, Jones and Blackey, 2010). Success in developing the use of TEL across the institution means that there is a perpetual challenge in providing support to meet increasing demands for both pedagogic and technical guidance and advice. In terms of the enhancement of academic staff, the TEL team are now working with the late majority, and meeting the challenge of those who are perhaps most resistant to changing their practice through the JISC Capacity building project (2011). Staff require increasing support in meeting student expectations that are raised by the University TEL agenda. Also, 37 TEL seminars have taken place since the start of the Gwella initiative, which have been attended by more than 958 delegates including representatives from several other Welsh HEIs. The TEL seminars continue to be a focus for enhancement at the institution, in their FE partners and across HE in Wales. A guide for course teams designing blended/e-learning programmes in Wales has been developed and is available in Welsh and English on the Centre for Welsh Medium Higher Education website. In addition as part of Gwella the CELT team provided key input and leadership to the development of 'Y Porth' the Welsh medium Virtual Learning Environment.

4 Challenges and Conclusion

The institutional enhacement activities at University level facilitated many major developments. Finally, while without being complacent, all those interviewed accepted that blended learning had developed considerably across the university in recent years. No faculty reported serious resistance to its implementation and all faculties indicated that, while there remained areas of non-involvement, significant progress had taken place. Digital literacy for students and technical competence for staff are two of the key areas to be improved. All faculties had important pedagogic initiatives that they felt were important. The new practices were designed to change the way technology was used to enhance learning teaching and assessment. Although there are continuing debates and discussions on the consistency of the technology usage and technical limitation, the discourse will be focused on student experience enhancement rather than the 'technical problems'.

Given the current economic climate, the support and enhancement structures which have been put in place have ensured that TEL remains a well-supported institutional priority in the coming years. For instance: (1) Glamorgan has led four Gwella funded Collaborative Approaches to the Management of e-Learning (CAMELS, 2010) in various TEL-related topics to empower the regional Gwella enhancement initiatives; (2) TEL team is continuing to strive for funded projects from both industry and The Higher Education Academy for research informed practice; (3) More dissemination and sources of support are available on our CELT and University websites and blogs such as CELT (2010), LearningZone (2010) and Blended Learning (2010); through the Higher Education Academy Special Interest Groups such as. LERSIG (2010),

ELESIG (2010 and MELSIG (2010)) and user groups (i.e. TurnitinUK & QMP); (5) We will continue the Gwella story on ELESIG Gwella group and to the world through wider dissemination. In sum, the figure below summarises the key messages for the sector which can be compared and contrasted with experiences in other institutions to inform others who are implementing similar developments while enhancing what the University of Glamorgan are doing.

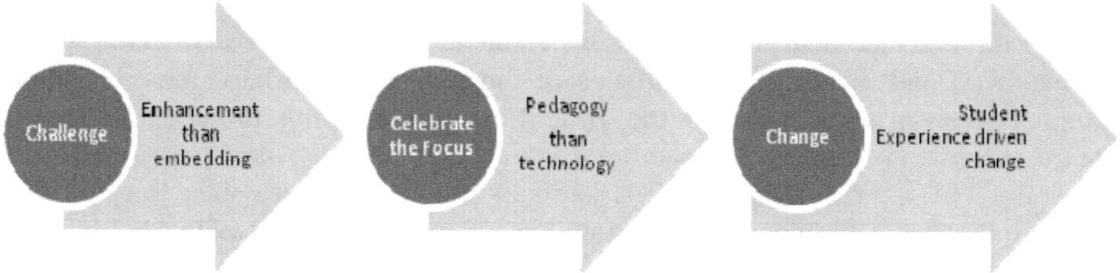

Fig. 3. 3Cs Framework for the Institutional Journey

References

1. Assessment Diary, JISC Case Studies for Digital Assessment (2009), http://www.jisc.ac.uk/media/documents/programmes/elearning/digiassess_puttingassess.pdf (retrieved January 24, 2011)
2. Assesment Policy, University of Glmaogran Assessment Policy (2010), http://celt.glam.ac.uk/Assessment-and-Feedback (retrieved January 24, 2011)
3. Blended Learning, LCSS Blended Leanring (2010), http://lcss.glam.ac.uk/blendedlearning/ (retrieved January 24, 2011)
4. CAMEL, Collaborative Approchaes to the Management of E-Learning (2010), http://www.jiscinfonet.ac.uk/camel (retrieved January 24, 2011)
5. CELT, Centre for Excellence in Learning and Teaching (2010), http://celt.glam.ac.uk/Enhancing-Learning-Teaching/Technology-Enhanced-Learning (retrieved January 24, 2011)
6. Chew, E., Price, R., Roger, C., Blakey, K., Noblett, N., Matins, A., Martins, I. : Turn it in or Turn it off – Confirming and Disconfirming Experience for Innovative Computer aided Assessment and Feedback. In: Proceedings of 9th European Conference on e-Learning, Instituto Superior de Engenharia do Porto, Portugal, November 4-5, pp. 155–162 (2010)
7. Chew, E., Jones, N., Blackey, H.: A UK Case Study - Technology Enhances Educational Experiences in the University of Glamorgan. In: The IEEE International Conference on Future Computer and Communication, Kuala Lumpur, April 3-5, pp. 212–216 (2009); IEEE No. 09PR3591; ISBN: 978-1-4244-3754-2, http://www.computer.org/portal/web/csdl/doi/10.1109/ICFCC.2009.109 (retrieved January 24, 2011)
8. Chew, E., Price, T.: Online Originality Checking and Online Assessment - an Extension of Academics or Disruption for Academics. In: Wong, S.L., et al. (eds.) Proceedings of the 18th International Conference on Computers in Education, November 29-December 3. Asia-Pacific Society for Computers in Education, Putrajaya (2010)

9. Chew, E., Jones, N., Blackey, H.: Implementing Institutional Online Assessment – Addressing the Challenges. In: Tsang, P., Cheung, S.K.S., Lee, V.S.K., Huang, R. (eds.) ICHL 2010. LNCS, vol. 6248, pp. 453–464. Springer, Heidelberg (2010), http://www.springerlink.com/content/0802v72064121055/ (retrieved January 24, 2011)
10. Chew, E., Jones, N., Turner, D.: The Marriage of Rousseau and Blended Learning: An Investigation of 3 Higher Educational Institutions Praxis. In: Leung, H., Li, F., Lau, R., Li, Q. (eds.) ICWL 2007. LNCS, vol. 4823, pp. 641–652. Springer, Heidelberg (2008), http://www.springerlink.com/content/b35336204387v576/ (retrieved January 24, 2011)
11. Christensen, C.: The Innovator's Dilemma: When New Technologies Cause Great Firms to Fail. Harvard Business Press, Mass (2000)
12. Connolly, M., Jones, N., Turner, D.: E-learning: a fresh look. Journal of Higher Education Management and Policy 18(3), 135–147 (2006)
13. ELESIG, Evaluation of Leaners Experiences of e-Learning Speical Interest Group (2010), http://elesig.ning.com/ (retrieved January 24, 2011)
14. Garrison, G.R., Anderson, T.: E-learning for the twentieth century. Routledge, London (2003)
15. Glamlife, Student Portal Glamlife (2009), http://inform.glam.ac.uk/glamlife/ (retrieved January 24, 2011)
16. GlamStart, GlamStart website (2010), http://gettingstarted.glam.ac.uk/glamstart/ (retrieved January 24, 2011)
17. iTuneU, University of Glamorgan iTuneU (2010), http://itunes.glam.ac.uk/ (retrieved January 24, 2011)
18. JISC Capacity Building Project, JISC Capacity Building Project (2011), http://learning.weblog.glam.ac.uk/building-capacity-project (retrieved January 24, 2011)
19. JISC, JISC Case Studies (2010), http://www.jisc.ac.uk/digiassess (retrieved January 24, 2011)
20. JICS e-learning, JISC e-Learning Evaluation Programme (2010), http://www.jisc.ac.uk/whatwedo/programmes/elearning/elearningcommsevaluation.aspx (retrieved January 24, 2011)
21. Jones, N.: Putting assessment at the heart of learning. University of Glamorgan Change Academy Report (2009)
22. LearningZone CELT Learning Zone Blog (2010), http://learning.weblog.glam.ac.uk/ (retrieved January 24, 2011)
23. LERSIG, Learning Environment Review Special Interest Group (2010), http://www.brad.ac.uk/lss/tqeg/conferences/lersig/ (retrieved January 24, 2011)
24. MELSIG, Media Enhanced Learning Special Interest Group (2010), http://ppp.chester.ac.uk/index.php?title=Main_Page (retrieved January 24, 2011)
25. Online Assessment Wiki, The University of Glamorgan Online Assessment Wiki (2009), http://glamorganonlineassessment.pbwiki.com/ (retrieved January 24, 2011)
26. Oliver, M., Dempster, E.: e-learning practices. In: Blackwell, R., Blackmorel, P. (eds.) Towards strategic staff development in higher education. Open University Press, Buckingham (2003)

27. Sharpe, R., Benfield, G., Roberts, G., Francis, R.: The undergraduate experience of blended e-learning: a review of UK literature and practice. Higher Education Academy, London (2006)
28. SLiDA, Study of how UK FE and HE institutions are supporting effective learners in a digital age, SLiDA (2010), http://www.jisc.ac.uk/whatwedo/programmes/elearning/slida.aspx (retrieved January 24, 2011)
29. SliDA Wiki, SliDA Case Studies (2010), https://wiki.brookes.ac.uk/display/slidacases/Glamorgan (retrieved January 24, 2011)
30. Turn it in or Turn it off, Turn it in or Turn it off Project (2010), http://turnitin.wetpaint.com/page/Turn+it+in+or+Turn+it+off+Project (retrieved January 24, 2011)
31. Turnitin and GradeMark, University of Glamorgan Turnitin wiki (2010), http://turnitin.wetpaint.com/ (retrieved January 24, 2011)
32. UCISA Award, UCISA Award of Excellence (2008), http://www.ucisa.ac.uk/members/awards/excellence/2008.aspx (retrieved January 24, 2011)

Policies and Strategies of Technology Enhanced Learning in Lifelong Education in China, Hong Kong, Macau, Taiwan and Singapore

J. Lam and P. Tsoi

Centre for Cyber Learning, School of Professional and Continue Education,
University of Hong Kong, Hong Kong SAR, China
ccl@hkuspace.hku.hk

Abstract. Policies and strategies of technology-enhanced learning issued by governments have played an important role in improving the quality of lifelong education. The objective of this study is to evaluate the effects of policies and strategies of technology-enhanced learning in lifelong education in China, Hong Kong, Macau, Taiwan and Singapore. A review of lifelong education policies and strategies in these countries is conducted in this study. The results show that these Asian societies input different levels of efforts in promoting technology-enhanced learning. Technology-enhanced learning provides for remarkably new avenues for learning and skills development. In order to educate the workforce in the future, governments should invest and develop more in these aspects.

Keywords: Technology Enhanced Learning, Lifelong Education, Information Technology Education.

1 Introduction

The idea of lifelong education can be traced back to Ancient Greek period. The Greek philosophers, Socrates, Plato and Aristotle considered lifelong learning to be the origin of happiness, root of the ordered society and source of life achievement [17]. Cross-Durrant [3] also studied the origins of lifelong education and identified that. Basil A. Yeaxlee, the author 'Lifelong Education', as the first person having made a formal attempt in the nineteenth century to address the issue of lifelong education and he attempted to combine the whole educational enterprise with formal, informal and non-formal education. In fact, Jarvis [13] pointed out that the concept of lifelong learning was published by J. Dewey early in 1916, in which Dewey opined education should not cease when one left school. Following Dewey's influential publication, lifelong learning and adult education were explicitly mentioned in the report published by the British Government in 1919.

In the literature, lifelong education is sometimes being used to refer to non-formal education and adult education. There have been debates over the last decades on the definition of lifelong learning. Shak [21] studied the term of lifelong education in the literature and he concluded his studies with seventeen characteristics of lifelong

R. Kwan et al. (Eds.): ICHL 2011, LNCS 6837, pp. 167–175, 2011.

education in the inherent, fundamental and desirable aspects. The editors of the International Journal of Lifelong Learning [14] discussed the phenomenon and concluded that lifelong education should be a wider and broader concept. Lifelong learning should be considered as the learning process running through one's life and should not simply be a form of adult learning or vocational learning. While schooling was a rather well-established mode for education delivery, most debates were in fact based on the topics relevant to adult education or continuing education. Among the definitions, Jarvis provided the best one by defining lifelong learning as a combination of processes throughout a lifetime whereby the whole person – body (genetic, physical and biological) and mind (knowledge, skills, attitudes, values, emotions, beliefs and senses) - experiences social situations, the perceived content of which is then transformed cognitively, emotively or practically (or through any combination) and integrated into the individual person's biography resulting in a continually changing (or more experienced) person [15]. Lifelong education should cover all types of education throughout lives of individuals.

2 Policies and Strategies of Technology-Enhanced Learning in Lifelong Education in China, Hong Kong, Macau, Taiwan and Singapore

The rapid and extensive development of lifelong education development first appeared in the 1970s under the leadership of various international organizations. The famous Faure Report of UNESCO in 1972 emphasized on lifelong education and the learning society, and lifelong education was proposed as the mater concept for educational policies for both developed and developing countries [10]. The ODEC addressed the issue of lifelong learning in the report 'Recurrent Education: A Strategy for Lifelong Learning' in 1973 but it was being criticized for the exclusion of formal schools when considering lifelong education [20]. Under the development of lifelong education for over twenty years, the UNESCO continued to emphasize the importance of learning throughout life [4]. With the mission of seeing all forms of education and learning to be recognized, valued and made available for meeting the demands of individuals and communities throughout the world, the Institute of Lifelong Learning was established as one of the six educational institutes of UNESCO to provide services in literacy, non-formal education, adult and lifelong learning to the member states, NGOs and grassroots community organizations [22]. Under the influence of globalization, the development of lifelong education has been expanded from regional to global scope. After the Second World War, the relationship between the East and the West became closer. Globalization has affected all countries in the world in the sense that education systems and policies in the Chinese societies has changed under Western influence. By adopting western theories and methods, the Chinese societies established the education structure with basic education, higher education, and more recently, lifelong education. In recent years, policies and strategies on technology-enhanced learning were introduced into Chinese countries and cities.

2.1 China

China introduced basic education to educate the new generation under the open-door policy adopted in 1978 and the economic reform in 1980s. The articulated education system of China was established in the mid-eighties. Nine-year general education, including primary and secondary school education, has been provided to all citizens in China since 1986. The lifelong education system of China was proposed in the 1990s [18] and physical implementation took place in the late 90s. The former president Jiang [16] emphasized that lifelong learning was the general trend for countries among the world and lifelong education system should be set up. Soon after the forceful direction enunciated by Jiang, four contexts of education, including general education, vocational education, adult education and higher education, were strengthened and integrated as the lifelong education system in China. The first Act of lifelong education in China was passed in 2005. In China, the draft of the National Outline for Medium and Long-term Education Reform and Development (2010-2020) was published in July 2010. The Chinese government pledged to improve the quality of lifelong learning education and to enable people to enjoy more education opportunities through a higher level of investment and reforms in the coming decade. Moreover, China would further develop on education reform through innovations and facilities upgrading for the coming years [1].

For technology-enhanced learning policy, China decided to carry out the strategy of rejuvenating the nation by relying on science and education in 1995 [2]. Technology-enhanced learning was highly emphasized by the former president Deng. The five main contents of the strategy were: education being the foundation of the nation, giving priority to science, technology and education in economic and social development; strengthening the national capabilities in science and technology and the ability to transfer scientific and technological findings into actual productivity; improving the quality of the whole nation in the spheres of science, technology and culture; setting economic construction on the road to relying on scientific and technological progress and the improvement of the quality of the workforce; and accelerating the pace toward the realization of national prosperity.

The objectives of the technology-enhanced learning policy have achieved the followings by the year 2000: established a scientific and technological system that fitted the socialist market economy system and the law of the development of science and technology; made considerable progress in scientific research and technological development in industry and agriculture, basic research and high-tech research; improved the contribution rate of science and technology to economic development; and moved economic construction and social development basically in the direction of relying on scientific and technological progress, and improving the quality of the workforce.

The policy has further achieved the following millstones by the year 2010: solidified and improved the newly established scientific and technological system, and combined science and technology with the economy; making scientific and technological undertakings prosper and fostering a high-quality team of gifted scientists and technicians; enhanced the quality of the whole nation in the fields of science, technology and culture to a large extent; spurred the scientific and technological strength of the major disciplines and some high-tech areas advanced world level; substantially raised the ability of scientific and technical personnel to innovate independently.

China has achieved remarkable outcomes from the policies and strategies over the past 16 years. Its strong authority and huge investment in technology-enhanced learning led to the establishment of many Television and Radio Universities and the transformation of these Universities into Open Universities in recent years.

2.2 Hong Kong

Hong Kong, being a British colony before 1997, is a special administrative region of China today. Due to the influence from the West, the basic education adopted in Hong Kong was initiated by the West and most schools established in early times were set up by Western religious bodies. It is found that the division between formal education and continuing education is blurred in Hong Kong and the lifelong learning system comprised of these sub-systems has formed [23]. The continuing education sector has developed well in Hong Kong. In 1957, the first department for adult education, the Department of Extra-Mural Studies, was formally established at the University of Hong Kong. By 2010, all government-funded universities in Hong Kong provide continuing education units. However, there is no legislation or policy on lifelong learning in Hong Kong.

There is no policy of technology-enhanced learning development in Hong Kong. However, there are strategic documents on the promotion of IT in education. The Hong Kong Government published the first strategy document promoting IT in education in November 1998 [7]. It had four key components. The first component was 'Teacher Enablement' which helped teachers to adjust to their new role as a "facilitator" and to become comfortable and habitual IT users; The second component was 'Curriculum and Software' which led to the incorporation of IT elements in the school curriculum and enhancement of provision of educational software in a more structured framework; The third component was 'Hardware Provision'. It progressively enhanced the provision of IT facilities for schools in line with their respective readiness, and worked with schools to overcome physical constraints in the process of adapting to IT-based teaching and learning; The fourth component was 'Network Infrastructure' where network infrastructures were built to facilitate the sharing of education resources and communications within the education sector, as well as between the education sector and the community.

The second strategy document was published in July 2004 [8]. It planned to continue with the measures in the first strategy. A series of new measures were introduced in the second strategy. These included providing more training opportunities for teachers as well as enabling a higher degree of development and dissemination of educational resources. It promoted research and development studies and provided more enhanced support. It also led to the organisation of activities during school years so as to sustain the implementation of the second strategy. The beneficiaries included all schools in the public sector.

The third strategy consultation document, titled "Right Technology at the Right Time for the Right Task", was published in October 2007 [9]. In the document, with its focus being placed upon IT education at schools, it was suggested that the use of technology should be put in the wider context of a learning environment where technology should only be one of many mediators in learning and teaching. Teachers and students would need to decide on whether the use of technology would serve as the most effective mediator for a particular learning and teaching activity.

After 2007, the Education Bureau (EDB) suggested a balanced baseline approach. The underlying thinking was to maximize the potential of technology as one of the many mediators of learning and teaching, and that there should be a balance between IT activities on the one hand and systematic guidance by teachers and perhaps parents on the other. The EDB was mindful of the differences in schools' priorities, teachers' readiness and students' motivation, and the danger of imposing additional workload on schools, teachers and students. Although the strategic focus was on human factor, the government did not ignore the need for providing extra resources and enhancing flexibility of existing operational grants to assist schools in making necessary upgrades and replacement of facilities which would support student learning.

In recent years, the EDB has not set goals according to a projection of what a future school would be. Instead, the EDB seeks to provide the necessary conditions and practical advice on pedagogical applications of technology to minimise the barriers to the integration of technology into education at present. The proposals in the third consultation strategy document were the necessary building blocks in light of the strategic focus on human factor. The ultimate result of using IT is to facilitate the achievement of learning goals in the curriculum reform.

2.3 Macau

Macau, similar to Hong Kong, was a colony of Portugal before the handover when the land was returned to China. As stated in 'Macau's Non-Higher Education System Principle', education in Macau is categorized into two major sections, one being formal education consisting of 15 years of free basic education, and the other being continuing education including community education and vocational education. The Government of Macau considers lifelong education one of the major missions in policy implementation. Macau promoted lifelong learning by issuing the 2004 Draft Law Consultation of Macau Educational System. In the annual report of the Education Department of Macau [5], development of lifelong learning was well-implemented in 2004 whereas 'Lifelong Education Week' was held with various education opportunities offered to citizens so as to encourage them to engage in lifelong learning.

In Macau, investments in technology-enhanced learning resources continue to take place to promote the development and improvement of school education in 2010. In the new academic year, the amount invested in the Education Development Fund for "School Development Plan" is found to be over 328 million patacas; there is an increase of about 10% in comparison to that of the previous academic year. The major subsidized items include the establishment of specific duty personnel, students' leisure activities, school-based training of teaching staff, school health promotion, renovation of school building, renewal of equipment, information technology education development, moral education and vocational-technical education [6].

The formulation of the technology-enhanced learning system for teaching staff will be further promoted, for the purposes of stabilizing the teaching team, defining their rights, obligations and working conditions clearly, and to encourage professional growth of the teaching team. DSEJ will improve the deployment of various types of specific duty personnel. It will promote school-based training. It also seeks to reinforce the training of main stem teachers, develop the Award Scheme of Instructional Design, and constantly enhance the overall quality of the teaching staff.

The Macau Government is putting more effort in technology-enhanced learning in lifelong learning by creating more opportunities for participation in learning and providing better learning conditions. The tools for learning via the Internet are developed, the environment and atmosphere which encourage reading will be created in a steadfast manner, and the concept of life-long learning will be reinforced. The recurrent education subsidy will be adjusted and the recurrent senior secondary education programme established in public schools will be extended to recurrent junior secondary education in order to enhance convenience and encourage residents to participate in recurrent education. The "Continuing Education Subsidy Scheme" will be improved by expanding the scope of provision and enhancing the effectiveness of the scheme. More institutions and residents are encouraged to join the "Life Long Learning Award Scheme". The informational and educational TV programmes will continue to be produced; the function of media in continuing education will be brought into full play through the use of diversified radio programmes and various types of video clips.

Macau has done a remarkable job in promoting the technology-enhanced learning in lifelong learning. The investments of Macau in technology and education have provided learners with additional opportunities to participate in learning under better learning condition.

2.4 Taiwan

Taiwan is another major Chinese society with over 20 million Chinese populations. The basic structure of education system in Taiwan was established in 1922 imitating the structure in the United States of America. The core structure of the education system has been kept since then with only minor amendments made subsequently. From 1968, the Taiwan Government has provided nine years of national education to the citizens. After studying at high schools or vocational schools, students can further their studies at universities or technical colleges. Continuing education is also provided for students pursuing further studies. The Taiwan Government published the White paper 'Towards a Learning Society' in 1998 and named the year as 'Year of Lifelong Learning'. In the proposal contained in the 'Development for Knowledge-Based Economy' announced in 2000, six knowledge-based economy development measures were being put forward. Among them, the fourth measure was to develop and import human resources actively. It can be seen that the implementation of lifelong education can encourage the development of human resources in the knowledge economy in Taiwan. The Taiwan Ministry of Education has set up policies in promoting technology-enhanced learning in lifelong learning in 2009 [19].

The first policy was to set up the Taiwan academic network. The Taiwan Academic Network (TANet) is a national computer network for teaching research, jointly established by major national universities and the Ministry of Education (MOE) in July 1990. TANet's main purpose is to support teaching research activities in schools and research institutes throughout the nation by providing a medium for sharing resources as well as to provide opportunities for cooperation. TANet has a backbone and a regional network structure as well as a research-related information infrastructure.

The second policy was the information security and management policies. The MOE has established the "Information Security Certification Center for Educational Institutions" to help educational institutions for procurement of certification. Currently, MOE mainly focuses on the introduction of ISMS in B Level institutions. In the future, MOE will implement the system at all levels of schools. Starting from 2008, the MOE has established a vulnerability scanning platform for website in region networks to prevent information leakage. MOE will also enact information security operation guidelines governing servers of online services and student record registration at all levels of admission examination systems MOE will also provide advising services on information protection and defense. These admission examination systems include junior high school basic abilities examination, unified admission examination for technical and vocational colleges, and university admission examination.

The third policy was about training Chinese language instructors of e-teaching ability training program. Chinese-learning has become a popular global trend, and in response the Taiwan Government has provided Chinese teaching services for foreigners through a variety of learning channels. The limited number of Chinese language instructors in Taiwan, however, means that the high demand cannot be met. Training and cultivating Chinese language instructors, therefore, should be a priority for the Government. The professional knowledge of Chinese language instructors is based on the principles and methods of language-teaching. Furthermore, with the rapid development of information communications technology, better Chinese teaching services can be provided through integration with digital information technology.

2.5 Singapore

The population in Singapore is composed of people from different nations and over half of the population, which is above 2 million, is Chinese. Similar to Hong Kong, Singapore was also a colony of Britain and the society was deeply affected by the Western culture. The Singapore Government provides ten years of basic education to the citizens. By passing the GCE examination, students can enter colleges, polytechnics, technical colleges or apprenticeship programmes. Universities and continuing education are available to the citizens. The educational reform in Singapore in 1997, with the vision of 'Thinking Schools, Learning Nation', emphasized on the fundamental review of the current system for better development of students' creative thinking and learning skills [11]. The Singapore Government has implemented policies in promoting technology-enhanced learning in lifelong education.

The first policy was the Masterplan for IT in Education (MPITE) launched early in 1997 with the aim of integrating information technology into the Singapore education system. It aimed to strategically deploy infocomm to provide a learner-centric, collaborative learning environment—extending beyond the classrooms, thereby enabling a diverse and vibrant schools landscape in the use of infocomm. [12] Building on the foundation, the Ministry of Education (MOE)'s IT in Education Masterplan II (mp2), which was launched in 2002, aimed to reinforce this transformation. The masterplan envisioned that the pervasive and effective use of IT for the enhancement of educational processes and structures would bring about engaged learning of pupils and enable the "ability-driven" paradigm. Schools were empowered to experiment, optimise, contextualise and integrate the use of IT in deeper levels. In 2008, the Ministry of Education launched its third masterplan. It represented a continuum of the visions of the first and second Masterplans i.e. to enrich and transform the learning environments of our students and equip them with the critical competencies and dispositions enabling success in a knowledge economy.

The EdVantage is a flagship programme provided by Info-communications Development Authority of Singapore (IDA) with the support of the Ministry of Education started from 2006. The programme seeks to harness infocomm to transform the education system in Singapore. Using innovative solutions to showcase Singapore as the leader in exploiting infocomm in education, it is also expected to create revenue and new capabilities for local infocomm enterprises in the education sector.

Among the Asian societies discussed above, Singapore did the best and it has stated the directions clearly for over 10 years. Throughout the years, Singapore obtained the most advanced technology for the purpose of learning enhancement.

3 Conclusion

Governments of different countries understand the importance of technology-enhanced learning in lifelong learning and addresses plan in policy or strategic documents. For examples: China will reinforce education reform through innovation and facilities upgrading. Hong Kong will concentrate on human factors rather than technological factors. Macau will emphasize on the renewal of equipments. Taiwan will set up specific policies and enforce them. Singapore will invest heavily in the lifelong learning Endowment Fund for sustainable and prolonged developments.

Among China, Hong Kong, Macau, Taiwan and Singapore, Singapore did the best and it has stated the directions clearly for over 10 years. Hong Kong does not have a clear policy on technology-enhanced learning development. Nevertheless, strategic directions had been developed in Hong Kong for three times. Practically, Hong Kong has advanced infrastructure in technology including T1 link network, high Internet access rate and high smart phone owning rate. In reality, both policies and practices are equally important in developing technology-enhanced learning for lifelong learning.

In conclusion, technology-enhanced learning opens up avenues for learning and skills development. In order to educate the workforce in the future, governments should further develop and invest in this aspect. This paper covers the study of policies and strategies only. Further studies should be conducted in assessing the effectiveness of implementation.

References

1. China News Agency National Outline for Medium and Long-term Education Reform and Development (2010-2020), `http://www.gov.cn/jrzg/2010-07/29/content_1667143.htm` (retrieved March 5, 2010)
2. CPC: CPC Central Committee and State Council on the decision to accelerate scientific and technological progress, China Government policy (8) (May 6, 1995) (in Chinese)

3. Cross-Durrant, A.: Basil Yeaxlee and the origins of lifelong education. In: Jarvis, P. (ed.) Twentieth-century Thinkers in Adult Education. Croom Helm, Beckenham (1987)
4. Delors, J., Mufti, I.A., Amagi, I., Carneiro, R., Chung, F., Grermek, B., Gorham, W., Kornhauser, A., Manley, M., Quero, M. P., Savane, M. A., Singh, K., Stavenhagen, R., Suhr, M. W., Nanzhao, Z.: Learning: the Treasure Within, Paris, UNESCO (1996), http://unesdoc.unesco.org/images/0010/001095/109590eo.pdf (retrieve September 24, 2010)
5. DSEJ, Annual Report, DSEJ, Macau (2004), http://www.dsej.gov.mo/~webdsej/www/magazine/dsej_book/2004/03e.pdf (retrieved December 7, 2010)
6. DSEJ, The General Situation of Non-tertiary Education in Macao Academic Year (2009/2010), http://portal.dsej.gov.mo/www/portalspace/discuz/dsej_viewnews_page.php?BoardName=enews&Title=News&board_searchvar=&board_orderby=&board_pg=&&msg_id=26 (retrieved March 5, 2010)
7. Education Bureau Consultation Document on the Third Strategy on Information Technology in Education, Education Bureau of HKSAR (1998–2007)
8. Education Bureau Consultation Document on the Third Strategy on Information Technology in Education, Education Bureau of HKSAR (2004–2007)
9. Education Bureau Consultation Document on the Third Strategy on Information Technology in Education, Education Bureau of HKSAR (2007)
10. Faure, E., Herrera, F., Kaddoura, A., Lopes, H., Petrovsky, A.V., Rahnema, M., Ward, F.C.: Learning to be, Paris, UNESCO (1972), http://unesdoc.unesco.org/images/0000/000018/001801e.pdf (retrieve September 24, 2010)
11. Goh, C.T.: Shaping Our Future: Thinking Schools, Learning Nation. In: International Conference on Thinking, Opening Speech by the Prime Minister, Singapore (1997)
12. ICTIE Information Communication Technology. In: Education: Singapore's Ict Masterplan 1997-2008. World Scientific Publishing Company (1997)
13. Jarvis, P.: Adult Education and Lifelong Learning: Theory and Practice, 3rd edn. Routledger Falmer, London (2004)
14. Javis, P.: Is lifelong learning adult education? International Journal of Lifelong Education 25(6), 545–546 (2006)
15. Jarvis, P.: Globalization, Lifelong Learning and the Learning Society: Sociological Perspectives. Routledge, London (2007)
16. Jiang, Z.: Improving the Quality of General Public Should be the Ultimate Purpose of Education. Speech presented at the National Education Conference, June 15, Beijing (1999) (in Chinese)
17. Lewis, R.B.: The Philosophical Roots of Lifelong Learning. Josh H. Russel Center for the Study of Higher Education, College of Education, University of Toledo, Toledo (1981)
18. Ministry of Education, National Education Law of China (1995)
19. Ministry of Education The Ministry of Education Main Policy (2009), http://english.moe.gov.tw/lp.asp?ctNode=783&CtUnit=137&BaseDSD=7&mp=1 (retrieved March 5, 2011)
20. Schuller, T.: The OECD and Lifelong Learning. In: Jarvis, P. (ed.) The Routledge International Handbook of Lifelong Learning, Routledge, London (2009)
21. Shak, W.H.: Lifelong education: Definition, Agreement and Prediction, HK: the Author (1989)
22. UNESCO, Website of Institute for Lifelong Learning, UNESCO (2005), http://www.unesco.org/uil/en/about/mission.htm (retrieved September 18, 2010)
23. Young, C.M.: Continuing Education in a Lifelong Learning Society: the Hong Kong Model. International Journal of Lifelong Education 27(5), 525–533 (2008)

Hybrid Learning: A Powerful Opportunity to Integrate SMEs in Courses as a Third Party

Tobias Fries and Andreas Henrich

University of Bamberg, D-96047 Bamberg, Germany
{tobias.fries,andreas.henrich}@uni-bamberg.de
www.uni-bamberg.de/minf/

Abstract. In typical teaching scenarios students and lecturers are involved. Nowadays, however, learning management systems (LMS) are used intensively to foster communication between students and lecturers and so reduce the need to meet in person in order to communicate. Additionally an increased involvement of practitioners and companies in teaching efforts at universities seems desirable for a variety of reasons. (1) Examples and comments from practitioners can augment teaching content. (2) Students can get in touch early and casually with potential future employers. (3) The lecturer might receive valuable feedback with respect to his/her teaching content and style and potentially more intense forms of co-operation might result. On the company side such co-operation might be especially appealing for Small and Medium-sized Enterprises (SMEs), because large companies usually have other options, as well. Therefore, we set up a project using a university wide LMS as an enabling platform to escalate the involvement of SMEs and their employees in teaching efforts. In the present paper we report on the experiences derived from this project.

1 Introduction

In contrast to large companies, Small and Medium-sized Enterprises (SMEs) cannot afford to run Research and Development (R&D) departments and also are disadvantaged in terms of Human Resources (HR) because university alumni prefer larger companies as employers [12, p. 135] (however, SME employees are more satisfied with their jobs [11, p. 16 and 161]). In addition, SMEs often do not have the time, money, and personnel to provide adequate further education opportunities for their employees. The fact that 99% of European Union companies (and even 99.8% of German companies [10, p. 59]) belong to the SME category and that they generate an estimated 55% to 60% of the economic wealth of the private sector [2, p. 9] helps clarify the seriousness of this issue.

Many authors see solutions to the above mentioned drawbacks of SMEs through inter-organisational networks and co-operation. In car manufacturing, in particular, close co-operation and networks between the big car manufacturers and the upstream SMEs in the value chain (car part producers) have become very common, but a lot of potential co-operation between networks of

R. Kwan et al. (Eds.): ICHL 2011, LNCS 6837, pp. 176–187, 2011.

SMEs remains unrealized. In recent times the phrase "co-opetition"—meaning co-operating with competitors—has become widespread. It usually means co-operation in one business function in order to realize economies of scale. In a similar manner, SMEs could establish R&D or further education co-operations with their competitors to avoid the costs of installing and running an R&D or further education department for every company. Co-operations with universities also provide two opportunities:

1. SMEs can get cost-effective access to recent research and inventions.
2. They can present their products and themselves to students as an actively recruiting company.

On seeing the benefits of co-operation networks between SMEs and of knowledge transfer between universities and SMEs, national and international institutions (like BMBF[1] and ESF[2]) have begun to fund projects for developing and establishing environments for this purpose. We run a project called "LMS4KMU 2.0"[3] (co-financed by the ESF) in which we study the possibilities of extending existing university courses for knowledge transfer to and from SMEs and for using a university-wide learning management system as a virtual co-operation infrastructure.

In the next sections of this chapter, we explain our motivation for incorporating SMEs into academic teaching and describe the situation at the University of Bamberg prior to the start of our project. We then present our approach to integrating SMEs into courses in Chap. 2, describing in more detail critical success factors, expedient co-operation types and how we implemented the co-operation infrastructure. In Chap. 3 we present the experiences of lecturers and SMEs with our project. The paper ends with Chap. 4, in which we consider the results and offer an overview of future prospects.

1.1 Motivation

In the past decade Learning Management Systems (LMS) have gained more and more importance in supporting learning processes. Nowadays they are widespread in all areas of education and learning. After the beginning of the process, when it was common at universities for different chairs to use different LMS, a phase of consolidation took place and today most universities provide a centrally administered university-wide LMS [8]. As we explained in last year's ICHL paper [7], a university-wide LMS forms a purposive basis for all lecturers and students to move from traditional to blended learning [1]. Since most lecturers and students are already conversant with the usage of their university's LMS and the technical teething problems of the systems are controlled by the computing centres, integrating third parties into these systems seems to be feasible.

---

[1] German Federal Ministry of Education and Research (Bundesministerium für Bildung und Forschung), http://www.bmbf.de, last checked May 12th 2011.

[2] European Social Fund, http://www.esf.de, last checked May 12th 2011.

[3] KMU is the German abbreviation for SME, http://www.uni-bamberg.de/minf/lms4kmu, last checked May 12th 2011.

University-wide LMS can be a powerful infrastructure to support knowledge transfer and co-operations between universities and SMEs, and this is worthwhile for the SMEs as we explained in the first part of this chapter. The question we want to address now is what motivates universities to incorporate SMEs into their LMS courses. One aspect is the legal background: The Bavarian Higher Education Act (BayHSchG), which is relevant for our university, explicitly mentions economic co-operations, knowledge transfer and further education as tasks of Bavarian universities. We will detail this in Sect. 2.1. For universities outside Bavaria similar regulations might apply explicitly or implicitly. In any case the idea that knowledge and technologies generated at universities should be transferred to companies for economic benefits seems obvious. Apart from this macroeconomic point of view, co-operation with SMEs is advantageous for a university and is in the best interest of the lecturers. Besides financial implications in terms of possible donations and contracted research, co-operations can also yield other benefits. The incorporation of companies into academic courses is not limited to knowledge transfer from universities to SMEs, but also implies transfer of knowledge and experiences from practitioners to the university and the possibility for students to tackle real-life problems together with company members.

1.2 Starting Point

Our project is based on the university-wide LMS Virtual Campus[4] (VC) of the University of Bamberg. It is an implementation of the wide-spread LMS moodle[5] and has been established in Bamberg since 2006. Before that time, several chairs at the University of Bamberg experimented with self-developed e-learning systems or provided out-of-the-box web discussion forums, but the majority of lecturers just provided their lecture notes for downloading onto their webpages (password protected by .htaccess files) and did not offer any further e-learning content. With the redesign of the university website in 2006, the chance was taken to divide public information (new website based on the Content Management System (CMS) Typo3[6]) and course-related content (uploaded to the new LMS) [9]. As the new Typo3-based website did not offer the possibility of password protection for the provision of lecture notes to the students, most lecturers accepted the need to create a course in the LMS for each of their lectures and to provide their lecture notes this way. Some lecturers still use the VC for this purpose only, but a lot of them experienced that moodle offers a wide range of intuitive but powerful e-learning tools and make use of some of them. So the usage ranges from the pure provisioning of slides, over discussion forums, video podcasts of lectures, exercises (including uploading of students' solutions and marking), to real interactive e-learning content. For the current summer semester 2011 over 1,400 courses are represented in the VC.

[4] http://vc.uni-bamberg.de/moodle, last checked May 12th 2011.
[5] http://moodle.org, last checked May 12th 2011.
[6] http://typo3.org, last checked May 12th 2011.

2 Our Approach

As the LMS Virtual Campus (VC) is very much accepted by lecturers and students at the University of Bamberg and co-operations and knowledge transfer between SMEs and universities are beneficial for companies, lecturers and students, the logical next step for us was to analyse the potential of partly opening the VC to companies. What we did not want to do was to prepare special further education courses just for SMEs, but to open those of the already existing courses which seemed to be appropriate for co-operations. In Sect. 2.1 we will describe the critical success factors of our approach, including incentives, necessary effort, legal issues and the first mover or critical mass problem when starting a co-operation network. Sect. 2.2 is about the co-operation types we have designed. We suggest in particular what influences assessment of the kind of co-operation to be recommended a particular course, and how we want to guide SMEs to find an appropriate co-operation. In Sect. 2.3 we describe our prototypical implementation, including configuration of the moodle system and development of a co-operation portal for the web, social networks, and smartphones.

2.1 Critical Success Factors

At first, we tried to identify the critical success factors which influence our project. A very important point is to cope with the legal challenges arising, when one provides companies access to the courses of an LMS which has been installed for the use of students and lecturers of a particular university. In Germany university-wide LMS make use of the eased copyright restrictions for the delimited circle of lecture attendees in education and research, which are no longer appropriate when practitioners get involved. Furthermore, we checked whether our approach is in line with the rights and duties of universities and considered data protection and privacy issues, too.

Apart from the legal challenges it is typical for any network, that the benefit one can get by joining is greater, the more people are already in the network. In our case, on the one hand, the more courses are offered the more likely SMEs will find a suitable co-operation. On the other hand, the more that SMEs are willing to co-operate with the university, the better the chance for lecturers to get feedback from practitioners and so increase the practical relevance for their students when they open a course. A crucial task is therefore to convince SMEs and lecturers to join the network from the beginning, by clearly pointing to the incentives and minimizing the efforts for starting and running co-operations.

Legal Issues. First of all, we ensured that our approach does not collide with the rights and duties of universities. The relevant code of law in our case is the Bavarian Higher Education Act (BayHSchG). In Art. 2 (1) and (5) the tasks of Bavarian universities are enumerated as research, teaching, studies, further education, economic co-operations, transfer of knowledge and technology, and to encourage acquisition of additional qualifications in co-operation with the business sector and the labour administration. Our approach is based on communication over the LMS and co-operations with bidirectional knowledge transfer and teamwork between students and company members, and hence in line with these tasks. As a clear borderline it was defined that in cases where a company member wishes to get a degree, he or she should instead enroll in a distance study programme.

As far as data protection is concerned, the Bavarian Data Protection Act (BayDSG) is relevant. Art. 16 to 18 deal with acquisition, storage, alteration, processing and transfer of personal data. At the University of Bamberg, students register for the VC themselves. They do this to access course contents and to communicate with other students and lecturers. To register, they have to input their real name and a valid email address, which are stored in the system. They also have the possibility of inserting additional personal data after registration. This personal data is visible to other users, enrolled in the same courses in the system. When company members gain access to courses in the system, the students have to be informed beforehand, so that they get the chance to delete personal data or unregister from the course opened to company members. Companies should also be informed, that they are not allowed to transfer personal data about students (e.g. for recruiting purposes) in their company without explicitly asking them for permission.

Last but not least, copyright issues have to be heeded. Of relevance here is the German Copyright Act (UrhG). As long as an LMS course is access protected by a password only known by the students attending a lecture, §52a (UrhG) absolves the lecturer from the need to ask authors of submitted third person content for permission and a framework agreement between the German federal states and the collecting societies covers the payment of compensations. When company members access a course, the lecturer has to hide critical content from them or strictly fulfil the preconditions of citations according to §51 in conjunction with §§62 and 63 (UrhG). More details can be found in our paper about legal pitfalls and circumventions [5].

Incentives. SMEs can take advantage of joining the project as they have the chance to contact universities directly which are in their neighbourhood, get to know students (and with it possible future employees), get a glimpse into fields of knowledge of those possible future employees and get to know results of research. The employees of the companies can increase their knowledge in topics of interest for their daily work and also can learn about new fields, which they can possibly use in their future work.

For lecturers, joining the project can offer the chance to intensify the business relevance of their teaching and research, establish contacts with possible project partners and present their research in a business context. Incentives for students are implicitly included in the incentives for lecturers: they receive more business oriented courses, start a dialogue with companies, gain insight into concrete business projects, problems, and solutions, and make contact with possible employers.

Effort. The incentives for lecturers and SMEs seem convincing, but in order to persuade lecturers to open their courses to companies and offer co-operations, it is also important that the effort of preparing and executing the co-operations is kept as low as possible. If a lecturer wants to let company members access his lecture notes and use a course's discussion forums, he can just enter the phrase "participates in the project LMS4KMU 2.0" in the course description of the moodle system. We have implemented a script, that retrieves all courses from the VC containing that phrase and prepares the courses for the co-operation.

For the SMEs it has to be easy to get an overview of available co-operation offers and to join a co-operation. For that purpose, we have developed a co-operation portal providing all the necessary information, a keyword search as well as an explorative search, recommendations, and direct access to the courses of the LMS (cf. Sect. 2.3).

First Mover or Critical Mass Problem. Convincing incentives, an intuitive search function for co-operations, easy access to courses and automatically adjusted course settings, all form a sound basis but are worthless without co-operation partners. To get the ball rolling, we started a pilot phase with a handful of SMEs which have already had successful co-operations with our university in the past using some lectures of our own and conversant chairs. Among our pilot phase partners were also some of the SME associations acting as communicators.

2.2 Co-operation Types

To give lecturers an idea of the typical kinds of co-operations mediated by a university-wide LMS and to support SMEs in finding suitable co-operations, we have depicted six prototypical co-operation types:

1. *Insight.* SMEs can limit their access to the lecture notes only and other content provided by the lecturer. They are not able to use the discussion forums and cannot access content provided by the students.
2. *Insight and Discussion.* In addition to no. 1, SMEs can also read the discussion forums and actively write contributions to them. They can also access content provided by students.
3. *Rework by Lecturer.* In contrast to no. 2, the lecturer provides special content for SMEs e.g. related to the current situation of the company.
4. *Rework by Students.* Students provide content for the companies.
5. *Arrangement with SME.* The lecturer includes the actual situation and challenges of an SME as a task for the students in a course.
6. *Prearrangement with SME.* The lecturer and an SME conjointly design a new lecture for the students on a given topic.

Co-operation types 1 to 3 are appropriate for typical lectures, whereas types 4 to 6 are more suitable for seminars, practicals and exercise courses. Combinations are often useful: it makes sense to allow SMEs insight into and discussion with the LMS course of a lecture and to co-operate with one of the companies according to type 4, 5 or 6 in overarching seminars. If the main co-operating SME permits it, other SMEs can also access the seminar course as co-operation type 2.

The co-operation types differ in activity and intensity of SME involvement. For us, the degree of activity means whether SME members merely download and read content, or if they provide content or problem definitions themselves. The intensity level indicates how often SMEs interact with the system. Fig. 1 depicts the relationship between co-operation type, SME activity and SME intensity on the left. The boxes symbolize the degrees of freedom, depending on the specifications of the lecturer and the attitude of the SME. Co-operation type

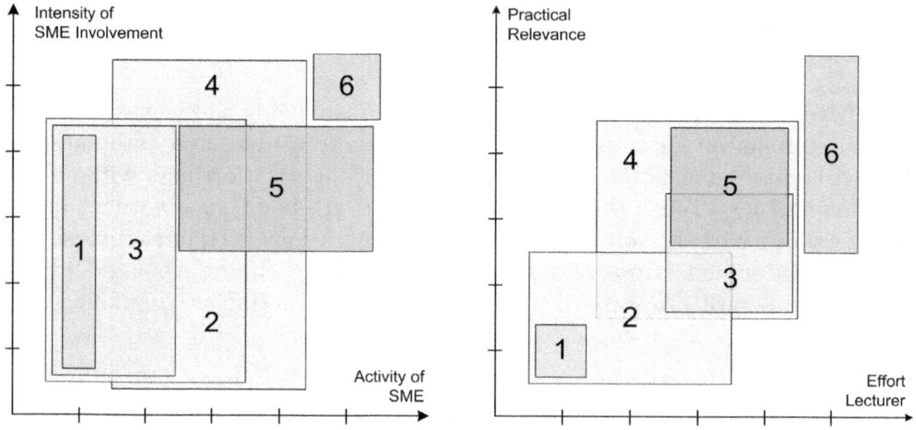

Fig. 1. On the left the relationship between co-operation type, activity, and intensity of SME involvement is depicted. The dashes on the co-ordinate axes always indicate values from *low* to *high*. On the right the relationship between co-operation type, practical relevance for the students, and the additional effort for the lecturer is shown.

1 allows almost no activity of the SME. They only consume content provided by the lecturer. The intensity is up to the SME member: from the date the lecture starts, the member can visit the LMS course and download, read or watch provided content. Co-operation type 2 allows the same range of intensity, but some more activity. The SME member can write postings addressing the lecturer or the students in the discussion forums. Co-operation type 3 allows the same intensity as the before mentioned types. The activity can be higher than in type 1, as discussion forums are accessible, but not as high as in type 2, as the SME and the students see different versions of the content and have therefore no common basis for discussions. Usually a forum just for students and the lecturer and another one exists just for the SMEs and the lecturer. In co-operation type 4, the lecturer has to decide whether the SMEs have to start the co-operation before the beginning of the course and how they have to interact with the students. One possibility is that students rework the content for SMEs in general, and concrete SMEs can give feedback if they want. Another possibility is that SMEs have to join the co-operation before the course starts so that the students can prepare the content for the concrete companies. In that

case, activity and intensity of SME involvement has to be higher. In co-operation type 5, the lecturer arranges the course (or parts of it) together with SMEs. A certain intensity and activity of the SMEs is therefore obligatory. A very high activity and intensity (starting before the beginning of the course and lasting until the end) of SMEs is needed to prearrange a new course conjointly (type 6).

It is clear, that a higher activity and intensity of SME involvement usually means more effort for the lecturer. On the other hand, the practical relevance of the courses will also be higher the more actively and intensively SMEs get involved. On the right of Fig. 1 you can see the relationship between co-operation type, practical relevance, and lecturer's effort.

2.3 Implementation

In this section we describe how we configured and extended the moodle system in order to allow the lecturer to hide content and forums from the company members and also to provide special content and forums only for SMEs. We also explain how we implemented the backend of our co-operation portal and the different frontends (website, social network app, and mobile phone app).

Configuration of the Moodle System. The VC is based upon version 1.9.7 of the open source LMS moodle. In moodle it is possible to define different user groups on the course level. When opening a course for SMEs, it is very useful to define a user group as "students" and another one for "SMEs". The lecturer can assign users to one of the groups manually, but moodle also offers the choice of defining different access keys for different user groups. The lecturer can inform the student of their access key in his lecture, and the access key for SMEs can be deposited in the co-operation portal. When a user matriculates to the LMS course, he will be automatically assigned to the correct user group because of his access key. The lecturer can now easily find out, whether a user is a student or an SME member and define, which group can access forums, questionnaires and other "activities". Unfortunately, it is not possible to hide files and other content from a user group. The solution is the so-called *groupings*, which are declared to be experimental, but these work well in moodle 1.9.7. Groupings are a type of "super groups", which means that groups can in turn be assigned to a grouping. So we enabled the groupings feature in the moodle configuration and now one can create groupings such as "grouping students" and "grouping SMEs" on the course level and assign the corresponding groups. In this way users are assigned to the right groupings transitively and the lecturer can hide copyright protected third person works from the SMEs.

Recently version 2.0 of moodle was released. Groupings are now activated by default, but it is still necessary to enable an experimental feature (this time called "enablegroupmembersonly") to allow files to be hidden from existing groupings.

Co-operation Portal. The co-operation portal has been designed to automate the process of offering co-operations and support the SMEs in finding suitable co-operations, enroll in the courses, and get into contact with lecturers. It allows the SMEs to get an overview of the available co-operations, get detailed information about the lectures, find out how they can get involved, and makes it possible, to join a co-operation directly. SMEs can also use a search and filter function to preselect appropriate co-operations. The use cases can be found in [4].

To minimize the effort for the lecturers and to avoid redundancies, the portal harvests the necessary information from the existing information systems at the University of Bamberg. It establishes a data connection to the VC via the web service extension WSPP[7] which can be added to moodle 1.9.7. WSPP provides most of the required features our portal needs to get information from the VC and to manipulate data inside the VC. The recently released moodle 2.0 offers four built-in web service APIs: AMF (for access from Adobe Flash), REST, SOAP and XML-RPC. The SOAP web service of moodle 2.0 works very similarly to the WSPP extension, but provides only a very limited amount of predefined functions so far. Fortunately, it is much easier to define own functions extending moodle 2.0's SOAP service than it was with the WSPP API in the past.

The portal's backend is a web service, implemented as an extension to the CMS Typo3 and coded in object-oriented PHP. The extension also includes a frontend, consisting of an HTML page serving as container for the actual application, coded in JavaScript and using DOM manipulation for the user interface and communicating with the backend via AJAX requests and JSON responses.

The portal is also available as a social network app using Google's OpenSocial API. In this way we try to exploit the viral effect of social networks to solve the critical mass problem for the collaboration platform [3]. For increased user convenience we are also currently implementing a mobile app of our portal for Android devices.

3 Experiences

We started our project LMS4KMU in October 2008 with seven industrial project partners, four SMEs and three SME alliance organisations (communicators). By the beginning of the summer semester 2009, we had met with our project partners to discuss our ideas and their wishes, roughly designed the co-operation types, prepared the VC for co-operations and implemented a first rudimentary version of our co-operation web portal so that we could launch the pilot phase. Between the summer semester of 2009 and the winter semester of 2010/11 seven lecturers offered 19 co-operations to SMEs, which in sum were joined by 45 practitioners. 10 of the co-operations offered were categorized as Insight and Discussion (type 2), 6 as Arrangement with SME (type 5), 1 as Rework by Students (type 4) and 2 as Prearrangement with SME (type 6). In the next two sections, experiences of the lecturers and SMEs are shown.

3.1 Lecturers

On the VC forum for course tutors we posted information about our project and announced that we were looking for lecturers to join the pilot phase in early

[7] WSPP was developed by OKTech and further developed by Patrick Pollet at INSA de Lyon (http://prope.insa-lyon.fr/~ppollet/pp.ssi).

2009. To our surprise only three lecturers were willing to participate. One opened the VC course of his seminar on business ethics, so that companies could post a question to the forum and students answered the questions in a report. A freelance marketing consultant joined the co-operation and provided the topic "compliance", which was assigned to a student for his report as it matched the general topic of the seminar. A lecturer from the history department wanted to digitalise a historical document with his students and was looking for a company with experiences in document management systems and electronic publishing formats. The seminar was held as a co-operation between the history and media informatics lecturer including students of both fields of study. One SME member joined the VC course because of personal interest in the topic, but no company with experiences in document management systems could be found. Another history lecturer wanted to prearrange courses with SMEs (type 6), but as he did not clearly describe what the topic of the co-operation would have been or what the involvement of the company would be, no industrial co-operation partner could be found. We had expected some lecturers would just open some of their courses for Insight or Insight and Discussion (types 1 or 2) as these were meant to be low-threshold entry co-operations without much effort for the lecturers. We opened our courses Web Engineering, Multimedia Techniques and Information Retrieval for Insight and Discussion. All of them contained the lecture notes, video podcasts of the current lectures and exercises. The Information Retrieval course was designed completely new, including additional interactive applets and other e-learning content [6], but Web Engineering was joined by many more SMEs. To find more lecturers to participate in our project, we sent personal emails to those who had courses that seemed to be interesting for SMEs to us. The chair for marketing offered co-operations of type 2 and 6 and the chair for communication sciences of type 2 and 5. SMEs joined the type 2 co-operations, but not those of types 5 and 6. The chair for cognitive systems offered a usability study for software developing companies. Two SMEs made use of the chance to present themselves and their software to the students and get a profound feedback about potential for increasing usability and customer satisfaction.

The fact that only very few lecturers allow Insight and Discussion indicates that many fear being exploited by the companies. It seems difficult to convince them of this co-operation type as an easy opportunity to get into contact with SMEs and as entrance to more sophisticated co-operations. The small number of participating SMEs is a problem, as lecturers can get into trouble if they plan to arrange or prearrange a course together with SMEs and no appropriate industrial partner can be found. In the case of the usability study, two appropriate companies applied and the lecturer divided the students into two groups. The students were critical, that the workload was higher in contrast to former courses, when only a theoretical problem had to be solved, but the benefits compensate that: the lecturer could establish a mutual trust with one of the companies for further co-operations, student apprentices and tutored bachelor theses.

3.2 SMEs

The feedback from our industrial project partners is largely positive. Apart from one person, everyone felt they had learned interesting new knowledge and the majority acknowledged the benefits for their job. Many also appreciates that they could get direct and fast benefit for low input. On the other hand, many participants regretted that they had not become part of a network. While this is not true for the SMEs participating in co-operation types 5 and 6, it is unfortunately true for co-operation type 2. Almost none of the SME members took the chance to use the discussion forums for talking with lecturers and students. Some SME members asked about the possibility of receiving certificates. As we explained in Chap. 2, certificates are at the moment only available for enrolled students. This may change in the near future, when the prospective so-called "modular studies" for company members becomes part of the study forms defined in the Bavarian Higher Education Act (BayHSchG).

We have seen that SMEs only joined co-operations that promised direct benefits. Two companies, which develop and sell document management systems were not interested in joining the co-operation about digitalising ancient documents, although they could have highlighted the merits of their software and tried to find future customers or employees. In contrast, both participated in the usability study and were impressed by the professional feedback and the concrete recommendations on how to improve their user interfaces. One of the companies offered to coach a bachelor thesis, where one of the students could design a web user interface according to the findings of the usability study, but when a student was found, the company withdrew because they were trying to gain a large new customer and had therefore no time to continue with the web user interface and the bachelor thesis. Such problems are typical for co-operations with SME.

4 Conclusion and Outlook

The experiences of the last four semesters show that a university-wide LMS can enable successful co-operations for the benefit of SMEs, lecturers, and students. Co-operations of type 2 can be set up very easily without noticeable extra work for the lecturers, but to achieve network buildung and bi-directional knowledge transfer more effort is needed. In the cases when participating SMEs could be found, the effort of the lecturers to arrange or prearrange courses with SMEs has been beneficial and had pay-offs in increased practical relevance for the students, job offerings for student apprentices, bachelor theses and the establishment of a co-operative culture.

As a next step, we will analyse the wishes and reservations of SMEs and lecturers concerning co-operations and knowledge transfer by interviewing them directly. We will then adapt our approach accordingly, so as to reach the critical mass of participants of both lecturers and SMEs to guarantee the sustainability of our project.

References

1. Chew, E., Jones, N., Turner, D.: Critical review of the blended learning models based on maslow's and vygotsky's educational theory. In: Fong, J., Kwan, R., Wang, F.L. (eds.) ICHL 2008. LNCS, vol. 5169, pp. 40–53. Springer, Heidelberg (2008)
2. Farvaque, N., Voss, E.: Guidelines for vocational education in small and medium-sized enterprises (SMEs) (in German). Amt für Veröff. der Europ. Union, Luxemburg (2010), Ms. abgeschl. im (August 2009), `http://dx.doi.org/10.2767/33248`
3. Fries, T., Boosz, S., Henrich, A.: Integrating industrial partners into e-teaching efforts – using social networks to support the initiation of co-operations (accepted for publication). In: Int'l Symposium of Information Science (ISI). Hochschulverband Informationswissenschaft and IuK-Initiative Wissenschaft, Hildesheim (2011) (in German)
4. Fries, T., Henrich, A.: Integrating industrial partners into e-teaching efforts – a portal to support the initiation of co-operations. In: Proceedings of the IADIS Int'l Conf. E-learning 2010, vol. 1, pp. 89–96. IADIS Press, Freiburg (2010)
5. Fries, T., Henrich, A.: Integrating industrial partners into e-teaching efforts – legal pitfalls and circumventions. In: Online Educa Berlin 2010, ICWE GmbH, Berlin (2010); STA72 Legal Challanges
6. Henrich, A., Sieber, S.: Blended learning and pure e-learning concepts for information retrieval: experiences and future directions. Information Retrieval 12(2), 117–147 (2009)
7. Henrich, A., Sieber, S.: Hybrid learning: "neither fish nor fowl" or "the golden mean". In: Tsang, P., Cheung, S.K., Lee, V.S., Huang, R. (eds.) ICHL 2010. LNCS, vol. 6248, pp. 82–93. Springer, Heidelberg (2010)
8. Henrich, A., Sieber, S., Wolf, S.U.: Integrating a university-wide LMS into the system landscape of a university – a pragmatic approach (in German). In: Dötsch, V., Hering, K., Schaar, F. (eds.) Flexibly integratable e-Learning – Near future or utopia? (in German), pp. 57–76. Dötsch, Volker and Hering, Klaus and Schaar, Florian, Leipzig (2007)
9. Henrich, A., Wolf, S.U.: Virtual Campus of the University of Bamberg: a comprehensive eLearning system based on moodle (in German). In: WEL 2006, HTWK Leipzig und Fachbereich Informatik, Mathematik und Naturwissenschaften HTWK Leipzig, Leipzig (2006)
10. Renker, C.: Marketing in Medium-sized Businesses – Requirements, Strategies, Activities (in German). Schmidt, Berlin (2009); 3., neu bearb. Aufl.
11. Wegmann, J.: Business Economics of Medium-sized Businesses – Textbook for Practitioners (in German). Oldenbourg, München, online-ausg. edn (2006), `http://dx.doi.org/10.1524/9783486593082`
12. Wesel, M.A.: Corporate Governance in Medium-sized Businesses – Requirements, Specialities, Implementation (in German): Univ., Diss. Osnabrück, 2009. Management und Wirtschaft Studien, vol. 69. Schmidt, Berlin (2010)

Optimization Based Multimedia Performance to Enhance Blended Learning Experience in Constrained Low Bandwidth Environment

Nazir Ahmad Suhail, Jude T. Lubega, and Gilbert Maiga

College of Computing and Information Sciences,
Makerere University, P.O. Box 7062, Kampala, Uganda
nazir_suhail@yahoo.co.uk, {jlubega,gmaiga}@cit.mak.ac.ug

Abstract. The efficient transmission of multimedia applications and time sensitive applications in particular, over the heterogeneous networks is a challenging research problem that requires investigation. This paper focuses on an experimental testbed designed to verify the theoretical concept; performance of multimedia content can be improved by optimizing both network and application. User-driven parameter 'latency' was used to achieve the objective, during transmission of multimedia files (video, audio, graphics, and text) over a wireless network. Results indicated that latency factor was reduced significantly, when optimization technique was applied on both network and multimedia content as compared to applying on each component individually. This work falls within the scope of "Optimization Technique for Implementation of Blended Learning in Constrained Low Bandwidth Environment" [1].

Keywords: Blended learning, constrained low bandwidth environment, optimization, QoS.

1 Introduction

Features that respond to offer new educational opportunities in a flexible and cost effective manner to meet the growing demand of education are changing the spectrum of higher education around the world. This rapidly changing environment and advances in Information Communications Technologies (ICTs) fueled the universities to adopt e-learning at a greater pace. And the introduction of the concept of blended learning model is a natural start for the universities in developing countries which is pursued by many organizations in developed world. Following the global trend many Higher Education (HE) institutions in developing countries are exploring the possibilities as how to embrace the new educational paradigm [10], driven by the demand coupled with other factors; convenience, lower costs, flexibility and advanced technologies [4]. Although blended learning is an effective and efficient instructional delivery mode, it is not a panacea, there can be some key challenges [8]such as constrained low bandwidth environment to its adoption, particularly in the context of organizations in Least Developed Countries (LDCs) [2], [9]. Despite the fact that a number of blended learning frameworks (e.g., [5], [6], [7], [8], [9], [11]) have been developed,

R. Kwan et al. (Eds.): ICHL 2011, LNCS 6837, pp. 188–199, 2011.

the issue of implementing an effective and efficient blended learning process in constrained low bandwidth environment has not been adequately addressed. The effective and efficient blended learning process in relation to this research, may include optimizing the multimedia (video, audio, graphics and text) performance by developing content that is specific to the needs and sensitive to the challenges of constrained low bandwidth environment [15], and optimizing the network efficiency. However, the issue was addressed in a recent work of Suhail and Lubega [1] that asserts that multimedia (video, audio, graphics, and text) performance can be improved by optimizing both network and the application.

There is significant evidence that researchers tested their theories through a scientific research process in the form of experimental studies [14], an authentic method. On that pretext, an experimental testbed was designed aimed to observe the behavior of various media types (video, audio, graphics, and text) to verify the theoretical concept "performance of multimedia content can be improved by optimizing both network and application" [1] to enhance the blended learning implementation process in LDCs. The performance metric 'latency' was used during transmission of various media files over a wireless network. The reason of choosing 'latency' as a performance evaluation metric among others, was that it is a perceived user-satisfaction parameter, where user satisfaction level is increased with reduced download time (latency) of e-learning content from a remote server that is a part of blended learning process and the choice is in line with ITU-recommendations [3]. Results indicated that latency in multimedia was reduced significantly when optimization technique was applied on both network and multimedia applications.

2 Technological Terms

2.1 Constrained Low Bandwidth Environment

In relation to this study, the constrained low bandwidth environment refers to low bandwidth (insufficient bandwidth as compared to needs) coupled with other bottlenecks such as; viruses, Internet worms, spam, misuse and mismanagement of bandwidth that contribute to network congestion[16].

2.2 Blended Learning

A variety of definitions exist in literature for the term blended learning. However, in education, blended learning may refer to a thoughtful combination of best experiences in traditional face-to-face classroom learning and e-learning [17]. And e-learning definition used in this paper is "a combination of network and multimedia learning" [1].

2.3 Quality of Service (QoS)

In computer network system, Quality of Service (QoS) refers to prioritizing a specific type of traffic (e.g., video and audio) over other network traffic by allocating specific amounts of bandwidth to various classes.

3 Experimental Testbed

To observe and evaluate the exact behavior of multimedia performance an experimental testbed as shown in Figure1 was designed. The testbed aimed to apply optimization technique on both network and multimedia content to determine the performance of application during transmission over wireless network. The User-driven multimedia performance 'latency' parameter [3] was used to achieve the goal.

3.1 Materials and Method

The experimental testbed of this research used following hardware and software:

- Cisco router 2801 software C2801-ADVIPSERVICES K9-M version 12.4(6)T7 & CISCO 2950 switch
- Indoor Wimax Internet Antena
- 2 Computers running Microsoft Window XP Professional
- Files converting and optimization tools from Internet resources (e.g., "Total Video Converter" etc.)
- VE Catchlite (Latency Measuring Tool that can also measure packet loss)
- Straight through UTP cables
- A Broad Band 128 kb Internet connection
- Video Files : .flv, .avi, and .mp4 (commonly used compression standard for video formats)
- Audio Files: wav, m4a, and mp3 (commonly used compression standard for audio formats)
- Graphic files: bmp, tiff, and JPEG (commonly used compression standard for graphics)
- Text Files: Power Point(PPT); PPT(unoptimized) and PPT(optimized)

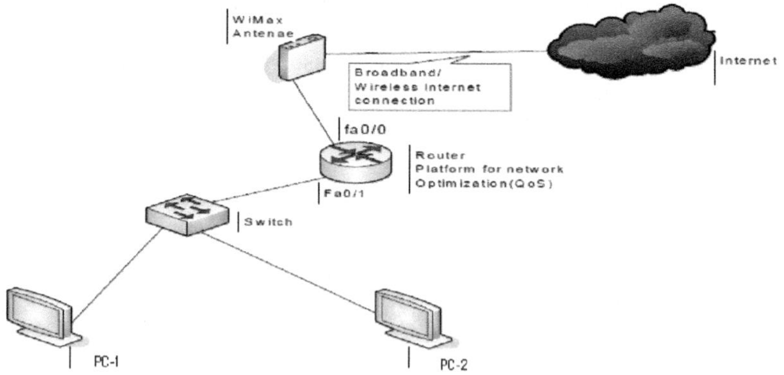

Fig. 1. Experimental Testbed System Architecture

Fig.1 describes the System Architecture of the experimental testbed where two client computers PC-1 and PC-2 are connected to a Cisco router through a switch. The router has two interfaces; fa0/0 connecting to the Internet and the other fa0/1 on network connects to our LAN. PC-1 receives multimedia files from the Internet and tests them for latency, whereas PC-2 congests the network and is used as a network "destabilizer". Table 1 shows the device addressing scheme used to configure router and router Interfaces to link PC-1and PC-2 and to provide Network Address Translation (NAT) service that translated our LAN IP addresses to Internet.

Table 1. Device Addressing Scheme

Device	IP Address	Subnet Mask
Interface fa0/0	216.104.203.125	255.255.255.224
Interface fa0/1	192.168.1.254	255.255.255.0
PC-1	192.168.1.1	255.255.255.0
PC-2	192.168.1.2	255.255.255.0

Unoptimized and optimized multimedia files of all types (video, audio, graphics, and text) mentioned above were uploaded on Internet aiming to download them in constrained low bandwidth environment and evaluate their performance by activating "VE Catchlite" tool installed on client computer PC-1.

For video files we captured .flv file from the Internet and by using a video conversion tool converted the same file to .avi, for the sake of consistency. Afterwards, all these files were optimized (converted-compressed) to.mp4. The same procedure was adopted for audio and graphic files. However, for text files we used inbuilt compression technique for optimizing the Power Point file but other optimizing tool on the Internet are also available for use.

4 Measuring Multimedia Performance

4.1 Multimedia Performance for Unoptimized Network

Below are screen shots taken by 'Net Catchlite' tool that measured latency, when unoptimized and optimized Multimedia files from various categories were transmitted over the unoptimized network. In the graph green curve shows the latency measured in milliseconds (ms) with minimum/average/maximum values shown at the bottom, and the other red curve is for 'packet loss' as latency and packet loss are inter-related.

Latency measurement for unoptimized and optimized video files: With unoptimized network state Fig. 2 and Fig. 3 present the screen shots for .flv, and .avi video files while Fig. 4 shows the screen shot when these files were converted-compressed (optimized) to .mp4. The average latency for .flv, .avi and .mp4 as shown in the graphs is 559, 581, and 422 ms, respectively.

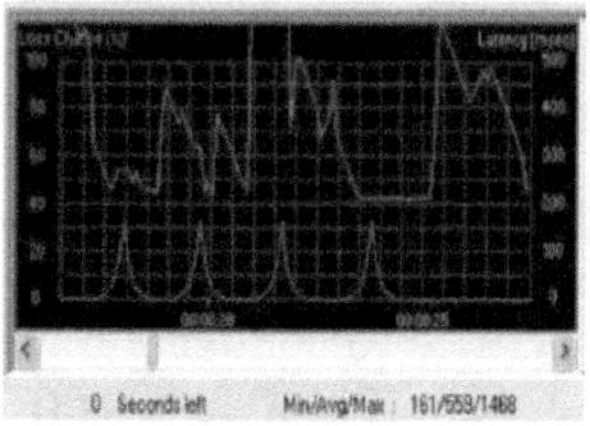

Fig. 2. Latency for .flv

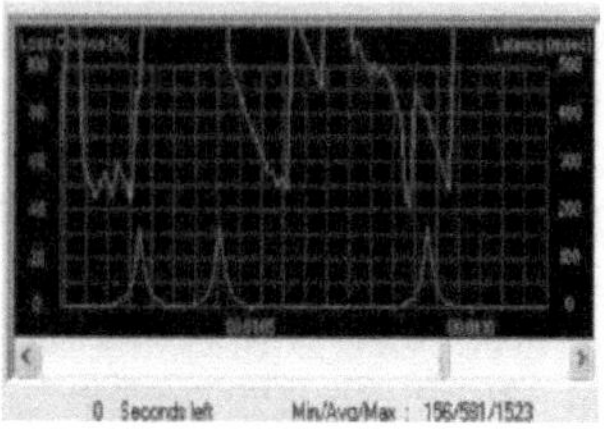

Fig. 3. Latency for .avi

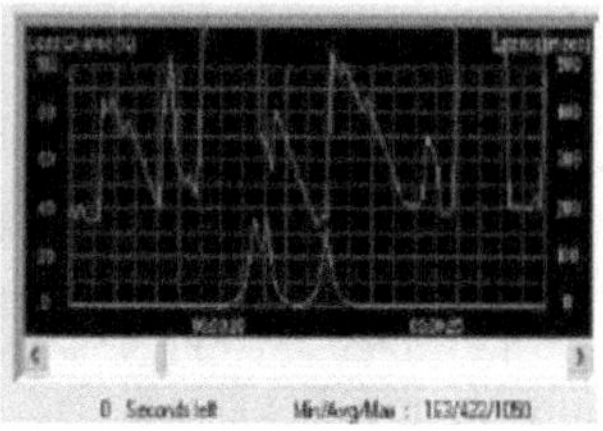

Fig. 4. Latency for .mp4

Latency measurement for unoptimized and optimized audio files: With unoptimized network state, Fig. 5 and Fig. 6 present the screen shots of wav and m4a audio files when they are unoptimized while Fig.7 shows the screen shot when they are converted-compressed (optimized) to mp3. The average latency for wav, m4a, and mp3 as shown in the graphs is 270, 249, and 217ms, respectively.

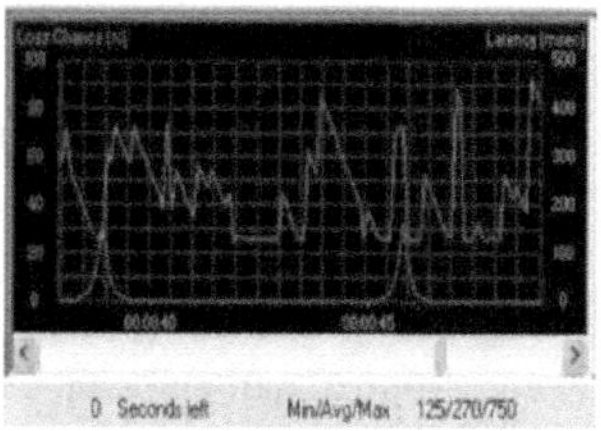

Fig. 5. Latency for wav

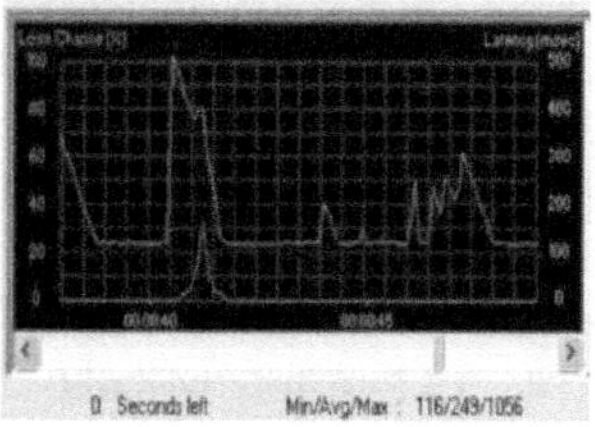

Fig. 6. Latency for m4a

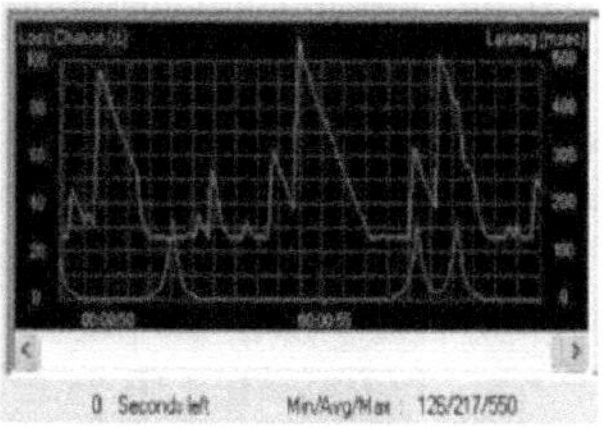

Fig. 7. Latency for mp3

Latency measurement for unoptimized and optimized graphic files: With unoptimized network state, Fig. 8 and Fig. 9 present the screen shots of bmp and tiff graphic files when they are unoptimized while Fig. 10 shows the screen shot when they are converted-compressed (optimized) to JPEG. The average latency for bmp, tiff and JPEG as shown in the graphs is 408, 323, and 286 ms, respectively.

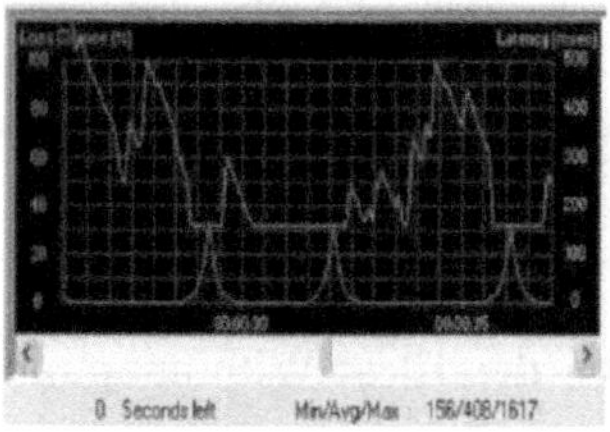

Fig. 8. Latency for bmp

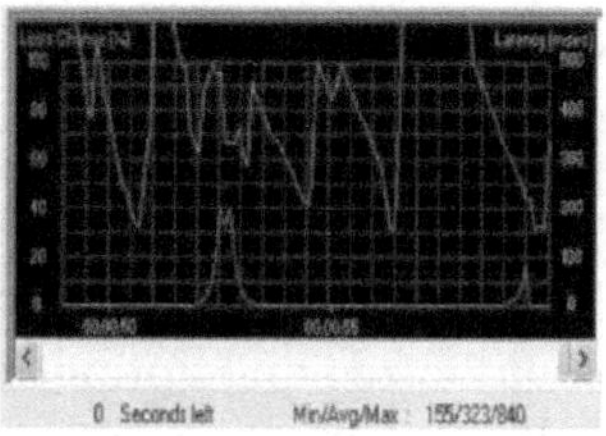

Fig. 9. Latency for tiff

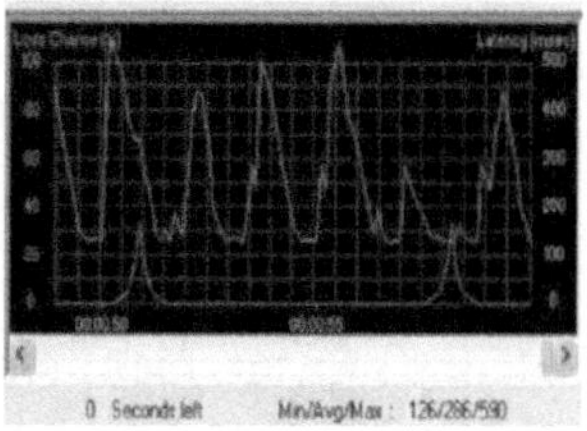

Fig. 10. Latency for JPEG

Latency measurement for unoptimized and optimized Text files: With unoptimized network state, Fig.11and Fig.12 present the screen shots of unoptimized and optimized Text (Power Point-PPT) files, having latency 246 and 203 ms, respectively.

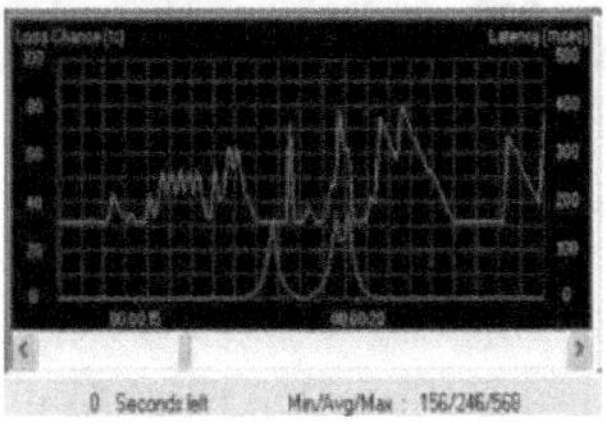

Fig. 11. Latency for PPT

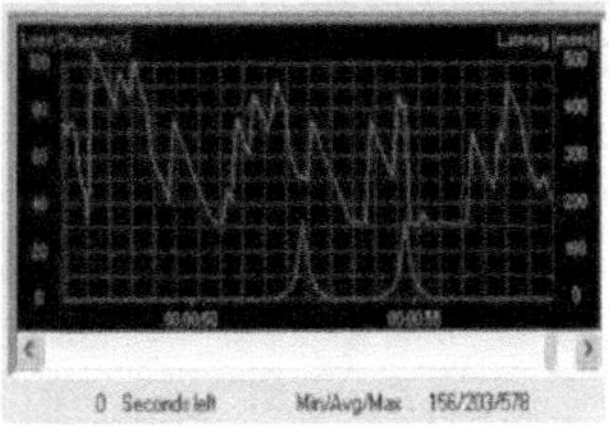

Fig. 12. Latency for PPT

4.2 Network Optimization

Next, this testbed optimized the network by configuring policy map on router interface by allocating specific amount of bandwidth to various classes and prioritizing a specific type of traffic (e.g., video and audio) over other network applications, in an attempt to apply Quality of Service (QoS). For efficient transmission of multimedia contents in constrained low bandwidth environment where network is congested, it is vital to apply QoS [18].

Latency measurement for unoptimized and optimized video files: With optimized network state, Fig.13 and Fig.14 provide the screen shots for video files .flv and .avi, respectively when they are unoptimized while Fig.15 presents the screen shot when they are converted-compressed (optimized) to .mp4. The average latency for .flv, .avi and .mp4 as shown in the graphs is 221, 242, and 212 ms, respectively.

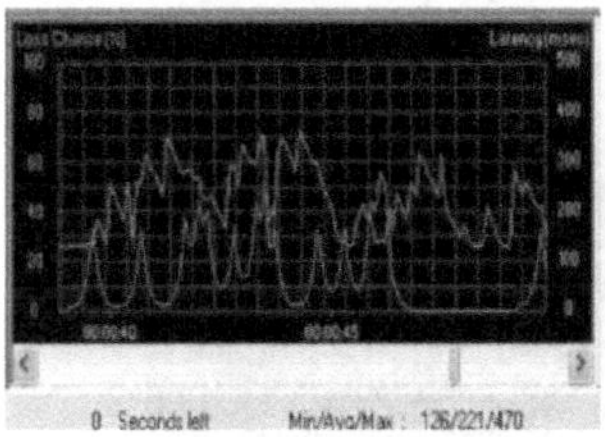

Fig. 13. Latency for .flv

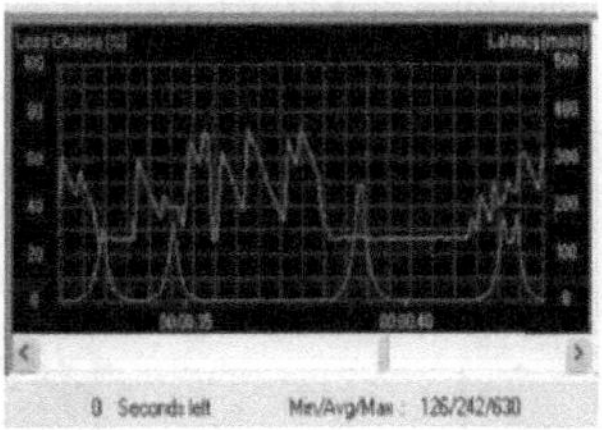

Fig. 14. Latency for .avi

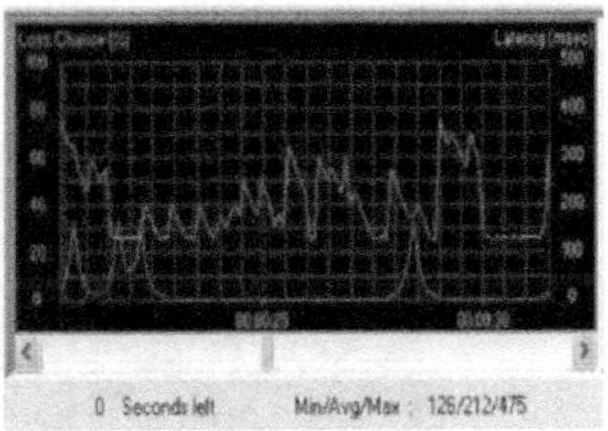

Fig. 15. Latency for .mp4

Latency measurement for unoptimized and optimized audio files: With optimized network state, Fig.16 and Fig. 17 present the screen shots for unoptimized wav and m4a audio files while Fig.18 presents the screen shot when they are converted-compressed (optimized) to mp3. The average latency for wav, m4a and mp3 as shown in the graphs is 186, 170, and 160 ms, respectively.

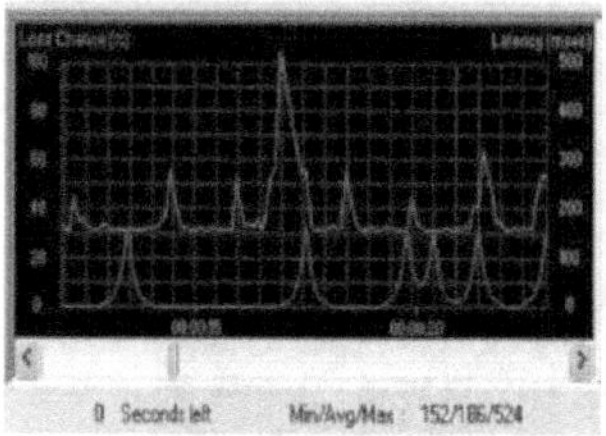

Fig. 16. Latency for wav

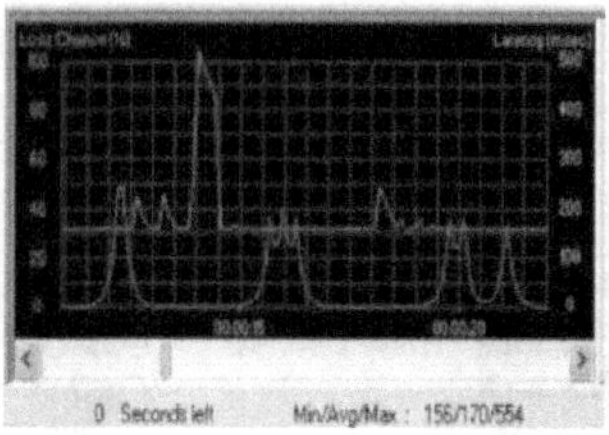

Fig. 17. Latency for m4a

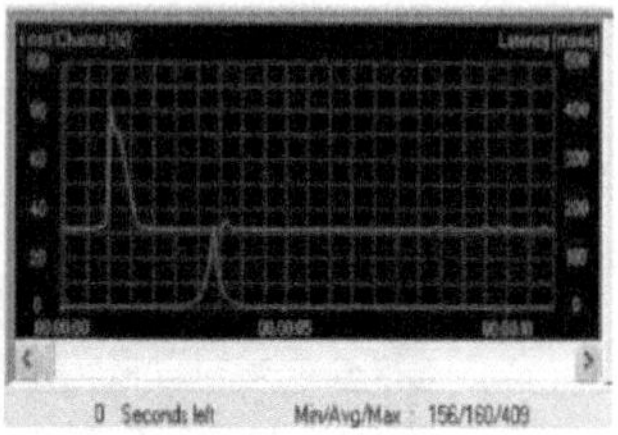

Fig. 18. Latency mp3

Latency measurement for unoptimized and optimized graphic files: With optimized network state, Fig. 19 and Fig. 20 present the screen shots for unoptimized bmp and tiff graphic files while Fig. 21 provides the screen shot when they are converted-compressed (optimized) to JPEG. The average latency as shown in the graphs for bmp, tiff, and JPEG is 264, 223, and 195ms, respectively.

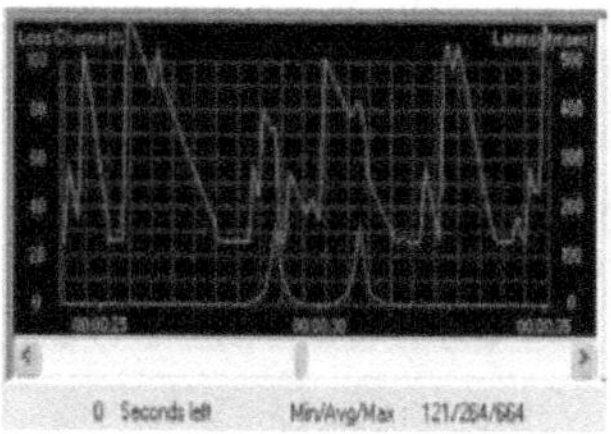

Fig. 19. Latency for bmp

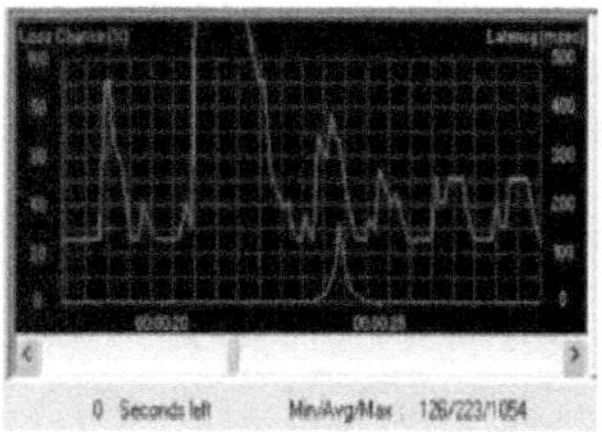

Fig. 20. Latency for tif

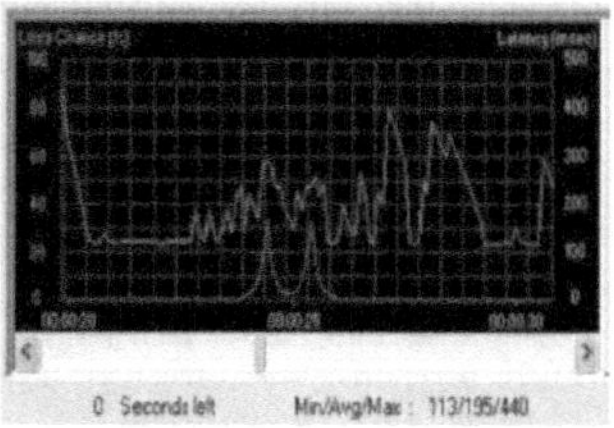

Fig. 21. Latency for JPEG

Latency measurement for unoptimized and optimized Text file: With optimized network state, Fig. 22 and Fig. 23 present the screen shots for unoptimized and optimized Text (PPT) files, respectively. The average latency for unoptimized and optimized PPT files as shown in the graphs is 209 and 193ms, respectively.

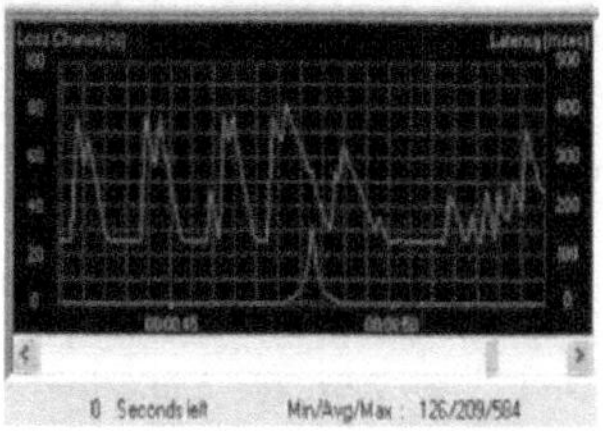

Fig. 22. Latency for PPT

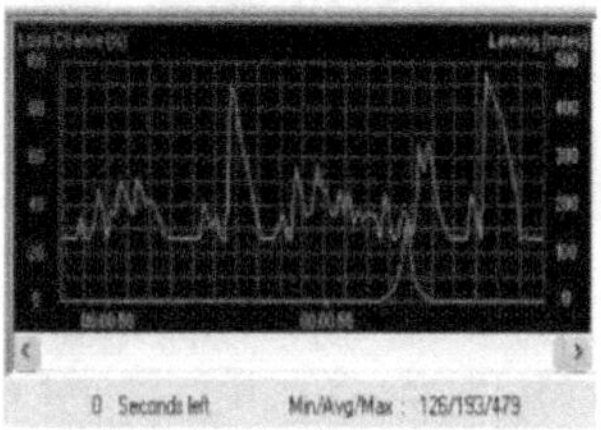

Fig. 23. Latency for PPT

5 Results and Analysis

Some of the multimedia performance improvement techniques have been used on both network and multimedia contents as described in the testbed, and results calculated in terms of the user–driven parameter 'latency' and plotted.

The performance of multimedia content was observed and evaluated in following four Phases:

Phase I: Unoptimized Network & Unoptimized Multimedia (UNUM)
Phase II: Unoptimized Network & Optimized Multimedia (UNOM
Phase III: Optimized Network & Unoptimized Multimedia (ONUM)
Phase IV: Optimized Network & Optimized Multimedia (ONOM)

The analysis of latency results for the identified video, audio, graphics, and text files is shown in Tables 2- 8.

Video Files

Table 2. Analysis of .flv latency results

Phases	Optimized Network	Optimized Multimedia	Average Latency (ms)	Percentage of Latency Reduction
I-(UNUM)	X	X	559	N/A
II-(UNOM)	X	√	422	24.51 %
III-(ONUM)	√	X	221	60.46 %
IV- (ONOM)	√	√	212	62.07 %

Table 3. Analysis of .avi latency results

Phases	Optimized Network	Optimized Multimedia	Average Latency (ms)	Percentage of Latency Reduction
I (UNUM)	X	X	581	N/A
II (UNOM)	X	√	422	27.37 %
III (ONUM)	√	X	242	58.34 %
IV (ONOM)	√	√	212	63.51.%

Audio Files

Table 4. Analysis of wav latency results

Phases	Optimized Network	Optimized Multimedia	Average Latency (ms)	Percentage of Latency Reduction
I (UNUM)	X	X	270	N/A
II (UNOM)	X	✓	217	19.62 %
III (ONUM)	✓	X	186	31.11 %
IV (ONOM)	✓	✓	160	40.74 %

Table 5. Analysis of m4a latency results

Phases	Optimized Network	Optimized Multimedia	Average Latency (ms)	Percentage of Latency Reduction
I (UNUM)	X	X	249	N/A
II (UNOM)	X	✓	217	12.85 %
III (ONUM)	✓	X	170	31.72%
IV (ONOM)	✓	✓	160	35.74 %

Graphics

Table 6. Analysis of bmp latency results

Phases	Optimized Network	Optimized Multimedia	Average Latency (ms)	Percentage of Latency Reduction
I (UNUM)	X	X	408	N/A
II (UNOM)	X	✓	286	29.90 %
III (ONUM)	✓	X	264	35.29 %
IV (ONOM)	✓	✓	195	52.20 %

Table 7. Analysis of tiff latency result

Phases	Optimized Network	Optimized Multimedia	Average Latency (ms)	Percentage of Latency Reduction
I (UNUM)	X	X	323	N/A
II (UNOM)	X	✓	286	11.45 %
III (ONUM)	✓	X	223	30.95 %
IV (ONOM)	✓	✓	195	39.62 %

Text Files

Table 8. Analysis of Power point (PPT) latency results

Phases	Optimized Network	Optimized Multimedia	Average Latency (ms)	Percentage of Latency Reduction
I (UNUM)	X	X	246	N/A
II (UNOM)	X	✓	203	17.47 %
III (ONUM)	✓	X	209	15.04 %
IV (ONOM)	✓	✓	193	21.54 %

An overview of the analysis of latency results for video, audio, and graphic files shown in above tables indicate that in phase II (Unoptimized Network & Optimized Multimedia) latency reduced, in phase III (Optimized Network & Unoptimized Multimedia) it further reduced, and it reduced significantly in phase IV(Optimized Network & Optimized Multimedia) in comparison with phase I (Unoptimized Network & Unoptimized Multimedia). However, for text files phase III latency was higher than phase II but in Phase IV the trend of latency reduction was preserved.

In summary, latency factor reduced significantly when both network and multimedia contents were optimized as compared to when each was optimized individually, verifying the fact that multimedia performance can be improved when network and application are both optimized.

6 Conclusion

The paper has verified and validated the theory, "performance of multimedia content can be improved by optimizing both network and application" [1] successfully by measuring the performance of various media types and achieved the main objective of the study. The performance evaluation was based on user-driven multimedia metric 'latency'. And at the same time, it has given a way forward of protecting the valuable institutional resource (bandwidth) through prioritizing time-sensitive applications to minimize delays [12] that would contribute to increase the perceived user-satisfaction level. Also it is worthy to note that to deliver a high performing multimedia content to users in the context of constrained low bandwidth environment is a big milestone indeed, as in return it would enhance the process of implementing blended learning in LDCs.

This research focused on evaluating the performance of learning content which is an integral part of blended learning process, linked practical to theoretical foundations and to the relevant literature aimed to make both practical and scientific contribution [14], which shows that there were sufficient theoretical background and principles that guided the practice. In other words, the study has bridged the gap between theory and practice and has laid the foundation stone for continuous further research in the area that can inform subsequent developments of blended learning intervention [13]. Future research may include finding a mechanism to improve the performance of multimedia content to increase further the level of user satisfaction by reducing latency factor more than shown in the current study, and to study multimedia performance in different context.

References

1. Suhail, N.A., Lubega, J.: Optimization Technique for Implementation of Blended Learning in Constrained Low Bandwidth Environment. In: Tatnall, A., Kereteletswe, O.C., Visscher, A. (eds.) ITEM 2010. IFIP Advances in Information and Communication Technology, vol. 348, pp. 166–173. Springer, Heidelberg (2011)
2. Hatakka, M.: Build it and They Will Come? - Inhibiting Factors for Reuse of Open Content in Developing Countries. The Elect. J. of Info Syst. in Dev. Count. 37(5), 1–16 (2009)
3. End-user multimedia QoS categories. In: ITU-T Recommendation G.1010 ITU-T, G-Series Recommandations, transmission systems and media, digital systems and networks (2001)
4. Hanna, D.E.: Higher Education in an Era of Digital Competition: Emerging Organizational Models. JALN 2(1) (1998)
5. Bersin and associates: 4-factor Blended Learning Framework, What Works in Blended Learning. In: ASTDs Source of E-learning, Learning Circuits (2003), http://www.bersin.20.com/ 510.654.8500
6. De Vries, J.: E-learning strategy: An e-learning Framework for Success. Blue Streak learning, quality learning solutions (2005), http://www.bottomlineresults.elearningcentre.typepad.com/whatsnew/2005/08/strat.html
7. Khan, B.H., Ealy, D.: A framework for Web-based authoring systems. In: Khan, B.H. (ed.) Web-based training, pp. 355–364 (2001)
8. PDSEN: Professional Development Series E-News letter. In: The National Youth Develop-ment Learning Network, A Blended Learning Strategy for the Professional Development of Youth workers (2005), http://www.nassembly.org

9. A Blended Learning Model. In: Training: A Critical Success Factor in Implementing a Technology Solution, North America Radiant Systems (2003), `http://www.radiantsystems.co`
10. Dakar+7 Education for all in Africa, Dakar, UNESCO (2007)
11. Faridha, M.: Towards Enhancing Learning with Information and Communication Technollogy in Universities. MCS Dissertation report, Makerere University, Kampala (2005)
12. Palmieri, F.: Streaming Networks: A Differentiated Service Approach. In: EC-VIP-MC, 4th EURASIP Conference focused on Video Image Processing and multimedia Communications, Zagreb (2003), `http://www.atics.info`
13. Heinze, A.: Blended Learning facilitated by Conversational Framework: An action research on the part time course in the University of Salford, PhD interim report (2005)
14. Botha, J., van der Westhuizen, D., De Swardt, E.: Towards appropriate methodologies to research interactive learning using a design experiment to assess a learning programme for complex thinking. I. J.of Edu. and Dev. using ICT 1(2), 105–117 (2005)
15. Omwenga, E., Waema, T., Wagacha, P.: A model for introducing and implementing e-learning for delivery of educational content within the African context. A. J. of Sc. and Eng. Series 5(1), 34–46 (2004)
16. Optimizing Internet bandwidth in developing countries higher education. In: INASP (2003)
17. Harvey, S.: Building Effective Blended Learning Programs. Issue of Educational Technology 43(6), 51–54 (2003)
18. Abbasi, A.A., Iqbal, J., Malik, A.N.A.: Novel QoS Optimization Architecture for 4G Netw-orks. World Academy of Science, Engineering and Technology (2010)

E-learning Readiness Assessment Model: A Case Study of Higher Institutions of Learning in Uganda

Godfrey Omoda-Onyait and Jude T. Lubega

Makerere University, School of Computing and Informatics Technology
Tel.: +256-41-540628
{Gonyait,jlubega}@cit.mak.ac.ug

Abstract. Uganda faces challenges in her efforts to achieve her goal "education for all", as a developing country. E-learning has been suggested as an alternative approach that can overcome these challenges involved in reaching underserved students. It is therefore important for an institution to know if it is ready for e-learning. This study examined the readiness for e-learning by Ugandan institutions of higher learning and proposed ways to encourage the use and development of e-learning systems aimed at up-lifting the education standards of the country. Data collected from eight Ugandan universities on analysis revealed that: awareness, culture, technology, pedagogy and content need to be considered in e-learning readiness assessment. These results together with the review of existing models for e-learning readiness assessment led to the development of a modified model for e-learning readiness assessment. Each layer corresponds to the attribute that is to be used for assessing the institutional e-learning readiness.

Keywords: E-learning, e-learning readiness, Higher Institutions of Learning.

1 Introduction

Uganda faces challenges in her efforts to achieve her goal "education for all", as a developing country. This is because of the increasing demand for higher education with limited resources and large numbers of students. The demand for education in Africa exceeds the ability to deliver thus, it is not offered to significant portions of the population [1]. E-Learning has been suggested as an alternative approach that can overcome many of the challenges involved in reaching underserved students [2]. The underserved students are those who have limited access to educational resources due to their location and their large numbers. E-learning has the potential to enable Africa to achieve education for all [1], which is in line with the goal for developing nations. While technology has enabled online education in many countries, the same cannot be said for African public universities [3]. E-learning is the use of ICT as mediating devices that allow learners to access learning resources that inform them of new ideas, reflected on them and integrate into their existing knowledge [4]. It can also be defined as a type of learning meant to enhance the learning process using electronic means. Most educational institutions in developing countries are unfamiliar with e-Learning, have low levels of computer availability, access, familiarity and Internet penetration which leads to skepticism about the feasibility of this approach [2].

R. Kwan et al. (Eds.): ICHL 2011, LNCS 6837, pp. 200–211, 2011.

E-learning has been identified as the future of learning worldwide since the powerful platform of the internet has accelerated the speed of communication [5]. E-learning is good for African nations; they can access recent and quality information for learning, hence increasing on their knowledge and their standard of education [7]. Adoption and implementation of e-learning needs to be done carefully because other researchers [9] have warned the stakeholders interested in it to take care in order to avoid cost overruns, unappealing training products and failure in general. The adoption of e-learning by many institutions in developing countries has been carried out in relation to specific models borrowed. The educational requirements and challenges faced by these developing countries vary from country to country. The borrowed models have greatly contributed to the challenges faced by institutions because they do not suit their contextual setting [12]. Meeting these challenges has been especially difficult for those looking forward to validate a measure for institutional readiness for e-learning. There are many examples of failed e-learning events [12]; hence it is necessary to modify such models in order to address the challenges faced by the developing countries in their attempts to embrace e-learning technology. This research work on e-learning readiness assessment is crucial because:

a) There is high demand for higher education in Uganda, with its limited resources.
b) The rapid growth and evolution of ICT and teaching-learning technologies makes it crucial that we understand what is needed for higher institutions to investment in e-learning.
c) Existing models have so far been designed for and tested only against business organizations and higher education institutions such as universities in developed countries [9]. Therefore, a design of a model for e-learning readiness assessment suitable for developing countries is necessary.

The purpose of this research is to investigate factors affecting e-learning readiness for an institution and design an e-learning readiness assessment model for institutions of higher learning in developing countries. This paper specifically includes:

a) To establish the factors influencing the e-learning readiness of an institution.
b) To design a model for assessing institutional e-learning readiness.

This study focuses on the Ugandan experience of higher education institutions of learning and will also benefit other developing countries that are exploring the use of e-learning technology. The next sections of this paper examine the existing literature on e-learning, identifying the existing models of e-learning readiness assessment in use and finally suggest a model suitable for use in developing countries.

2 E-learning in Higher Institutions of Learning

Despite the efforts of the developing countries to integrate e-learning into education institutions of higher learning, it has not been effectively done. Several challenges hinder its successful integration in higher education system. Just having all the technological hardware and software available for learning is not enough to start an e-learning course. There is a need for organizations to define clear and comprehensive strategies for the integration of e-learning in their delivery processes in order to respond to the new learner market demands, their changing needs and expectations. If Higher Education Institutions of learning do not embrace e-learning technology, they will be left behind the globalization era [19]. Most educational institutions and organizations are interested in making use of e-learning but they are not sure of the parameters to use in order to assess their readiness for e-learning technology. Therefore, it is necessary to come up with a model for e-learning readiness assessment to guide the institutions and organization in how to embrace e-learning technology.

The development and implementation of ICT in the education sector has posed a challenge to the traditional learning environment by introducing new educational tools, including e-learning [14]. ICT integration in learning processes depends on the support of stakeholders [15]. This explains why the importation of ICT related equipment is not taxed in Uganda. In this ICT driven education delivery, the major weaknesses in the implementation of a comprehensive e-learning strategy that would make a sustainable and viable economic and pedagogical solution in the long – term are: the lack of good quality e-learning content, provision of training and support to teachers/trainers in parallel with the organizational changes in the educational systems [20]. Most African countries have inefficient ICT related infrastructure [1]. A survey carried out by African Virtual University revealed that, internet connectivity in tertiary institutions in Africa is inadequate, expensive and poorly managed [16].

2.1 E-learning Readiness Assessment Models

Several readiness assessment and measurement models have been proposed some of which are summarized in table 1 below.

Table 1. A Summary of the E-learning Readiness Assessment and Measurement Models

A Seven Category Model Aydin and Tasci (2005)	**An Eight Category Model** Chapnic (2005)	**A Three Category Model** Psycharis (2005)	**A Five Category Model** Mohd (2001)
1. Human resource **2. LMS** **3. IT** **4. Finance** **5. Vendor**	**1. Human resource** **2. Equipment readiness** **3. Technological skill** **4. Financial readiness**	**1. Resources** - Technological readiness - Economic readiness - Human readiness	**1. Technology**
6. Content	**5. Content readiness**	**2. Education** - Content availability - Structure of content	**2. Pedagogic aspects**
7. Learners	**6. Environmental readiness** **7. Sociological readiness** **8. Psychological readiness**	**3. Environment** - Culture - Political context - Legal context	**3. Environment** **4. Learners** **5. Context**

A comparison of the four models shows some common attributes namely: 1. **Resources**, 2. **Content**, 3. **Environment**. These models were developed based on developed countries; which are not suitable for Uganda. Based on this research and literature review, a modified model is proposed as in figure 1.

3 Methodology

3.1 Data Collection

Questionnaires were used to collect data from instructors, lecturers and learners. Questionnaires have five - point Likert scale: 1 = represents strongly disagree, disagree, neutral, agree and 5 = strongly agree was administered to both the staff and the students from the selected universities. Among the respondent were students of computer science, bachelor of Information Technology and students from distance education. Public universities and the private universities were chosen because of their popularity and exposure to e-learning technology. Random selection of staff members in the department of ICT, distance education and students were selected to a total of 100 respondents. To achieve the objectives of the study seventeen questions were used. Question one was meant to collect demographic data while the other questions were grouped as follows: Availability of resources (7, 8, 11, and 15); Attitude towards e-learning (2, 3,4,14 and 17); Resistance to change (6, 12, 13 and 16); Usefulness of the new technology (5, 9 and 10).

3.2 Data Analysis Technique

The Wilcoxon signed rank test is a non-parametric analytical technique that focuses on the association of grouped data looking at all levels of possible interaction effects. Therefore it is used to find out which variables are related during interaction. This technique is used when considering interactions among variables rather than the main effects when analyzing them.

3.3 Data Analysis

The Wilcoxon signed rank test was used in the study to identify what interaction and interrelationships existed within the variables that were being investigated. The test was carried out by calculating for each factor the difference between the level of agreement and disagreement. We then ranked the differences by their absolute value that is ignoring the sign giving 1 for the smallest difference, 2 for the next smallest and so on. Then we sum the ranks of the positive (T^+) differences and sum the ranks of the negative differences. The test statistic is the lesser of these two sums. If the null hypothesis was true and there was no difference, then we would expect the rank sums for positive and negative ranks to be the same H_0: $E(x) = E(y)$; hence we accept the null hypothesis. While if the null hypothesis is to be rejected against the alternative hypothesis H_1: $E(x) < E(y)$, there must be a difference between the positive and negative ranks. During analysis the test level α is at 5% which is equivalent to 0.05. The critical region is determined using this expression $T^+ \leq T_{0.1\ ,\ n,}$ T^+ is calculated by adding all the positive signed ranks.

Where:
H_0 = the null hypothesis; H_1 = the alternative hypothesis; $E_{(x)}$ = expected level of disagreement of variable x in question; $E_{(y)}$ = expected level of agreement of variable y in question; N = number of ranks; $T_{0.1,\ n}$ = tabulated values read from signed rank test table; T^+ = sum of positive signed ranks; α = level of test (read from Wilcoxon signed rank test table) / significance; W = sampling distribution; μ_W - mean sampling distribution; z = ratio showing level of significance; δ_W = standard deviation of sampling distribution.

4 Presentation of Results and Discussion

The results collected from the questionnaires were analyzed and presented in two tables 2 and 3.

Table 2. A Summary of the results on the various attributes

Attributes	Q.NO	Level of Disagreement ($E_{(x)}$)	Level of Agreement ($E_{(y)}$)	Difference $E_{(x)} - E_{(y)}$	Modulus	Rank	Signed Rank
a) vailability of resources for E-learning	7	49	16	-33	33	4	-4
	8	32	30	-2	2	2	-2
	11	43	19	-24	24	3	-3
	15	26	25	-1	1	1	-1
b) Attitude towards E-learning	2	25	31	-6	6	1	-1
	3	25	39	-14	14	2	-2
	4	15	42	-27	27	3	-3
	14	8	57	-49	49	5	-5
	17	11	54	-43	43	4	-4
c) Resistance to change	6	17	34	-17	17	3	-3
	12	18	27	-9	9	1	-1
	13	14	44	-30	30	4	-4
	16	34	21	13	13	2	2
d) Usefulness of the new technology	5	25	29	-4	4	1.5	-1.5
	9	24	28	-4	4	1.5	-1.5
	10	5	48	-43	-43	3	-3

a) Availability of Resources for E-Learning
The questions below were used to assess the availability of resources for e-learning:

> ***Q7***. *There are enough computers in our laboratory.* ***Q8.*** *We have reasonably fast and stable internet services in our institute.* ***Q10.*** *Power supply in our institute is stable.* ***Q15.*** *We do have meaningful support systems and opportunities to actively participate in e-learning programs.*

H_0: There are enough resources available for e-learning in our institution; H_1: There are no enough resources available for e-learning in our institution.

The results from table 2 were used for computing the variables in table3. Results on availability of resources for e-learning summarized in table 3 were computed as follows: The maximum possible value of W:

$$\text{Sum} = \frac{N\,(N+1)}{2}$$

$$\text{Sum} = \frac{4(4+1)}{2} = 10 \tag{1}$$

We noted earlier on in the null hypothesis that there are enough resources available for e-learning; we would expect the value of W to approximate to zero within the limits of random variability. This implies that any particular observed value of W belongs to a sampling distribution whose mean is equal to zero, hence $-\mu_W = 0$. For any particular value of N, it can be shown that the standard deviation of the sampling distribution of W is equal to:

$$-\delta_W = \sqrt{\left[\frac{N(N+1)(2N+1)}{6}\right]}$$

$$= \sqrt{\left[\frac{4(4+1)(2*4+1)}{6}\right]} \tag{2}$$

$$= \pm 5.48.$$

This value is used for computing the z-ratio. The z-ratio must include ± 0.5 corrections for continuity in Wilcoxon test. Thus, the structure of the z-ratio for the Wilcoxon test is:

$$z = \frac{(W-\mu w) \pm 0.5}{\delta w} \tag{3}$$

The correction for the connectivity is "- 0.5" when W is greater than $-\mu_W$ and "+ 0.5" when W is less than $-\mu_{W.}$ Since $-\mu_{W\ is}$ in all instances are equal to zero, the simpler computational formula is:

$$z = \frac{W-0.5}{\delta w}$$

$$z = \frac{10-0.5}{5.48}$$

$$z = +1.734.\ (W = 10,\ -\delta_W = \pm 5.48)$$

From the table of critical values of z read from Wilcoxon signed rank test table, we observed that the value of z = +1.734 is significant. We reject the null hypothesis H_0 and accept the alternative hypothesis H_1 that there are no enough resources available for e-learning. The variables in table 3 for parts b), c) and d) that follow are computed in a similar way as shown above.

Table 3. Summary of the Variables Computed

NO	Attribute	N	W	δ_W	Z
a)	Availability of resources for E-learning	4	10	± 5.48.	+1.734
b)	Attitude towards e-learning	5	15	± 7.42.	+1.950
c)	Resistance to change	4	10	± 5.48.	+1.734
d)	Usefulness of the new technology	3	6	± 3.74.	+1.470

b) Attitude towards e-learning
The questions below were used to assess the attitude of the users towards e-learning:

> ***Q2**. I have known e-learning for a long time. **Q3.** I have used or I am making use of e-learning. **Q4.** I find using e-learning technology simple. **Q14.** In cooperation of e-learning technology into Ugandan education system is a wise move. **Q17**. I would recommend e-learning as one of the alternatives for the traditional teaching-learning approaches.*

H_0: Stakeholders have negative attitude towards e-learning; H_1: Stakeholders have a positive attitude towards e-learning.

The data for these questions summarized in table 2 was used to compute the variables in table 3 part b). Using the variables in corresponding to row b) for attitude towards e-learning, we observed that the value for z = +1.95 is significant. We reject the hypothesis H_0 and accept the alternative one H_1 that there is positive attitude towards e-learning.

c) Resistance to Change
The questions below were used to assess resistance to change:

> ***Q6**. The cost for implementing e-learning is high. **Q12.** The organization is willing to invest in e-learning technology. **Q13.** E-learning has more challenges than the current teaching-learning approaches in our education system. **Q16**. The use of computers is a health hazard.*

H_0: There is sufficient resistance to change hindering the e-learning adoption in Uganda; H1: There is no sufficient resistance to change hindering e-learning adoption in Uganda.

The results from these questions were used to compute the variables in table 3. From the table of critical values of z read from Wilcoxon signed rank test table, we observed that the value of z = +1.734 is significant. We reject the null hypothesis H_0 and accept the alternative hypothesis H_1 that there is no sufficient resistance to change hindering the e-learning adoption in Uganda.

d) Usefulness of the New Technology

The questions below were used to assess the usefulness of the new technology:

> ***Q5***. *E-learning motivates me to learn.* ***Q9.*** *My frequency of using internet and surfing is high. and* ***Q10.*** *I have the basic ICT skills that will enable me to feel at ease with e-learning technology.*

H_0: The new technology (e-learning) is not useful in our situation.

H_1: The new technology is useful in our situation.

The data obtained from these questions were used for computing the variables shown in table 3 in row d) corresponding to usefulness of the new technology. In the table of critical values of z read from Wilcoxon signed rank test table, we can see that the observed value of z + 1.47 is significant. We reject the null hypothesis H_0 and accept the alternative H_1 that the new technology is useful.

5 Descriptions and Discussion of the Proposed Model for Institutional Readnessfor E-learning

Data analysis and review of the existing e-learning readiness models led to the development of this proposed model for e-learning readiness assessment for institutions of higher learning.

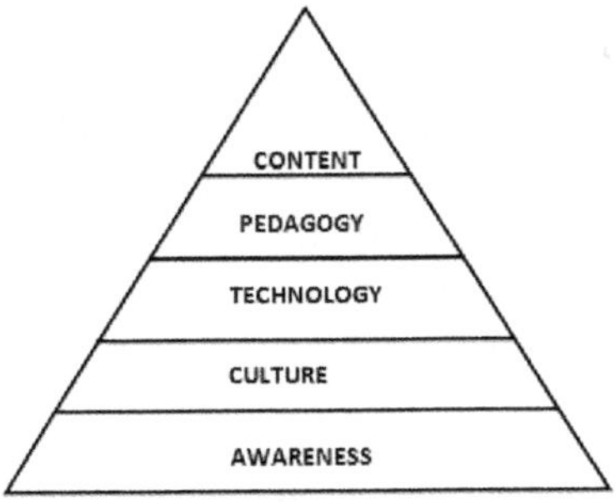

Fig. 1. A Model for E-learning Institutional Readiness Assessment (Adapted from [17])

The model for assessing institutional readiness for e-learning is represented in figure 1, as a five-layered triangle. Each layer corresponds to an attribute that is to be used for assessing the institutional readiness for e-learning namely: awareness, culture, technology, pedagogy and content. Based on the proposed model for e-learning readiness assessment for an institution, awareness at the base of the triangle is considered to be a key factor, followed by the culture of the society or an institution, then technology available, pedagogy to match with the technology for creating an inviting, demanding, engaging and motivating learning environment for the learner and the content at the apex.

i) Awareness

This involves making the public get to know of the new technology in place hence, preparing the stakeholders for it. E-learning has many stakeholders including: learners, developers, educationists, the government, donors, parents and other funders of the projects. This calls for careful and gradual integration of e-learning technology into educational systems for institutions of higher learning. This will help avoid failure to benefit from the e-learning technology. In awareness, learners as part of the stakeholders need to be ready for e-learning because they are the direct beneficiaries of the new technology. Not only that, human resource too play a big role in the successful implementation of e-learning. According to the results of a study in Turkey human resources need to be the priority for development of e-learning implementation [9].

ii) Culture

Organizations need to focus on what really matters; creating an environment that truly values learning, which for many may involve a substantial culture change [18]. However, organizations wanting to embrace a successful e-learning strategy must ensure that they are fully prepared both culturally and technologically [19]. Each developing and developed nation has her own culture that governs the way things are done. In order for a successful change to take place, there is a need to understand the culture of the society in order to prepare for cultural and technological change. In African culture, stakeholders choose what they already know works with only limited room for innovation. The culture of Ghanian public universities was identified as a major barrier to adoption of e-learning systems and in particular their policy that a student's physical presence determines the number of credit hours earned in a discipline counted towards a degree [3]. If cultural and technological foundations are not in place, the e-learning strategy will not succeed [19]. This is an indication that culture plays a key role in the successful integration of e-learning into education systems in Africa. Use of modern technology in education systems in Africa is limited to mainly PowerPoint slide shows.

iii) Technology

Selection of technology is important as this can be a limiting factor to further e-learning development [18]. Integrating e-learning in a higher education institution's curriculum requires a gradual process because it involves a range of stakeholders namely policy makers, learners, developers, parents, instructors and others. Recent learning research has demonstrated that interaction is a critical factor for learner satisfaction, higher level of achievement, higher learner engagement, and a positive attitude toward digital learning [17]. According to a workshop held in Ghana on e-learning, workshop participants indicated that their universities provide no or minimal support for technology in teaching and learning [3]. At Makerere University, under the end user training project (EUTP) sponsored by Netherlands' government (NUFFIC project) teaching and non-teaching staff were trained in the basics of ICT. This exposed lecturers and other staff members to online resources.

iv) Pedagogy

Pedagogy in this context is used to refer to the correct use of teaching strategies in knowledge delivery. In planning to develop an e-learning content, the pedagogical approaches need to be identified and evaluated. Suitable pedagogical approaches make it easier to create content that is rich and flexible to suit the learner needs. A learning environment must invite and even demand the active engagement of the learner [20]. It is important to facilitate students' ability to learn successfully on an individual basis [6]. Therefore it is necessary to modify the structure of teaching and learning to one that seeks to promote individual learning identities. The success of e-learning depends on how learning takes place online, that is the underlying pedagogy and real value of e-learning lies in our ability to deploy its attributes to train the right people to gain the right knowledge and skills at the right time [6]. In the pedagogical aspect, most lecturers who did not pass through pedagogical training lack the basic skills necessary in the delivery process. Awidi [3], pointed out that in addition to the lack of technology for teaching, most lecturers had no formal training in instructional methods. There is need for every lecturer to undergo a formal training in instructional methods in order to teach. Getting good grades at the end of the degree program does not necessarily mean that, the product has also acquired delivery skills that can help in the teaching-learning process. Most institutions of learning in Uganda employ graduates to lecture who do not have formal training in delivery process. Institutional design needs to be done in line with the new technology.

v) Content

In order to provide high quality e-Learning, content is important. This will make it easier for learners, curriculum designers and intelligent software to make use of the content in a wide variety of contexts. Ideally, you will be able to obtain emotional reactions. As designers and developers, one of our purposes in life is to help novices in a particular skill or content area gain new levels of competency. Effective content is among the greatest challenges facing any on-line learning initiative. If the content does not teach, it has no value, regardless of how "high-tech" or cost-effective it might be.

6 Conclusion, Recommendations and Future Work

The paper presented the model for e-learning readiness assessment for higher institutions of learning. It provides institutions with guidelines on readiness for e-learning technology. A qualitative review was based on each level that included: awareness, culture, technology, pedagogy and content. The model also identifies practical study and necessary technical skills that should be developed before embarking on integrating e-learning into the education system. This study suggests integration of e-learning into higher institutions of learning by breaking down these problems identified into smaller solvable units. Below is a list of challenges that need to be addressed: Fear of new technology; Resistance to change; High cost of e-learning infrastructure; Low level of computer literacy; unstable power supply; Low level of e-learning awareness. From the findings of this research, there is need for the government to come up with clear ICT policies to back-up the introduction of e-learning in the Ugandan education system. A second aspect is the provision of finances to universities from the government, private sector, donors...etc. appropriate supervision of university management in line with acquisition of the necessary e-learning infrastructure and establishment of e-learning centers in higher institutions of learning.

More work needs to be done on the introduction of e-learning technology in a Ugandan education system especially in the use of agents for personalized learning and real-time feedback generation to address the cultural diversity of the learners and their varying learner needs. Due to the diversity in a learner's knowledge, background, skills, learning styles and preferences, personalization plays an important role in taking these factors into considerations [21]. Increasing the level of e-learning in African Universities would solve the problems of overcrowding in lecture rooms, hostels, low lecturer to students ratios, insufficient laboratory equipment, too many applicants for too few institutions, transport costs among others. This has led to depreciation of the universities human resource and accounts for many of the social ills observed in most of the Universities today in Uganda. The common evil among others is strikes by students, academic, non-academic staff or both. Apparently e-learning technology has the ability to provide a remedy for these problems and it should be encouraged in accordance with the policies of the government [20].

References

1. Gunga, O.S., Ricketts, W.I.: Facing the Challenges of E-learning Initiatives in African Universities. British Journal of Educational Technology 38(5), 896–906 (2007)
2. Buenafe, R. A., Ninomiya, S.: E-Learning in Higher Education Makes Its Debut in Cambodia: Implications of the Provincial Business Education Project (2007)
3. Awidi, T.I.: Developing An E-learning Strategy for Public Universities in Ghana. EDUCAUSE Quarterly 31(2) (2008)
4. Littlejohn, A.: Key Issues in the Design and delivery of technology-enhanced learning (2007), http://www.facetpublishing.co/UK.ch4.pdf (accessed on June 23, 2008)
5. Vate-U-Lan, P.: Readiness of e-Learning Connectivity in Thailand. In: Fourth International Conference on e- Learning for Knowledge-Based Society, Bangkok (2007)
6. Uhomoibhi, J.O.: Implementing e-learning in Northern Ireland: prospects and challenges. Campus Wide Information Systems 23(1), 4–14 (2006)
7. Hamel, J.L.: Knowledge for Sustainable Development in Africa towards New Policy Initiatives. World Review of Science, Technology and Sustainable Development 2(3), 217–229 (2005)
8. Wong, A.L.: Cross-Cultural delivery of e-Learning Programmes: Perspectives from Hong Kong. The International Review of Research in Open and Distance Learning 8(3) (2007)
9. Ayudin, C.H., Tasci, D.: Measuring Readiness for e-Learning: reflections from an Emerging Country. Educational Technology and Society 8(4), 244–257 (2005)
10. Downes, S.: Learning Networks and Connective Knowledge. Institutional Technology Forum (2006)
11. Lubega, J.: E-Learning; opportunities and Institutional Changes. In: East African Inter-University Conference in Nairobi (2008)

12. Hill, J.R., Raven, A., Han, S.: Connections in Web-Based Learning Environments: A Research-Based Model for Community Building. The Quarterly Review of Distance Education 3(4), 383–393 (2002)
13. Noonan, J.: Online Collaboration: how can it boost personalized learning? Development and Learning in Organizations 21(6), 3–10 (2007)
14. Debande, O.: ICTs and the Development of e-Learning in Europe: the role of the public and private Sector. European Journal of Education 39(2), 191–208 (2004)
15. Bryderup, I.M., Kowalski, K.: The role of local authorities in the integration of ICT in learning. Journal of Computer Assisted Learning 18, 470–479 (2002)
16. Twinomugisha, A., Magochi, J., Aluoch, S.: Investigation of bandwidth consolidation for partnership universities, Nairobi: The African Virtual University (2004), `http://www.avu.org/documents` (accessed on 13th December, 2005)
17. Huitt, W.: Maslow's hierarchy of needs. Educational Psychology Interactive. Valdosta State University Valdosta, GA (2007), `http://www.edpsycinteractive.org/topics/regsys/maslow.html` (accessed on March 6, 2003)
18. Ettinger, A., Holton, V.: E-learner experiences: What is the future for e-learning? Journal of Industrial and Commercial Training 39(4), 208–212 (2006)
19. Macpherson, A., Homan, G., Wilkinson, K.: Adopting an E-learning Strategy. The Practical Considerations of Delivering a Successful e-Learning Program, Development and Learning in Organizations 20(3), 23–25 (2006)
20. Olusegun, F., Oluwafem, S.O., Sharma, S.K.: An Exploratory Study of the Critical factors affecting the acceptability of E-learning in Nigerian Universities. Journal of Information Management and Computer Security 14(5), 496–505 (2006)
21. Ong, S.S., Hawryszkiewycz, I.: Towards Personalized and Collaborative Learning Management Systems. In: Proceedings of the 3rd IEEE International Conference on Advanced Learning Technologies (ICALT 2003), Sydney NSW 2032 Australia (2003)
22. Chapnic, S.: Are you ready for e-learning? Learning Circuits: ASTD's Online Magazine All abouit e- learning (2005)
23. Psycharis, S.: Presumptions and actions affecting an e-learning adoption by the educational system. Implementation using Virtual Private Networks Eurodl (2005), `http://www.eurodl.org/materials/contrib/2005/Sarantos_Psycharis.htm`)

A Study on Effective Math Teaching Strategy Design in Hybrid Learning Environment

Liming Zhang[1] and Jianli Jiao[2]

[1] University of Macau,
Av.Padre Tomas Pereire, Taipa, Macao
lmzhang@umac.mo
[2] South China Normal University,
Guangzhou, Guangdong Province, 510631, China
jiaojianli@126.com

Abstract. Computer supported instruction can easily facilitate different learning environments, different teaching models and learning styles. In hybrid learning environment, the teachers face a big challenge to find the suitable teaching strategies for a specific content. In this study, three experiments were conducted to explore the different math teaching strategies for different contents and different characteristics of the students in hybrid learning environment. The results indicated that traditional teaching was more suitable for the algebra related topics. Computer supported hybrid teaching was more effective for the graph related topics. Towards different students' characteristics, medium and low performance students benefited more from the computer supported hybrid teaching. The traditional teaching was more suitable for the high performance students. The student-centered hybrid learning requested significant more teaching hours to facilitate effective learning results.

Keywords: Math teaching strategy, Hybrid learning, Cognitive load theory, Teach-centered, Student-centered.

1 Introduction

Recent advances of information technology have facilitated a convergence between traditional face-to-face and technology-mediated learning environment, which is so-called hybrid or blended learning. The hybrid learning environments try to take advantage of the merits of both learning environments [1]. Hybrid learning usually refers to using multiple approaches in teaching, including combining technology-based materials and traditional print materials, group and individual studies, structured pace study and self-paced study. So besides the computer supported learning environments, hybrid learning also emphasizes the effective combination of different modes of delivery, models of teaching and styles of learning [2].

Mathematics is one of the most difficulty subjects in the secondary studies. Many researchers have been seeking for new pedagogies to improve the student performance in math. Technology based math teaching is one of the choices and

R. Kwan et al. (Eds.): ICHL 2011, LNCS 6837, pp. 212–223, 2011.

playing an increasingly important role in teaching and learning. Commonly used hybrid math teaching approaches could fall into two categories. One category is the courseware or online learning environment based teaching and learning, in which the teaching contents have been developed already. Teachers can use it to demonstrate the abstract math concepts in class, and students can use it to further explore the concepts or practice the exercises by themselves in class or after class. Another category is the dynamic math software based teaching and learning, such as the Geometer's Sketchpad (GSP), in which the teaching contents have not been developed yet and could be easily developed at the same time during the teaching. Dynamic math software is a dynamic construction and exploration tool that enables teachers and students to explore the mathematics in the way of learning by doing that is simply not possible with traditional tools. Teachers and students can construct an object and then explore its mathematical properties by dragging the object with the mouse in class during teaching and learning. It can easily be integrated into traditional teaching by teachers and effectively support the students' active self-explorations. Both courseware and dynamic math software could be online or offline versions.

To explore the effective hybrid math teaching strategies, we have the following research questions.

- What is the effective teaching strategy in using courseware based hybrid math teaching?
- What is the effective teaching strategy in using dynamic math software based hybrid math teaching?
- Which way is more effective between teach-centered and student-centered hybrid math teaching?

In this paper, a series of three experiments were conducted. Experiment 1 focused on the effectiveness comparison between courseware based and traditional teachings. Experiment 2 was conducted to compare the effectiveness between the dynamic software based and traditional teachings. Experiment 3 concentrated on the dynamic math software based effectiveness comparison between teacher-centered teaching and student-centered learning. The effective math teaching strategy design is suggested based on the experiment results.

2 Hybrid Learning Environments and Cognitive Load Theory

2.1 Hybrid Learning Environments

There were two different kinds of computer supported learning environments used in the experiments in this study. One was interactive courseware on trigonometric functions. It was developed by using GSP. There were seven sections totally about 70 pages in the courseware, including tutorials, examples, interactive graphs, and exercises in each section [3]. It took about one year to develop it. One page of the courseware in its section 2 is illustrated in Figure 1.

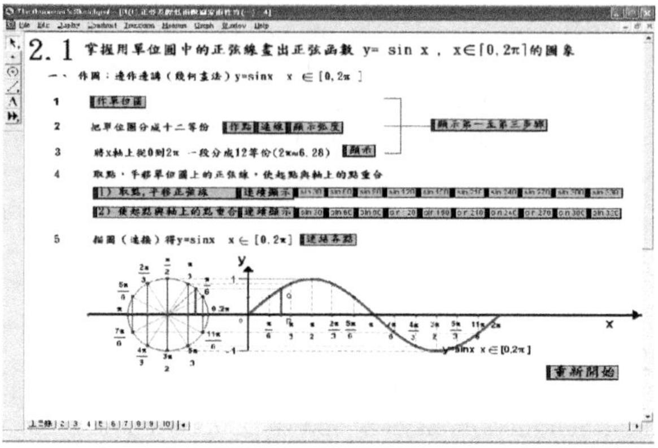

Fig. 1. Example of the developed courseware

Another learning environment was Dynamic Mathematical Laboratory (DM_Lab), which was one of dynamic math software series developed by the experiment school. This tool had been applied in many math courses in the experiment school and proved to be a useful instructional tool. DM_Lab interface is illustrated in Figure 2 [4]. Both the software used in the experiments are CD ROM and are used in class.

2.2 Cognitive Load Theory

Cognitive Load Theory (CLT) was introduced in this paper to evaluate whether computer supported instruction could support more efficient and deeper learning activities so as to increase the learning effectiveness.

Cognitive load theory is mainly concerned with how cognitive psychology has influenced pedagogy [5]. It builds on an information-processing view of cognition, defining long-term and working memory as main structures of human cognitive architecture. Learning is proceeding well only when the amount of information to be processed in the task is within the bounds of working memory. Once exceeded, it would lead to a shortage in allocations of cognitive resources to impede learning, which is so-called cognition overload. CLT is concerned with engineering of instructional designs in order to avoid overload of learners' cognitive systems.

CLT researchers have recognized three categories of load during instruction. They are Intrinsic, Extraneous and Germane cognitive loads [6]. First, *Intrinsic cognitive load* refers to the load placed on working memory by the intrinsic of the materials to be learnt. It is entirely determined by levels of element interactivity. Simultaneously, it is affected by the expertise levels of leaner [7]. Second, *Extraneous cognitive load* is the load placed on working memory by the instructional design itself. Unlike intrinsic cognitive load, extraneous cognitive load is imposed by inappropriate instructional procedures. It is under control of the instructor. Last, *Germane cognitive load* is the load placed on working memory during schema formation and automation. CLT assumes a limited working memory connected to an unlimited long-term memory [8]. How to decrease the extraneous cognitive load, in order to free the working memory for tasks associated with the germane cognitive load is the prime goal of instruction.

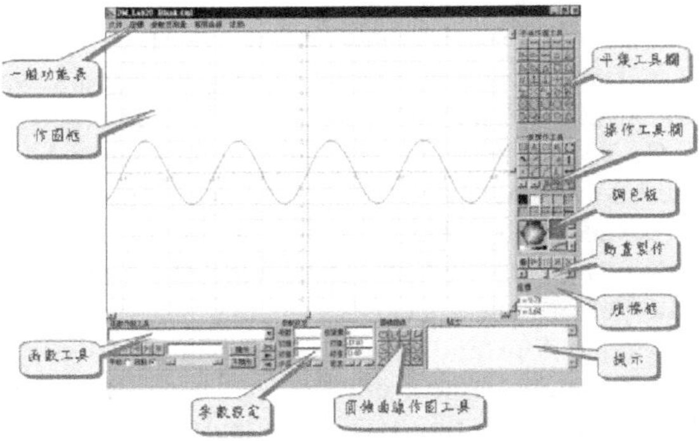

Fig. 2. DM_Lab Interface

There are three classic categories of cognitive load measurement techniques: Subjective, Physiological and Task Performance. Subject techniques use rating scales to report the experienced effort or the capacity expenditure [6]. The direct subject measurement was used in this study to assess the extraneous cognitive load of the subject who was learning in the computer supported environment. The NASA-Task Load Index [9] is a kind of subjective measures which consists of rating scales, providing participants six dimensions to perceive cognitive load: mental demand, physical demand, temporal demand, effort, frustration tolerance, and performance. Because NASA-TLX is a multidimensional scale, it is usually administered only once, at the end of a learning or test phase [10]. There is another un-dimensional 9-point scale developed by Paas [11]. Because it has only one item asking participants to rate their perceived mental effort, it can be used during the process of performance as well. Both questionnaires were used in the experiments in this study.

3 Experiments and Data Analysis

There were three experiments being conducted. Since the students during the experiments could not be randomly assigned, quasi-experiments were used in this study. CLT was introduced into the experiment 2 and 3.

3.1 Experiment 1

Experiment 1 was designed to investigate the effective teaching strategy in using courseware based hybrid math teaching.

An experiment was conducted to compare the students' achievement in two groups. Trigonometric functions were selected as the instruction topic. One class of students served as control group with 40 students was taught by traditional instruction alone. The teaching contents included trigonometric algebraic properties deduction and trigonometric graphs drawing on the blackboard. A similar class of students served as experimental group with 41 students used the courseware as a supplement to traditional instruction. The courseware was designed and developed by the same teacher who gave lectures to both the student groups [6]. He had taught the corresponding topic for three years in traditional way with well-designed lecture notes and good experience. The instructional strategy design in courseware was consistent with his traditional instruction. The GSP was used to develop the courseware.

Two classes of Grade 10 students from the same high school in Macao were selected in the experiment. They were randomly designated as experimental group and control group, respectively. Based on the previous semester's math averages, each group of students were divided into three clusters: high performance, medium performance and low performance. The experiment lasted four weeks. Pretest and posttest were conducted before and after the experiment to compare the students' achievements. The test papers came from the Teachers' Book of the trigonometry textbook used in Macao. The question types in pretest and posttest were similar. The questions themselves basically were same. The flow chart of the experiment procedure is illustrated in Figure 3.

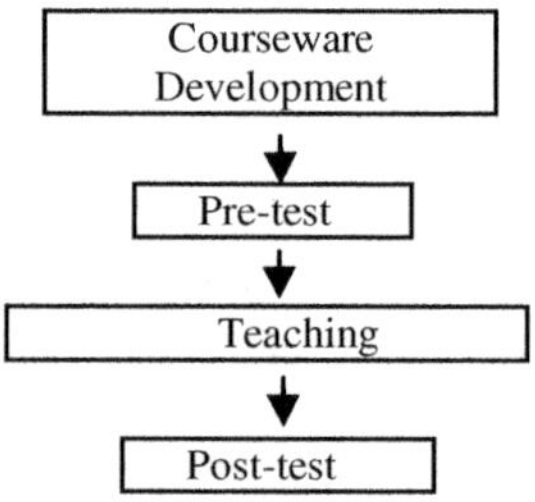

Fig. 3. Flowchart of the experiment 1 procedure

Data Analysis. SPSS ANOVA analysis results indicated that though there was no significant difference on students' achievement from both groups, the difference between the mean of posttest, however, were noticeably greater in the experimental group than those in the control group. It indicated that the courseware supplemental instruction produced achievement effects superior to the traditional instruction alone in this experiment.

The correct answer rate of the examination papers was further analyzed. There were total 30 questions in the pretest and posttest papers. Of which, there were 19 questions related to the trigonometric graphs and 11 questions related to the trigonometric algebra deduction. The correct answer rate in trigonometric graph related questions was obviously higher in the experimental group than that in the control group. In the meanwhile, the correct answer rate in trigonometric algebra deduction related questions was comparatively lower in the experimental group than that in the control group. The results indicated that courseware supported hybrid teaching design can help the students to understand the principle of the graphs better than the traditional blackboard drawing did. To the algebra deduction, however, courseware was not more effective than the traditional blackboard deduction, though all the same deduction was included in the courseware.

Though there was no significant difference on students' achievement between high performance clusters, the average score of high performance cluster in the control group was higher than that in the experiment group. It indicated that the traditional teaching was more suitable for the high performance students.

On the contrary, the average scores of medium and low performance clusters in the experiment group was higher than that in the control group, though there was no significant difference on the final achievement. Moreover, the medium performance cluster in experiment group made greatest progresses among all the students. It indicated that the courseware supported hybrid teaching could help the medium and low performance students to better understand the math concepts. The medium performance students benefit most from courseware based hybrid teaching.

3.2 Experiment 2

Experiment 2 was designed to explore the effective teaching strategy in using dynamic math software based hybrid math teaching.

An experiment was conducted to compare student achievements and cognitive load from two groups of students [12]. The participants consisted of 71 F2 students in a secondary school in Macao. Class A with 36 students was selected as the control group. This group was taught by the traditional teaching alone. Class B with 35 students was selected as the experimental group and was taught by the dynamic math software based hybrid teaching. Based on the previous semester's math averages, each group of students were divided into three clusters: high performance, medium performance and low performance. The Parallelogram Unit in elementary geometry was selected as the content which was to be taught to the students in the experiment. The content primarily consisted of two sections: Basic Properties and Determinants of Parallelogram, Basic Properties and Determinants of Rectangle, Rhombus, and Square.

The measurement tool for student achievement was the school-based test papers "Parallelogram Unit Quiz I, II, and III". The Self-reporting Questionnaire of Cognitive Load (CL) was also used in the experiment to measure the perceived cognitive load. The questionnaire, which consisted of a single question with a 9 points scale, was adopted in this study. The experiment took place over two weeks during the routine hours of the school day. Both the experiment and control group took 14 geometric lessons. Each lesson lasted 40 minutes. The topic "Basic Properties and Determinants of Parallelogram" was the stage one and was taught in 7 lessons; while the topic "Basic Properties and Determinants of Rectangle, Rhombus, and Square" was the stage two and was taught in further 7 lessons. The same math teacher delivered the entire courses to both groups. The instructional software used in the study was DM_Lab. The flowchart of the experiment procedure is illustrated in Figure 4.

The data of the study came from test papers of pre-test, Parallelogram Unit Quiz I, II, III and Self-reporting Questionnaire of Cognitive Load. Quiz I, Quiz II, and Quiz III were regarded as the mid-test, final-test, and post-test, respectively. The former two tests were conducted during the experiment period with the cognitive load questionnaire together. The post-test was conducted one month after the experiment with no cognitive load questionnaire assessment. All data was analyzed by independent sample *t*-tests on SPSS 15.0.

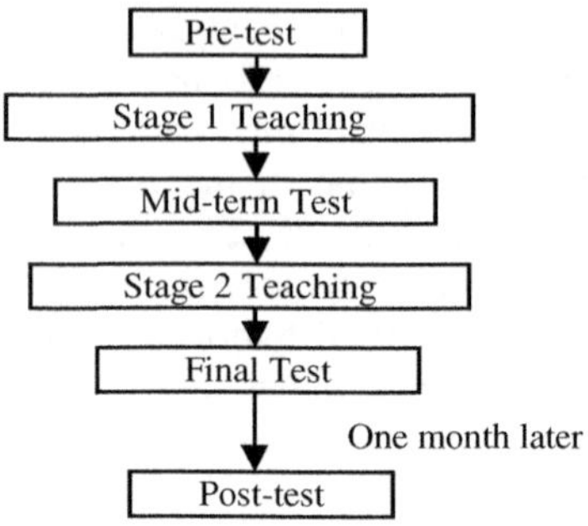

Fig. 4. Flowchart of the experiment procedure

Data Analysis. The result showed that there was no significant difference on both math achievements and students' self-reported CL between the experiment and control groups. Figure 5 illustrates that in the pre-test, the mean of the control group was higher than that of the experiment group. After the stage 1 teaching, the mean of the experiment group became higher than that of the control group. The means of the control group, however, turned to be higher in the final and posttests than those in the experiment group. To explore the reason, further analysis was conducted to the different performance clusters – high performance, medium performance and low performance students in both the control and experiment groups, which are illustrated in Figure 6.

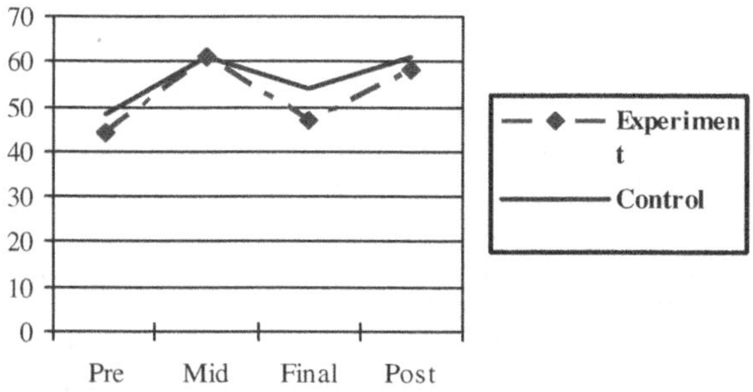

Fig. 5. DM_Lab Interface

Based on the test scores, the dynamic math software based teaching method had negative effect to the high performance students. The traditional teaching method was more suitable for them. In a short term, the dynamic math software based teaching was more suitable for the medium and low performance students to improve their learning achievements, where the low performance cluster made greatest progresses among all the students after the first stage. In a long term, however, there was no advantage.

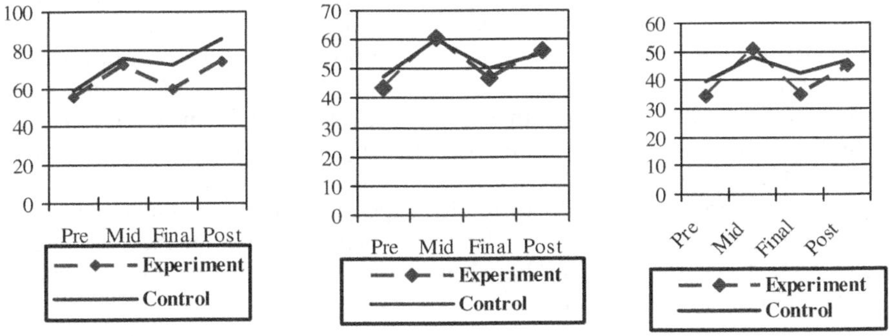

Fig. 6. Students' math achievement of high, medium, and low performance clusters

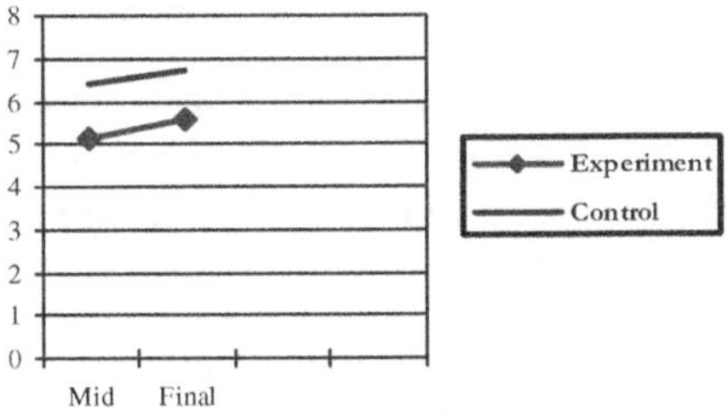

Fig. 7. Students' self-reported CL

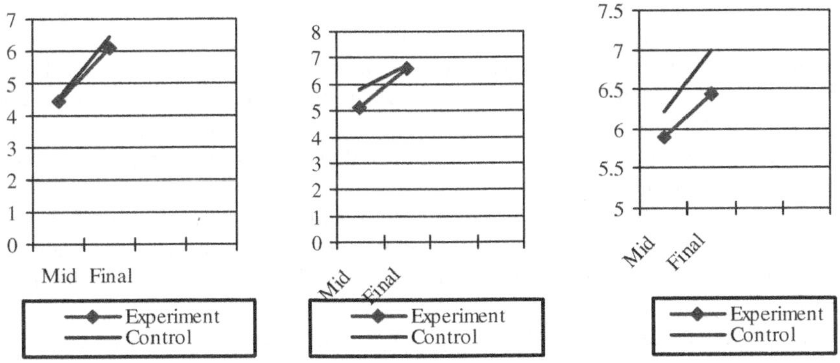

Fig. 8. Students' math achievement of high, medium, and low performance clusters

Though there was no significant difference on CL between the experiment and control groups, all high, medium and low performance students in the experiment group claimed lower CL than those in the control group as illustrated in Figure 7 and 8, respectively. It indicated that the dynamic math software based teaching method could help the students to reduce their CL in understanding the math concepts.

In the second stage, the traditional teaching outperformed the dynamic math software based teaching method. Interview was conducted after the experiment to explore the reason. The students in the experiment group complained too much learning materials and tight time schedule in using software in the second stage. It indicated that dynamic software based hybrid teaching requested more teaching time than the traditional teaching did.

3.3 Experiment 3

Experiment 3 was designed to investigate effectiveness between teach-centered and student-centered hybrid math teaching.

An experiment was conducted to compare students' achievement and cognitive load between two groups [13]. The dynamic math software was used in both groups. One group was teacher-centered, in which the teacher used the software in supporting the traditional teaching. The other group was student-centered, in which the students used the software to explore the math concepts by themselves guided by the teacher. The participants in this study consisted of 83 Form 5 students in a secondary school in Macao. Class A with 42 students was selected as the control group. This group was taught by the teacher-centered hybrid teaching. Class B with 41 students was selected as the experiment group and was taught using the student-centered learning method. Based on the previous semester's math averages, each group of students were divided into three clusters: high performance, medium performance and low performance.

The Ellipse Unit was selected as the content which was to be taught to the students in the experiment. The content primarily consisted of three sections: Ellipse's formula, Ellipse's geometric properties and Ellipse's parameter equation. The instructional software used in the study was DM_Lab.

The measurement tool for student achievement was the school-based final test paper. Experiment cognitive load scale used in the study was a Chinese edition revised from NASA-Task Load Index. This scale has 6 dimensions: (1). mental demand; (2). physical demand; (3). temporal demand; (4). effort; (5). frustration tolerance; (6). performance.

The experiment took place over two weeks during the routine hours of the school day. Both the experiment and control group took 12 Ellipse lessons. Each lesson lasted 40 minutes. The same math teacher delivered the entire courses to both the experiment and control groups.

Pre-test was conducted before the experiment to investigate participant's mathematics ability in Ellipse. There was significant difference in expertise experience between the experiment group and control group. The reason was that there were several students in the experiment group failed to go up to the next grade and stayed in the same grade for an additional year. To exclude the pre-test effect, the repeated-measures were used in the data analysis in this study. The final math test scores in last semester were also analyzed by SPSS. There was no significant difference between two groups.

Besides the test, the tasks were also conducted on lessons 2, 3, 6 and 11. The task topics were usually one question and related with the corresponding lecture. The students were requested to finish the task individually within 10 minutes. The 9-point scale Self-report Cognitive Load Questionnaire was conducted directly after the task paper collected. The question was "How difficult was this task?" The flowchart of experiment 3 is illustrated in Figure 9.

Data analysis. The data were analyzed on SPSS. UNIANOVA was used to measure the students' achievement based on the final test performance. There was no significant difference between the control and experiment group in students' achievement. The mean in the control group was slightly better than the one in the experiment group. However, there was significant difference in the final question in the test paper between the control and experiment group. The control group achieved significantly higher scores in that question than the experiment group did (t=-3.396, Sig=.001). The question was graphic related question.

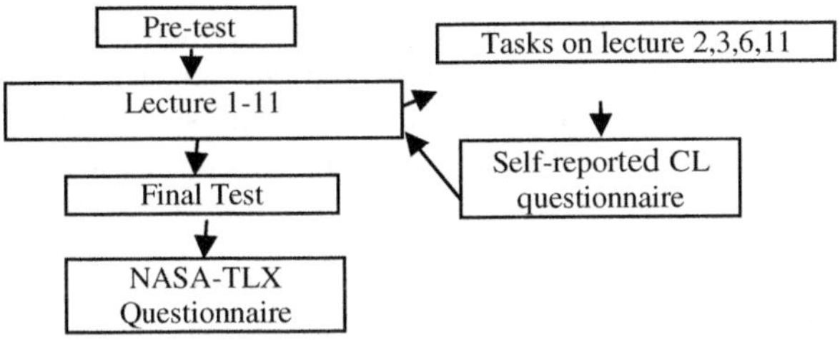

Fig. 9. Students' self-reported CL

There was no significant difference on the sum of CL dimensions between the control and experiment groups. However, there was significant difference in Temporal Demand dimension between the control and experiment groups. The experiment group claimed more time required in learning during the experiment. Based on the higher marks in final test and lower time required in learning, the control group performed better than the experiment did.

In the view of students' Task, and Task CL, the experiment group performed significantly better in most of the situation, especially in the graph related questions. Considering the combination results of the Task performance and Task CL, the student-centered hybrid learning method could facilitate more efficient learning in non-test performance.

The students' performance in graph related problems was much better during the non-test performance than those in the test. It indicated that DM_Lab could help the students understanding better the graph related problems; meanwhile it might cause the students' dependence on the software tool which resulted in worse performance during the test without the software support.

There was no significant difference on the sum of CL dimensions between different performance clusters; however, the medium and low performance clusters in experiment group claimed significant high CL in Temporal Demand dimension. It indicated that teacher-centered method was more effective to the medium and low performance students for the final test. Meanwhile, student-centered method was better to them for the non-test results. Teacher-centered and leaner-centered dynamic software based hybrid math teaching methods had the same effectiveness to the high performance students.

4 Conclusions and Suggestions

Experiment 1 demonstrated that courseware based hybrid math teaching method was more effective in teaching graph related topics, though the significant difference between two groups did not reach. Meanwhile, the traditional teaching was more effective in teaching algebra related topics. It seems that courseware might distract the students' attention from the algebra deduction. It is recommended that teachers should spend more time in class on algebra related topics when they would use courseware supported teaching. If it could be possible to use different teaching methods towards different performance students, traditional teaching would be recommended for the high performance students and courseware supported hybrid learning would be recommended for the medium and low performance ones.

The results of experiment 2 showed that the dynamic software based hybrid teaching method had negative effect to the high performance students. The traditional teaching was more suitable for them. If there could be sufficient teaching hours, the dynamic software based hybrid teaching method was more suitable for the medium and low performance students to improve their learning achievements and reduce their CL in understanding the math concepts.

The results of experiment 3 indicated that the teacher-centered hybrid teaching performed slightly better than the student-centered hybrid learning method in the average marks in the final test. However, the student-centered hybrid learning method performed better than the teacher-centered hybrid teaching in non-test marks. It showed that the normal test paper might not be a good evaluation tool for the student centered instruction. Regarding the experiment CL, the student-centered hybrid learning method requested significantly more time to facilitate the teaching and learning. Considering the combination results of the students' final test and the experiment CL, the teacher-centered hybrid teaching could be more effective.

In general, the three experiment results indicated in one aspect that only if the teacher could make the same effort in teaching, there would be no significant difference among different teaching methods on overall students' achievements. In other aspect, however, different teaching methods did have different effects on students' learning time as well as their understanding towards graph and algebra related topics.

Based on the experiments results, there are following suggestions towards hybrid math teaching strategy design.

- Computer supported hybrid leaning, no matter courseware based or dynamic software based, is certainly more effective in teaching graph related math topics. It is highly recommended to be used in teaching.
- Computer supported hybrid leaning, no matter courseware based or dynamic software based, has negative effect in teaching algebra related math topics. It is suggested to use traditional teaching method on those topics. Furthermore, if the algebra related topics were taught within the hybrid teaching period,

the teacher should pay extra effort to attract the students' attention to the algebra related math topics for better understanding.

- Computer supported hybrid leaning, no matter courseware based or dynamic software based, has slightly negative effect on high performance students. Traditional teaching would be recommended for them.
- Teacher-centered hybrid teaching, no matter courseware based or dynamic software based, has positive effect for the medium and low performance students.
- Dynamic software based student-centered hybrid learning requests significant more teaching hours. It would have positive effect for the medium and low performance students if sufficient learning time could be provided.

References

1. Graham, C.R.: Blended learning systems: definition, current trends, and future directions. In: Bonk, C.J., Graham, C.R. (eds.) Handbook of Blended Learning: Global Perspectives, Local Designs, pp. 21–33. Pfeiffer Publishing, San Francisco (2006)
2. Heinze, A., Procter, C.: Reflections on the Use of Blended Learning. Education in a Changing Environment. University of Salford, Salford, Education Development Unit (2004)
3. Zhang, L.M., Ho., P.K.: A Case Study on the Necessity of the Teaching Method Design Associated with CAI Implementation in Mathematics Teaching. In: Proceedings of the World Conference on Educational Multimedia, Hypermedia & Telecommunication, Florida, USA, June 26-30 (2006)
4. Wai, F.L.: DM_Lab and experimental geometry instruction. Macao Foundation, Macao (2002)
5. Sweller, J.: Cognitive load during problem solving: Effects on learning. Cognitive Science 12, 257–285 (1988)
6. Sweller, J., van Merrienboer, J.G., Paas, F.: Cognitive architecture and instructional design. Educational Psychology Review 10(3), 251–296 (1998)
7. Kalyuga, S., Ayres, P., Chandler, P., Sweller, J.: The Expertise Reversal Effect. Educational Psychologist 38(1), 23–31 (2003)
8. Kirschner, P.A.: Cognitive load theory: implications of cognitive load theory on the design of learning. Learning and Instruction 12, 1–10 (2002)
9. NASA-TLX. Task Load Index, `http://humansystems.arc.nasa.gov/groups/TLX/` (retrieved on February 7, 2011)
10. van Gog, T., Pass, F.: Instructional efficiency: revisiting the original construct in educational research. Educational Psychologist 43(1), 16–26 (2008)
11. Paas, F.: Training strategies for attaining transfer of problem-solving skill in statistics: A cognitive load approach. Journal of Educational Psychology 84, 429–434 (1992)
12. Ouyang, S.Y., Zhang, L.M., Chan, N.H.: A Study on Effectiveness and Cognitive Load of Secondary Math Teaching Using Dynamic Geometry Software PG_Lab. In: Proceedings of International Conference on Information and Communication Technologies in Education (ICICTE 2009), Corfu, Greece, July 9-11 (2009)
13. Zhang, L.M., Chan, N.H., Chu, Y.L.: Cognitive Load Theory Based Effectiveness Evaluation on Dynamic Math Teaching. In: Tsang, P., Cheung, S.K.S., Lee, V.S.K., Huang, R. (eds.) ICHL 2010. LNCS, vol. 6248, pp. 427–438. Springer, Heidelberg (2010)

EduPunks and Learning Management Systems – Conflict or Chance?

Martin Ebner[1], Andreas Holzinger[2], Nick Scerbakov[2], and Philip Tsang[3]

[1] Graz University of Technology, Computing and Information Services, Division of Social Learning, Graz, Austria
martin.ebner@tugraz.at
[2] Graz University of Technology, Computing and Information Services, Institute for Information Systems and Computer Media (IICM), Graz, Austria
martin.ebner@tugraz.at
[3] Caritas Institute of Higher Education, President's Office
HKSAR, China
ptsang@cihe.edu.hk

Abstract. The term Edupunk coined by Jim Groom defines a do-it-yourself concept of using the most recent Web tools available for teaching, instead of relying only on commercial learning platforms – it is the information, the content, the knowledge which matters. Technology itself does not make education valuable per se, it is the creation of individual knowledge which is of paramount importance. However, today, so much free technology is available, which can be used as hands-on tools to enhance learning and teaching of students. However, in this article, we demonstrate that such issues can also be included in a large university wide LMS, which has been developed at Graz University of Technology (TU Graz) during the last years. The development was initiated by the necessity to emphasize and implement three crucial factors for learning: communication, active participation and social interaction. We assess the potential of current Web 2.0 technologies for implementing such factors. We show that the development process was not technology driven; on the contrary, end user requirements of all end user groups engaged into university learning (students, teachers and administrators) were thoroughly investigated and mapped onto functional components of the LMS. Finally, we provide an overview of the platform functionalities with an emphasis on Web 2.0 elements and EduPunk concepts.

Keywords: EduPunk, Learning Management System, e-Learning 2.0, Web 2.0.

1 Introduction

E-learning technologies have changed significantly over the last 10 years - from the development of all kinds of Learning Management Systems (LMS) to the application of Web 2.0 technologies in educational settings. However the solution of a didactic problem is what ought to drive change in educational settings. Consequently Multimedia and e-Learning must be considered as one of many possible elements required to solve a didactical problem (Holzinger, 2002).

R. Kwan et al. (Eds.): ICHL 2011, LNCS 6837, pp. 224–238, 2011.

Tim O'Reilly (O'Reilly, 2005) introduced the term Web 2.0, and described a "read-write-Web" that changes the Web landscape from a huge collection of individual documents to a set of interoperable Web applications. The role of a Web user switched from a passive reader to an active author/writer – as a thinker; and thinking is a central process for effective learning. Such significant changes in the whole Web concept inevitably affected the teaching and learning via Internet. Downes (2005) summarized educational activities by means of using Web 2.0 approaches and concluded that a shift from closed, rigid, passive systems to a more open, collaborative, communicative and sharing philosophy is required. Moreover experiments with Weblogs (Luca & McLoughlin, 2005), Wikis (Augar et al., 2004), (Holzinger, Kickmeier-Rust & Ebner, 2009) and Podcast (Evans, 2007) showed positive effects on Web-Based Learning – if it is used in an appropriate didactical setting. Web 2.0 technologies can be applied for the encouragement of reflective practices (Beale, 2007), or as a support to student-centred approaches (Motschnig-Pitrik & Holzinger, 2002).

In particular, Weblogs can facilitate and stimulate a more distributed learning behaviour, consequently they can be an appropriate instrument to improve learning performance by supplementing traditional lecturing (Holzinger, Kickmeier-Rust, & Ebner, 2009). Since e-learning can generally be defined as a computer-supported communication between teachers and learners, or learners and learners (Preece et al. 2002), new communication facilities have been examined; for example, as an application of microblogging in education (Ebner & Schiefner, 2008). The use of freely available Web resources by means of a combination of different Web applications, such as MashUps (Kulathuramaiyer & Maurer, 2007), (Auinger, Ebner, Nedbal, & Holzinger, 2009) or the utilization of different Web services are a promising approach to overcome the increasing problem of having too much information.

Although technological innovation plays a central role in e-Learning (Ebner & Schiefner, 2009), the success of any application depends on how fast and seamlessly these technological innovations are incorporated into a practical classroom setting. In this paper, we provide an overview on the Edupunk concept through the integration of open and large Web resources into a classroom setting. We present a specially designed and implemented technological solution for 10,000 students from the Graz University of Technology and demonstrate how various services are used in the daily educational practice.

2 EduPunk

On May 25, 2008 Jim Groom coined, on his Weblog, a new term: EduPunk[1]. With this term he expressed his anger about the rigidness and inflexibility of costly commercial learning platforms: "but that survival (of a LMS) is not necessarily dependent on a technology or an innovation, rather it is a means of taking the imaginative experimentation of others and wrapping them up as a product that can be bought and sold like a pair of shoes[2]". According to Jim Groom's Edupunk, there is a "necessity for a

[1] http://bavatuesdays.com/the-glass-bees/ (last visited: May 2010).

[2] http://www.downes.ca/cgi-bin/page.cgi?post=44760 (last visited May 2010).

communal vision of educational technology to fight capital's will to power at the expense of community". Stephen Downes[3], who coined the term e-Learning 2.0, expanded the definition into three facets (Rowell, 2008):

1. As a reaction against the commercialization of learning
2. To symbolize the do-it-yourself (DIY) aspect of educational technology
3. As a way of thinking for yourself instead of being told what to think and learning for yourself instead of being told what to learn

Consequently, Stephen Downes addresses elements of the anti-authoritarian education of the 1960s to be interpreted by the modern digital world of the present time. Gualtieri compared EduPunk with a kind of chaos, made necessary by a low budget. She asked whether chaos 'will ensue if all instructors do that?' (Gualtiere, 2008, Page ref). Some educational institutions provide appropriate, internal systems for their educational aims, however, there are lecturers who like to teach in different, unsupported ways. In the future, upcoming technologies may even broaden the gap between what is possible and what teachers want. Increasing mobility, a huge quantity of mobile devices with access to teaching and learning processes, as well as cloud computing, are trends strengthening the philosophy of distributed learning and the concept of EduPunk.

Consequently, rather than seeing EduPunk as a pure concept or theory, we have to see it as a possible way to foster and strengthen future approached to teaching and learning. Teachers will be able to consider learner individuality by integrating different Web resources; will be able to strengthen their own didactical scenarios by using the Web applications most appropriate for their needs; and, will be able to enhance education using the largest database that has ever been available. Obviously, there are opposing opinions, e.g. that not everyone wants to be an Edupunk as Mark Notess recently pointed out: 'cobbling together unique collections of social media tools to craft the customized toolset for each learning event. In fact, quite a few instructors prefer the technology of instruction to be as invisible as possible and do not themselves have the expertise, time, nor interest to make it so if they had to build their own learning environment (Notess, 2009)'.

Since teaching is also a form of learning for the teachers, as they acquire knowledge through new information, educational institutes have to think about how they can integrate Edupunks in an appropriate way.

3 The General Concept

Graz University of Technology can look back on a long history of technology enhanced learning generally and has profound experience in applying e-learning specifically. First experiments were carried out to enhance online education by developing special authoring tools (Maurer & Scerbakov, 1996) and information systems with a special focus on e-learning needs (Andrews et al, 1994) along with the general recognition of the enormous potential of the Web for higher education. Such experiences

[3] "Introducing EduPunk" http://www.downes.ca/cgi-bin/page.cgi?post=44760 (last visited: May 2009).

provided a solid know how for the development of a very large Content Management System (Kappe et al., 1994), followed by a recent Learning Management System, the "WBT-Master" (Helic et al, 2004). Initially, a database portal system, called TU-GRAZonline was developed and deployed (Haselbacher, 2002) to support solely administrative tasks.

Typical administrative tasks are:

- Target group - students: Students are able to enroll for university courses and get a personal planer, where all course appointments are scheduled. Students may register for examinations, and practical exercises. Information about each student's progress according to courses is also kept in the database.
- Target group - teachers: Teachers define actual courses, provide course descriptions, including learning goals and prerequisites, and define course appointments.
- Target group – administrative staff: There are some further administrative tasks, such as booking rooms, handling exceptional enrolments for courses and examinations; and providing final student marks.

It was recognized that the existing administrative environment needs to be enhanced with a modern learning management system (LMS). Such a LMS should support innovative Web 2.0 technologies to encourage teachers to follow the Edupunk concept by using appropriate tools enhancing their didactical practice. For media didactics, the three following questions are particularly important (Holzinger, 2002):

- How should the communication space of a medium be designed, in order to secure and/or to increase learning success?
- Should the interaction by means of defined learning methods progress sequentially?
- Should the possibility of free movement within an open interaction space, in a net of informational units be given?

These questions have been intensely studied by media didactic researchers for some years. The decisive criteria for the structure of an interaction space can be summarized as follows:

Previous Knowledge: A cross linked communication room is of more use when the target audience has a basic knowledge of the subject (Holzinger, Kickmeier-Rust, Wassertheurer, & Hessinger, 2009). Learner can then freely select the information of individual interest.

Motivation: The term intrinsic motivation (Brehm & Self, 1989) is used when learners wish to know more of the subject as a result of a personal interest in the subject itself, rather than from a primary interest in the possible rewards of learning, such as good notes in an imminent examination. In the case of a sufficiently large intrinsic motivation, an open learning environment can be created.

Independent Learning: A strongly cross linked and open learning environment is suitable for learners accustomed to, or preferring, independent study. Learners who are, as yet, unfamiliar with this method require sequential learning methods at the beginning (Graf, Lin, & Kinshuk, 2008).

4 The Technological Solution

A Learning Management System (LMS) can be seen as a special type of Web based Content Management System (CMS) providing tools for uploading learning materials, access to such materials and special learning-oriented functionalities including communication, collaboration, and evaluation.

An LMS works in a rich Web context and obviously has to be integrated with general functionalities available on the Web. In former times, the LMS did not suffer from an isolation effect. That is, any materials available on the Web might be easily reused within an LMS simply by an URL – computer navigable links; similarly, documents inside an LMS were accessible via generic URLs leading to a particular document. However, the following Web 2.0 concept changed the connotation of the Web dramatically.

Instead of a huge number of individual documents interrelated by navigable links, we see now diverse Web applications. Such isolated systems such as CMS, LMS, Wikis, Blogs, Social Communities, Podcasts, and Image repositories, are accessible by means of Internet protocols. This situation resulted in a certain isolation of the LMS – rich functionality of modern Internet applications cannot be seamlessly integrated into an LMS, thus the content of an LMS becomes isolated from other systems.

4.1 Synchronous Web Services

A synchronous Web service can be defined as follows – a Web server (service-client) forms an XML encoded request to another Web server (service-server), and sends the package via an HTTP protocol to the service-server. Essentially, the service-client cannot continue the task and waits for a response from the service-server. Normally, the REST (REpresentational State Transfer) and RPC (Remote Procedure Call) protocols are used for such a communication. A precondition for using this architectural style is a short response time, (time needed to transfer and process a request).

Obviously, such a communication architectural style might be used very extensively, but we will point out only actually implemented tasks that have verifiably provided a robust functionality.

- Export LMS content as RSS (really simple syndication) feed; it has become almost a common way nowadays to inform users of latest modifications by dynamically generating topical RSS feeds and requesting them via a REST Web service.
- Export LMS content as RDF (resource definition framework) map. While RSS feeds provide information on latest modifications, an RDF map provides a standard structured view on a topical resource (say, a training course) that can be further integrated with other maps and browsed using third party applications. RDF maps can easily be requested via a REST Web service.
- Remote publishing. Needless to say that acceptance of almost any Web application essentially depends on the tools that are available for content authoring. It is also well recognized that from the user interface point of view, stand-alone applications on a user desktop have serious advantages in comparison with a Web interface. Simply speaking or authoring a document should be as convenient as, for example, as using a favorite text editor tool and uploading must not be more complex than

reshuffling files between local folders. RPC Web services are extremely suitable for providing robust interfaces between such stand-alone applications as remote WYSIWYG (What-You-Get-Is-What-You-See) HTML editors, as well as file managers, and a remote server. For example, we use well-known blog editors such as Windows Live Writer and ScribeFire as end-user authoring tools connected via an RPC Web service to the LMS system.

- Creating a personal portfolio. The LMS provides access to material that might be of interest to teachers. Very often, some materials are of a particular interest for a certain user and need to be kept in a way defined by that user; it might be a personal blog, a CMS on another server or even a special database application. In this context, an LMS must provide tools to export selected elements in the most convenient way. Obviously, using the RPC protocol with personal adjustments seems to be the simplest way to achieve this. For example, any document from the LMS server might be copied into a personal user blog with just one mouse click.
- Import RSS/RDF. This is an obvious task that allows a seamless integration of materials from another server into a training topic (training course). Using a REST Web service is almost a standard way of implementing such a task.

4.2 Asynchronous Web Services

The only difference between asynchronous and synchronous Web services is the behavior of the service-client that sends a package to the service–server, and continues without receiving data from the server. In this case, the client provides an additional entry where the server would send a response as soon as it is ready. Using asynchronous Web services becomes necessary when processing information, and creating a response by the server, may require substantial time.

Normally, so-called SOAP (Simple Object Access Protocol) is used for such communication. Asynchronous Web services are typically used for different types of automatic assessment of user uploads, for example, plagiarism control, compiling/running a programming source, and automatic essay grading.

Some typical e-learning tasks that have proved to provide a robust functionality by using asynchronous Web services are:

- Plagiarism control. Files are simply delivered to a server providing such plagiarism detection functionality, and final results (reports) are sent back afterwards to the LMS as the task is completed.
- Checking programming sources. Source texts along with selected test cases are delivered to a specially allocated Internet application where they are compiled and run. Reports on performing all the tasks are sent back to the LMS.
- Automatic Essay Grading. From a technical point of view, the process looks similar to previously mentioned usage of asynchronous Web services.

4.3 Mashup Technologies

The mashup technology relies on end-user client functionality. A user screen may be divided into a number of areas allocated for communication with different servers, and, thus, functionality of a number of applications is integrated (mashed up) on a single screen.

Note that applications used in such a way must provide a so-called JavaScript API to implement the necessary communication between the applications. Nowadays, providing such a JavaScript API is almost a hallmark for any more or less wide spread internet application such as Facebook, Twitter, GoogleMap, GoogleSearch, GoogleWave, Microsoft Bing, to mention just a few.

Mashup technology can be used within a LMS and in almost all settings.We have implemented so far:

- A Spatial Content Management training component where users can both provide and browse training content using a geographical location (Google Map).
- A geographical chat component where users can share information on their current location.
- Interface to Facebook allowing use of this huge social network for training purposes.
- Interface to Twitter to allow the sharing of twitter messages and discussions as a training component.

As new Web applications appear and gain wide recognition, this technology will attract more and more attention. Right now many experts have started experimenting with GoogleWaves and its JavaScript API; Microsoft offers Enterprise Mashups that would provide a possibility of reusing the whole Microsoft office and sharing its applications.

5 Discussion, Examples, Field Studies

Currently more than 500 training courses are implemented and deployed at Graz University of Technology to

- deliver online content to students;
- support different communication scenarios (forums, chats, announcements, emails, SMS-Service and push-notifications) ;
- provide additional functionality, such as online examinations, appointments and student upload areas.

Shown below are some examples of using Web 2.0 components by teachers in a real training context by means of the previously mentioned technological solutions. It is interesting to note that the teachers were not forced to use the technology just for the sake of technology; rather, they simply enhanced an existing didactic concept with technological innovations, hence, the teachers functioned as Edupunks. In a typical case, the teachers switched from isolated Web 2.0 tools to the same tools seamlessly integrated into the LMS. Personal feedback from students, including their motivation, which was gathered through an immediate feedback round, showed quite positive results. Our task was to integrate widely accepted and recognized concepts into a modern LMS so that teachers, as well as students, benefited most in their teaching and learning activities.

5.1 Integration of a Weblog (Synchronous Web Service)

The course "knowledge management" for students of Mechanical Engineering and Economic Sciences serves more than 30 learners each study term. Students are supposed to learn main concepts, methods and trends in knowledge management; its actual applications and benefits. Weblogs were traditionally used for practical exercises to reflect the lecture content, discuss results and support collaboration among students, teachers and especially invited experts. For example, the Weblog on "knowledge identification" is accessed at http://tugll.tugraz.at/wm09ident/Weblog/ (last visited: 25-02-2010). Since the teacher allocated five Weblogs on slightly different topics, students suffered from *lost syndrome* and often could not find a relevant Weblog.

In this particular case, the synchronous Web service "Import RSS" was used to integrate all different RSS feeds into a single course Internet panel (see Fig.1), and thus provide a convenient overview and access to the Weblogs.

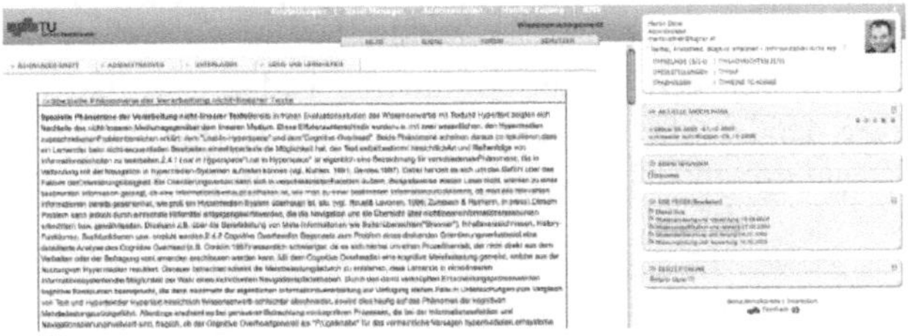

Fig. 1. Web service "Import RSS"

Fig. 1 shows the latest post in the Weblog "knowledge identification" as a component within the learning management system. There is a box "RSS Feeds" on the right side bar where numerous feeds can be imported. The content from an external resource (in this case a student's Weblog) is imported, parsed and finally visualized within the system by clicking on one Weblog title. Thus, students are provided with an overview of the online activity of their colleagues and teachers, along with basic functionality of the LMS.

Another important aspect of integrating training materials from different sources is the so-called homogeneous time line. All the material must be provided with a time stamp in the course context. Such time stamps are often used to access materials as "latest", "most recent", and "modified after my latest visit". Fig. 1 (German title "Aktuelle Änderungen"), shows that the imported feed elements are properly integrated into the course time-line and any changes in such blogs are marked as changes in the course materials.

Teachers of the course "Application Software and Programming" use the same technical concept in a slightly different way. They run their own Web server (separated from the LMS) and notify students on its actual content by generating a RSS feed that is automatically imported into the LMS. Thus, the content of those external servers is provided to students in the same way as usual LMS content. In this particular case, teachers use this feature to obtain the advantages of the LMS - use of online administration and online communication tools, along with their own proprietary programmed environment for uploading content from TEX-scripts.

5.2 Exporting a Podcast (Synchronous Web Service)

One mandatory course (*Strength of Materials*) in Mechanical Engineering and Economic Sciences, is attended by more than 250 students every year. This course is about stresses, deformations, material laws, normal stresses in bars and plates, bending of straight beams, torsion of straight bars, special problems in strength of materials, work and energy methods in elastostatics and buckling of materials. Traditionally, teachers of this course have used a tablet PC in combination with a projector and screen casting software to record the contents of the whole lecture and related exercises (Ebner and Nagler, 2008). The videos were supposed to be provided in different formats (.avi, .mp3, .mov and .mp4) to the students after each lecture (Nagler et al, 2008). The process of selecting an appropriate file format for a particular end-user device is far from a trivial one, especially for non computer-science students. The support of different and easily maintainable lists of podcasts for downloading to different devices or for online viewers is very much desired. For this purpose, the synchronous Web service "Export LMS content as RSS" is used to provide students with a facility to download files as special podcast series.

Fig. 2 shows a recorded lecture within the LMS. The listed files are provided through the RSS feeds, which can be booked on the right side ("RSS Feed", select "This course") and downloaded directly to a particular end-user's device.

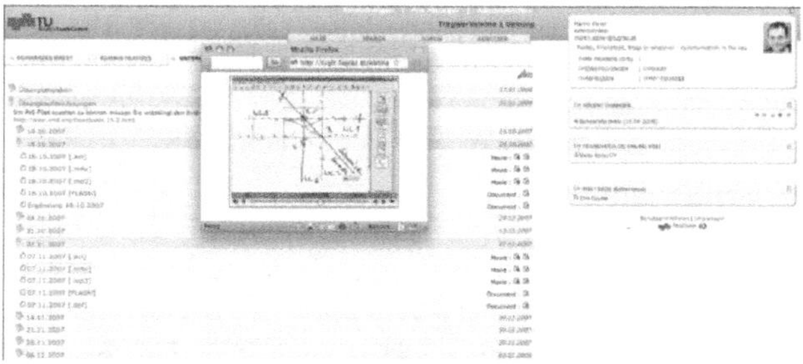

Fig. 2. Web service "Export LMS content as RSS"

5.3 Evaluating Programming Sources (Asynchronous Web Service)

The course *Programming in Fortran* is offered to students of Technical Chemistry, Chemical Process Engineering and Biotechnology on a voluntary basis. The course teaches students to perform electronic data processing by means of the Fortran programming language. Therefore, students have to develop small program samples on their own, testing them by compiling the source code and presenting it to the teacher for grading. In former times, the teacher needed to manually compile/run student sources on a local computer. Recently a special, asynchronous Web service was implemented to provide a consistent interface for students to compile/run their sources under teacher monitoring. Source texts, along with selected test cases, are automatically delivered to a specially allocated Internet application as a so-called SOAP package. A separate internet application (service-server) compiles and runs the files automatically. All reports (error messages or program output) are sent back to the

LMS, hence, the students see results as soon as the results are ready. An additional communication feature allows discussions/assessment of reports.

5.4 Integrating Live Web Streaming (Mashup Technology)

The course *Introduction to Structured Programming* is perhaps the largest course at the Graz University of Technology. Every year about 800 students are required to attend the lecture to get a first impression on C-programming. Since the largest lecture room of the university is designed for a maximum of 500 students, an alternative teaching scenario needs to be applied. Formerly, the lecture content was recorded and provided as podcast with some delay necessary to produce and deploy the video files.

To avoid this delay and provide students with a possibility of viewing the lecture and asking questions in real time, a live streaming broadcast was deployed. Thus, a special Web application (streaming server) with appropriate equipment has been installed to stream a lecture. The audio and video signals as well as slides from the desktop computer are sent directly to the Web streaming server which allows the lecture to be seen on demand.

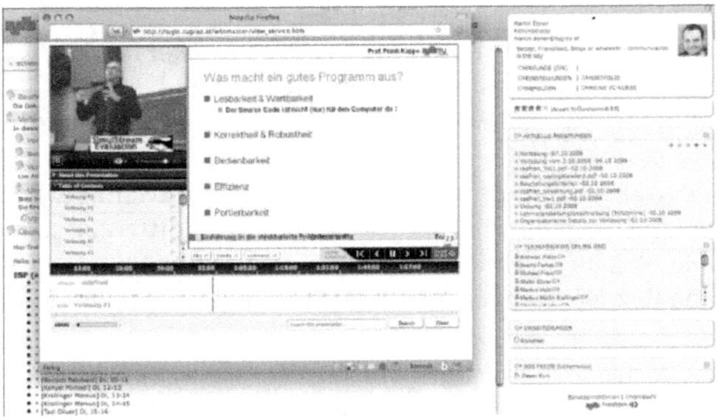

Fig. 3. Mashup Technology via embedded code

The streaming session is archived and made accessible for students as back-up after each lecture. Mashup technology is used to seamlessly integrate such live lecture recordings to the Learning Management System. Thus, the videos are placed at the streaming server and the integration to the LMS is achieved by reuse of a special JavaScript Code (Fig. 3). Similar to the world's biggest video platform YouTube[4], streaming videos are directly embedded into the existing learning context.

5.5 Integrating Blogs and Microblogs (Mashup Technology)

Since the geographic location of objects provides essential information in many training areas (for example, architecture, and civil engineering), embedding such information into an e-learning context constitutes an obvious need. A combination of pictures with global coordinates is called "geotagging" and gained significant interest once

[4] http://youtube.com (last visited May 2010).

mobile devices had GPS receivers on board. One interesting didactical scenario is that students take their pictures, combine them automatically with coordinates, upload them, for example, onto an adapted wiki site and collaborate further by writing essays about them (Safran et al, 2009).

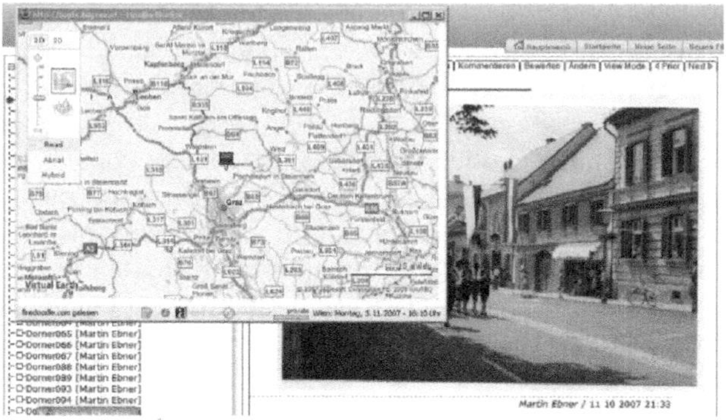

Fig. 4. Geotagging by using Microsoft Map API

The course *Urban development and town planning, history and theory* utilizes this scenario. Students have to choose an existing building and develop a project on renovation of that building or embedding new buildings into an existing architectural landscape.

Geographic coordinates are provided for each picture to show where the buildings are exactly located as well as what they look like from different perspectives. Fig. 4 shows an example of such a geotagged picture mashed up with a so-called "Microsoft Maps" application that allows zooming in and out or switching between map, satellite and a 3D view.

5.6 Integrating Widgets (Mashup Technology)

Another example of the integration of different Web applications was successfully implemented for the course *Social Aspects of Information Technology*. The course deals with different forms of communication (Weblogs, collaboration and microblogs) to reflect experiences and research results by students (Ebner and Maurer, 2009). Thus, eight student groups were supposed to use a Weblog server, and eight other student groups were established to work with the open-source microblogging platform called Laconica. Results of all the student groups needed to be integrated with the content of the course, providing inter-communication facilities for students from different groups.

Obviously, providing an overview on all incoming information is not a trivial task since more than 200 students are permanently working on their contributions, providing upwards of 100 microblogs and 160 Weblog posts each week.

Fig. 5 shows the multiple ways the different Web resources are combined and presented within the LMS course panel. Similar to the course *Knowledge Management*, the external Weblogs are integrated via RSS feeds. Furthermore, an upload possibility is integrated via an additional tool. Finally, the external microblogging activities are implemented via a small widget. Widgets are tiny embeddable applications that can be included into an HTML code or even executed on a desktop. Such client side code can be simple JavaScript, Java-applets or anything that can be embedded into a valid HTML or XHTML document (Taraghi et al, 2009). The LMS was extended to accept small code parts and allow integrating external resources through the use of widgets. In this way, each student may access individual blogs or microblogs in the context of current course materials.

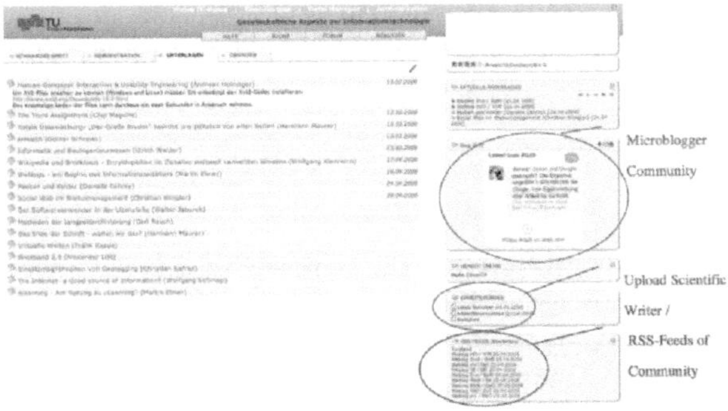

Fig. 5. Widgets use – another example of mashup technology

6 Conclusion

If we summarize our more than 10 years experience in the design, development, experimental and practical application of LMS, we can point out that a general LMS provides course administration, communication support and extended content management, online examinations, and upload possibilities. Most of the Austrian universities are running courses that have these functionalities. As Web 2.0 technologies become more and more wide-spread, teachers seek to enhance their teaching strategies with these functionalities. At Graz University of Technology, we permanently adapt the existing e-learning environment to the requirements, needs and demands of the teachers, following learner centered approaches (Holzinger & Motschnik-Pitrik, 2005). Synchronous/asynchronous Web services and mashup technologies are used to overcome information isolation of such an LMS and to avoid the endless reproduction of functionalities of already existing Web applications – not reinventing the wheel.

The power of a modern LMS must focus on the ability to implement a potentially large number of Web applications. Such distributed architectures may well equal rather ambitious goals that might be formulated as follows:

- Individuality: The large amount of online data will help to assist learner's individual learning needs. It is imaginable that in the near future students can choose any content from the Web that fits best.
- Creativity: The large number of tools allows teachers to create new didactical approaches and thereby enhance learner motivation.

- Live collaboration: One of the next major steps on the Web will be real-time collaboration as already implemented by tools like etherpad[5] or GoogleWave [6].
- Personalization: An LMS must be much more flexible and adaptable to user needs. A very first step has been made by beginning to develop a so-called Personal Learning Environment (Taraghi et al, 2009a). Based on a widget concept and distributed technology, learners should be able to choose their own different (learning) resources as well as to integrate their daily Web applications.
- Mobility: Access to Web resources tends to rely more and more on mobile devices. Since devices like the iPhone or netbooks allow constant internet access, it may be feasible that learners as well as teachers will learn or even teach on the move (Ebner et al, 2008).

References

1. Andrews, K., Kappe, F., Maurer, H.: The Hyper-G Network Information System. Journal of Universal Computer Science (j-jucs) 1(4), 206–220 (1995)
2. Augar, N., Raitman, R., Zhou, W.: Teaching and learning online with wikis. In: Atkinson, R., McBeath, C., Jonas-Dwyer, D., Phillips, R. (eds.) Beyond the comfort zone: Proceedings of the 21st ASCILITE Conference, Perth, Australia, December 5-8, pp. 95–104 (2004)
3. Auinger, A., Ebner, M., Nedbal, D., Holzinger, A.: Mixing Content and Endless Collaboration – MashUps: Towards Future Personal Learning Environments. In: Stephanidis, C. (ed.) UAHCI 2009. LNCS, vol. 5616, pp. 14–23. Springer, Heidelberg (2009)
4. Beale, R.: Blogs, reflective practice and student-centered learning (2007), `http://www.bcs.org/upload/pdf/ewic_hc07_sppaper1.pdf`
5. Brehm, J.W., Self, E.A.: The Intensity of Motivation. Annual Review of Psychology 40, 109–131 (1989)
6. Downes, S.: e-Learning 2.0. ACM e-Learn Magazine 10 (October 2005)
7. Ebner, M., Schiefner, M.: Microblogging - more than fun? In: Proceedings of IADIS Mobile Learning Conference (2008)
8. Ebner, M., Nagler, W.: Has the end of chalkboard come? A survey about the limits of Interactive Pen Displays in Higher Education. In: Bruck, P.A., Lindner, M. (eds.) Proceeding of the 4th International Microlearning 2008 Conference on Microlearning and Capacity Building, pp. 79–91. Innsbruck University Press, Innsbruck (2008)
9. Ebner, M., Scerbakov, N., Stickel, C., Maurer, H.: Mobile Information Access in Higher Education. In: Proceedings of E-Learn 2008, Las Vegas, pp. 777–782 (2008)
10. Ebner, M., Maurer, H.: Can Weblogs and Microblogs Change Traditional Scientific Writing? Future Internet 1(1), 47–58 (2009)
11. Ebner, M., Schiefner, M.: Looking Toward the Future of Technology-Enhanced Education: Ubiquitous Learning and the Digital Native. IGI Global (2009)
12. Evans, C.: The effectiveness of m-Learning in the form of podcast revision lectures in higher education. Computers & Education 50(2), 491–498 (2007)
13. Graf, S., Lin, T., Kinshuk, J.: The relationship between learning styles and cognitive traits - Getting additional information for improving student modelling. Computers in Human Behavior 24(2), 122–137 (2008)

[5] http://etherpad.com (last visited May 2010).
[6] http://googlewave.com (last visited May 2010).

14. Gualtieri, L.N.: Once a Edupunk, Always an Edupunk. eLearn Magazine (2008), http://elearnmag.org/subpage.cfm?section=opinion&article=101-1
15. Haselbacher, F.: Design and operation of a WEB-databased university-information-management-system. In: The Changing Universities: The Challenge of New Technologies 2002, International Conference of European University Information Systems, vol. 8 (2002)
16. Helic, D., Maurer, H., Scerbakov, N.: Knowledge Transfer Processes in a Modern WBT System. Journal of Network and Computer Applications 27(3), 163–190 (2004)
17. Holzinger, A.: Multimedia Basics. In: Learning. Cognitive Fundamentals of multimedial Information Systems, Laxmi, New Delhi, vol. 2 (2002)
18. Holzinger, A., Motschnik-Pitrik, R.: Considering the Human in Multimedia: Learner-Centered Design (LCD) & Person-Centered e-Learning (PCeL). In: Mittermeir, R.T. (ed.) Innovative Concepts for Teaching Informatics, Carl Ueberreuter, Vienna, pp. 102–112 (2005)
19. Holzinger, A., Kickmeier-Rust, M.D., Ebner, M.: Interactive Technology for Enhancing Distributed Learning: A Study on Weblogs. Paper presented at the HCI 2009 The 23nd British HCI Group Annual Conference, Cambridge (2009)
20. Holzinger, A., Kickmeier-Rust, M.D., Wassertheurer, S., Hessinger, M.: Learning performance with interactive simulations in medical education: Lessons learned from results of learning complex physiological models with the HAEMOdynamics SIMulator. Computers & Education 52(2), 292–301 (2009)
21. Kappe, F., Andrews, K., Schmaranz, K., Maurer, H.: Hyper-G: A Distributed Hypermedia System of the Second Generation. In: Proc. EEOS Workshop on European Data Networks and Earth Observation User Information Services: Survey and Consultation, Marino (Rome), Italy. European Commission Joint Research Centre and ESA/ESRIN, pp. 305–318 (1994)
22. Kulathuramaiyer, N., Maurer, H.: Current Developments of Mashups in Shaping Web Applications. In: Proc. of ED-MEDIA 2007, pp. 1172–1177. ACCE, USA (2007)
23. Luca, J., McLoughlin, C.: Can blogs promote fair and equitable teamwork? In: Proceeding of ASCILITE 2005: Balance, Fidelity, Mobility: maintaining the momentum?, pp. 379–385 (2005)
24. Maurer, H., Scerbakov, N.: Multimedia Authoring for Presentation and Education: The Official Guide to HM-Card, vol. 250. Addison-Wesley, Bonn (1996)
25. Motschnig-Pitrik, R., Holzinger, A.: Student-Centered Teaching Meets New Media: Concept and Case Study. IEEE Journal of Educational Technology & Society 5(4), 160–172 (2002)
26. Nagler, W., Saranti, A., Ebner, M.: Podcasting at TU Graz: How to Implement Podcasting as a Didactical Method for Teaching and Learning Purposes at a University of Technology. In: Proceeding of the 20th World Conference on Educational Multimedia, Hypermedia and Telecommunications (ED-Media), pp. 3858–3863 (2008)
27. Notess, M.: Not Dead Yet: Why the Institutional LMS is Worth Saving. eLearn (7) (2009)
28. O'Reilly, T.: What is Web 2.0? – Design Patterns and Business Models for the Next Generation Software (2010), http://oreilly.com/Web2/archive/what-is-Web-20.html
29. Preece, J., Sharp, H., Rogers, Y.: Interaction Design: Beyond Human-Computer Interaction. Wiley, New York (2002)
30. Rowell, L.: "Edupunk" Rocks the (Virtual) House, eLearn Magazin (2008), http://www.elearnmag.org/subpage.cfm?section=articles&article=65-1

31. Safran, C., Garcia-Barrios, V.M., Ebner, M.: The Benefits of Geo Tagging and Microblogging in m-Learning: a Use Case. In: Proceedings of ACM Academic MindTrek 2009 - Everyday Life in the Ubiquitous Area, MindTrek 2009, Tampere, Finland, pp. 135–141 (2009)
32. Taraghi, B., Ebner, M., Till, G., Mühlburger, H.: Personal Learning Environment - A Conceptual Study. In: International Conference on Interactive Computer Aided Learning (ICL 2009), Villach (2009)
33. Taraghi, B., Ebner, M., Schaffert, S.: Personal Learning Environment for Higher Education - A MashUp Based Widget Concept. In: Proceedings of the Second International Workshop on Mashup Personal Learning Environments (MUPPLE 2009), Nice, France (2009)
34. Holzinger, A., Kickmeier-Rust, M.D., Ebner, M.: Interactive Technology for Enhancing Distributed Learning: A Study on Weblogs. In: HCI 2009 23rd British HCI Group Annual Conference on People and Computers: Celebrating People and Technology. British Computer Society, Cambridge University (2009)

Students' Perceptions of Different Delivery Methods in Hybrid Language Learning

Yoko Hirata and Yoshihiro Hirata

Hokkai-Gakuen University
Sapporo, Japan
{hira,hirata}@eli.hokkai-s-u.ac.jp

Abstract. In the last decade, a wide variety of computer applications for language learning have been introduced into Japanese educational settings. According to this recent trend, various computer-based courseware or commercial software for language learning plays an indispensable role in higher educational organizations. However, not enough research has been done concerning which and how courseware can be adapted to the particular students' needs and skills. Even the instructor is often unaware of what methodological approaches work well for students' needs. The present study aims at understanding how Japanese students view certain courseware when they use it and determine how the courseware should be incorporated into the hybrid language learning environment. The study focuses on a hybrid English learning course offered to improve students' scores in The Test of English for International Communication (TOEIC®). The results of this study provide instructors with many insights into how to facilitate hybrid learning for students using courseware. The results also suggest some significant implications concerning how to maximize the effectiveness of hybrid learning for future language learning.

Keywords: evaluation, courseware, language learning, hybrid learning.

1 Introduction

Recently the number of hybrid-learning courses which combine a face-to-face teaching module with technology support have increased in Japan. Unlike traditional language learning settings, this new environment is supposed to provide students, having different needs and proficiency levels, with ample opportunities to learn individually without the direct intervention of an instructor [1]. As this type of educational setting becomes more widely available, various computer-based courseware and platforms have been developed and a large amount of money has been spent on them [2]. Courseware includes "tutorial software" and software packages which can be used without an instructor [3]. In Japan, commercial test preparation courseware is currently abundant and using this kind of computer program in English language classrooms is an area which has gained in popularity.

R. Kwan et al. (Eds.): ICHL 2011, LNCS 6837, pp. 239–250, 2011.

One of the reasons includes the fact that English is a compulsory subject and has traditionally been taught to large classes which have students of various levels [4]. As a result the courseware is often used as a cost-effective and time-efficient solution for language learning [1]. However, one of the problems of this system is the fact that technology is often viewed as a substitute for the instructor [5]. Another problem is that, in Japanese educational settings, learning is still very teacher-centered. Traditionally, students have been conditioned to follow what the authorities decide without little thought [6]. In spite of this situation, relatively little is actually known about how these receptive students view the courseware. Although computer users have been compared with a control group using traditional learning methods, the instructor needs to ensure students' learning opportunities are maximized.

2 Research Background

The Test of English for International Communication (TOEIC®) has been used worldwide as a means of measuring communication abilities of non-native speakers of English. The language skills they are required to obtain include everyday English listening and reading skills similar to people working in an international environment. Recently, companies in Japan tend to use TOEIC scores to estimate university students' English levels for the purpose of hiring suitable employees. As the TOEIC scores are also used as a requirement for job promotion in the company, in 2009 the test was adopted by 2,700 companies and educational organizations in Japan [7]. As there is another belief that success in examinations appears to be seen as the key to success in life in Japan [8], improving university students' TOEIC scores has been an integral part of the English curriculum. In response to these needs, various kinds of commercial courseware and platforms have increasingly been developed in order for students to gain high TOEIC scores [9] [10]. These tools have been used for the purpose of the promotion of individualization and autonomy in learning, since they provide students with opportunities to do the tasks, select the contents and sequence of learning according to their own choice and preferences [11]. A number of research publications in the past decade have discussed the potential contributions of courseware to the improvement of students' language skills [10] [12]. However, the studies indicate that these learning environments are often completely machine-dependent and there is no meaningful interaction between the instructor and the students [6]. In addition, little empirical data has been collected on students' views on these computer technologies. In Japan, despite the fact that adaptation of courseware in tertiary language education has become a mainstream practice, not much is known about how it can be integrated into the course which supports these students in preparing for the tests. There is still a strong need for comprehensive studies on the possible relationship of the courseware with the rest of the curriculum, and how it relates to students' educational background and needs [3].

3 Purpose of the Study

The purpose of this study was to examine university students' own learning preferences and attitudes toward relatively new courseware-based language learning. The focus was placed on the students' views on the advantages and disadvantages of the tutorial role of the courseware. The research questions are summed up as follows:

Research questions

1. How do students perceive two different modes of teaching: conventional paper-based learning and new courseware-based learning?
2. Is there any relationship between the students' background, such as computer skills and motivation, and their perception of the different learning styles?

4 Methodology

4.1 The Setting and Participants

A class of non-English majors in a university in Japan was chosen as participants for the present study. The participants (n=43) were lower-intermediate learners of English enrolled in a "TOEIC English" course in an undergraduate English program. The students, who inclined to rely heavily on the instructor, consisted of 31 males and 12 females were between the age of eighteen and twenty. The objective of this course was to help students develop the four language skills and it was specifically designed for them to gain higher TOEIC scores. The results of their performances on the placement test at the beginning of the course showed that their English proficiency was similar. The course, which was a hybrid learning course, continued for two semesters and was offered for ninety minutes a week in a computer assisted language learning (CALL) classroom. About half of the class hours were devoted to working on the courseware-based learning. The majority of students themselves thought that they were not fully skilled in using computers, although they had been using the Internet and mobiles in their everyday lives.

4.2 Procedures

At the beginning of this course, the instructor explained the benefits of taking the TOEIC test and the aim of this course is achieving at least a score of 450 TOEIC points. During the class, approximately half of it was used for direct, instructor lead teaching, using the textbook. The rest of the class was spent on the computer which included a classroom management system. During the computer session, students worked on a courseware full of multiple-choice exercises. At the same time, they used the classroom management system as their main tool for engaging vocabulary activities. The classroom management system enabled the instructor to monitor the students' activities on their screens. The system also allowed the instructor to restrict students' web browsing and even control their computers. While the students' were working on their computers, the instructor was available to answer the students' questions.

At the end of the course, the students were provided with a questionnaire which attempted to find out their views on different modes of learning. The questions in the questionnaire were based on the previous study examining students' attitudes to learning grammar with web- and book-based contexts [3]. Only twenty eight questions from the questionnaire referring to the evaluation of paper-based learning and courseware-based learning were used. Most of the questions had a 10-point Likert scale, with "1" representing "strongly disagree" and "10" representing "strongly agree". The questionnaire had an area where students could write comments in relation to the questions. The points were totaled and averaged, and a standard deviation was also attained. The data is presented in this paper as mean ±SD. As well, the questionnaire was analyzed by using Spearman's correlation. In addition, although initially the students' computer levels were divided into four groups: 'very low', 'low', 'high', and 'very high', there was only one student who answered 'very high'. As only one student answered 'very high', the levels were divided into two groups: 'high' and 'low'. The different computer levels were compared by a one-way ANOVA with the results of the students' ratings based on the 28 questions mentioned above. In addition, the results of the students' ratings were analyzed by a one-way ANOVA with the students' perception of the importance of the TOEIC preparation as well as their motivation for taking the TOEIC tests.

4.3 Teaching Tools

The textbook used in the classroom was THE TOEIC TEST TRAINER Target 650 [13]. This textbook is a conventional test-preparation book and is comprised of two major parts; one part consists of an explanation of grammar and vocabulary, and the other part has exercises. The textbook which contains twelve units has various language exercises, including multiple-choice questions, true or false practice questions, and fill-in-the-blank comprehension tests. The courseware used in the classroom was an online TOEIC preparatory program named TOEIC® Test Super Practice Exam 730 [14] and is designed to help students develop test-taking skills to get higher scores. This multiple-choice TOEIC preparation courseware, which is not relevant to the content of the textbook, has a user friendly interface and allows students to listen to the audio files on their own. The courseware requires students to have basic computer skills, such as being able to scroll texts and click on text, to tackle the questions. The courseware is comprised of two parts; the first part consists of three training units, and the second part deals with three test units. Students were allowed to make their own choices as to how to work through these exercises and tests. After each unit, the program provides students with scores as well as explanations of the right answers, so that students get instant feedback on the answers they have given. The students were recommended to use this courseware for their independent study as well.

5 Findings

The results gained by the questionnaire are presented below. First of all, with regard to computer skills, 67.4% of the students stated that they have 'low' or 'very low' computer skills, whereas there was only one student who stated that he/she has a very high level of computer skills.

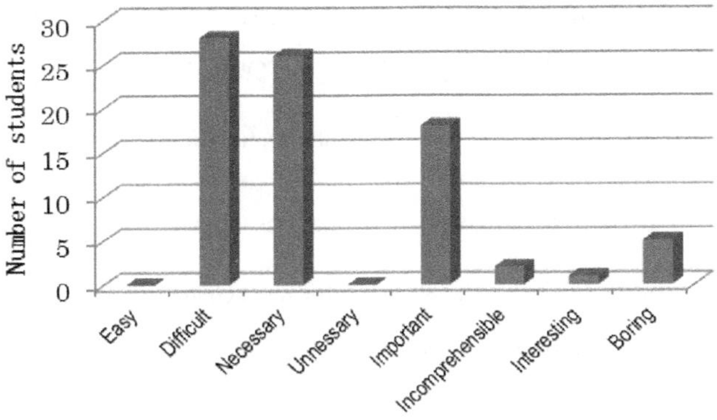

Fig. 1. Students' views on TOEIC tests

As shown in Figure 1, the students thought studying for the preparation of the TOEIC tests was 'difficult', but, at the same time, 'necessary' and 'important'. The majority of the students recognized the importance of the study. With regard to the level of importance of taking the TOEIC test, more than 93% of the students considered preparing for the test was 'important' or 'very important'. Despite the students' recognized importance of taking the test and the fact that they have registered for this course, 74.4% of the students declared that they were going to take the test before graduating from the university. Those who are not going to take the test stated the reasons including the enormous difficulties with the test. However, only 10 out of 32 students, who stated they are going to take the test, were actually studying for the test on their own. In addition, for the majority of students who were studying by themselves, the frequency of study is less than once a week. Twenty three out of 32 students, who were going to take the test, stated that getting a good TOEIC score would look good on their resume as a reason of taking the test.

Table 1 shows the students' view on the courseware. As shown in Table 1, many students stated that the courseware provided them with various TOEIC exercises. The Average (±SD) of this response was 6.86 (±1.85). The findings also indicate that many students thought that the courseware had an easy-to-use audio playback system. The Average (±SD) of this response was 6.58 (±2.29). Only a few students thought that the courseware was easy to navigate. The Average (±SD) of this response was 4.42 (±2.29). In addition, not many students valued the usefulness of navigating the courseware.

Table 1. Students' view on the courseware

	Mean (SD)
1. The courseware was appropriate to my English level.	5.21 (2.04)
2. The courseware was appropriate to my study needs.	5.07 (2.00)
3. The courseware provided me with various exercises.	6.86 (1.85)
4. The courseware helped me enjoy studying the TOEIC exercises.	5.14 (2.12)
5. The courseware gave me practical advice about studying for the TOEIC test.	5.19 (2.04)
6. The courseware had comprehensive explanations of exercises.	5.63 (2.23)
7. The courseware was effective in studying for the TOEIC test.	5.44 (2.16)
8. The courseware helped me understand the importance of studying for the TOEIC test.	5.21 (1.88)
9. The courseware had a simple and clear screen layout.	5.72 (2.14)
10. The courseware was easy to navigate.	4.42 (2.29)
11. The courseware displayed beautiful digital pictures.	5.93 (2.28)
12. The courseware had an easy-to-use audio playback system.	6.58 (2.29)
13. The courseware was easier to use than the textbook.	5.00 (2.27)
14. The courseware would help me improve my TOEIC score.	5.63 (2.14)

(N = 43)

Table 2 shows the students' views on the textbook. Compared with Table 1, the results presented in Table 2 clearly indicate that the students highly valued the simple and clear page layout and the easiness of turning the pages of the textbook. The Averages (±SD) of these response were 6.05 (±2.03) and 6.02 (±2.76) respectively. Unlike the students' views on the courseware, with regard to the comprehensive explanations of the exercises, the students did not value this as highly as the courseware. Likewise, compared with the results of the courseware evaluation, the students did not think of the benefits of the textbook, such as enjoyment and the advice provided by the textbook, as much as those provided by the courseware.

The results of the one-way ANOVA showed that there were no significant differences between the students' perception of the importance of the TOEIC preparation and the students' views on both the courseware and the textbook. The analysis with the usability of the courseware indicated by a difference in the students'

Table 2. Students' view on the textbook

	Mean (SD)
1. The textbook was appropriate to my English level.	4.86 (1.74)
2. The textbook was appropriate to my study needs.	5.26 (1.65)
3. The textbook provided me with various exercises.	5.58 (3.58)
4. The textbook helped me enjoy studying the TOEIC exercises.	4.44 (1.84)
5. The textbook gave me practical advice about studying for the TOEIC test.	4.44 (2.12)
6. The textbook had comprehensive explanations of exercises.	4.12 (2.15)
7. The textbook was effective in studying for the TOEIC test.	4.58 (2.03)
8. The textbook helped me understand the importance of studying for the TOEIC test.	5.05 (1.84)
9. The textbook had a simple and clear page layout.	6.05 (2.03)
10. The textbook was easy to navigate.	6.02 (2.76)
11. The textbook displayed beautiful pictures.	5.30 (2.26)
12. The textbook had an easy-to-use CD.	4.53 (1.71)
13. The textbook was easier to use than the courseware.	5.93 (2.23)
14. The textbook would help me improve my TOEIC score.	5.58 (2.05)

(N = 43)

Table 3. Averages of usability of courseware based on students' computer skills

The level of computer skill is…	Low	High
Average (S.D.)	4.48 (2.06)	6.07 (2.40)

computer skills F (1,41) = 5.032, p = .030 (see Table 3). As shown in Table 4, the analysis was conducted in order to check the appropriate English level of the courseware, and showed a significant effect of the students' motivation for taking the TOEIC test, F (1,41) = 5.774, p = .021. In addition, the same analysis was conducted in order to check the variety of the exercises provided by the courseware, and indicated a significant effect of students' motivation for taking the TOEIC test, F (1,41) = 4.289, p = .045. This result was consistent with the results of the clear screen layout F (1,41) = 5.885, p = .020 and the beautiful digital pictures provided by the courseware F (1,41) = 4.526, p = .039.

Table 4. Factors affected significantly by students' motivation

The courseware...	Less motivated	Well motivated
was appropriate to English level	4.00 (1.61)	5.63 (2.03)
provided me with various exercises	7.82 (1.47)	6.53 (1.87)
had a simple and clear screen layout	7.00 (2.00)	5.28 (2.04)
was easy to navigate	5.64 (1.96)	4.00 (2.27)

Table 5. Correlation between factors for using the courseware

The courseware...	gave me practical advice about studying for the TOEIC test.	was effective in studying for the TOEIC test.	had a simple and clear screen layout.	was easier to use than the textbook.	helped me improve my TOEIC score.
helped me enjoy studying the TOEIC exercises.	-----	.702	.637	-----	.617
had comprehensive explanations of exercises.	.708	.648	-----	-----	-----
was effective in studying for the TOEIC test.	-----	-----	-----	.623	.809

Notes: Correlation Matrix (N=43), p < .01.

Table 5 shows that there was a strong correlation (r < .8) between those who thought the courseware was effective in studying for the TOEIC test and those who thought the courseware helped them improve their TOEIC score (r = .809, p < .01). There was also a moderate correlation (r < .6) between those who thought the courseware had comprehensive explanations of exercises and those who thought the courseware was effective in studying for the TOEIC test (r = .648, p < .01). The correlation of .637 was significant between those who thought the courseware helped them enjoy studying the TOEIC exercises and the simple and clear screen layout. There was a moderate correlation between those who thought the courseware helped them enjoy studying the TOEIC exercises and those who thought the courseware helped them improve their TOEIC score ($r = .617$, $p < .01$).

In Table 6 below, there was a strong correlation between those who thought the textbook had comprehensive explanations of exercises and those who thought the textbook was effective in studying for the TOEIC test ($r = .820$, $p < .01$). There was also a strong correlation between those who considered the textbook gave them practical advice about studying for the TOEIC test and those who thought the textbook had comprehensive explanations of exercises ($r = .808$, $p < .01$). The correlation of .627 was significant between those who thought the textbook had comprehensive explanations of exercises and those who thought the textbook helped them improve their TOEIC score.

Table 6. Correlation between factors for using the textbook

The textbook...	had comprehensive explanations of exercise .	was effective in studying for the TOEIC test.	helped me understand the importance of studying the TOEIC tests.	was easier to use than the courseware.	helped me improve my TOEIC score.
helped me enjoy studying the TOEIC exercises.	.689	.637	-----	.657	.655
gave me practical advice about studying for the TOEIC test.	.808	.732	.624	-----	-----
had comprehensive explanations of exercises.	-----	.820	-----	-----	.627

Notes: Correlation Matrix (N=43), $p < .01$.

The findings also indicated that, in relation to the listening activities, the majority of students thought online learning was better than paper-based learning. However, in relation to the grammar activities, more than 80% of students stated that they preferred paper-based study. Similarly, 83% of students preferred paper-based reading exercises compared to online counterparts.

6 Discussion of Findings

With respect to the students' general views on the TOEIC test, the results indicate that almost all the students understood taking the TOEIC test was important and necessary. This illustrates how important the TOEIC test was in the minds of the students, because they were concerned about applying for jobs that need a high TOEIC score. At the same time, however, because of the differences in style between TOEIC and the university admission English test, many students seemed to think the TOEIC test was very difficult. Also, interestingly, two thirds of students who actually planned to take the test were reluctant to study on their own for the test. The students were not proactive in preparing the TOEIC tests.

Although there were some minor variations in the results between the students' views on the paper-based style and the courseware-based style, there were consistent patterns in students' feedback. First of all, the findings from the analysis of the data indicate that the students didn't favor the courseware in general. The students preferred the listening sections of the courseware because they highly rated the easy-to-use audio playback system. However, the reading and grammar exercises provided by the courseware were not highly appreciated. In addition, the communication with some students indicates that they thought the textbook is better than the online program because they can take notes on the book. This is in accordance with a relatively new study which has investigated students' attitudes to learning grammar in autonomous contexts and indicated that students prefer working with paper-based materials to online materials [15]. As Enright et al claimed, the potential problem with computerized reading and/or online reading is that it is "less appealing" than paper-based reading [16].

With respect to the difference in students' computer skills, the findings suggest that those who thought themselves skilled computer users appreciated the usability of the courseware more than unskilled users. This suggests that the courseware-based system used in the present study is more suitable for skilled computer users. In addition, the findings from the analysis of the data indicate that those, who were highly motivated to take the test, considered the English level of the exercises provided by the courseware appropriate. Also, in comparison with those who were less motivated to take the test, those who were highly motivated were less satisfied with the digital pictures and the page layout of the courseware. For those who were less motivated to take the test, the large number of exercises provided by the courseware was too much. These results clearly indicate that the students' appreciation of the courseware differs depending on their level of computer skills and motivation.

Another aspect of students' views on the courseware and the textbook to consider is the fact that the students highly valued the detailed instructions on how to accomplish the TOEIC exercises successfully. The findings suggest that students were motivated by the possibility of improving their scores through the comprehensive instructions provided by the authorities [6]. The same tendency was also seen among students who used the textbook in the face-to-face classroom. This result suggests that, although the courseware was introduced for students who can study without any help from the instructor, step-by-step instructions and detailed guidance for less experienced online users are absolutely indispensable. It is important to note that, as recent studies have shown, effective, meaningful communication between the instructor and the students is still a prerequisite for an effective hybrid learning environment [11] [17].

Although studies have indicated that using any types of technology can motivate students [1], the present study shows that the balance between the intake of traditional instruction and that of online systems is important for successful hybrid learning. In order to maximize active and sustainable student engagement, having learner-training sessions or preparatory activities before students actually engage in the technology-enhanced activities is also essential [3]. In addition, as Sharma & Barrett claim, the instructor should understand the potential possibility and influence of technology based on students' cultural and educational backgrounds [1]. For the purpose of developing better online courses for Japanese students, more emphasis should be placed on how students learn rather than what they are taught [6]. The students should be carefully monitored and provided with an opportunity to evaluate what they have been doing in the classroom [3].

7 Conclusions

This study examines how Japanese university students perceive conventional paper-based learning and courseware-based learning in a hybrid language learning environment. The study also focuses on the influence of students' computer skills and motivation on their perception of these different learning styles. The results suggest that even if students performed the study with paper-based activities before, it does not mean that they can perform the same types of activities online successfully. The students surveyed are not yet ready to fully utilize and are not content with online modes of language learning. As technology is likely to develop further and the hybrid learning environments play a major role in students' language education, more focus should be placed on, firstly, the students' previous educational backgrounds and careful selection of appropriate teaching modes. Secondly, students should not be encouraged to study online in a mechanical way. We conclude that the instructor needs to examine students' e-readiness when the instructor decides to introduce courseware into the classroom. Furthermore, although the development of students as effective online learners is a challenge for the instructor, on-going research is indispensable in relation to students in online learning environments.

Acknowledgement. This study was supported by a research grant provided by Hokkai-Gakuen.

References

1. Sharma, P., Barrett, B.: Blended Learning. Using Technology in and beyond the Language Classroom. Macmillan Education, Oxford (2007)
2. Pagel, J., Reedy, L.: Integrating e-Learning in all English classes: Success at the half-way point of a 5-year project. The JALT CALL Journal 3(3), 94–109 (2005)
3. An Invitation to CALL. Foundations of Computer-Assisted Language Learning. Linguistics Department, Stanford University, `http://www.stanford.edu/~efs/callcourse/` (retrieved February 20, 2011)
4. Hinkelman, D., Grose, T.: Placement Testing and Audio Quiz-Making With Open Source Software. In: Proceedings of CLaSIC. CLS International Conference (2004)
5. Reedy, D., Pagel, J.: Integrating e-Learning into an English curriculum. Selected Proceedings of The Thirteenth Annual JALT CALL SIG Conference, pp. 97–101 (2008)

6. Chia, C.: Autonomy in Language Learning. The Use of IT and Internet Resources. McGraw-Hill Education, Singapore (2007)
7. Trends Survey of TOEIC® test Utilization 2007. The TOEIC Steering Committee of the Institute for International Business Communication. Educational Testing Service, Tokyo (2007)
8. Garant, M.: EFL Testing and University Admission in Finland and Japan. Asian Journal of English Language Teaching 10, 115–135 (2000)
9. Brown, I., Campbell, A.P., Weatherford, Y.: Using DynEd and Alc with low-level university freshmen. The JALT CALL Journal 4(3), 37–53 (2008)
10. Bringham, S., Larson, E.: Using CALL as the major element of study for a university English class in Japan. The JALT CALL Journal 2(3), 39–52 (2006)
11. Wolff, D.: Computers and new technologies: Will they change language learning and teaching? In: Kohn, J., Ruschoff, B., Wolff, D. (eds.) New horizons in CALL, Proceedings of EuroCALL 1996, vol. 96, pp. 65–82. Szombathely, Hungary (1997)
12. Hubbard, P.: An integrated framework for CALL courseware evaluation. CALICO Journal 6(2), 51–72 (1988)
13. Yamaguchi, M., et al.: The TOEIC test trainer target 650. Ask Co., Ltd. (2007)
14. TOEIC® Test Super Practice Exam 730. CHIeru
15. Jarvis, H., Szymczyk, M.: Student views on learning grammar with web- and book-based materials. ELT Journal 64(1), 32–44 (2009)
16. Enright, M.K., Grabe, W., Koda, K., Mosenthal, P., Mulcahy-Ernt, O., Schedl, M.: TOEFL 2000 reading framework: A working paper (TOEFL Monograph No. MS-17). ETS, Princeton, NJ (2000)
17. Thomas, M., Reinders, H.: Task-Based Language Learning and Teaching with Technology. Continuum, London (2010)

Improving Flexibility of Teaching and Learning with Blended Learning: A Case Study Analysis

Le Jun and Zhou Ling

Information Network Center
Guangdong Radio & TV University, Guangzhou, 510091, China
lejun@gdrtvu.edu.cn

Abstract. Although blended learning has emerged in higher education for a few years and people generally think that it can bring effective learning and increase flexibility, it is not easy to introduce this instruction method to higher education. There are many major issues are relevant to designing blended learning systems. As we move into the future, it is important that we continue to identify successful models of blended learning at the institutional, program, course, and activity levels that can be adapted to work in varied contexts. In this paper, we show our experiences in a blended course. At first, we introduce our blended learning system and analyze the components. Secondly, we show our systematic instruction design method and strategies to support learning flexibility with open course structure, self-pace learning resource, learner-centered learning strategy, technology-mediated interaction, online learning community, technique tool support, and integrated assessment method in the course. In the end, we introduce a few data analysis results.

Keywords: blended learning, learning flexibility, instruction design, interaction, learning strategy.

1 Introduction

Blended learning is an integrated learning mode which combines online and face-to-face instruction and it has emerged in higher education for about ten years (Young, 2002; Huang et al., 2006; Allen, Burrell & Timmerman et al., 2007, Garrison & Vaughan, 2008). Baesd on several successful cases, some people think that it can improve learning and increase learning flexibility (Lorenzetti, 2005; Bonk & Graham, 2005; Garrison & Vaughan, 2008; Fong, Kwan & Wang, 2008; Wang, Fong, Zhang & Lee, 2009; Tsang, Cheung, Lee & Huang, 2010).

Blended learning is emerging as the organizing concept in transforming teaching and learning while preserving the core values of higher education (Garrison & Vaughan, 2008). Albrecht (2006) reports high satisfaction with blended learning, and other have reported faculty satisfaction (Vaughan & Garrison, 2006a). In a survey, Marquis (2004) found that 94 percent of lecturers believed that blended learning is more effective than classroom-based teaching alone. This conclusion is also consistent with a study by Bourne and Seaman (2005), who found that the primary interest in blended learning is to benefit the educational process.

R. Kwan et al. (Eds.): ICHL 2011, LNCS 6837, pp. 251–261, 2011.

In fact, it is a complex process introducing blended learning into higher education. There are six major issues are relevant to designing blended learning systems: (1)the role of live interaction, (2)the role of learner choice and self-regulation, (3)models for support and training, (4)finding balance between innovation and production, (5)cultural adaptation, and (6)dealing with the digital divide[1]. How to blend effectively is one of the most important we can consider (Graham, 2006). Ross and Gage state that the future learning systems will be differentiated not based on whether they blend but rather by how they blend[2].

As we move into the future it is important that we continue to identify successful models of blended learning at the institutional , program, course, and activity levels that can be adapted to work in contexts (Graham, 2006). In practice, people continue to seek the best practices that take advantages of blended learning in different contexts and levels in recent year (Graham, 2005; Bonk, Kim & Zeng, 2005; Draffan & Rainger, 2006; Norman, 2007; Yoon & Lim, 2007; Garrison & Vaughan, 2008; Zhao & Yuan, 2010; Si & Cai, et al., 2010).

In the follow section, we will show our experiences on implementing blended learning in a course for improving the flexibility in teaching and learning. The course name is the management practice of tax and accounting in company. All the data here are from one semester and the time is from September to December in 2008.

2 Course Analysis

2.1 Course Object

The course is established for the college students who learn company accounting curriculums or company financial affair management curriculums in the polytechnic college in the university. The college provides three-year professional training courses and college diploma.

The course is a 3-credit course, which is designed for professional skill training and isn't designed for learning theory. Based on past instruction plan, the lecture in face-to-face is arranged three hours each week.

There were 335 students to register this course. Among them, 234 students comes from the department of company accounting and 101 students belonged to the department of company financial affair management.

2.2 Course Content

The knowledge contents are composed of the introduction of the rule of tax administration and accounting affair in company, management skill training and practicing in workplace.

It has three preparing courses which are accounting foundation, financial accounting management in practice and accounting information system training. It also has three related follow-up courses which are plan of pay taxes, tax agency in practice and accounting profession certificate examination.

The instructional objectives are understanding the basic tax regulations and guides, knowing about the accounting affair management related the tax, and possessing the skills about tax accounting affair management in a company as an assistant tax accountant or an accountant.

2.3 Learning Activity Space

According to the course requirement, the students have to practice for one week in a workplace in the end of the course. This means that the practice workplace outside the college campus is a new learning activity space.

Except classroom and practice workplace, Internet-based virtual space for e-learning is another important activity space for learning. We need to design corresponding instruction strategies to adapt to theses different learning spaces.

2.4 Motivation

There are some factors from different dimensions in the context to drive us to adopt blended learning mode.

The university encourages teachers to innovate traditional face-to-face teaching model. The college has set up an integrated e-learning platform and cooperation relation with business circle. The college also supports the teachers to form instruction teams and invite some experts from business circle to participate teaching activities by the college instruction support fund.

For the teachers, they chose blended learning model to save their work time and manage instructional materials effectively. They need to improve teaching relying on the feedbacks and supplement different learning resources in a new term.

The students have some learning expectations. They want learning flexibility and share their learning experiences in different backgrounds. They want to build a bridge between students and business fields.

Some people maybe think that technology tools can help us solve our problems. But based on some experiences, we think that it isn't natural. We need to find an integrated model to design a blended learning system. Blended learning is a selectable mode. Improved pedagogy and increased flexibility are our main reasons for blended learning mode.

3 Instruction Design

Instruction design is one of issues and challenges when we implement blended learning (Graham, 2006).

In some cases, why blended learning has not yet fulfilled its promise of being the best way to deliver information. Hofmann (2006) think that lack of a formal instructional design process is much more obvious, even worse, the participants are most often aware of the issues before the blended learning facilitator[3].

Therefore, designing is an important part in our process of blended learning.

3.1 Definition of Blended Learning

Although blended learning has become somewhat of a buzzword in higher education settings, there are still quite a bit of ambiguity about what it means (Jones, 2006). Therefore, we need to give our clear definition of blended learning.

Graham, Allen and Ure (2003) think that there are three kind of common definitions[4]:

- Combining instructional modalities (or delivery media) (Bersin & Associates, 2003; Orey, 2002a, 2002b; Singh & Reed, 2001; Thomson, 2002).
- Combining instructional methods (Driscoll, 2002; House, 2002; Rossett, 2002).
- Combining online and face-to-face instruction (Reay, 2001; Ronney, 2003; Sands, 2002; Ward & LaBranche, 2003; Young, 2002).

Here, we use the definition (Graham, 2006):

Blended learning systems combine face-to-face instruction with computer-mediated instruction.

This definition is our working foundation. Our blending is course-level blending. It combines face-to-face instruction activities and online instruction activities, and combines teacher-centered instructional method and learner-centered instructional method. It also combines digital media resources and printing materials.

3.2 Design Model

System theory is an important research method for us to understand the complexity of blended learning and to design a blended learning system. We apply this method to analyze all possible factors and construct an adaptive blended learning system.

We integrated the following models as our instruction design models.

- The Dick and Carey model for systematic instructional design [5][6].
- The Bonk and Dennen framework for instructional design [7].
- The Naidu guide for instructional design for optimal learning [8].

The Dick and Carey model suggests the following process for the instructional design.

- Identification of instructional goals.
- Subordinate skill analysis.
- Learner and context analysis.
- Construction of performance objectives.
- Identification of assessment techniques.
- Identification of instructional strategies.
- Determination of appropriate delivery media.
- Course development.
- Evaluation

In blended learning, the step 7 is the key (Hofmann, 2006). But We think that isn't enough. Technology mediated interaction is an important factor in blended learning. For interaction design, we follow the processes of the Bonk and Dennen model and Naidu model here.

3.3 Elementary Components

A blended learning system has some elementary components. Before we construct the structure of the system, we need to make sure which are components in the system. They must be reviewed prior to even considering how a course will be presented. They come into play in determining the design of a course before we even look at its learning goals[9].

Following some blended learning systems[10][11], we add some elements to our system in the design process as following:

- Course structure.
- Learning objective and expectation.
- Teaching and learning strategy.
- The role of learner and teacher.
- Technology tool.
- Learning resource and medium.
- Interaction.
- Learning community.
- Support and facilitating.

These elements are different from the 9 steps which Dick and Carey model has suggested.

3.4 Teaching and Learning Strategies

The blended strategies of teaching and learning are important conditions to ensure learning flexibility in the varied learning spaces for the students. We chose a mixed instruction strategies with teacher-centered teaching, learner-centered self-directed learning and group collaborative learning.

Some knowledge units in the course are difficult for these students without work experiences to understand and hold operative skills. For these units, teachers often give lectures, show a few operative demonstrations, and hold varied discussions in the classroom. Sometime experts from some business companies are invited to hold lectures. These teaching behaviors are controlled by the teachers. The instruction design, learning resources and actives are teacher-centered and controlled by the teachers. There are about one -third knowledge units using teacher-centered instruction strategy.

About one-third units are designed based on learner-centered learning strategy. Web-based self-testing, extended reading, virtual training and learner-to-learner interaction can be controlled by the students based on learner-centered learning strategy. The students can learn individually and self-directed. In this time, the roles of teachers are coordinators, backers and guiders. Before the students learning, we have to finish some web-based learning materials and interactive topics to support computer-mediated learning and self-directed learning.

For a few group collaborative works, learning strategies are mixed with these two strategies. The teachers intervene their activities only in problem appearing time.

3.5 Interaction

For technology-mediated learning, interaction is a key value proposition[12]. Moore [13] thought that there were three types of interaction: learner to learner; learner to teacher, tutor, and service worker; learner to learning content. He thought that the depth of talk, the flexibleness of self-paced learning and the structure intension of the course design affect the learning efficiency.

Above three types of technology-based interaction are introduced in the learning process. Specially, the interactions between the student and the teacher are led by the designed problems and group collaborative works. The teachers design sixteen open problems for asynchronous discussing. All students need to present their group answers or individual responses in the course online forum. The teachers put forward views and assess students' works.

For the interaction between learner to learning content, all the web-based reading materials and files in the course web site and online virtual experiments support this interaction. We develop eight web-based operational training cases. The cases are student-centered designed to simulating the true environments of the tax bureau of the local government. The system can be manipulated by the students in anytime and anywhere. With these learning materials, the students can simulate to make some business tax return, such as value-added tax, consumption tax, valued-tax, business-tax, business-income tax, individual income tax, urban construction tax, and stamp tax. The virtual system can response to their submitting in time[14].

For the interaction between learner and learner, the roles of the teacher only are equal guiders and participants. In the course forum , these interaction behaviors are autonomous. Their topics are open, and some topics are independent the course.

3.6 Online Learning Community

Some people have found that a community is associated with higher levels of perceived learning (Rovai, 2002; Schrite, 2004; Shea et al., 2006). Empirically, Rovai and Jordan (2004) found that blended courses produce a stronger sense of community among students than either traditional or fully online course.

In the process of blended learning, it is one of important works for us to create and sustain an online learning community. It has strong ties and enables people to develop social networks for collaborative knowledge sharing (Lin, 2007).

There are a few advantages to set up a online learning community. Because all the students are from different classes and departments, they are short of the chances of face-to-face talk. But they want to share different experiences. When they meet some problems, they may look for helps from other students. They also hope to build connections with business company and the alumni with the same specialty background. In the college, many students have formed varied small groups by QQ system, which is the most common Chinese instant message tool in China.

With the community, the teachers can find some problems and adjust some learning factors in the process. They can continue to accumulate teaching knowledge and diminish workloads in the future. In fact, the learners and their knowledge contributions are our important learning resources.

Based on the model of a community of inquiry[15], cognitive presence, social presence, and teaching presence are three essential elements. Here we introduce a few development strategies to construct an online learning community in course-level. For social presence, the community is open and all students register in authentic name. We encourage our learners presenting personal and group's learning experiences by reforming formative assessment. The conversations are emotional and equal.

For cognitive presence, our cases, works, and discussions can cause the students to deep learning, exploration, exchanging different ideas, and making knowledge nodes. The purpose, content, conversation, connection are our four key factors to promote knowledge-building and cognitive presence.

For teaching presence, teachers always appear in the community. The open problems are well designed. The teachers need to finish the following works during the process.

- Giving responses to the students in time in one day.
- Providing some support services to some students in need.
- Improving teaching and learning strategy.
- Improving instruction design.
- Analyzing the instructional data and making knowledge management.

3.7 Web-Based Learning Resource

Web-based learning resources are classified into static resources and dynamic resources (Hill & Hannafin, 2001). There are employed to support specific learning outcomes. We use them to support self-paced learning, interaction and group cooperative learning.

Static resources are fixed in nature and they can provide reliable information and knowledge. They are often made before the instruction and have no change in the process. In the course, these resources include instruction information, objective, plan, scheduled task, the class video records in realtime with flow media form, reference papers and books, lecture PowerPoint files, FAQ, some experiences from the previous students, and demo demonstrating materials, etc. The students can use in any time, any place, and any step by Internet.

Dynamic resources are changing in the learning process, such as knowledge databases, new learning cases, and the talks and topics in the course forum. The learner experiences in the Blog, the BBS, and the workplaces also are new added resource for blended learning [16].

We get some new dynamic learning resources by discovering in the interaction and talk in the online learning community. Some new cases, tasks, problems, dialogs, and lectures are always added and made in the process to improve our former instruction designs. Specially, these dynamic learning resources show cognitive presence and teaching presence in the online community.

3.8 Support and Software Tool

During the process, the learners usually have some problems and they need individual supports (Francis & Raftery, 2005; Trapp, 2006). For example, we need to explain the students the special resources and software applications and to show how they can access support.

Based on our experiences, developing learning skill, providing feedback in time, and facilitating software tools are our typical supports. In fact, the biggest difficulty is short of computer-mediated learning skill in our environments. In the beginning, the proportion is about 60%. Some students are short of e-learning self-efficacy. These problems aren't from the course itself, but they affect learning effects.

In our blended learning system, web-based learning management system and learning content management system are our basic learning tools whose functions are similar to Blackboard. The course discussion forum is an asynchronous or synchronous interaction space. The QQ tool only is an assistant synchronous interaction tool for group online talks.

We design an online tax declaration management system in the course. It is a virtual training system and can be controlled by distance terminal. Sometime several students send some help requests and then teachers need to reply in time.

3.9 Assessment

Assessment is the biggest challenge and is a driving force for the students in the blended learning. Before the course, we need to design the whole assessment method and explain to all the students clearly. The assessment method is a process evaluation covering the whole activities and results.

We use both formative assessment and summative assessment in the course. We set up an integrated formative assessment method. We evaluate the most of the learning activities and their results in the processes. For each student, he or she needs to finish individually eight assignments, eight online virtual experiments, a five-day practical activity in workplace and a work experience report.

All the students are divided into different learning groups. Each group has about five students. There are four group assignments. Each student needs to participate these group assignments and share their works in the course online discussion forum.

Other important survey points are each student's interaction participating rate and his contribution. The participating discussion time, the number of putting forward to question and answering the question in the course online discussion forum.

In the end of the semester, each student needs to finish simulation tax declaration report.

Above four parts are formative assessment contents. Each part has equal score, each is 25 points. A student can get summative assessment only when he finish the four works. The course summative assessment score is 100 points.

4 Result Analysis

4.1 Interaction Data

We select the learner-to-learner interaction data in the course online discussion forum. The time was a term from 2008-9-9 to 2008-12-27. During the interaction, teachers were only equal participants and didn't evaluate students'talking.

During the time, there were 49 students to put forward 145 questions and talk topics. This student number was about 14.63% of the whole registered students. Here we called these students as the first kind of student. The 143 topics result in interaction talking during the students and only one topic hadn't any response.

There were 73 students to participate in the interaction talking and to give their questions. These 73 students were called as the second kind of student. They gave 727 responses on the problems of the first kind of student. The second kind of student was 21.79% of the whole registered students.

In the first kind of student, each student average gave 2.96 request problems average. The most number of the request problems from a single student is 9 and they were from 2 students. There were 28 students that gave only one problems, about 20% of the first kind of students. The following tab.1 shows the student numbers and their request problems.

Table 1. The student numbers to give different amount problems

The problem number	1	2	3	4	5	6	7	8	9
The student number	28	5	1	1	3	2	3	4	2

Here we use the response number to describe the interaction talking depth. The total response number was 755, and 727 was from the student. For each topic, average response number from the student is 11.69. The biggest response number is 40, which means that there were 40 students who have take part in discussing and gave their remarks. The following tab.2 shows the topic number and its' corresponding response number.

Table 2. The problem number and its' response number

The topic number	2	11	14	10	33	30	14	13	7	2	4	1	1	1	1	1
The response number	0	1	2	3	4	5	6	7	8	9	10	11	14	23	27	40

For example, the first column shows that there are 2 request problems which each one of them has 0 response, the second column shows that there are 11 request problems which each one of them has 1 response separately, etc.

For all the interaction talking and their remarks, the total browsing number for the all remarks in the forum is 6391 during the whole term, average browsing number of one topic is 44.69. Average browsing number of one student in the term is 19.66.

In the course online discussion forum, all the interactions are asynchronous. We divided the interaction time into six parts. We find that their activities happened in the evening from 7 p.m. to 12 p.m. in most cases. The following tab.3 shows the appearing number of times of the topics and the time interval of presenting topic.

Table 3. The appearing number of times and the time interval

The time interval	8 – 12 a.m.	12 – 14 noon	14 – 18 p.m.	18 – 19 p.m.	19 – 24 evening	other time
The appearing number of times	9	16	8	5	104	7
The percentage number (%)	6.21	11.03	5.52	3.45	71.72	4.83

4.2 Questionnaire Survey

At the end of the semester, the administrations office gives an online questionnaire, 331 students give their remarks and 297 questionnaires are valid. The course grade is excellent in the college.

On a five-point scale (Likert score), the teacher's score is 4.709 and The learning resource score is 4.502.

On a ten-point scale, the score of each part is as following.

- The multimedia resources and application is 9.293.
- The designing of the assignment,group work and problem is 9.071.
- The feedback is 9.091.
- The support to operation training is 8.943.
- The information content is 9.481.
- Developing the professional skill is 9.172.
- Independent learning flexibility for self-paced is 8.848.
- Instruction design on in practice to improve the operative skill is 8.943.

5 Conclusion

Based on the instruction design and data analysis, the students have got learning flexibility in the choice of learning resources, learning pace, learning time, learning activity space and learning strategies.

For a successful blended learning course, it is very important for us to set open course structure and provide different learning resources, virtual activity spaces and learning strategies. It is also critical to make interaction in the course online forum and to form an online learning community with some interaction strategies. In the other hand, an integrated assessment method is the successful guarantee to gain feedback and maintain the credibility of the blended course.

Like many design problems, there are many choice solutions in varied environments. Our experiences show that the systematic design, integrated action strategies and some supports can improve traditional face-to-face learning flexibility. In the future, we will further research on this subject.

Acknowledgements. We thank the Guangdong Province Education Science Foundation for her supporting our research project (No.07SJY021).

References

1. Graham, C.R.: Blended Learning Systems: Definition,Current Trends, and Future Directions. In: Bonk, C.J., Graham, C.R. (eds.) The Handbook of Blended Learning, pp. 14–19. Pfeiffer (2006)
2. Ross, B., Gage, K.: Global Perspectives on Blended Learning: Insight from WebCT and Our Customers in Higher Education. In: Bonk, C.J., Graham, C.R. (eds.) The Handbook of Blended Learning, pp. 155–168. Pfeiffer (2006)
3. Hofmann, J.: Why Blended Learning Hasn't(Yet) Fulfilled Its Promises:Answers to Those Questions That Keep You Up at Night. In: Bonk, C.J., Graham, C.R. (eds.) The Handbook of Blended Learning, pp. 27–40. Pfeiffer (2006)
4. Graham, C.R.: Blended Learning Systems: Definition,Current Trends, and Future Directions. In: Bonk, C.J., Graham, C.R. (eds.) The Handbook of Blended Learning, pp. 3–5. Pfeiffer (2006)
5. Dick, W., Carey, L., Carey, J.O.: The Systematic Design of Instruction, 5th edn. Simplified Chinese Edition, pp. 1–23. Higher Education Press, Beijing (2004)
6. Dick, W.: A Model for the Systematic Design of Instruction. In: Tennyson, R.D., Schott, F., Seel, N.M., Dijkstra, S. (eds.) Instructional Design: International Perspectives. Theory, Research, and Model, Chinese Edition, vol. 1, pp. 405–414. Educational Science Publishing, Beijing (2005)
7. Bonk, C.J., Dennen, P.V.: Frameworks for Design and Instruction. In: Moore, M.G. (ed.) Handbook of Distance Education, pp. 233–246. Lawrence Erlbaum Associates, Mahwah (2007)
8. Naidu, S.: Instructional Designs for Optimal Learning. In: Moore, M.G. (ed.) Handbook of Distance Education, pp. 247–258. Lawrence Erlbaum Associates, Mahwah (2007)
9. Shearer, R.: Instructional Design and the Technologies: An Overview. In: Moore, M.G. (ed.) Handbook of Distance Education, pp. 219–232. Lawrence Erlbaum Associates, Mahwah (2007)
10. Qi, H., Le, J.: Theory and Application of Feedback Information in Distance Instruction, pp. 102–107. China Central Radio & TV University Press, Beijing (2006)
11. Garrison, D.R., Vaughan, N.D.: Blended Learning in Higher Education: Framework, Principles, and Guidelines, pp. 104–141. Jossey-Bass, A Wiley Imprint, San Francisco (2008)
12. Wagner, E.D.: On designing interaction experiences for the next generation of blended learning. In: Bonk, C.J., Graham, C.R. (eds.) Handbook of Blended Learning: Global Perspectives, Local Designs, pp. 41–54. Pfeiffer Publishing, San Francisco (2005)
13. Moore, M.G.: The Theory of Transactional Distance. In: Moore, M.G. (ed.) Handbook of Distance Education, pp. 89–105. Lawrence Erlbaum Associates, Mahwah (2007)
14. `http://210.38.32.42/801/801/default.htm`
15. Garrison, D.R., Anderson, T., Archer, W.: Critical Inquiry in a Text-Based Environment: Computer Conferencing in Higher Education. The Internet and Higher Education 2(2-3), 87–105
16. Qi, H., Le, J.: Theory and Application of Feedback Information in Distance Instruction, pp. 173–189. China Central Radio & TV University Press, Beijing (2006)

A Teaching System Design Based on Website of Course Theory and Practice of Futures

Shan Zhao

Department of Economics, Beijing Radio and Television University, Beijing, China
zhaos@mail.btvu.org

Abstract. In the 21st century online distance and open education has broken the concept of traditional education system, in which the hybrid teaching system based on website blending diversified interactive multimedia course resources with network can comply with the requirements of new times and has been playing a more and more important role.

The features of futures determine that the course Theory and Practice of Futures, one of the financial curricula of Beijing Radio and Television University, is a difficult and practical financial subject with its imperative requirements of precise logic and skillful operation. In the past few years the course Theory and Practice of Futures has build up various multimedia interactive education resources gradually such as CAI courseware based on network, network course, course resources database, course cases and streamline course etc. It's necessary to design a new and optimal hybrid teaching system to congregate all the multimedia resources of course with the use of advanced computer technology. It's well known that the multimedia interactive teaching system based on .Net is a better choice to recompose learning resources and perform the responsibility of multimedia interactive teaching. But how to design and realize it is the key problem and should be researched, which is just the purpose of this paper.

Based on Browser/Server operation module, making use of three tier structure of Microsoft .NET, that is, data tier, logic tier and representation tier, the paper presents the interactive multimedia teaching system of course platform selection and macro-design, concrete function design and realization. The research results has been typically used in financial courses education as an experiment with new teaching system and has achieved excellent effects, which proved that as a new method the design and module showed by the paper are practical and have great applying and promoting value.

Keywords: Theory and Practice of Futures Multimedia interactive teaching system, Browser/Server operation module, Data tier, Logic tier, Representation tier.

1 Course Features Request Hybrid Teaching System

With the development of psychics, constructivist learning theory put forward in the late of 1980 has become the top mainstream in learning theory and influenced current

R. Kwan et al. (Eds.): ICHL 2011, LNCS 6837, pp. 262–271, 2011.

teaching module. Constructivist learning theory emphasizes that students are center, that is, learning involves more than just receiving transmitted information and teaching must be interactive and encourage student's engagement. It requires not only students should change from passive information receiver to the active knowledge self-operator, but teachers should be converted from information initiator and irrigator to the helper and promoter for student's knowledge construction.

The blended or hybrid teaching system is a mixture of classroom and online instruction that has an abundance of benefits. Hybrid courses blend face-to-face interaction with online learning and customarily involve the delivery of curricular materials, access to resources, submission of assignments, project based learning, activities that support higher order thinking, and online discussions that may be asynchronous or synchronous in nature. The hybrid teaching system based on website blending diversified interactive multimedia learning course resources with network can comply with the requirements of constructivist learning theory and provide solutions to the demands of a changing environment, allowing flexibility for learning from home or work, and breaking the traditional concept of "in-classroom study" with its ideal of anytime and anyplace education for anyone.

The course Theory and Practice of Futures is one of the corn financial curricula of financial and economics department in Beijing Radio and Television University. Futures dealings play an important role in business and financial transactions with its special functions of hedge and venture investment. It has been one of the most important and effective venture management and investment facilities for merchandise manufactures and franchisers or financial service institutions. All features of futures determine that the course Theory and Practice of Futures is a difficult and practical financial subject with its imperative requirements of precise logic and skillful operation. So if in practice we only depend on spoon-feeding with the use of textbooks in classroom and one-sided teaching face to face, it's so difficult for students to understand well the contents of this subject that it ultimately influences the effects of teaching. Through analyzing the features of this course, it's necessary and suitable to construct a multimedia interactive teaching system and in some sense to compensate the disadvantages of traditional school teaching. In the past few years the course Theory and Practice of Futures has build up various multimedia interactive education resources gradually such as CAI courseware based on network, network course, course resources database, course cases and streamline course etc. It's necessary to design a new and optimal hybrid teaching system to congregate all the multimedia resources of course with the use of advanced computer technology.

It's well known that the multimedia interactive teaching system based on .Net is a better choice to recompose learning resources and perform the responsibility of multimedia interactive teaching. But how to design and realize it is the key problem and should be researched, which is just the purpose of this paper. This article firstly designs education resources data structure with the use of database management system, then a data structure module is given, applying ASP.NET□JavaScript computer developing languages, based on Browser/Server operation module, making use of three tier structure of Microsoft .NET, that is, data tier, logic tier and exhibition tier. The research results has been typically used in financial courses Theory and Practice of Futures education and has achieved excellent effects, which proved that the way and module shown by the thesis are practical and have great applying and promoting value.

2 Course Teaching System Platform Selection and Macro-design

At present as a potential and preponderant network education resources multimedia interactive teaching system based on .Net has showed its flourish and vigorous vitality. With its powerful advantages on super learning resources supply multimedia interactive education system based on .Net performs knowledge in multiple dimensionality and allows students to browse all the learning resources freely and flexibly in non-linear way. It is a new type of education resources based on network combining information technology and curriculum, which sufficiently fulfills its characteristics of opening, interaction, sharing, and super-media with its safety, big capacity and persistent stability.

2.1 Selection of System Development Platform

It will be planed to select Microsoft .NET technology as the development platform for the multimedia interactive system. At present Microsoft .NET is one of the most important application framework in the Web Service platform markets. With its powerful and flourishing advantages on design, integration, capability, security and reliability etc in the scope of development for distributed N-Tier application, Microsoft .NET provides general guides and rules, on which technology suppliers have provided corresponding platform, facilities and programming environments. In the application framework there are such contents in details as exhibition tier services, server processes, conversation management, logic framework, applying data cache, application logic, permanence, affairs, security and log services etc.

Microsoft .NET is a platform consisted of Server, Client and Service. .NET includes basic processing base, CLR, C#, C++, VB.NET, Jscript.NET, ASP.NET etc.

2.2 Selection of Web Server

Since the whole system is built only on the Windows operation platform and developed on the Microsoft .NET development platform, the web server will certainly be Microsoft IIS that is the abbreviation of Internet Information Server. IIS as one of current dominant Web servers provides formidable services for Internet and Intranet, which transits information through HTTP and provides FTP and other services such as NNTP, SMTP etc with configuration of IIS.

2.3 System Framework Structure

The system will use C#.NET platform to construct three tiers application system based on Browse /Server (B/S in abbreviation) structure as shown in figure 1. Logically the three tiers respectively are database tier, application service tier and user interface tier. In this system mostly functions and operations will be fulfilled in the application service tier and the database tier will be used to store data while the responsibilities for interaction with users are going to be managed in the interface tier. In figure 1 we can see that database tier is further divided into database and popedom database, the application service tier comprised of data access tier, popedom control, public API, CSS, XML and operation logic tier, the Web Form responsible for communication with users.

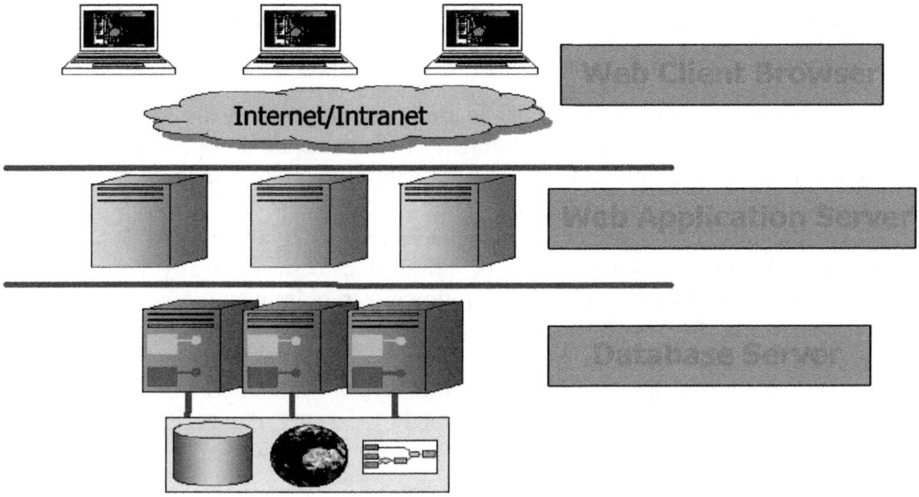

Fig. 1. System framework structure

2.4 Course Multimedia Teaching System Macro-structure

Multimedia interactive system consists of learning resources database including CAI courseware database, multimedia database, video and audio database, file database, popedom management database and basic information database, GUI that is the users interface of multimedia interactive education system, database management system that is used as an instrument to maintain and renew system database, system access interface that is developed for other system accessing or facilitating collection and updating as the obligated access interface. Macro-structure of interactive multimedia education system is as in figure 2.

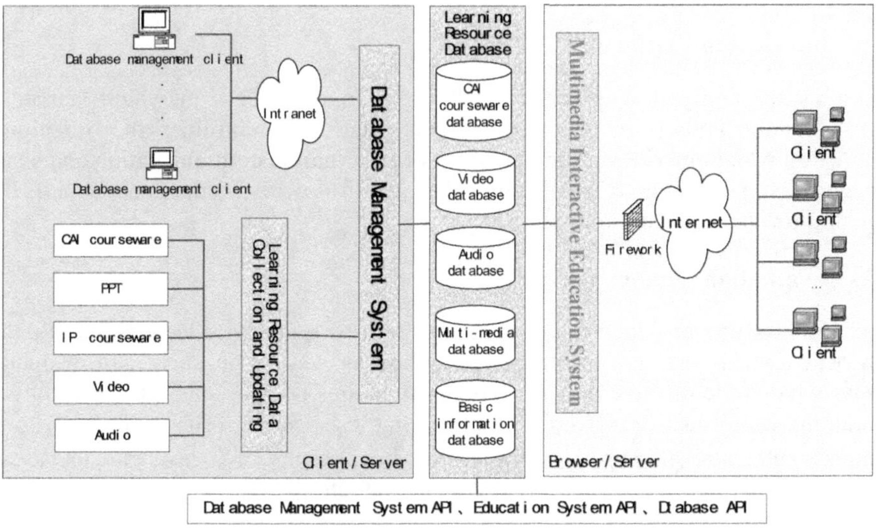

Fig. 2. Macro-structure of interactive multimedia education system

3 Concrete Function Design of Course Interactive Multimedia Teaching System

With the advocation of constructivist learning theory that in an education system teacher should act as mentor while student is backbone, the application module of course teaching system should be a kind of exploring teaching module by the means of network.

Before the design the principle and characteristics orientation of a multimedia interactive education system should be confirmed first. Basically a successfully education website should satisfy the following requirements that is diversified learning resources, favorable education interaction, direct and amicable interface and lively, vivid teaching strategies.

Generally a multimedia interactive education system should comprise of three parts that is essential learning contents, multimedia learning database and interaction learning support platform. Its concrete functions are as followings.

3.1 Text Resources

Text resources supply all the basic text information mainly with the explanation of textbook used, contents, character, cases about futures dealings as well as some emphases or difficulties introduction and reviews.

3.2 Multimedia Resources Database

This part undertakes the function of vivid reappearance of courses information with the use of multifarious media such as CAI courseware, futures streamline courseware, images, graphics, sound, video and radio etc. At the same time all the multimedia resources can be downloaded, uploaded, added and deleted conveniently for teachers or students.

3.3 Interaction Platform

Learning autonomy is a dynamic, multidimensional process in which learner and instructor are equally active. Cooperating platform centralize the function of interaction which provides an environment of information communication and sharing for teachers or students. It usually includes such following methods as E-mail, BBS, teaching forum or discussion online etc.

3.4 Evaluation Online

Evaluation online provides some relative exercises, quizzes or tests online. Students can do exercises or have examinations online as well as teachers can evaluate or assess what students have done. It has the functions such as on—line assigning and submitting exercises, or dynamically producing test papers, self—evaluation, online testing, automatic grading, integrating the final results of a test with the average performance of learning etc. This part facilitates the individual measurement of self learning as well as the assigning, grading, testing, adjusting teaching or learning and helping the learners for the teachers.

3.5 Information Search

This function supplies an information searching index, which will facilitate information query about text materials, multimedia database, users information, exercise evaluation and examination score etc in a multimedia interactive education system. It can be realized by storing all the various resources in a database with the ASP database technology.

3.6 Popedom Management

Multimedia interactive system administrates popedom in the way of role, which through authorizing roles users will naturally enjoy popedom distributed to them. This function allows teachers or students to register with their user name and password to modify individual resources and undertake other popedom authorized to them.

According to the above basic function module, system frame structure is as shown in figure 3.

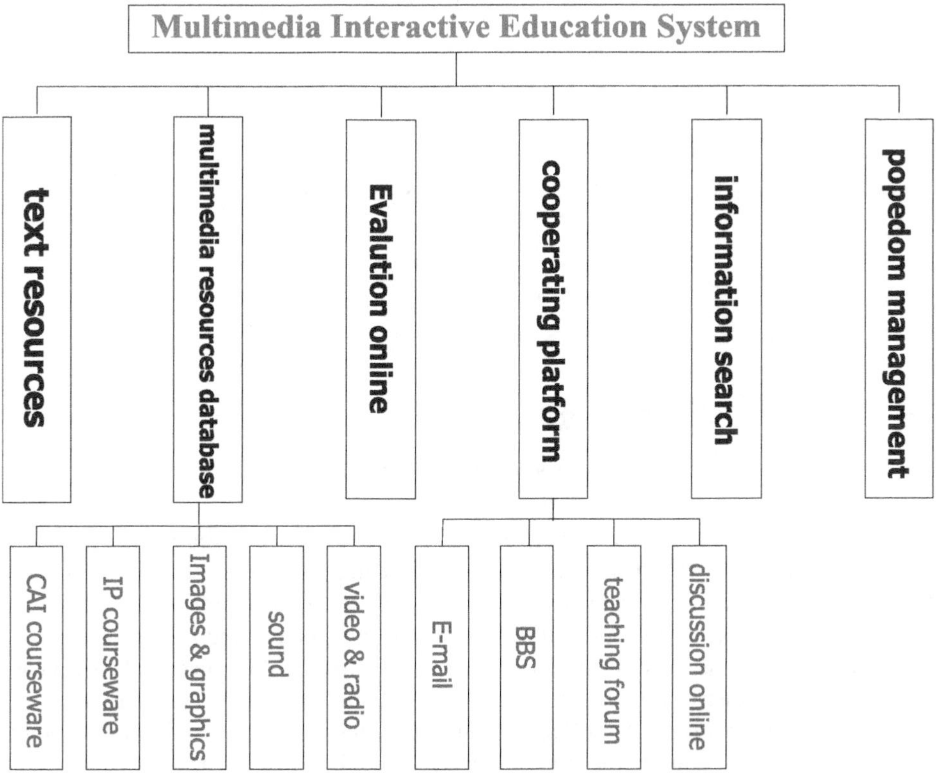

Fig. 3. System frame structure

4 Realization of a Teaching System Based on .net of Theory and Practice of Futures

According to the macro-design of framework, macro-structure and function about the multimedia interactive education system, the multimedia interactive teaching system based on .NET could be developed and applied in practice. Now we put forward the teaching system of course Theory and Practice of Futures as an example.

4.1 Functions of Multimedia Interactive Education System for Course

The multimedia interactive teaching system constructed for the course of Theory and Practice of Futures should have the following basic functions in details as shown in figure 4.

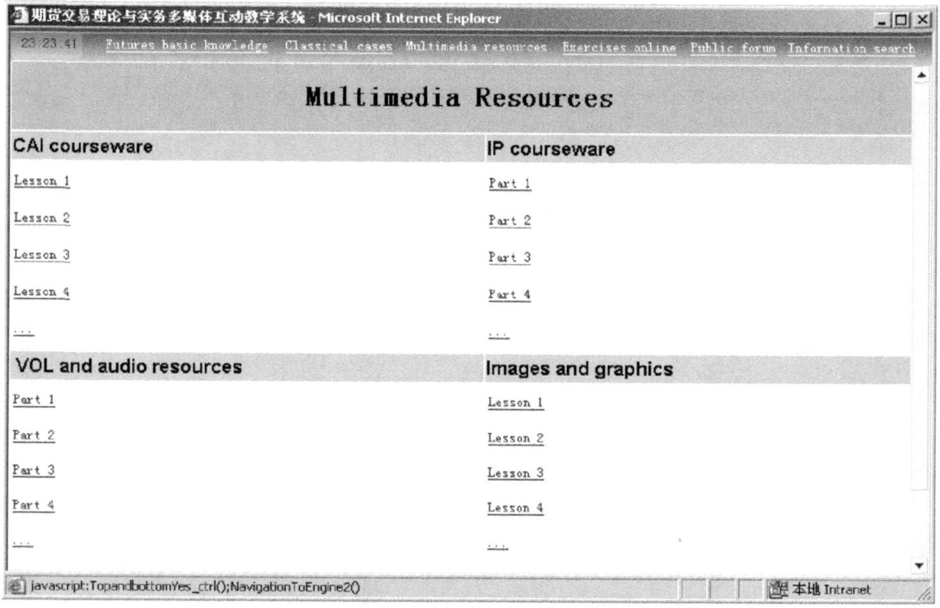

Fig. 4. Application example

Futures basic knowledge: This area includes two part : course text data and classical cases course text data mainly show text materials to explain basic theories, rules and terms about futures investment as well as some emphases or difficulties about this course according to textbook,such as futures hedge and futures speculation. Classical cases: This menu is to collect and display historical or current classical cases successful or failure in futures investment to teach students practical experiences.

Teaching interacion: An effective and dynamic learning environment should provide heightened interaction for the learner. Teaching interaction area in website of courses Theory and Practice of Futures provide a platform in way of BBS, campus

QQ, discussion online or E-mail etc. for discussion among students, online exchanging between teachers and students, and tools for e-learning. Students can access site at any time for self-learning, and through the human-computer interaction to complete interactive learning. "Interactive teaching" area in website provide network platform for learning, discussion, exchange and question among students; teachers to open site at any time for Q & A and guide students.

Synchronous chat: The synchronicity of an online environment allows for flexibility for the learner but also an open connection to the learning at all times. Synchronous connections provide an immediate connection that promotes a sense of community for the learners. The synchronous chat session is one of the most dynamic interactions with students. The chat session would run for one hour with a specific discussion topic and using a chat technology that provide electronic whiteboard as well as text. I would lead the sessions or have a student group leader lead. The class was divided into smaller groups and would be asked to read certain futures readings or research certain futures dealing topics before the discussion. As an instructor, these sessions helped me "hear" each student; sometimes students can remain quiet in a class setting yet will become quite verbal online. When the discussion was extremely directed and in the online chat, we covered more topic area than in a typical class discussion that would typically have more people and more distractions. In fact, it was quite usual following a synchronous chat session for students to feel effectiveness and efficiency because they had focused intensely for that period of time.

Multimedia resources: This function will display collectively various multimedia resources that have been created or taped for Futures such as CAI courseware, streamline courseware, VOL and audio resources etc. At the same time all the multimedia resources will be easily download for students, add and delete conveniently for teachers. Especially the streamline courseware of Theory and Practice of Futures in the highest flight in its learning autonomy has been used frequently by students. Learning autonomy is a dynamic, multidimensional process in which learner and instructor are equally active. The challenge to reach learning autonomy is for students of all ages : learning how to learn for oneself. Offering video and audio resources of futures dealings streamline courseware maximizes student self-direction, content choice and organization and heightened interaction, students become central to their own learning process. This, in turn, increases autonomous learning skills and students become more aware of how they learn, what they want to learn, and how they need to apply futures theory to their practical investments.

Virtual market: With the use of database, Internet and communication technology, a virtual futures market will be shown. Students can use it to carry out virtual futures buy in or sell at a price and teacher can also use it to explain cases. Virtual market function will benefit to enhance liveliness of this course and attract students to participate and interact.

Exercises online: Exercises online will provide the course exercises, quizzes or tests online. Students can do exercises or have examinations online assigned automatically and after their submitting scores, evaluation and answers will be displayed simultaneously.

Public forum: Public forum will include student-to-student forum and student-to-teacher communication both in real time and non-real time way as

Information search: This function allows students to search for what they want in resources that are provided in the course of Theory and Practice of Futures quickly and conveniently.

4.2 Course Teaching System Evaluation

The research results has been typically used in financial courses education as an experiment with new methods of teaching and has achieved excellent effects, which proved that the way and module showed by the paper are practical and have great applying and promoting value.

The teaching system of course Theory and Practice of Futures proves that teaching system based on .Net is a super computer technology platform. With its powerful advantages on capacity, sharing and interaction it provides a system platform to collect all multimedia resources and facilitate learning anytime even at work. It will be helpful to reach the aim of study anytime and anywhere for anyone.

The teaching system of course Theory and Practice of Futures shows that multimedia interactive teaching system based on .Net will be useful to promote learning efficiency. Interactive multimedia presents an opportunity for using technology to improve and enhance student's learning environment. Studies conclude that students best learn if they are active participants in their education and are exposed, in varying degrees, to each discerned learning style. Students are more attentive to visual, audial and participating lessons, seem to retain more of what they see over what they hear, and are more comfortable with visual and audial learning. At the same time the wide accessibility of the network offers educators a new medium to deliver those multimedia interactive teaching and learning materials– one that can be an alternative to traditional teaching techniques.

The teaching system of course Theory and Practice of Futures demonstrates that multimedia interactive teaching system based on .Net will be beneficial to individual studies. It can be used to store, dispose and transit multimedia learning information, to cooperate and communicate what students have learned in self-teaching way with the use of multimedia resources. Through giving exercises evaluation and feedback to students online, students can check up what they learn all by themselves. All of the above will be helpful for students to arrange their individual learning schedules.

The teaching system of course Theory and Practice of Futures displays that multimedia interactive teaching system based on .Net will be useful to enhance students' abilities to settle practical problems. Cases explain intentionally guide students to research more widely, deeply about corresponding knowledge and stimulate them to collect more texts, images or visual resources for further comprehension and creation by themselves, ultimately which will steer students to digest all the knowledge and upgrade their abilities to settle practical problems gradually.

In generally speaking, through our practical design, development and application about the multimedia interactive education system in financial courses education as an experiment the research results put forward in this paper has proved that the macro-design especially the three tier structure module showed by this paper are practical and have great applying and promoting value.

References

1. Mooney, G.A., Bligh, J.G.: Information technology in medical education: current and future application. Post grad. Med. J (February 2005)
2. Jacobson, M.J., Levin, J.: Network Learning Environment s and Hypertext: Const rusting Personal Shared Knowledge Spaces. In: Proceedings of Tel - Ed93 Dells, International Society for Technology in education, Texas (June 2005)
3. Kansan, R., Bento, A.M: A Learning Centered Approach to Education Using Hypermedia and the Internet [DB], http://worfubalt.edu/abento/ais/teach.html
4. Mouser, D., Marin, M.S.: Students, construction of structured knowledge representation. Journal of Research on computing in Education
5. Spiro, R., Cousin, R., Feltovich, P.J: Cognitive flexibility theory: Advanced knowledge acquisition in structured domains. In: Proceeding of the Tenth Annual conference of the Cognitive Science Society, Hillsdale. Lawrence Erlbaum Associates, New jersey
6. Spiro, R.J., Feltovich, P.J., Jacobson, M., et al.: Cognitive flexibility, Constructivism and Hypertext: Random Access Instruction for Advanced knowledge acquisition in structured Domains. In: Constructivism and the Technology of instruction: Conversation Hillsdale. Lawrence Erlbaum Associates, New Jersey

User Loyalty of Reader's Space: A Case Study of Social Network Services

Zhiwu Gong and Di Wu

Guangzhou Open University, Guangzhou, China
kungcw@126.com

Abstract. The paper analyses one of the Social Network Services, Reader's Space to explore how to improve the user loyalty by tracing the repeated times, length of visit and depth of visit for 2 years. The result shows that the designed Reader's Space is suitable for distance learners to participate and sharing each other, User loyalty is determined by the service quality and the trust between the users. Either the length or depth is critical to retain new users and find the sense of belonging.

Keywords: Social Network Service, User Loyalty, Bounce Rate, Page Views, Length of visit, Depth of visit.

1 Introduction

Social Network Services (SNS) is becoming a new issue in the field of distance education, how could the students be involved and engaged in the designed activities without any boring or reluctance?

In order to explore how the SNS works, we developed a website called Reader's Space(RS) in 2007, which is a sort of social network site focusing on creating a set of reading, entertainment, social integration that enables network users to build and reflect social relations among themselves, and share interests and activities together. The website adopts real-name registration, and open to all the staffs and students in our university.

As we know, SNSs usually allow users to express themselves, keep in touch with friends, and interact with others. As a sort of SNS, RS should have some characteristics, our online survey indicates that the top 5 factors to motivate users to log on RS are: trust(19%); sharing(19%); curiosity(16%); interaction and communication(16%); make friends(9%). While the least factors are: sense of identification(3%); value(3%); self-expression(3%); just try(3%); others(3%).

According to community characteristics and behavior of users, analyze their form of reflection, logs, experience sharing, knowledge, communication emotional support, design virtual community activities and organizations, design and organization of open, flexible and virtual community activities and tasks, the use of effective strategies to organize and guide the design of progressive involvement of members in activities to promote the process to complete the task of virtual community development and self-improvement and build each other's social knowledge base.

R. Kwan et al. (Eds.): ICHL 2011, LNCS 6837, pp. 272–278, 2011.

2 Overview

All traffic sources sent a total of 19,846 visits at the period of Sep.1st, 2010 to Jan.1st, 2011 on Reader's Space.

Data were: Direct Traffic 12,937.00 (65.19%), Referring Sites 5,228.00 (26.34%), and Search Engines 1,681.00 (8.47%).

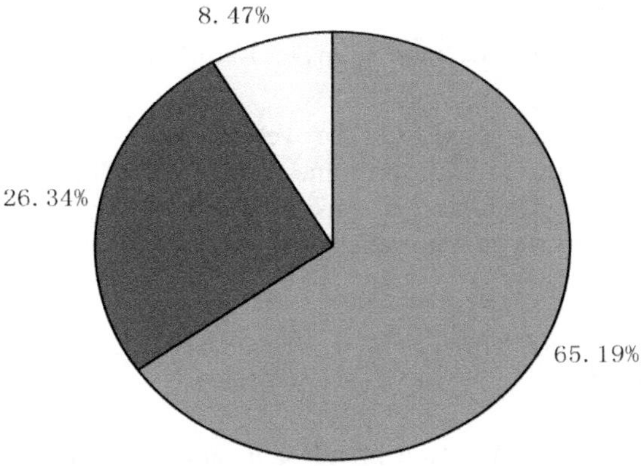

Fig. 1. Traffic sources on Readers Space during the period of Sep.1st, 2010 to Jan.1st, 2011

Table 1. Rate of change for RS vs benchmark

item	RS	benchmark	rate of change
Visits	19,846	28	+70,778.57%
Pageviews	178,994	45	+397,664.45%
Bounce Rate	21.79%	31.22%	-30.20%
New Visits	37.49%	51.69%	-27.46%
Avg. Time on Site	00:07:22	00:00:02	+24,808.44%
Pages/Visit	9.02	1.58	+471.20%

In order to improve the website better, we conduct a comparative study during the period of Sep.1st, 2010 to Jan.1st, 2011 and the same period last year.

Table 2. Comparative study result during the period of Sep.1st, 2010 to Jan.1st, 2011

item	2010 Autumn term	2009 Autumn term	rate of change
Visits	19,846	11,726	+69.25%
Visits / Day	161.35	95.33	+69.25%
Absolute Unique Visitors	7,770	2,529	+207.24%
Pageviews	178,994	72,700	+146.21%
Pages/Visit	9.02	6.20	+45.47%
Avg. Time on Site	00:07:22		
Bounce Rate	21.79%	23.78%	-8.40%

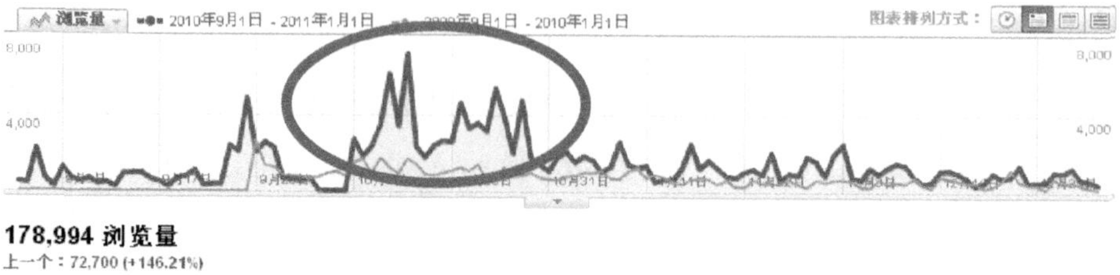

Fig. 2. Website traffic from Sep.1st, 2010 to Jan.1st, 2011

Form the curve above, we can see the website traffic was significantly active in 2010 autumn term compared with the same period of 2009, which reached a peak in October and November. That trend is consistent with the rhythm of teaching schedule. So we should design proper and substantial interactive activities to stimulate and attract distance learners.

3 User Loyalty

Loyalty is a deep commitment to a brand or a service provider (Oliver 1999). User loyalty can be explained as commitment to continued use and recommendations to others (Yi Maggie Guo & Chung-Tzer Liu, 2010) [1]. Especially when users get the services they really need from one site, they would prefer to visit the site over and over.

Take an example of Twitter, recent research has indicated that more than 60 percent of those who sign up to Twitter quit after just one month. According to Nielsen Online, "Twitter has languished below 30 percent retention, the percentage of a given month's users who come back the following month is currently about 40 percent." (Marc Chacksfield, 2009) [2].

Eric T. Peterson suggests that the visitor engagement metric can be composed of six sub-metrics, which are Click-Depth Index, Recency Index, Duration Index, Brand Index, Blog Index and Conversion Index [3].

Although we never know when our user will lose interests at our site, it is time for website developer to focus on how to keep their current user to stay at the website and make strong link with them. We take Google Analytics as tool and take three sub-metrics to analyze the user loyalty, which are repeated times, length of visit and depth of visit.

Table 3. Returning Visitor and New Visitor Counts of the website

Returning Visitor	12,393	62.45%
New Visitor	7,453	37.55%

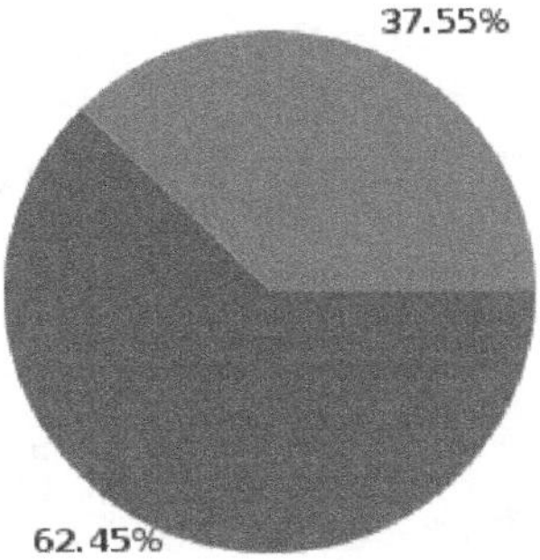

Fig. 3. Graph of Returning Visitor and New Visitor Counts of the website

However, for our site, from the chart above, we can see that the percentage of returning visitors is 62.45%, much higher than the average level of SNSs. Even though we cannot take it for granted, there is still much room for us to improve. We would analyze it from the three dimensions below.

3.1 Repeated Times

How many times do users visit this website? Most visitors visit the site 1 time, including newcomers, but as the number of visitors grows, the more they come. More and more users tend to visit the site over 100 times, even triple over 200 times. That means there is large room for SNSs to improve services to attract the users.

Table 4. Count of visits from users

Count of visits from this visitor including current	Visits that were the visitor's nth visit	Percentage of all visits
1 times		
1 Sep 2009 - 1 Jan 2010	2,515.00	21.45%
1 Sep 2010 - 1 Jan 2011	7,453.00	37.55%
2 times		
1 Sep 2009 - 1 Jan 2010	751.00	6.40%
1 Sep 2010 - 1 Jan 2011	2,393.00	12.06%
101-200 times		
1 Sep 2009 - 1 Jan 2010	783.00	6.68%
1 Sep 2010 - 1 Jan 2011	1,027.00	5.17%
201+ times		
1 Sep 2009 - 1 Jan 2010	227.00	1.94%
1 Sep 2010 - 1 Jan 2011	997.00	5.02%

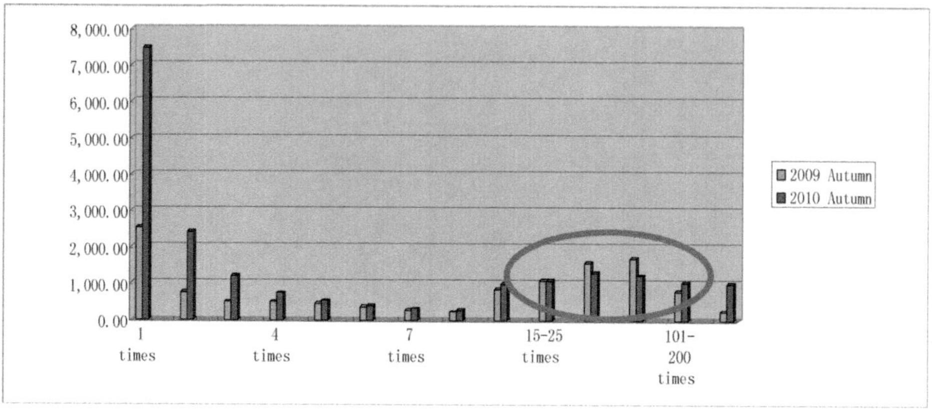

Fig. 4. Chart of the visits of users

3.2 Length of Visit

Social network services have to get adapted to the rapid changing situation both in traffic and length of visit. Nielsen NetView data indicates that social media companies such as facebook, twitter.com, MySpace.com have fluctuations in length of visit [4]. They start to react on how to make their users stay longer. So do us.

Most visits lasted no more than 10 seconds, secondly users will last for more than 3 minutes, if the website are interesting enough to attract them for 3-30 minutes, then the users number will falling down sharply after 30minutes. So 3-30 minutes are critical for instructors to design proper learning activity for distance learners to surf and explore.

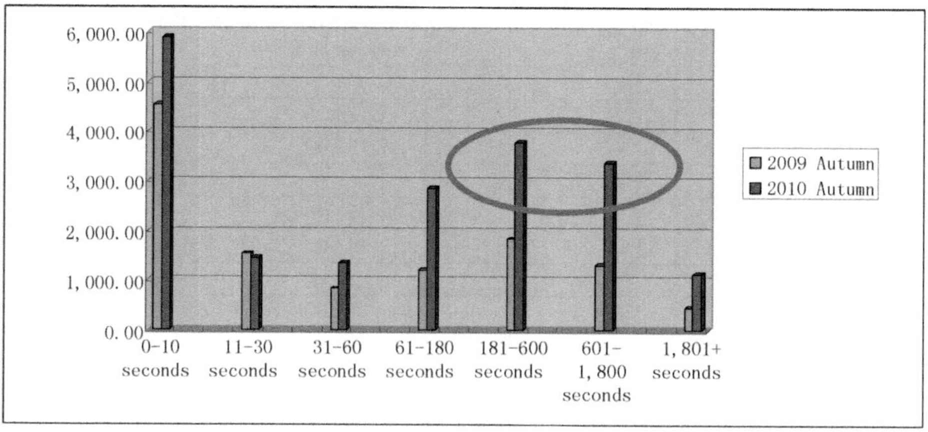

Fig. 5. Chart of the Length of visits of users

3.3 Depth of Visit

When comparing two date ranges, we can see from the chart below clearly that most visits tracked are 1-2 pageviews with the percentage of 43.85% and 35.4% respectively, since then there appears a typical long-tail phenomenon. However, when it comes to over 20 pageviews, there comes a sharp climb to 2323 visits compared with 689 visits previous year, near 6% increase.

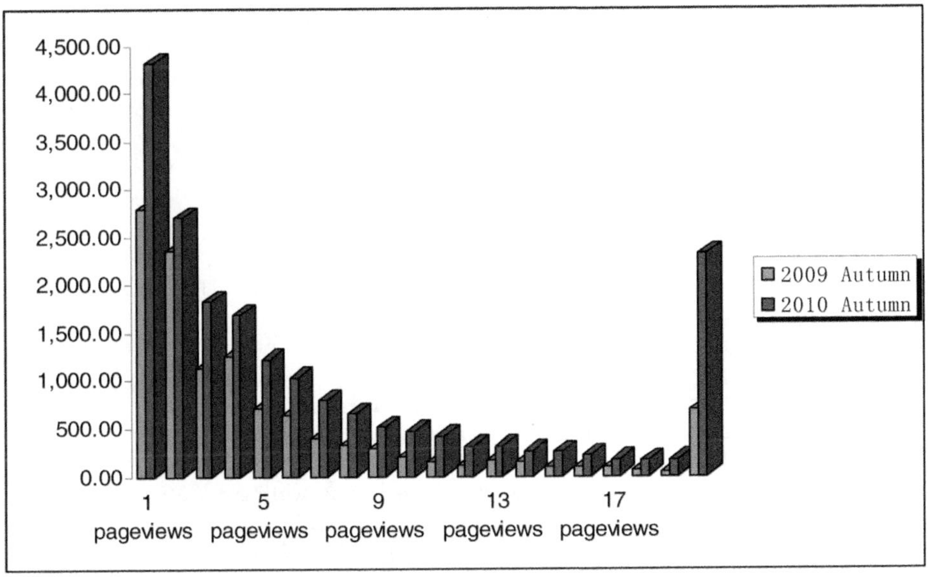

Fig. 6. Chart of the Depth of visits of users

4 Discussion and Conclusion

Firstly, the number of page views for site analysis to analyze site traffic trends gives us much valuable clues. Over three years for running the site, the site number of page views in a clear upward trend matches the characteristics of the site development stage. Page views reflect the stability and improvement of the websites relevant support services and content, which is especially noteworthy in distance learning.

Secondly, the number of page views per visitor trends of real growth in website visits. The number of page views per user reflects the user to access information from the website much higher the average, indicating that the greater the amount of information the more users access. By the proportion of each part of the number of page views, we can see the user content or product information on the level of interest, At present users pay more attention to personal home page, followed by site games, notification and tasks, which means there need to be further guidance for users to switch to logs, knowledge management, results-sharing column.

Thirdly, user loyalty is determined by the service quality and the trust between the users. At the early stage of the website, the trust is built through friends and acquaintance, later it spread to newcomers. There is over 60% direct traffic on our website, which means the visitors have strong interest and clear purpose in this site.

In conclusion, to retain more users, we should try to offer substantial content to attract users keep surfing in the net. The date shows that 3-30 minutes are critical for them to stay on. If there is no effective activity to keep them, the bounce rate would be definitely high.

However, as a social network website, users have their rights to choose whether they would or would not to log on the website without any constraint. While in the context of distance learning, things are different. Once enrolling the course, distance learners are required to access the e-learning platform. It seems that there is nothing to do with whether the learner has royalty or not. In other words, can the research on user royalty be applied to distance learning is still a tough issue, we would do more work on it.

References

1. Guo, Y.M., Liu, C.-T.: Loyalty Of Web 2.0 Sites: The Role Of Sense Of Belonging[DB/OL]. (2010), http://www.pacis-net.org/file/2010/S24-01.pdf
2. Chacksfield, M.: 60% of Twitter users 'quit after a month' [DB/OL] (2009), http://www.techradar.com/news/internet/60-of-twitter-users-quit-after-a-month—595710
3. Peterson's, E.: Blog at Web Analytics Demystified [DB/OL], http://blog.webanalyticsdemystified.com/weblog/2007/01/engagement-metric-defined-part-iv-in.html
4. Sherman, E.: Social Network User Loyalty Erratic [DB/OL] (2009), http://www.bnet.com/blog/technology-business/social-network-user-loyalty-erratic/1144

Assessing the Role of Mobile Learning Systems in Graduate Management Education

Owen P. Hall Jr. and David M. Smith

Pepperdine University, Graziadio School of Business and Management,
24255 Pacific Coast Highway, Malibu, California, USA
{owen.hall,david.smith}@pepperdine.edu

Abstract. Mobile learning has come a long way since Sir Isaac Pitman initiated the first correspondence course in the early 1840s. The demands of globalization call for new and innovative learning systems for enhancing graduate management education. One approach for meeting these challenges is through the increased use of mobile learning systems like the iPad. The purpose of this paper is to highlight the results from an iPad initiative in a program of graduate management education. The preliminary data shows that while learning outcomes did not vary between the iPad and non-iPad sections student convenience and flexibility along with energy and environmental sustainability were enhanced.

Keywords: Mobile learning, iPad, energy and environmental sustainability, graduate management education, student flexibility and convenience.

1 Introduction

Globalization is bringing about a radical *rethink* regarding the content and delivery of graduate management education. Today, hybrid learning, e-learning, distance learning and mobile learning are all playing an increasingly significant role in higher education. [16] Mobile learning systems (MLS), in particular, offers the student both a customized and an integrated knowledge experience. MLS embrace many options for presenting flexible content to students in both individual and collaborative contexts. [19] MLS are well-suited to meet the challenges associated with graduate management education since they provide instructional content at a time, location and pace convenient to the student. Today, the use of MLS throughout management education is growing rapidly. [2], [18], [26] MLS is also seeing wide spread use in the business community. For example, the Assessment & Learning in Practice Settings at five major UK medical universities is using mobile devices to deliver learning resources and assessments to enrich, enhance and extend practice learning. A basic goal of the program is to build student confidence at the beginning of their professional careers. [29]

Mobile based learning systems are designed to leverage the strengths of face-to-face instructional contacts with web-based knowledge acquisition which focuses on distance learning and virtual collaboration. The degree and nature of the use of MLS depends heavily on the goals and characteristics of the specific graduate management

R. Kwan et al. (Eds.): ICHL 2011, LNCS 6837, pp. 279–288, 2011.

program. [15] For example, most executive MBA programs tend to focus on broad based issues like leadership and strategic management. This is in contrast to the more "technical" focus of a residential MBA program. One of the advantages of MLS is that it provides a flexible learning environment that can be customized to meet the needs of a wide portfolio of graduate management programs. This article is organized as follows 1) a review of the current trends in mobile learning systems; 2) an introduction to the iPad initiative; 3) an assessment of preliminary empirical results associated with hybrid learning technologies; and 4) a discussion on the impact of increased MLS usage on economic, environmental, and energy sustainability.

2 Mobile Learning

Typically mobile learning is defined as the acquisition of knowledge through conversations across multiple contexts via interactive technologies. [21] Mobile learning is designed to significantly alter the three pillars of traditional MBA instruction—fixed time, fixed location, and fixed learning pace—with a more flexible and customized learning environment. Specific characteristics of the MLS paradigm for MBA programs include:

- Provides increased student convenience and flexibility
- Offers the capability to receive *live* webcasts on a worldwide basis
- Affords an integrated perspective on the course/program
- Presents instructional-rich content including real-time feedback
- Increases opportunities for student and team participation and interaction
- Improves quality control through content integration
- Provides direct linkage with Internet and library resources
- Supports environmental, and energy sustainability

For example, the traditional classroom setting tends to be effective for team presentations that require a great deal of face-to-face interaction while a threaded chatroom learning experience supports the student's requirement for flexibility. Another learning focus for students is to develop the capability to access business information. The continuing enhancement of search engines and digital libraries provides an opportunity for students to "drill down" on topics such as industry analysis, technology, and globalization. Mobile learning devices offer the potential for supporting these learning challenges.

The mobile learning model highlighted in this paper is predicated on the following three learning theories:

- A Theory of Mobile Learning. [25] This theory offers a framework about mobile learning as a complement to the classroom, workplace and informal learning. A related aim is to identify new environments and technologies to support mobile learning.
- Instructional Management System (IMS) cooperative initiative. [12] This initiative is designed to promote systematic thinking regarding the delivery of higher education, to improve learning outcomes, and to increase return on

instructional investments. The IMS initiative calls for the increased use of mobile technologies to promote integrated learning and to provide customized content.

- E-Learning Success Model. [9] This model suggests that the overall effectiveness of mobile learning depends on the attainment of success at each of three stages: system design, system delivery, and system outcomes. The effective use of mobile learning will require the integration of all three stages.

The E-Learning Success Model represents an important ingredient of the MLS paradigm. The model design, highlighted in Figure 1, suggests that the overall effectiveness of MLS depends on the attainment of success at each of three stages: system design, system delivery, and system outcomes. The efficacious use of this paradigm will require the integration of all three stages.

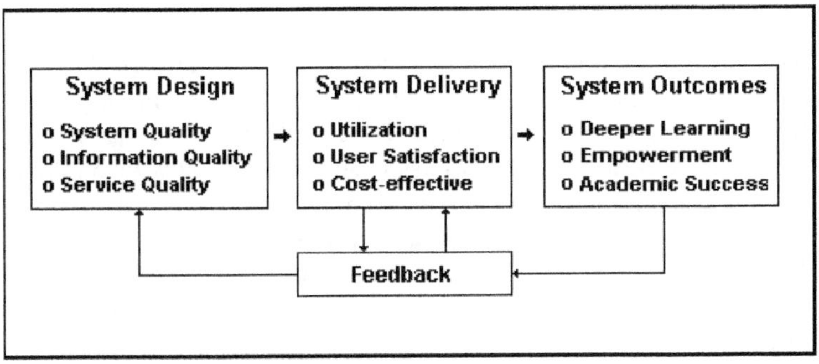

Fig. 1. E-learning Success Model

Each stage consists of a number of specific performance metrics. For example, service quality can be measured using availability, reliability, and response time. Assessment rubrics can be used for evaluating each performance metric. [14]

Mobile learning systems like the iPad, offer students engaged in graduate management education both synchronous and asynchronous learning opportunities. [6] Furthermore, the use of artificial agents to assist in the learning process is receiving increased attention. [17] More specifically, synthetic agents, which by design are compatible with the MLS paradigm, can generate customized learning plans based on student accomplishments, backgrounds, and expectations. Another advantage of mobile learning technology is that it provides a 24/7 learning environment which is an increasing requirement for student, particularly working adults. Additionally, students tend to participate more in learning systems that are content rich and that feature extensive variety which is a hallmark of mobile learning systems. Student interest in the use of mobile learning technology, like the iPad, for delivering content and know-how is growing. [23] Furthermore, students that are technologically ready are more likely to be interested in engaging in so-called hybrid-based learning programs [30].

Another recent study on the use of mobile learning technologies found: [27]

- Students consistently recognized that watching Internet based video lectures provided the highest degree of choice and control since students could choose which portions to watch at any time of their choosing.
- Students found themselves generally more engaged in the face-to-face tutorial that gave them the highest level of bandwidth and engagement without technological interference or blockage.
- Students noted the exam to be the most challenging activity; this is not an unexpected finding given the lack of control, i.e., the students had a relatively fixed amount of time and were constrained to a fixed date and time.

There are a number of criteria that educational managers should use to assess whether new technological advances improve teaching and learning. [3] Some specific examples include:

- What are the learning curves in deploying new technologies?
- To what extent does the introduction of new technologies require the diversion of teaching time to instructing students how to use them?
- What are the benefits and costs associated with the new technologies?
- How are technological advances changing our notions of time and space in regards to the management education classroom?
- What opportunities and challenges does this change represent?
- Do certain technologies appeal more to specific categories of students or particular course objectives?
- Are new technologies more effective with specific categories of students, or particular course objectives?

Mobile learning technologies also make it possible to provide educational opportunities to those students that are either without the traditional infrastructure or those individuals that are constantly on the move. [5] In this regard further research is needed at the course, curriculum, and delivery levels to assess both the effectiveness and direction of MLS compared with traditional and online delivery modes. [4], [20], [22].

3 iPad Initiative

An iPad initiative was launched in the fall of 2011. The purpose of this research initiative was threefold:

- Assess the impact of the iPad on learning outcomes
- Characterize the use of the iPad on student convenience and flexibility
- Evaluate the efficacy of the iPad on energy and environmental sustainability

A Phase I evaluation of the iPad was conducted in the fall of 2010. Two sections of the same graduate management level course were selected for evaluation with the students of one section receiving iPads from the University. The cohort groups for both courses consisted of working professionals with five to ten years of business experience. The students also received a gift card from the University for the acquisition of specific iPad related applications (e.g., Numbers). The curriculum for both sections was the same as well as the grading methodology. The iPad assessment initiative will continue throughout the remainder of 2011 (Phase II). Course content for both sections was delivered via the Internet.

The two sample groups, in effect, were selected at random since none of the students were informed of the iPad initiative until the night the iPads were distributed. No student transfer was allowed between the two sections. To confirm that the two samples were randomized a standard t-test assuming equal variance was performed using undergraduate GPA scores. The results indicated there was no significance difference between the two samples using GPA at the 0.05 level.

A student pre-survey on the use of computer technology (CT) was conducted on both sections. The highlights of the survey are presented in Table 1.

Table 1. Student Computer Technology Pre-survey Results

Statistic	iPad Section	Non-iPad Section
Own laptop (%)	100	95
Use CT at work (%)	94	91
Use CT at school (%)	61	59

One of the overall learning goals of both sections (iPad and non-iPad) was to develop an understanding of the interactive nature of modern business management. Specifically to show how finance, marketing, and operations are linked together in developing an aggregate plan. Aggregate planning is a core notion associated with a course in operations management. Generally, the planning process begins with a forecast or forecasts regarding future demand and customer requirements. Based on these forecasts the specific process for fulfilling these requirements can be identified (process management). Next, the size of internal capability can be determined (capacity planning). The final step is to determine how this capacity is to be used (aggregate planning). Aggregate planning is a macro approach for determining how an organization plans to meet demand. Typically, this process involves finding the most effective way to meet demand through a combination of adjusting production rates, pricing, promotions and manpower. An aggregate plan can be based on a variety of goals including minimizing total costs or maximizing customer satisfaction. The primary purpose of aggregate planning is to develop a strategy that meets demand in the most cost-effective manner.

In the iPad section an app named *Hotel Tycoon* was used to reinforce aggregate planning principles. Students in both courses were exposed to both reading materials and lectures on aggregate planning, however, only the iPad course utilized the *Hotel Tycoon* simulation. Hotel Tycoon is an operations management simulation which can be played both individually or in a team environment. The goal of *Hotel Tycoon* is to develop one four-star hotel and one five-star hotel over a four year period. The game begins with the student (or student team) owning a three-star hotel. The game involves a wide variety of finance, marketing and operations decision-making. Typically, the simulation can be completed in approximately two hours. The final course exercise involved a competition between four student teams. These were the same study teams that had been formed at the beginning of the trimester. The *Hotel Tycoon* is only one example of the many iPad apps that are currently available or will soon be available to support graduate management education.

4 Preliminary Results

The database consisted of student records on undergraduate GPA, undergraduate degree type and gender. The sample sizes for the iPad and non-iPad sections were 17 and 23, respectively. Table 2 provides descriptive statistics for the combined database (N=40). For example, approximately 48 percent of the students held an undergraduate degree in business and economics and about 43 percent were female.

Table 2. Descriptive Statistics (N=40)

Variable	Average	S.D.	Max	Min
GPA	3.05	0.42	3.92	2.07
UB/E (B/E=1)	0.475	-	1	0
Gender (F=1)	0.425	-	1	0
iPad (iPad=1)	0.425	-	1	0
Final Grade	89.1	2.83	95.2	83.7

To control for these other factors a stepwise SPSS regression analysis of the database using final numerical grade score as the target variable was performed. The results revealed that only GPA from the above variable set, including the iPad dummy variable, was statistically significant when taken in combination at the 0.05 level. GPA showed a positive correlation with the target variable ($r = 0.42$). The corresponding R-square was 0.17. The iPad variable when analyzed separately with the target variable was found *not* to be statistically significant at the 0.05 level. This result suggests that the learning outcomes were about the same for the two sections.

Each student in the iPad section was tasked with maintaining a blog over the course of the trimester. The participation rate was 82 percent. Approximately 70 percent of the participating students generated three or fewer separate blogs while the remainder generated four or more blogs. Nearly 80 percent of the students indicated that they found the iPad useful for the reading assignments.

The following selected blog comments are representative of the overall student experience.

- I found note taking to be very useful. When I was in a conference call it was easy to take notes. One problem is that the notes can't be directly exported to my laptop.
- It's easy to carry an iPad instead of heavy text books. There are still many of my classmates who prefer print books because they don't want to view the screen for long hours.

- Using the iPad has been cool, but I'm not sure yet that I would recommend changing from a laptop completely to an iPad. I think that the iPad is great for virtual books, and may even be effective for note taking if a person was able to become proficient at typing. For a quantitative class, until the iPad can run Java, it has some significant shortfalls.
- I am happy to report that IPAD use for this week has been extensive. I realized that having an IPAD on-the-go is obviously more convenient, than having to open your laptop and waiting for it to load. I've been able to read stuff for school in a variety of venues. The only thing that still bothers me is the keyboard.

5 Sustainability

Institutions of higher learning are becoming increasingly concerned regarding economic and environmental sustainability. [8], [11] One strategy for helping ameliorate this growing challenge is the delivery of "green-based" learning. Rising gasoline prices has generated increased interest using mobile learning systems. The inefficient use of fossil fuel energy in commuting to campus coupled with the high energy content associated with the production and distribution of printed materials suggests an expanded role for mobile learning. Increasing the use of MLS throughout higher education can contribute to the goal of achieving sustainable growth in a globalized economy as well as improve learning outcomes. With respect to environmental sustainability, U.S. universities have taken a lead role with the founding of the American College & University Presidents Climate Committee (ACUPCC) and the Association for the Advancement of Sustainability in Higher Education (AASHE). [1] The mission of the AASHE is to advance the efforts of the entire campus sustainability community by uniting diverse initiatives and connecting practitioners to resources and professional development opportunities.

One area receiving specific attention from academia is student commuting. This activity represents a significant sustainability issue, especially for those participating in non-residential programs. A recent study found that distance learning higher education programs consumes 87 percent less energy and 85 percent lower CO_2 emissions compared with full-time campus-based courses. [24] The study also discovered that part-time campus programs reduce energy and CO_2 emissions by 65 and 61 percent, respectively, compared with full-time campus courses. The lower impacts of part-time and distance compared with full-time campus courses is mainly due to a reduction in student travel and elimination of much energy consumption of students' housing, plus economies in campus site utilization.

Another university-oriented opportunity for enhancing sustainability is the print book and print materials industries. Presently, the print book sector alone emits approximately nine pounds of carbon per book, with most of the impact connected to forest carbon loss. [13] E-books represent a basic alternative to the traditional print book (p-book). An e-book is a digitized learning resource that is both readable and downloadable. E-books need only contain the required material for the specific course as compared with the often unused material in many p-books. The transition from printed materials to electronic based materials in higher education, for example, can reduce energy consumption and carbon emissions associated with the print industry by upwards of 90 percent.[10] Furthermore, e-books, in particular, and digital material, in general, can be easily distributed via distance learning networks. E-books appears to offer only relatively small energy and emissions reductions (20 and 12 percent, respectively) compared with mainly print-based distance learning courses, primarily because online learning requires more energy for computing and paper for printing. However, these estimates are based on the assumption that students will print the instructional material distributed via the web. There is a growing body of evidence that students are becoming more comfortable in reading on line [28] In this case the amount of energy and emission savings could rival those associated with reduced driving. From a MLS perspective one could assume that the energy and environmental savings might be on the order of one-half of those reported for a completely on-line program. Furthermore, e-books also provide a low cost alternative to increasingly expensive p-books. [7], [31]

6 Conclusion

Mobile learning systems (MLS) like the iPad hold out considerable promise for enhancing graduate management education in a changing global environment. Many MBA programs are increasingly focused on customization, experiential learning, and results assessment. MLSs provide an opportunity for collaborative learning that can have a positive impact on the educational experience. Providing the broadest range of tutorial instruction options optimizes students' opportunities for effective learning. Specific benefits of MLS for management education programs are highlighted below:

- Affords an integrated perspective on the course/program
- Presents instructional-rich content including real-time feedback
- Offers courses designed for specific learning applications
- Increases opportunities for student and team participation and interaction
- Improves quality control through content integration
- Supports quality through learning assurance
- Provides direct linkage with Internet and library resources
- Supports economic, environmental, and energy sustainability

Higher education, in general, and management education, in particular, is undergoing a fundamental shift from a teacher-centric process to a learning-centric environment that focuses on customized learning. In graduate management education this transformation is being fueled by the need to produce educated managers that can compete on a global basis. The vehicle for facilitating this reformation is the Internet. MLS, which combine the best in classical learning with web-based support systems, provide both the rigor and flexibility to meet the challenges and requirements of today's and tomorrow's managers.

The preliminary results from the iPad initiative showed that there was no difference in learning outcomes as measured by the final numerical course grade between the iPad and non-iPad sections. Additionally, students indicated that they found the iPad useful for the reading assignments and in playing the *Hotel Tycoon* simulation. Nevertheless, they also reported a number of draw-backs including the inability to run Java or flash screen applications. Furthermore, the students indicated that the keyboard was hard to use and that the *Numbers* app does not permit extensive calculations like Excel. Finally, the iPad initiative contributed to both energy and environmental sustainability by reducing student commuting and eliminating the use of print books.

References

1. Alexsson, H., Sonesson, K., Wickenberg, P.: Why and How Do Universities Work for Sustainability in Higher Education? International Journal of Sustainability in Higher Education 9(4), 469 (2009)
2. Banerjee, J., Bose, I.: Higher Education Through Mobile Learning. Indian Journal of Commerce & Management Studies 2(1), 123 (2011)
3. Billsberry, J., Rollag, K.: New Technological Advances Applied to Management Education. Journal of Management Education 34(2), 329 (2010)
4. Brannon, T.: Learner Interactivity in Higher Education: Comparing Face-to-Face, Hybrid and On-line Instruction. Distance Learning 2(2), 1 (2005)
5. Brown, T.: Towards a Model of M-Learning in Africa. International Journal on E-Learning 4(3), 299 (2005)
6. Chang, C.: Acceptability of an asynchronous learning forum on mobile. Devices. Behavior and Information Technology 29(1), 23 (2010)
7. Christopher, L.: Academic Publishing: Digital Alternatives to Expensive Print Books. The Seybolt Report 8(19), 11 (2008)
8. Clegg, P.: Creativity and Critical Thinking in the Globalised University. Innovations in Education and Teaching International 45(3), 219 (2008)
9. Delone, W., Mclean, E.: The Delone and Mclean Model of Information Systems Success: A Ten-Year Update. Journal of Management information Systems 19(4), 9 (2003)
10. Engelhaupt, E.: Would You Like that Book in Paper or Plastic? Environmental Science & Technology 42(12), 4242 (2008)
11. Forrant, R.: Globalization, Universities and Sustainable Human Development. Development 45(3), 102 (2002)
12. Graves, W.: The Instructional Management System Cooperative: Converting Random Acts of Progress into Global Progress. Educom Review 34(6), 32 (1999)
13. Healy, M.: Environmental Trends and Climate Impacts: Finding from the US Book Industry. Book Industry Study Group, New York (2008)
14. Hughes, G.: Using Hybrid Learning to Increase Learner Support and Improve Retention. Teaching in Higher Education 12(3), 15 (2007)
15. Kleiman, L., Kass, D.: Giving MBA Programs the Third Degree. Journal of Management Education 31(1), 81 (2007)
16. Li, F., Liu, W.: Emerging eLearning Technologies. International Journal of Distance Education Technologies 5(2), 2 (2007)
17. Lin, F.: Designing Distributed Learning Environments with Intelligent Software Agents. Information Science Publishing, Hershey (2005)
18. Lopez, J. et al.: Methods of Adapting Digital Content for the Learning Process via Mobile Devices. Procedia Social and Behavioral Sciences, 1 (2009)
19. Normand, C., Littlejohn, A., Falconer, I.: A Model for Effective Implementation of Flexible Program Delivery. Innovations in Teaching and Education International 45(1), 25 (2008)

20. Orr, G.: A Review of Literature in Mobile Learning: Affordances And Constraints. In: 6th IEEE International Conference on Wireless Mobile and Ubiquitous Technologies in Education (2010)
21. Peng, H.: Ubiquitous knowledge construction: Mobile learning redefined and a conceptual framework. Innovations in Teaching Education International 46(2), 171 (2009)
22. Petrova, K., Li, C.: Focus and Setting in Mobile Learning Research. A Review of the Literature. Communications of the IBIMA 10, 1943 (2009)
23. Rhee, B., et al.: Technology Readiness, Learning Goals, and eLearning. Searching for Synergy, Decision Sciences Journal of Innovative Education 5(1), 127 (2007)
24. Roy, R., Potter, S.: Designing Low Carbon Higher Education Systems. International Journal of Sustainability in Higher Education 9(2), 116 (2008)
25. Sharples, M., Taylor, J., Vavoula, G.: Towards a Theory of Mobile Learning. In: Proceedings of mLearn 2005 Conference, Cape Town (2005)
26. Shen, R., et al.: Mobile Learning in a Large Blended Computer Science Classroom: System Function, Pedagogies, and Their Impact on Learning. IEEE Transactions on Education 52(4), 538 (2009)
27. Shroff, R., Vogel, D., Coombes, J.: Student E-Learning Intrinsic Motivation: A Qualitative Study. Communications of the Association for Information Systems 19, 241 (2007)
28. Tang, M., Byme, R.: Regular Versus Online Versus Blended: A Qualitative Description of the Advantages of the Electronic Modes and a Quantitative Evaluation. International Journal on ELearning 6(2), 257 (2007)
29. Taylor, J., et al.: Developing a Mobile Learning Solution for Health and Social Care Practice. Distance Education 31(2), 175 (2010)
30. Traxler, J.: Current State of Mobile Learning. International Review on Research in Open and Distance Learning 8(2), 52 (2007)
31. Young, J.: To Save Students Money, Colleges May Force a Switch to E-Textbooks, The Chronicle of Higher Education (February 9, 2011)

YouLearn Portal: Hybrid Learning with Archived Lectures and Tutorials

Joseph Fong[1], Tracy Au[2], and Simon K.S. Cheung[3]

[1,2] City University of Hong Kong, Tat Chee Avenue, Kowloon, Hong Kong
csjfong@cityu.edu.hk, hkhahawai@hotmail.com
[3] Open University of Hong Kong, Good Shepherd Street, Kowloon, Hong Kong
kscheung@ouhk.edu.hk

Abstract. YouTube portal is a popular video-sharing tool for entertainment. On similar ideas, we propose a YouLearn portal to support university students' learning. Very often, owing to heavy study load and tight study schedule, it is difficult for many students to 'digest' the lecture materials. Borrowing the ideas of YouTube portal, these lectures and tutorials can be recorded, archived and posted onto the Internet so that students can watch back the video archive of lectures and tutorials. This paper shows a solution called YouLearn portal by synchronizing video, audio and image, three-in-one files, used in the lectures and tutorials, and deploying them through web podcasting. The portal also facilitates hybrid learning by encouraging the students to learn from each other through open forum chat room activities.

Keywords: YouLearn portal, hybrid learning, podcasting, chat room, blog.

1 Introduction

Although the existing e-learning systems provide many useful features to support students' learning, there are still a number of shortcomings:

Lack of interactivity. The existing e-learning systems are informative for learning. They are however not interactive enough. Although video demonstration and multi-media features are offered, users can only act as "knowledge receivers". There is a lack of real-time and face-to-face discussions. As a result, students are not motivated to use the systems for learning.

Lack of up-to-date information. System administrators of the existing e-learning systems need to update the materials periodically. The updates are made less often. Sometimes, the materials may be out-dated due to the change of syllabus or due to some new concepts. Using out-dated materials in e-learning systems may have bad effects in students' learning and studying.

Lack of multi-courses platform. Most of the existing e-learning systems have limitations on the courses supported. Some e-learning systems only provide learning in one language, for example, either English or Putonghua. As a result, these e-learning systems are not well-rounded.

R. Kwan et al. (Eds.): ICHL 2011, LNCS 6837, pp. 289–297, 2011.

Nowadays, people are familiar with the internet. They often use networking tools like MSN, weblogs and social platforms and discussion forums like Facebook, Twitters and Uwants to meet friends, getting latest information and communicating with others around the world. They also use searching engines, such as Google and Yahoo, for finding information they need. For leisure, they browse the web or play some online games.

For studying, students use e-learning systems to clarify their misunderstandings and uncertainties in different courses by asking questions directly to their lecturers or tutors. Since communication in e-learning system is different from that in daily life, students can discuss with each other in e-learning system in a more relaxing mode, and are more willing to ask questions [1]. Students can also get some supplementary materials related to their courses via some multimedia components in the e-learning systems in order to get much understanding to their courses.

Students often have heavy study load and tight study schedules. If the lectures can be recorded and posted into the Internet, they can check content and review difficult aspects of the lecture. Many universities are responding to the issues by video recording tutoring. However, in most cases the video recording cannot cover all aspects of a class (hand-written notes, and/or power point slides) in one file.

A possible solution is the use of Podcasting which is a digital media file, or a series of such files, distributed over the Internet using syndication feeds for playback on portable media players and personal computers. A podcast is a specific type of webcast which can be either the content itself or the method by which it is syndicated; the latter is also termed podcasting. Another similar term is Video podcast which refers to a term used for the online delivery of video on demand video clip content. The following is the definition of Podcasting in this project: 'A podcast is a web-based technology to synchronize multimedia element including video, audio, any graphic files and animations. It also refers to the distribution of the mentioned elements which users can retrieve them by using a podcast player.'

YouLearn portal uses the podcast technology to synchronize video, audio and image files into an archived podcast file, for posting onto the web. It enables hosting and archiving of an open forum discussion with a shareable whiteboard. The objective is to record and archive their lectures and tutorials. Teachers may use the portal to record and archive their tutorials using a whiteboard through a real time open forum or chat room. Participants may share drawings, messages and verbal communications among lecturers and students; both can draw on a shared whiteboard. This function is particularly useful when there are ideas in art and language studies that can better be communicated through diagrams.

This paper aims at providing a YouLearn portal for students to ask questions and get more knowledge related to their courses taught at university. The main feature of the portal is providing a real time video-based chat room. In the chat room, lecturers will be available in the chat room at a certain period of time for students to ask questions related to their courses. Students can also share their idea about the courses in the chat room. Many students can go into the chat room at the same time to communicate with their lectures via their webcam and message board in the chat room. Beside the chat room, some tools, such as lecturer online schedules and news announcement, are provided by the YouLearn portal.

2 Related Work in e-Learning

The section briefly described some related work in e-learning.

iClassroom interactive e-learning channel [2] offers interactive educational flash games to assist primary schools in implementing information technology teaching materials. The purpose is to make use of interactive e-learning format to allow more flexibility, nurture students' learning interest and encourage communication between the parents and their children via the interactive educational flash games.

HKedCity has established an e-learning platform for primary and secondary teachers, parents and students. Its "Sport Classroom" e-learning platform [3] provides teaching videos of sports coaches, letting students know different techniques and skills of sports. The platform also provide some real-time interactive flash quizzes for students to strengthen the knowledge of sports, as well as some video illustration for students to know how to use the techniques and skills practically.

British Council offers different sorts of interactive English-learning materials, classified into kindergarten, primary school, secondary school, adult learning, summer learning and also lecturer training [4].

Taiwan civil servants e-learning website [5, 6] offers online learning materials for Taiwan civil servants to enhance their knowledge in the leisure time. The website provide online classroom and learning records, discussion forum and weblogs, as well as some description of the courses provided to civil servants.

WWF has established a my-IT school website [7], which makes use of informative flash animation and their statistics to introduce birds' wetland life in Hong Kong. It also let students record their statistics via the system after explore to wetland area in Hong Kong.

Learning Management System (LMS) provides a centralized and consolidated method for the delivery of online training programs [8]. Its built-in assessment and reporting tools allow for automated certificate generation. LMS also enables lecturers to provide speedy teaching materials in e-learning system. It enables students to have independent information in their own accounts and at the same time students can have the same teaching materials retrieved from lecturers [9]. However, it did not support multiple lecturers and students at the same time.

3 YouLearn Portal

In general, the YouLearn portal will store the archive of classroom lectures by means of podcast files and tutorial session whiteboard files. The YouLearn portal will be available for students as a substitute for physical attendance in case they cannot attend the class, and also as a means to review and reflect upon classes that have been attended. The YouLearn portal can also help lecturers to archive their lectures and tutorial sessions as supplementary teaching materials for reuse in their future classes. The design of YouLearn portal screen layout can be illustrated as follows for student to select which archived and tutorial to browse or download as shown in Figure 1.

Title key word Search: Putonghua

Title of lesson / tutorial	Name of Teacher	Duration in hours	Ranking in 1-5 stars	Creation Date
Putonghua	John Doe	1 Hour	***	10-5-2010
SQL	Joseph Fong	2 hours	****	1-2-2011
VB Programming	Mary Kim	3 hours	*****	10-5-2010

Fig. 1. Directory of Archived Lectures and Tutorials on YouLearn Portal

Figure 2 shows a screen layout of an archived podcasting lecture file created by CALS(Computer Assist Lecturing System), in which, lecturers' video image on upper left hand side, power point slides on upper right hand side, and hand written notes on lower part of the following screen layout are all archived in a podcasting file.

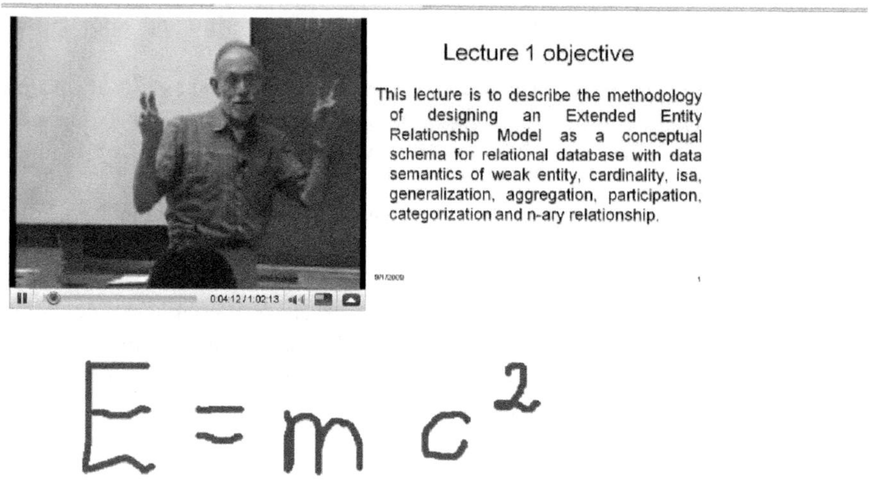

Fig. 2. A sample Podcasting slide of an archived lecture

To use CHAT(Chat room shareable whiteboard) system, a student notes a list of chat room. The student finds the chat room, which is created by a lecturer. After that, the student joins the chat room by clicking the list and enters Join. After that, the system changes the menu to Handwritten Notes and display lecturer in the second chat box. At the same time, the student also appears in the lecturer's browser as shown in Figure 3.

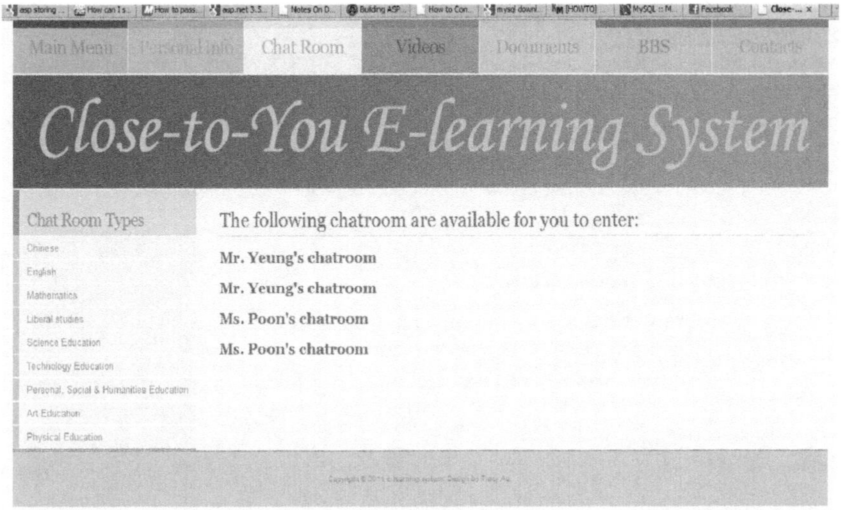

Fig. 3. A sample whiteboard drawing chat room slide of an archived tutorial

After viewing the archived lecture and tutorial slide, the student may want to post a question for the lecturer and tutor to answer by uploading a message attached to the slide as shown in Figure 4.

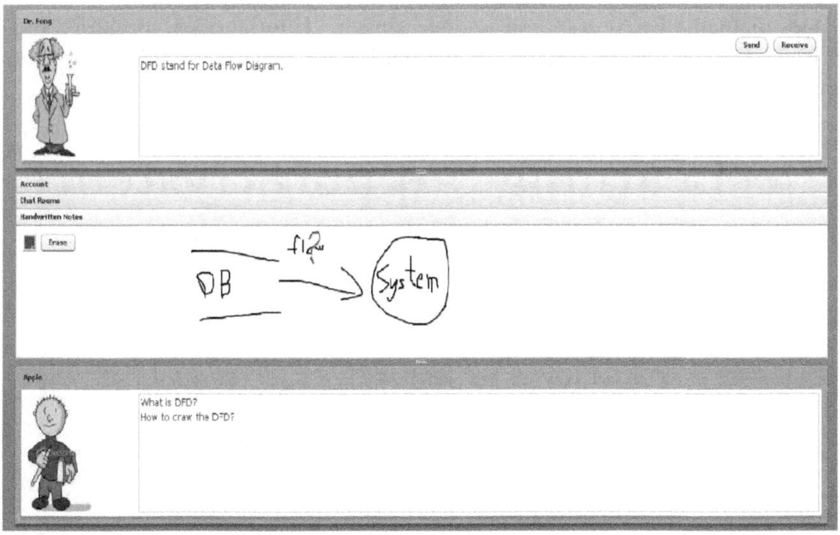

Fig. 4. A sample open forum chat room slide for student to post question

In viewing the question, the lecturer and other students can post an answer to the student's question by uploading a solution to the problem in the same open forum chat room slide in a blog system as shown in Figure 5.

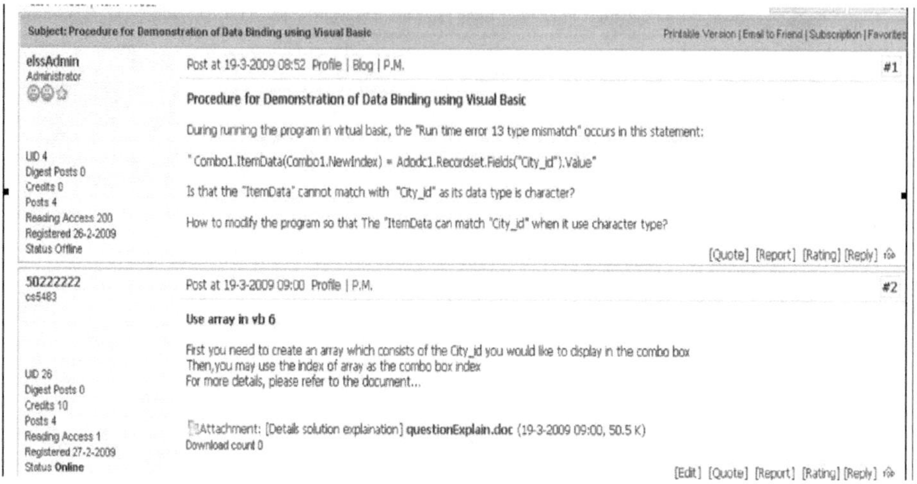

Fig. 5. Lecturer or another student posts a solution to the problem in a blog

After the students and lecturer blogging messages into the archived lecture or tutorial, another viewer may want to rank the usefulness of the archived lectures for his/her study with number of stars 1 to 5 as shown in Figure 6.

This portal signals a solution to the issues raised above by way of an archival system for both lectures and tutorials. The lectures can be archived by synchronizing video, audio and the lecturer image into a podcast file. Handwritten notes are used for language, mathematics, design and science classes. Tutorial sessions can be recorded by writing notes on an interactive whiteboard. This can be shared by students and lecturers in real time or can be accessed at a later date.

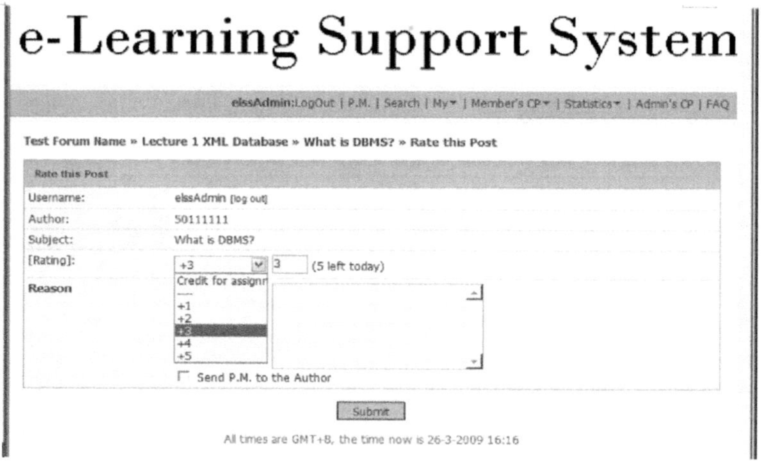

Fig. 6. Viewer assigns ranking to archived lecture/tutorial for its learning effectiveness

The YouLearn portal combines multimedia elements with web technologies. The portal will be searchable by lecture topics and other tags. It is interactive in real time but will also offer an archive of files. The archive will underpin opportunities for enhancement of teaching and time for in depth reflection and revision. YouLearn demonstrates the feasibility of applying tablet personal computers to make a podcast file, consisting of power point presentations, hand written notes, computerization, and lecturer images together with a CALS. Students are enabled to learn independent of time or location. Students may access files for the first time as a supplement to classroom learning or may use the archive to enable them to review lectures. The CHAT function enriches interaction among students and build reflective opportunities beyond what is available in traditional tutorial sessions. It also provides immediate feedback to lecturers.

The success of this portal depends on the usage by lecturers to conduct lectures and tutorials as well as the usage by students to review lectures and tutorials. YouLearn portal will enhance the student experience. Students will supplement their lecturer led learning with peer-to-peer interaction from their portal tablet personal computer.

The statistics of the lecturer and students using the YouLearn portal for a particular archived lecture and tutorial will be stored. Hence, the lecturer can make the future teaching planning according to the statistics as shown in Figure 7, such as the number of users, number of users having posts via the system, and number of user not having posts via the system, average number of posts per user, number of new posts in a day, number of forums created, the forum with highest number of posts, number of questions raised, number of questions raised from the hot forums, average number of replies per question, and forum activity level.

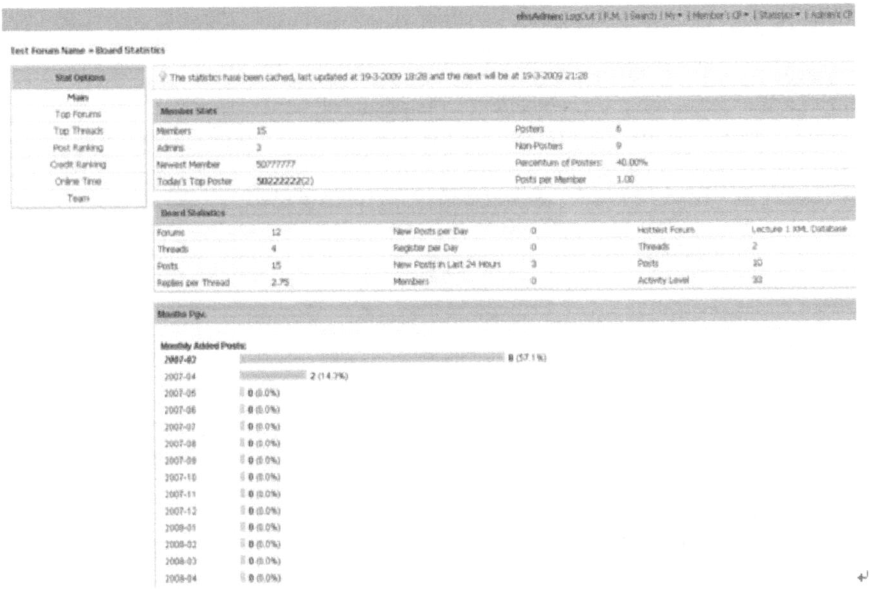

Fig. 7. Statistical figures of the history of posting problems and solutions

4 Conclusion

Borrowing the ideas of YouTube portal, in this paper, we proposed the YouLearn portal to synchronize and archive the video, audio and image used in lectures and tutorials, and to deploy them through web podcasting. With the portal, lecturers, tutors and instructors can record and archive their tutorial sessions in an open forum and real time chat room. The portal stores the archive of classroom lectures by means of podcast files and tutorial session whiteboard files, which are available for students as a substitute for physical attendance and as a means to review and reflect upon classes. It also help instructors to archive their lectures and tutorial sessions as supplementary teaching materials for reuse in their future classes.

Students can benefit from the use of the YouLearn portal because it enables much greater flexibility in accessing current teaching and access to archived teaching materials, anytime and anywhere. Lecturers and tutors will be given enhanced opportunity for timely feedback on the quality of their materials in a non-threatening environment. The portal will provide useful feedback on the comparative popularity of online access. This feedback will loop into corporate decision making about blended delivery. Moreover, the University management will be able to use of the archives for marketing courses and to provide extended opportunities for networks with community. External course appraisal by the Government Education Bureau (and others) will be much more transparent and extensive.

References

1. White, S.: Pros and cons of e-learning. Article Alley (August 1, 2006), http://www.articlealley.com/article_78603_45.html (retrieved August 23, 2010)
2. Homepage of iClassroom interactive e-learning channel, http://www.iclassroom.com.hk/iclass2010/index.html (retrieved August 30, 2010)
3. Homepage of HKedCity "Sports Classroom" e-learning platform, http://www.hkedcity.net/pe/cht/racket/table_tennis.html (retrieved August 30, 2010)
4. Homepage of British Council e-learning platform for the kids, http://learnenglishkids.britishcouncil.org/ (retrieved August 30, 2010)
5. Homepage of Taiwan Servants e-learning website, https://itschool.dgbas.gov.tw/hotForum.do?page_offset=20&method=topicList (retrieved September 1, 2010)
6. Demonstration video for newbie using Taiwan Servants e-learning website, https://itschool.dgbas.gov.tw/newbie1/player.html (retrieved September 1, 2010)
7. Homepage of World Wide Fund for Nature my-IT school, http://apps.wwf.org.hk/wetlandecologist/chi/index.php (retrieved September 2, 2010)

8. Anonymous. What's the difference between a Learning Management System (LMS) and a Learning Content Management System (LCMS)? Knowledge Direct (2008), http://www.knowledgedirectweb.com/content.cfm/Resources/Learning-Management-systems/ (retrieved October 18, 2010)
9. Ellis, R.K.: A field guide to Learning Management Systems. (2009), http://www.astd.org/NR/rdonlyres/12ECDB99-3B91-403E-9B15-7E597444645D/23395/LMS_fieldguide_20091.pdf (retrieved October 18, 2010)

From Web 2.0 to Classroom 3.0

Wilfred W. Fong

School of Continuing Studies, University of Toronto
wilfred.fong@utoronto.ca,
http://learn.utoronto.ca

Abstract. Web 2.0 has changed the way people communicate and learn. It has entered into the millennial classroom. This article discusses the Web 2.0 phenomenon and how it evolves the traditional classroom into Classroom 3.0 incorporating mobile technology with Web 2.0 technology. The impact on the implementation of Classroom 3.0 is also discussed and how it may affect the teaching and learning process of the millennial students.

Keywords: Social Media, Social Networking, Virtual Classroom, Virtual Learning Environment.

1 Introduction

Web 2.0 has created a new phenomenon on how people communicate and interact with each other. The term Web 2.0 was introduced in 2004 to describe the changes in the use of tools and applications available on the Internet.[1] In the initial implementation of the Internet, content was generally created and published by organizations and consumed by web users.[2] The exuberance displayed by the general public was due to the fact that anyone with a computer and web browser now had access to an unprecedented amount of information. Unlike its paper counterpart, the availability of this online data was immediate, timely, global, and on-demand.

The Web 2.0 technologies can be defined as tools available on the Internet to provide users with the capabilities of social media and networking.[3] It can also be defined as "how people use the Internet to create and form new waves of communicate mode. They build their own circle of friends in *Facebook,* contribute their own expertise to *Wikipedia* articles, develop their professional connections via *LinkedIn,* and transmit their daily experiences on *Twitter* as it happens."[4] Web 2.0 allows users to create their own interactive content and make them available to other users. It brings out creativity and innovation of many people to contribute to the building of a mass knowledge network. Many will result in commercialization of their contents or technology applied.

Web 2.0 has already found its way to educators and online learning. However, before Web 2.0, there was course management system (CMS) such as WebCT, Blackboard, etc. CMS has been used as supplementary materials for in-class courses as well as online courses. Institutions started using CMS to offer online courses in additional to traditional classrooms back in the late 90s. But CMS is considered a one-dimensional interaction as instructors would post lecture notes on those systems

R. Kwan et al. (Eds.): ICHL 2011, LNCS 6837, pp. 298–305, 2011.

via a link or click. There is limited interaction between the instructors and students except through the email system and the discussion board or chat room available on the CMS. Some instructors might use video conferencing tools such as Adobe Connect to enhance the communication and learning process in their courses.

With the availability of Web 2.0, the next generation of classroom, Classroom 3.0, a term coined by the author, should have no physical boundaries and will be accessible anytime and anywhere. Students will be able to attend classes and access course materials via a mobile device. The role of the instructors will become a mentor and coordinator of the contents. Students will be expected to contribute actively in creating and building the contents. This type of approach is achievable via the Web 2.0 technologies and we will discuss more in the next section of this paper.

2 Web 2.0 and Learning

Web 2.0 includes Internet tools or applications for social media and social networking. Some of these tools can be interconnected with both social media and social networking simultaneously. The differences on the use of terms reflect the evolution of this new type of communication media on the Internet. Social media is a medium or tool that allows people to network virtually while using various multimedia such as YouTube. This does not require face-to-face contact, except in the case of using a video camera. Social media may be used to include applications such as blogs. It is mostly a one-way direction of authoring, however. Only the original author can contribute to the contents. Others may add their comments to the media contents only if the author allows it.

On the other hand, social networking, such as Wikis, Facebook, etc., allows multiple connections among users who contribute to the contents. Some of these sites are invitation-only while some are open to the public. But it is the concept of a community to create and build together a set of contents or knowledge that makes this an effective instructional tool if used appropriately and effectively. Some even believe that the Web 2.0 tools are great tools to engage and motivate students to practice their writing skills.[5]

2.1 Web 2.0 as Instructional Tools

In recent years, educators have used many Internet tools to enhance their teaching and go beyond the physical classroom where learners can access a vast base of information available on the Internet at their fingertips. Using Web 2.0, learners can be encouraged to use their creativity and collaboration skills in working with their peers. As a study observed, educators had used Web 2.0 tools in their teaching, an example of using the Wiki would include quick and informative website publishing, collaborative website posting, student assignments with peer review capabilities, problem solving, focused discussions, interdisciplinary projects, community building amongst students, collaboration practice and more.[6] Another study found that weblogs could be used to improve students' critical thinking, literacy skills and their ability to use the Internet for research purposes; they allowed for instant publishing, sharing and collaboration with other students.[7]

A recent study on using Facebook in a university level course found that "many students already had a Facebook account and were familiar with the system. As they were already checking on the site every day, it was a convenient way for them to keep themselves up-to-date with the postings on the course site on Facebook. One student even commented that they visited the Facebook group more frequently than going to the university course site. They could post and share their feedback on Facebook as well as communicating with the instructor and fellow students. Access to the Facebook group was limited to students and invited "friends" only."[8]

Twitter has also been used in education for learners to express their opinions or exchange ideas. Some instructors asked students to follow people in their field of studies or related subject areas. Some even had learners tweet for a day pretending to be a character in a book that they were studying.[9] Although each tweet is limited to 140 characters, it can be used creatively to enhance the learning and to encourage learners to communicate more effectively. Nevertheless, Twitter has to be used cautiously. As one University of Texas-Dallas' instructor (@academicdave) who tweeted about the use of Twitter in education, "If you log into Facebook and see somebody else you know on there, you start connecting. Google is really simple. Wikis are not hard to figure out. But Twitter has so many different purposes, you have to have a clear idea when you go in about what you want to get out of it."[10]

2.2 Studies in Web 2.0

A number of research studies support the fact that web-based learning not only helps learners create a new body of knowledge but also improves their teamwork in collaborating with others online while get the learners to feel more enthusiastic about learning.[11] Through using Wiki and blogging, it was also found that learners felt freer to express and share their own views as well as to contemplate how their views could be interpreted by others. This helps them understand more the limitation of the technology and grasp a much better appreciation of effective communication as part of lifelong learning and prepares them for the real world in their careers.

3 Classroom 3.0

Before defining Classroom 3.0, one must understand the evolution of classrooms. A traditional classroom is a physical room with tables and chairs in a confined area with blackboard or marker broad, perhaps with an overhead or opaque projector. The second generation of classroom, Classroom 2.0, is a traditional classroom with technologies incorporated in it. It may have a computer connected to the Internet and instructors can teach using PowerPoint or other presentation software. Smart classroom is an example of Classroom 2.0 where students can have access to the course site or Internet using their own laptops/PCs with Internet connection available in their seat.

The next generation of classroom will have neither physical walls nor furniture. Classroom 3.0 will be powered by a mobile device. Some would call this "m-learning" (mobile learning) but m-learning is only a means. Not only should Classroom 3.0 be defined as borderless classroom but also the course contents or in-classroom lectures can be access virtually and completely digital.

3.1 Mobile Technology

Mobile technology has been used in teaching and education for a few years. It is considered a rapidly growing area of educational research in the field.[12] In recent years, mobile devices have already become an indispensable item in our daily life. In fact, this generation is known as "net generation" and is being called the "digital natives." They have grown up in an era of mobile and on-demand technology. They are comfortable in using it. Educators need to rethink on how to adapt this type of technology in teaching and to create new experience and capabilities in the classroom for this generation of millennial students. The concept of Classroom 3.0 revolves around the concept of mobile technology as part of m-learning. Mobile handheld technology makes this possible.

Before Apple introduced iPad in 2010, there was tablet PC. It was an innovation at the time when the user can use a stylus pen to write on a PC running Windows program. It had fairly accurate built-in handwriting recognition program. Many schools had adapted this new tablet PC in their classrooms. Besides iPad, several other companies also introduced their own version of "iPad," such as Viewsonic's Viewpad. These devices have now become more affordable. With the introduction of iPad, a mobile device has changed from laptop to a handheld device while providing the users same, if not less, amount of computing power. An electronic pad does not require a stylus pen. Its touch screen technology has made it convenience and easy access along with Wi-Fi Internet connection capability. This has made the "pad" devices quite popular among the digital natives. In many cases, a "iPad" type device has a much longer battery life than a laptop. Using this type of handheld mobile devices, the entire course contents are now possible to make in the form of e-book.

The e-book has evolved since the introduction of handheld book devices, such as the Amazon Kindle, Barnes and Noble Nook, Sony Reader, in early 2000. Although the market has not grown as fast as what the book sellers had hoped for, the sales have been steadily increased. The introduction of iPad and the Google Android based devices has helped increase the popularity of e-books. The cost of an e-book is cheaper than a paper copy, not to mention the hard cover price. It is also easier to take note and the convenience in carrying multiple book titles in one device is no comparison to books in paper format.

3.2 e-Book

The e-book market has also entered the textbook market by major textbook publishers such as McGraw-Hill and Pearson. According to the National Association of College Store (NACS), digital books currently account for less than 3 percent of textbook sales while Simba Information Research predicts that more than 11 percent of textbook sales will be on e-textbooks by 2013.[13] It was also predicted that it could be 100 percent to 200 percent increase in digital textbooks sale over the next few years.[14] Google is now working on its own cloud-based e-book service and this will not only have a great impact on book sellers but also on the textbook industry.

In addition, many universities have made textbooks as e-Book available on their library website for students to access the materials at anytime and anywhere. However, there is lack of studies on the effectiveness of using e-book as e-textbook in comparison with paper-based textbook in academic achievement. Questions such as can e-textbook enhance the learning environment and help student receive better grades should be explored. Only further studies can confirm if this is a fact or myth.

The e-book revolution may take some time to take off unless the reader has experienced significant value over the print version. With advanced media technology and Internet connection, an e-book should not be constrained to only the concept of a traditional "book." E-book can now simulate page turning even adding page-turning sound to give the readers a real experience like holding and reading a traditional paper book. But an e-book should be beyond that. The major difference between a digital version and the print version is the flexibility of content update and the availability of incorporating certain types of interaction with the reads. Any update of the contents can be done easily via new edition download instead of waiting for a new edition to be printed and bounded and to be made available in the bookstore. Any typographical or content errors can be corrected effortlessly.

The most valuable component is that interaction can be added in the digital version. Interaction, such as links to websites or additional resources as well as social media or network, can be integrated into the e-book contents to provide the reader or learner with a complete interactive learning environment. For example, links can be made available in the e-book to allow access a lecture or demonstration video in YouTube; or connect the link to the course site built within Facebook to give the students opportunities to participate in the discussions and post their comments on the "wall"; or simply contribute their knowledge to build the course contents on Wiki. Imagine an e-book on learning classical music by Beethoven with text-based contents about the composer along with links to sample of his symphonies, that the students can listen to on a YouTube Channel, or may be added commentaries from the instructors or reflections of conductors via Tweets. This type of learning environment is far beyond a traditional classroom or even a smart classroom environment. Best of all, these can be achieved through a mobile device.

Many of these handheld devices have built-in camera. This makes video conferencing at ease and increases the interactivity between instructors and learners. Regular scheduled office hours can be done via video conferencing. Paper-based textbook and notebook will be replaced by the new type of pads or tablets. The cost of these handheld devices has become more affordable and high speed Internet connection is also available in more places, even at the corner coffee shops. Most importantly, many students are already familiar with the technology and, in fact, may even use it in their daily lives.

3.3 Challenges

On the contrary, the gap in using an interactive e-book is the learning curve of the instructors to adopt this new technology and the expectation of students. It will take plenty of time to develop an effective e-book to incorporate different types of Web 2.0 technologies. It is not just the content of the e-book but also development of resources on social media or social network sites. The process can be costly and time consuming. The instructors must have a good understanding of the technology and apply it appropriately when developing e-books. To read a paper-based book is linear but e-book content is dynamic. You can go to any points in an e-book or any external resources by a simple click. The concept seems simple, but it is more difficult to choose and implement the right types of technology for the right contents. Training is key to implementing m-learning project.[15]

Another challenge in using e-book extensively is its accessibility for the blind. Some e-book devices, such as Kindle, have text-to-speech capabilities within the text it displays, but those capabilities do not extend to the menu interface. The National Federation of the Bind (NFB) and the American Council of the Blind (ACB) reached a settlement agreement in 2010 with Arizona State University and other universities that participated in the Kindle DX pilot program, prohibiting the named universities from further using the Kindle or any other e-book devices as their campus standard e-book adoption until the technology is made assessable to sight-impaired students.[16] Before adopting the e-book, one has to consider this major factor. But as text-to-speech technologies advance, this problem should be easier to overcome and e-books will become more widely adapted by universities for sight-impaired students.

Instructors also have to know how to develop support strategies when designing a mobile course using e-book technology. For example, if the learner has a technical question, there should be support procedures in place.

To avoid extensive wandering, students needed to develop self-discipline and good skills to manage their time and behavior. Instructors have to know how to control the class in postings and to carefully plan for the contents. Instructors should always develop and enforce guidelines and etiquettes in using the tools.

Before students enrolled in this type of course, they should be warned of the potential distraction and advised on self-discipline and time management to complete the required course work. Previous work has identified that personality traits and maturity in learning are likely to be equally important with computer literacy.[17] A study was conducted to examine students' experience on the opportunities and challenges of learning with social software.[18] Not surprisingly, the results suggested that success in online learning depended on the discipline and commitment of a student. An online learner is expected to take more responsibility for learning but the process can be personalized.[19]

The other restriction is the Internet connection in some countries that restrict Internet traffic. Some of the Web 2.0 tools might not be available. Even if the tools were available, the learners could have difficulties in accessing certain types of materials using those tools due to the country's government policies.

The principle of Web 2.0 is that it is "always on" and there is no closing time. The learners can complete the course at their own pace and on their own scheduled time. Learners can access to the course materials anytime and anywhere as long as they have access to the device. They can have interaction with others throughout the day while the instructors are not available.

The next generation of e-book will have the capability and function to contain more dynamic contents due to HTML5 and Flash. This may introduce a fresh new look of e-book and the concept of "book" will then change forever.

4 Conclusion

Mobile learning has been receiving more attention as the technology becomes more available and affordable as well as being popular in this generation of learners. Many educational institutions and corporations have already started using them. This article introduced the concept of Classroom 3.0. Planning to implement and deploy such technology is extremely important. Technical support must be in place for the instructors and learners. The fundamental question for further study will be: Is e-book Classroom 3.0?

It is important to collect data to track learning activities and learners' expectation.[20] Further research needs to be conducted to understand the cost effectiveness, level of quality assurance and maintaining IT infrastructure in the deployment of Classroom 3.0. Large scale study is also needed to accomplish to verify the feasibility of m-learning in active curriculum development.

Millennial students are able to develop deep relationships with others over the network, whereas many older teachers belong to a generation where deep relationships are only developed with personal meetings. Interactions using computer mediated technologies have the potential to be "as rich as face-to-face communication but this is dependent upon the extent to which the users are willing to suspend disbelief and immerse themselves in the environment."[21] While members of the millennial generation are generally able to fully commit themselves emotionally when communicating electronically, more traditional members of older generations are often unable to immerse themselves to the same degree. The trend toward the consumer use of social media is inevitable as the technology become more readily available and costs have decreased. Thus, as usage increases in the general public, it is unavoidable that it will be used for educational purposes. Even as teachers hand out homework assignments, students will likely be collaborating with classmates over Facebook or Twitter in an unstructured, self-initiated manner. Educators must decide whether or not they want to acknowledge that learning is happening on social media sites. The question then becomes, do they want to participate, embrace, and guide these learning activities, or do they want to ignore these activities as not part of the student learning process.[22]

New technologies will always bring new users and create new opportunities for learning. If they are being used in the right way, technologies can engage learners, foster profound and meaningful learning, and result in an enriched learning environment.

References

1. Graham, P.: Web 2.0, `http://www.paulgraham.com/` web20.html; O'Reilly, Tim: O'Reilly Network (2005), `http://www.paulgraham.com//pub/a/oreilly/tim/news/2005/09/30/what-is-web-20.html`
2. Tapscott, D., Williams, A. D.: Wikinomics: How Mass Collaboration Changes Everything, New York (2006) The exact year for the beginning of the Internet is debatable. In 1968, ARPANET was established, and this gave rise to the Internet. For an extensive examination of the history of Internet, see Fong, Wilfred W.: Information Resources on the Information Highway, Kendall-Hunt, Iowa (1998)
3. Cheung, C.M.K., Lee, M.K.O.: A Theoretical Model of Intentional Social Action in Online Social Networks. Decision Support Systems 49, 24–30 (2010)
4. Fong, W., Lee, G.: Social Media, Social Networking, and Communication. In: Newton, D., Fong, W.W., Van Leuven, N. (eds.) Communications For Everyday Life, pp. 203–222. Ginger Press, Toronto (2011)

5. Light, D.: Do Web 2.0 Right. Learning & Leading with Technology (February 10-14, 2011)
6. Synteta, V.: What is a wiki? http://tecfa.unige.ch/guides/tie/html/wikis/wikis-2.html
7. Oravec, J.A.: Bookmarking the world: weblog applications in education. Journal of Adolescent & Adult Literacy 45, 616–621 (2002)
8. Fong, W. W., Lee, G., Chan, A. B.: Learning Intercultural Communication in an Immersive Environment with Web 2.0 Tools. In: Proceedings of Canadian International Conference on Education, Toronto (2010)
9. Schaffhauser, D.: The Super-Secret, Never-Before-Revealed Guide to Web 2.0 in the Classroom. Campus Technology 24, 33–35 (2010)
10. http://campustechnology.com/articles/2010/10/01/15-twitter-tips.aspx (2010)
11. Ashcraft, D.: Collaborative online learning: a constructivist example. Journal of Online Learning and Teacher 4, 109–117 (2008); Jia, Y.: Building a Web-based collaborative learning environment. In: Proceedings of international conference, Vol. 7 pp. F2D/7–F2D/9, Santo Domingo, Dominican Republic (2005); Perry, B.: Using photographic images as an interactive online teaching strategy. Internet and Higher Education 9, 229-240 (2006)
12. Frohberg, D.: Communities- the MOBIlearn perspective. In: Workshop on ubiquitous and mobile computing for educational communities: enriching and enlarging community spaces. In: International Conference on communities and technologies, Amsterdam (September 19, 2003), http://www.idi.ntnu.no/~divitini/umocec2003/Final/frohberg.pdf Vavoula, G., Pachler, N. Kukulska-Hulme, A.: Researching mobile learning: frameworks, tools and research designs. Peter Lang, Oxford, UK. (2009)
13. Waters, J.: Can Tech Transcend the Textbook? Campus Technology (2011), http://campustechnology.com/articles/2011/03/01/can-tech-transcend-the-textbook.aspx?sc_lang=en
14. McCrea, B.: When Textbooks and Social Media Collide. Campus Technology (2011), http://campustechnology.com/articles/2011/03/09/when-textbooks-and-social-media-collide.aspx
15. Ramanau, R., Sharpe, R., Benfield, G.: Exploring Patterns of Student Learning Technology in their Relationship to Self-regulation and Perceptions of Learning Community. In: Sixth International Conference of Networked Learning (2008), http://www.networkedlearningconference.org.uk/abstracts/PDFs/Ramanau_334-341.pdf
16. Demski, J.: The Device Versus The Book. Campus Technology 23, 27–33 (2010)
17. Coulby, C., et al.: The Use of Mobile Technology for Work-based Assessment: The Student Experience. British Journal of Educational Technology 42, 251–265 (2011)
18. Jones, N., Blackey, H., Fitzgibbon, K., Chew, E.: Get Out of MySpace. Computers & Education 54, 776–782 (2010)
19. Sanders, J.: Social Software and Digital Competences. InnovA/T 3, 306–309 (2010)
20. Brink, J.: M-Learning: The Future of Training Technology, T+D. 27-29 (2011)
21. Gaimster, J.: Reflections on Interactions in Virtual Worlds and Their Implication for Learning Art and Design. Art, Design & Communication in Higher Education 6, 187–199 (2008)
22. Fong, W., Lee, G.: Social Media, Social Networking, and Communication. In: Newton, D., Fong, W.W., Van Leuven, N. (eds.) Communications For Everyday Life, pp. 203–222. Ginger Press, Toronto (2011)

Digital Microscope Recording System to Enhance Students' Understanding of Biological Observation

Ming-Hsiang Su, Yuan-Hsun Liao, Cheng-Yu Tsai,
Bo-Yen Wang, and Pao-Ta Yu

Dept. of Computer Science and Information Engineering,
National Chung Cheng University, Chiayi, Taiwan
{sumh,lyh96p,tcy97p,wangpy,csipty}@cs.ccu.edu.tw

Abstract. Electronic microscopy is a widely used instrument to observe micro movement or system of an object. Keeping the snapshot and phenomenon of the observing object is an important theme during the observation process. However, much literature described that people have to record the observed phenomenon under a microscope into text by hands, meaning that they need to spend more time and cost on handling the text records after the observation. A system to improve such a situation is needed, particularly in the teaching process. Therefore, we propose a Digital Microscope Recording System (DMRS) to help to digitalize the observation. DMRS can receive the real-time images captured by a USB digital microscope and the then students can select the pictures they want, draw symbols on them and add textual descriptions for these symbols. Finally, students can convert these records into a web page file or a document file so that they can discuss the observed biological phenomenon with the classmate easily or poste the results via internet.

Keywords: biological, observation, Digital Microscope Recording System, USB digital microscope.

1 Introduction

In the era of advanced technology, one would be hardly to ignore the use of electronic microscopes in the observation of biological [1]. Typically, biological record data was required to integrate the text description as the multimedia reports for behaviors observation. However, it is not easy for behavioral researchers to use technology to create multimedia reports, because the required technology is supported by several computerized tools for coding and annotating videotapes [2]-[4].

In the traditional observation methods, people often observed directly and wrote scripts to record the biological behavior [5]. In this view of point, the results of the observations were often dependent on the observer's memory and the observers' subjective consciousness may lead to be incorrect. Observer may ignore the important details of the observation by the limited memory and distraction. In some cases, observers had the difficulty to understand the meaning and importance of the biological behavior, so that he could not use the appropriate words to record the occurrence of the behavior.

R. Kwan et al. (Eds.): ICHL 2011, LNCS 6837, pp. 306–315, 2011.

This study proposes a DMRS to help students observe and record biological behavior and to improve the limits of memory and distraction. Students use USB digital microscope to capture biological activities under the microscope and send the real-time images to DMRS. Through the DMRS, students can exactly choice the picture from those captured images that they want to observe and draw some symbols on it. Then students can add text descriptions for these symbols. Finally, students can easily convert these records into a web page file or a document file so that they can discuss the observed behavior with their biological to improve the interaction between students and scholars.

The remainder of this paper was organized as follows. First, we introduce the related background techniques and theories. Then, we describe the construction of observation environment and the system implementation. Finally, concluding remarks were given.

2 Literature Review

2.1 Microteaching

Effective teaching has long been acknowledged as desirable goals of teacher education programs [6]. But the crucial question is: How should we go about it? In 2003, Pringle said "the use of microteaching within teacher education is seen as an on-campus way of introducing pre-service teacher to the complexities of teaching and as a bridge that connects theory to practice." In other words, teachers can be trained by microteaching to achieve effective teaching.

Microteaching is one of the most important developments in the field of teaching practice [7]. It originated in the early 1960s at Stanford University by Dr. Dwight Allen and Ryan, and its purpose is to provide teachers with the opportunity for the safe practice of an enlarged cluster of teaching skills while learning how to develop simple, single-concept lessons in any teaching subject [8].

There are some benefits of microteaching: It exposes pre-service teacher to realities of teaching; It introduces pre-service teachers to their roles as teachers [9]; It helps them to see the importance of planning, decision making, and implementation of instruction [10]; It enables them to develop and improve teaching skill (communication, public presentation, etc.); It helps them build their confidence for teaching.

2.2 Science Writing

Science writing is a form of expression that students can represent their science concepts in research by their words [11] [12]. Writing can promote the level of thinking and help students to realize their own thoughts, feelings, and experience [13] [14]. Nowadays, writing is not only used in application of language and literature, but also employed in instructions of nature science and daily technology [14].

Science writing is a tool used for communication, thoughts organization, and improvement of structuring concepts [15]. Students learn actively during the process of writing. They restructure the information and knowledge that they gained, collected, and integrates them. Science writing also helps students correlate with concepts.

Flower and Hayes [16] advanced a model to describe the writing process. In their study, Flower and Hayes asked subjects to think aloud when they were writing, and then researcher recorded the content and analyzed the subjects' mental progress. The model is illustrated in Fig. 1.

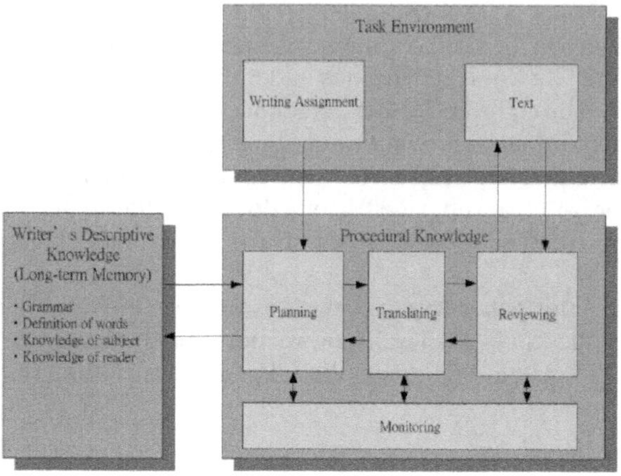

Fig. 1. Hayes-Flower writing process model

This model divides into two parts: one is the external task environment and the other is the writer's internal knowledge. In addition, the writer's internal knowledge also separates into two parts: descriptive knowledge and procedural knowledge. In brief, learning by writing is a process of planning what to write, translating concepts into contents, and review what writer done. In Flower and Hayes' opinion, these three activities of writing process are alternative rather than straightforward.

2.3 Knowledge Restructuring

The theory of knowledge restructuring is originally described as one of the three models of knowledge acquisition models advanced by Rumelhart and Norman [17]. These three models are accretion, tuning, and restructuring. Accretion refers to concept change that occurs through existent schemata to accumulate new knowledge gradually. Tuning depicts that a learner would modify the schema to accept new information if the existent schemata do not match new knowledge. Restructuring describes the changes in knowledge that involve establishing new knowledge structure and reorganizing existent schemata.

The role of learners in the process of restructuring is that the learner is a creator of knowledge rather than a consumer of knowledge, a disseminator of concept, or a knowledge keeper. Stella and William [18] stated that knowledge restructuring is "the most radical form of knowledge acquisition within prior-knowledge framework". Stephan, Mike, and Thomas [19] also announced that knowledge restructuring is defined as "a shift to a new set of rules, strategies, or declarative knowledge to perform a task without overt changes to the stimuli or learning environment". This shows that a learner can create new knowledge structures when gaining new information. A learner can also recombines what he or she has known rather than tunes existent schemata.

There are two kinds of restructuring advanced by Stella and William [18]: the first being global restructuring and the second being kinds of domain-specific restructuring. These two models are similar to "theory theories" and "knowledge-in-pieces theories" advanced by diSessa [20]. The global restructuring refers a learner arranging and restructuring all knowledge in his/her mind as rearranging the knowledge into theory-like structures. However, the kinds of domain-specific restructuring are regarded as the learner separating knowledge into pieces of specific domain. Learners restructure their knowledge in specific domain so that they can enhance the efficiency of creating new knowledge structures.

3 The Construction of Observation Environment

DMRS allows students to observe their biological behavior and mark annotations in their concern to the incident. In this section, we will introduce the system architecture. The architecture of the DMRS is shown in Fig. 2.

Fig. 2. Architecture of the Child-Behavior Observation System

3.1 Video Recording Module

A detailed description of the diagram is as follows:

(1) The students first connect USB digital microscope to PC.
(2) After connecting USB digital microscope, the students can launch DMRS, and the system will detect the connection of USB digital microscope to PC.
(3) After that, students can (1) change default setting of the recording system (2) encode the signal to a WMV file.
   A. When (1) is selected, the system will show a dialog to indicate how to change System settings, including frame rate, video bit rate, etc.
   B. When (2) is selected, the system will show a preview image which will be recorded later. And students can click start to encode and save it as a WMV file.
(4) When the steps end, the students can enter the observation record module.

3.2 Observation Record Module

The observation record module was divided into two parts: authoring mode and presentation mode. The authoring mode is described as the mode when students are designing content. When the system is in the authoring mode, five system components are available to the designers. They are the customized video tool, the indexing notation editor, the scene flow controller, the annotated video adding tool, the web-based presentation, and the e-Learning object generator. The authoring mode is shown in Fig. 3, and the flow diagram of authoring mode is shown in Fig. 4.

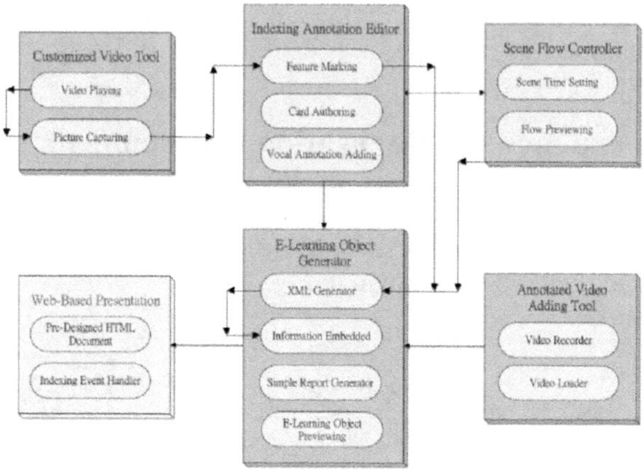

Fig. 3. Component diagram of authoring mode

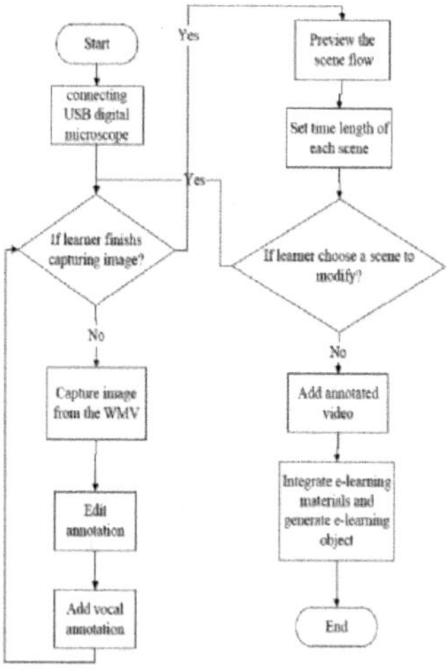

Fig. 4. Flow diagram of authoring mode

The customized video tool allows the students to display the video which is transmitted by the video record module and captures pictures from played video. The indexing annotation editing module allows the students to add the information of captured pictures. The scene flow controller enables the students to set the video pause time for each scene so that the content can display embedded information. The annotated video adding is a tool for adding video of introduction or conclusion before or after the main video. The e-Learning object generator module provides four main functions to transfer the authored content into a web-based learning object after the user finish editing. These four functions are XML generator, information embedded, simple report generator and e-Learning object previewing. The web-based presentation can be divided into two parts: the pre-designed HTML document and the indexing events handler. A pre-designed HTML document is used to unfold all the e-Learning materials, such as video, audio, images and cards as webpages. Therefore, students does not worry how to present their products using web on Internet. The indexing event handler provides a set of JavaScript functions that execute the commands in the embedded-information when it receives trigger messages issued from the WMV file. These functions control the video playing procedure, show annotations, and display the feature image. The viewer can also discretionarily choose certain feature parts of the video to study in details.

When the system is in presentation mode, it presents the content from pre-designed HTML documents that include both video and cards of annotations. the flow diagram of presentation mode is shown in Fig. 5.

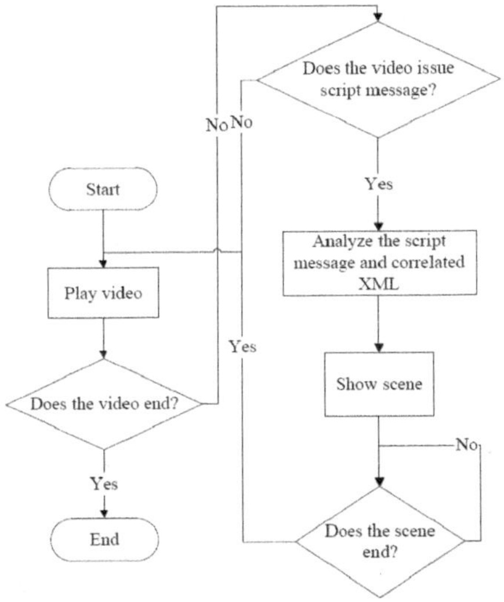

Fig. 5. Flow diagram of presentation mode

4 System Implementation

In the beginning, the DMRS system will pop a window to detect electromechanical devices. It will provide a list of hardware name that students can use. After setting all the requirements, the button of start is allowed to click. The procedure of setting up the DMRS system is shown in Fig. 6.

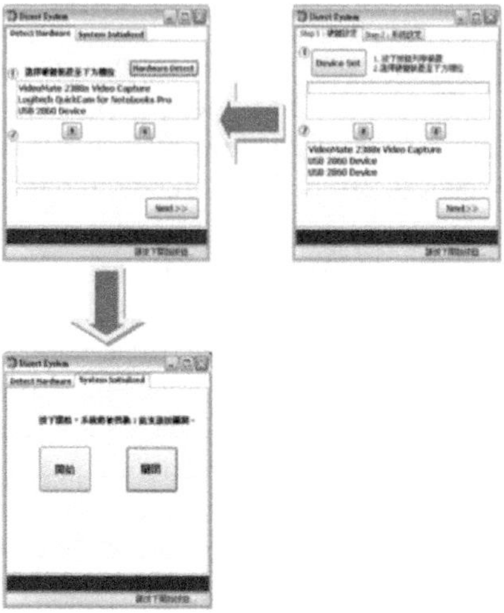

Fig. 6. Procedure of setting up the DMRS

After students capture stream from USB digital microscope, user can capture images he think are interested in the captures stream. Then the DMRS system changes the state into editing annotation. When students find a feature on the image, he/she can mark circle or rectangle graph on the featured part of the image. Finally the students can edit the annotation and adds audio to emphasize this annotation.

The State of editing annotation is shown in Fig. 7. When students find a feature on the image, he/she can use the button marked Label 1 in Fig. 7 to circle the featured part. The students can edit the annotation and adds audio to emphasize this annotation at Label 2 in Fig. 7.

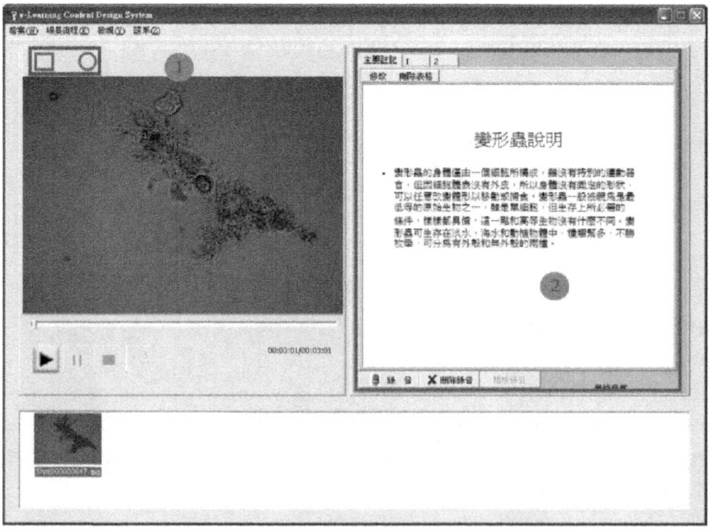

Fig. 7. The State of editing annotation

When the images were captured and authoring correlative annotations were completed, students enter the step of controlling scene flow is shown in Fig. 8.

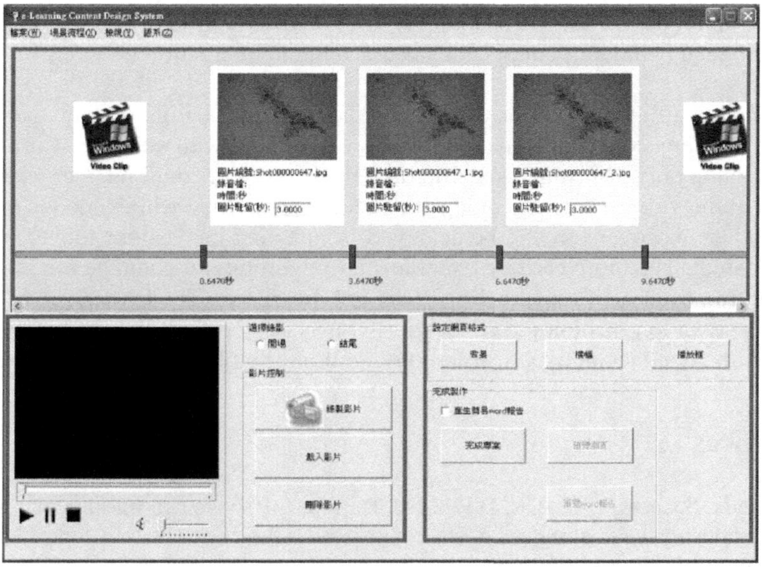

Fig. 8. The step of controlling scene flow

In this step, students can add the title sequence of the video or the trailers of the video. Students also can design web pages related to the output screen. Finally students can output document files and web pages as shown in Fig. 9.

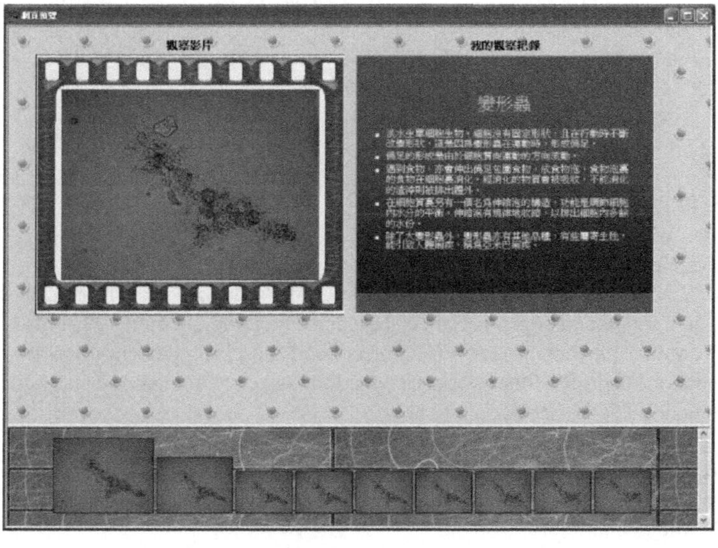

Fig. 9. User interface of the webpage

5 Conclusions and Future Works

The purpose of this study is to provide a simple way for students to participate in observing and documenting. Students can use the results of observation to understand their biological behavior patterns, thus increasing the interaction between students and scholars.

There are still many opportunities for the system to improve. In the system's function, the embedded information video can interact with students. Currently, the information is only issued at a specific time. If the system could interact with specific subjects in the video, students could get annotations anytime while video is playing.

The other improvement can be achieved in indexing card editor tool. This system provides students editing card by Excel form. In the future, it could be modified to add different frameworks of card, such as Word or PowerPoint. The DMRS is a helpful tool for the observation of biological behavior. Our next step will keep improving on our interface and conduct an experimental observation of biological behavior in research.

References

1. Veilleux, Spencer, J.A., Biss, D.P., Cote, D., Lin, C.P.: vivo cell tracking with video rate multimodality laser scanning microscopy. IEEE Journal of selected topics in quantum electronics 14(1), 10–18 (2008)
2. Sanderson, P.M., Scott, J.J.P., Johnston, T., Mainzer, J., Watanabe, L.M., James, J.M.: MacSHAPA and the enterprise of exploratory sequential data analysis (ESDA). International Journal of Human–Computer Studies 41, 633–668 (1994)
3. Tapp, J.T., Walden, T.A.: Procoder: A professional tape control, coding and analysis system for behavioral research using videotape. Behavior Research Methods, Instruments, & Computers 25, 53–56 (1993)
4. Vlugt, M.J., van der Kruk, M.R., van Erp, A.M.M., Geuze, R.H.: CAMERA: A system for fast and reliable acquisition of multiple ethological records. Behavior Research Methods, Instruments, & Computers 24, 147–149 (1992)
5. Slee, P.T.: Child observation skills. Croom Helm, New York (1987)
6. Wahba, E.H.: Microteaching. A journal for the teacher of English outside the United States 37(4) (1999)
7. McGarvey, B., Swallow, D.: Microteaching in teacher education and training. Croom Helm, Dover (1986)
8. Brent, R., Wheatley, E., Thomson, W.S.: Videotaped microteaching: Bridging the gap from the university to the classroom. The Teacher Educator 31(3) (1996)
9. Amobi, F.A.: Preservice teachers' reflectivity on the sequence and consequences of teaching actions in a microteaching experience. Teacher Education Quarterly 32, 115–130 (2005)
10. Gess-Newsome, J., Lederman, N.G.: Preservice biological teachers' knowledge structures as a function of professional teacher education: A year-long assessment. Science Teacher Education 77, 25–43 (1993)
11. Britton, J.: Language and learning. Penguin Books, New York (1970)
12. Britton, J., et al.: The development of writing abilities. Macmillan, London (1975)
13. Bulter, S.: The writing connection, whole-language practice and theory. Prentice-Hall Canada, Inc., Ontario (1990)
14. Shelly, C.: The write approach. Science Scope 22(1), 36–39 (1998)

15. Rivard, L.P., Straw, S.B.: The effect of talk and writing on learning science: An exploratory study. Science Education 84, 566–593 (2000)
16. Flower, L., Hayes, J.R.: A cognitive process of writing. College Composition and Communication 32, 365–379 (1981)
17. Rumelhart, D.E., Norman, D.A.: Accretion, tuning, and restructuring: Three modes of learning. In: Cotton, J.W., Klatzky, R. (eds.) Semantic factors in cognition, pp. 37–60 (1981)
18. Stella, V., William, F.B.: Theories of knowledge restructuring in development. Review of Education Research 57(1), 51–67 (1987)
19. Stephan, L., Mike, K., Thomas, L.G.: Competing strategies in categorization: Expediency and resistance to knowledge restructuring. Journal of Experimental Psychology: Learning, Memory, and Cognition 26(6), 1666–1684 (2000)
20. diSessa, A.A.: Knowledge in pieces. In: Forman, G., Pufall, P.B. (eds.) Constructivism in the computer age, pp. 49–70 (1988)

An Exploration of Using Facebook to Build a Virtual Community of Practice

Kenneth Wong, Reggie Kwan, and Kat Leung

Caritas Institute of Higher Education
{kfwong,rkwan,kleung}@cihe.edu.hk

Abstract. Students at all levels are heavily immersed in social network sites such as Facebook and YouTube. Social networking is indeed not only playing an increasingly important role in students' social life, but also for teachers. Educators are now turning to use Web 2.0 tools to promote students' ability to assist in creating, collaborating and sharing content. Facebook is a free and most popular social network site. Its primary purpose is to provide an online communication platform for users to make new friends and interact with them. A Community of Practice (COP) is a group of people who share their knowledge, ideas and practices in a common domain or topic [1]. A virtual COP means the communication between members are using electronic channels, such as email, discuss forums, blogs and wikis, etc. Since virtual COPs encourage collaborative and sharing recourses in knowledge domain on the Web, it may be an ideal model for the online learning community. This research aims to explore the use of Facebook features to foster virtual COPs. We further intend to investigate how Facebook can enhance collaborative learning and knowledge building in this virtual COP. Two classes of sub-degree students have been chosen to participate in this study. The data will be collected quantitatively and qualitatively in nature, consisting of students' posting messages and comments on the Facebook, surveys on the students' reflective experiences using Facebook as communication and collaboration tools, and group interview with each instructor. This research will shed some lights on effective ways to promote virtual Community of Practice.

Keywords: Web 2.0, Social Networking, Facebook, Community of Practice, Learning Community, Collaborative Learning.

1 Introduction

The concept of Web 2.0 is a new generation web applications that facilitate information sharing, interaction and collaboration among its users. Social networking is a sample of Web 2.0 technology. It is designed for the social interaction purpose. During our interaction with our sub-degree students, we notice that they are heavily immersed in social network sites, such as Facebook and YouTube. They spend a lot of time on Facebook daily. Interestingly, the social networking is not only playing an increasingly important role in students' social life, but also for teachers. Educators are now turning to use Web 2.0 tools to promote students' ability to assist in creating,

R. Kwan et al. (Eds.): ICHL 2011, LNCS 6837, pp. 316–324, 2011.

collaborating and sharing content. Although Facebook's primary purpose is to provide an online communication platform for users to make new friends and interact with them, it also can foster virtual communities for students to work together to enhance collaborative learning. The fact that it is free and the most popular social network site played a big part in our tool selection.

The theory of Community of practice has gained significant ground in higher education institutes [2] in recent years. COP puts an emphasis on communication, sharing of ideas, passions, common problems and issues, and learning together as a team. The main features of Faecbook are ideal for online communication and sharing resources, it is an ideal platform to implement the COP in virtual learning environments. This research aims to explore the use of Facebook to build a virtual Community of Practice. We intend to use the communication environment with which students are familiar to establish a virtual COP and promote collaborative learning and knowledge building.

2 Communities of Practice

Lave & Wenger [1] introduce a new theory of learning called "situated learning" as well as the concept of COP. They used the term Communities of Practice to describe learning through practice and participation. A COP is a group of people who share a common interest and a desire to learn from and contribute to the community with their variety of experiences. In fact, communities of practice are everywhere and that we are generally involved in a number of them whether that is at work, school, home, or in our civic and leisure interests [3][4]. This phenomenon is nothing new but the term COP is relatively new.

Wenger [3] has further elaborated the idea of the COP:

> *Communities of practice are formed by people who engage in a process of collective learning in a shared domain of human endeavor: a tribe learning to survive, a band of artists seeking new forms of expression, a group of engineers working on similar problems, a clique of pupils defining their identity in the school, a network of surgeons exploring novel techniques, a gathering of first-time managers helping each other cope. In a nutshell: Communities of practice are groups of people who share a concern or a passion for something they do and learn how to do it better as they interact regularly.*

To understand how communities of practice represent the foundation of a knowledge strategy, there are fundamental characteristics of COPs: (i) Domain; (ii) Community; and (iii) Practice. Firstly, a domain of knowledge creates a common ground, inspires members to participate, guides their learning and gives meaning to their actions. Secondly, a community is a necessary component that members of a specific domain interact and engage in shared activities, help each other, and share information with each other. Thirdly, members are all practitioners in the community. They develop a shared repertoire of resources which can include stories, helpful tools, experiences, stories, ways of handling typical problems, etc. [5]. A virtual COP means the communication between members is through electronic channels, such as email, discuss forums, blogs and wikis, etc. All interactions in the community are web-based.

3 Application of Virtual Community of Practice in Education

Thanks for the blooming of technologies, we now have the opportunity to operate in an improved learning environments through increased communication, interactivity among participants, and incorporation of collaborative pedagogical models. One of the suggest applications is virtual COP in which group members are able to explore their knowledge and exchange information through blogs and wiki [6]. The nature of the COP, its goals, and its communicative procedures are all codetermined by the individual members in a way that allows for continuous change and self-development. As a consequence, a COP usually serves as an effective platform for people to exchange knowledge and publicize new information based on their personal needs and living environment [7]. Furthermore, a COP tends to encourage every member to take responsibility for information-sharing and problem-solving, to develop their personal identities in the community, and to foster unification of the community. Wenger [3] suggests that communities of practice can apply in teacher training and in providing isolated administrators with access to colleagues. There is a wave of interest in these peer-to-peer professional-development activities. Indeed, communities of practice can apply to students' peer-to-peer learning and collaborative learning. Since virtual COPs are web-based in nature, people with common interests or passions can easily work on a collaborative project beyond the barriers of geographical boundaries. By using the virtual COPs, for example, researchers are able to exchange ideas and provide instant feedback to one another effectively even though they are scattered around different parts of the world.

4 Facebook

Facebook, launched in February 2004, is the most popular social network website. As of January 2011, Facebook has more than 600 million active users. Users may create a personal profile, add other users as friends, and exchange messages, including automatic notifications when they update their profile. Additionally, users may join common interest user groups, organized by their workplace, school, college, or other characteristics. Facebook is continually upgraded and thus new features pop up on a regular basis. Facebook has been found to be used to reinforce current offline relationships [8]. We have already integrated some communication technologies (such as email, chat rooms and discussion forum) into the way we teach and administer our courses. Therefore, social network sites may also have a place in our classroom.

5 Facebook in Education

As Facebook is built to provide a social networking environment, one application in education may be on using Facebook to build learning and promote virtual COP.

Facebook has quickly become the social network site of choice by college students. They are not only registered on social networking sites, but they are also very active users. One research shows 85% of college students that have adopted Facebook as a college network [9]. Other researches show that students are "comfortable" with faculty on Facebook and want regular on-line discussions with faculty [10]. Since Facebook is free and open to the public, it allows users to make comments, post messages, upload photos and sharing resources. Teachers can use Facebook to ask students questions, share viewpoints, and encourage students to discuss issues and express their concerns. Certain evidence such as discussion threads created, resources collected and comments given can be recorded automatically. This information can be useful for teacher to identify students' individual contributions and engagement in the collaborative learning progress [11] [12] [13]. Students can collaborate with others to establish a particular topic of mutual interest. More specifically, Facebook has many features that people can be used to share their mutual interests, to collaboratively set objectives, regulations, and formats, and this is what distinguishes Facebook from other forms of websites, such as blogs and wiki.

6 Facebook Features for Building Online Community of Practice

There are a number of unique features that make it suitable in education. Facebook is equipped with discussion forums, instant messaging, email, and the ability to post videos and pictures. Most notably, Group feature on Facebook seems to be a powerful tool for collaborative learning. Students can use this Group feature on Facebook to perform various tasks and share resources at the same time. Students create a "Group" to pertain to their interests. An online COP is a network of individuals who share a domain of interest about which they communicate online. Facebook group features are very suitable for building online COP. Since there are three fundamental characteristics of communities: (i) Domain; (ii) Community; and (iii) Practice. Features in Facebook such as Groups, Chats and Docs are perfect for sharing. In this article, we intent to explore the effectively ways to use group features in Facebook with all three crucial characteristics of communities in mind.

Firstly, students can form groups for a specific purpose, members can post message, have discussions and share resources on a specific domain within the group. Furthermore, members can make use of other Internet resources for the specific domain. Students and teachers can share more learning resources by adding hyperlinks within the group. Secondly, Facebook itself is a real online community with features that are conducive to establishing the online communities. Facebook Chat provides a new way for group members to communicate each other in real-time. Like online chart software, the messages are delivered and displayed to members as soon as they're sent, so it is more interactive than only text messages. Thirdly, members of a COP are practitioners. They can develop a shared repertoire of resources. "Docs" feature in Facebook can help with collaborative tasks, it allows members collectively write and edit notes with one another. Similar to a wiki, these resources can be viewed and edited by all members of a group, and any group member may add or remove sections of the "Doc" [14]. Recently, Facebook and Skype are forming a partnership to offer video-conference service for Facebook users. The new video-conference system is currently being tested and, when released, it will be incorporated in Facebook's platform [15].

7 The Research Methodology

7.1 Participants

Two classes of sub-degree students will be included in this study. They are all first year students taking a course called "Introduction of Information Technology" in the Spring semester. The courses mainly covered the basic concepts, capabilities and limitations of Information Technology (IT) and the impact IT have on individuals, organizations and the general public.

7.2 Setting

In this course, students have to complete a group project for the course. They are encouraged to form a learning group in Facebook on a project work. For instance, they can specify what topics or themes of interest for the project according to the course syllabus. Each group contains 4 to 6 members and the instructor will participate in all groups as an ordinary member. The role of the instructor likes an old-timers and students are like newcomers in the community as in a COP [1]. As the newcomers moves from the periphery of the community to its center, they become more active and engaged within the culture and hence assume the role of expert or old-timers. In order to promote collaborative learning in the community, students' work process will be separated into a number of tasks, with each task performed by an individual student.

7.3 Research Questions

The aim of the study was to investigate the learning process in Facebook. In order to see what they have learned and enhance the effectiveness of COP, three specific research questions served as guides in the data analysis:

1. Would students like to use, or are they comfortable using, Facebook to perform the task?
2. Could Facebook enhance collaborative learning for students?
3. How can use of Facebook promote COP?

7.4 Data Collection

The primary data for this study consisted of: (1) student teachers' posting messages and comments on the Facebook; (2) group interviews by instructors in meetings; and (3) end-of-semester questionnaires given to each student.

The quantitative data will be obtained from counting number of messages posted and comments of students in Facebook. The qualitative date can be obtained from group interview which aims to gather students' reflective experiences using Facebook as a communication and collaboration tool. The end-of-semester questionnaire will be given to all students to gather their opinions about Facebook's role in their project.

8 Formation of Groups

Students were requested to form a couple of learning groups on the Facebook to support their collaboration work. As shown in Figure 1, 17 groups were formed in the Facebook. Each group selected their own project topics based on the guidelines listed in the course syllabus, shown in table 1. Each group contained 4 to 6 members and formed a private group in the Facebook. Once the individual private group was formed, group leaders would invite the instructor and other students to join their groups as an ordinary member, shown in figure 2. Serving as consultants, the role of the instructor is to provide group members with constructive advice or challenging feedback in order to monitor the project progress. Group members were advised encouraged to collaborate with one another as much as possible using Facebook. Collaborative activities such as message posting, discussion forum and resources sharing were highly encouraged. Furthermore, student members were allowed to make use of Internet resources for the specific domain. Students and instructor were able to share learning resources by means of hyperlinks within the group. An example of information sharing using Interactive Whiteboard was shown in Figure 3. On the other hand, Facebook itself is a real online community with features that are conducive to build and maintain communities in the virtual world. Users are encouraged to exchange idea, share information and work collaboratively within the community.

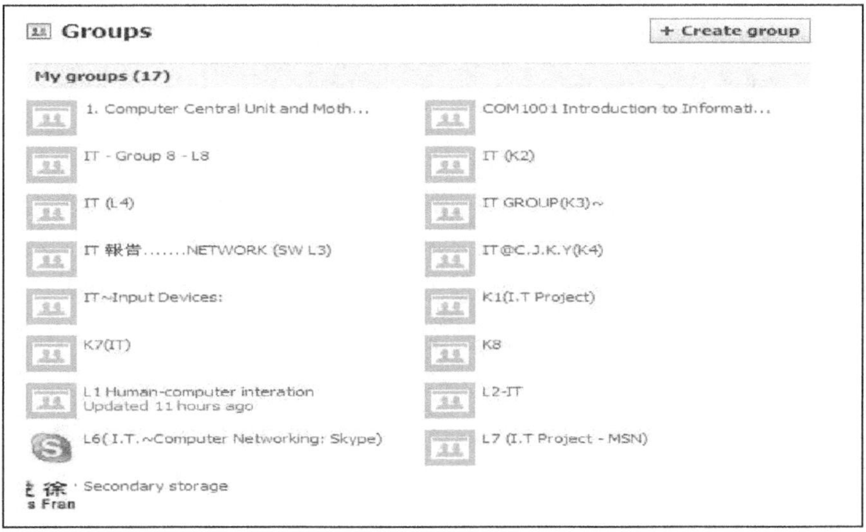

Fig. 1. Students Learning Groups Formed in the Facebook

Table 1. Specific topics for the projects

	Interested Topics
1.	**Computer Central Unit and Motherboard**
2.	**Primary Storage**
3.	**Secondary Storage I**
4.	**Secondary Storage II**
5.	**Input Devices (Keyboard, Mouse & Scanner)**
6.	**Output Devices**
7.	**Output Devices (Laser Printer)**
8.	**Computer Networking-Skype**
9.	**Web browsers**
10.	**Social aspect of IT: Cyber bully**
11.	**Computer Network – MSN**
12.	**Modern Applications of IT - Blogging**
13.	**Smartphone**
14.	**WIFI-networking**
15.	**MSN & ICQ**
16.	**Social Networking – Facebook**
17.	**Human-Computer Interaction**

Fig. 2. Group leader invites instructor and members to join the group

Fig. 3. An example of formation sharing using Interactive Whiteboard

9 Summary

Web 2.0 puts an emphasis on facilitation, sharing, interaction and collaboration among its users. In this regard, Facebook can be viewed as the epitome of a Web 2.0 tool. Besides its popularity, Facebook supports innovative learning approaches, motivates students' participation, presents multimedia materials and enables students to share resources. Students can interact in a small group or even a whole class, they can communicate with text messages in both asynchronous and synchronous mode. Facebook's imminent launching of video conference feature has great potentials for teaching and learning.

Communities of practice are groups of people who share a concern or a passion for something they do and learn how to do it better as they interact regularly [3]. A COP is a process of social learning that occurs when people who have a common interest in a subject or area collaborate over an extended period of time, sharing ideas and strategies, determine solutions, and build innovations. The three required components of COPs, namely Domain, Community and Practice, can easily be dealt with in Facebook. Involvement in a COP means sharing of ideas, stories, common problems and issues, in effect it means learning together as a team. By sharing information and experiences [1], group members learn from each other, heighten their appreciation of the opportunities and challenges. However, COPs need tools to implement. The major features in Facebook are focused on interaction, sharing concerns and empowering collaborative work and thus it seems to be an ideal tool to implement COPs. The features like Group, Chats, Docs and video conference (to be launched), they are all match the COP's characteristics. Thus, we intent to explore the use of Facebook features to implement a virtual COP. We further intend to investigate how Facebook can enhance collaborative learning and knowledge building in virtual COPs. Two classes of sub-degree students will be chosen in this study. The data will be collected quantitatively and qualitatively in nature, consisting of students' posting messages and comments on the Facebook, surveys on the students' reflective experiences using Facebook as communication and collaboration tools, and group interviews with instructors. Hopefully through this research, we can find effective ways in using Facebook to promote virtual COP.

References

1. Lave, J., Wenger, E.: Situated Learning: Legitimate Peripheral Participation. Cambridge University Press, Cambridge (1991)
2. Gannon-Leary, P. M., Fontainha, E.: Communities of Practice and virtual learning communities: benefits, barriers and success factors. eLearning Papers, no. 5. ISSN 1887-1542. (2007).
3. Wenger, E.: Communities of practice. A brief introduction. Communities of practice, http://www.ewenger.com/theory/ (retrieved on December 30, 2010)
4. Smith, M.K.: Communities of practice, the encyclopedia of informal education, http://www.infed.org/biblio/communities_of_practice.htm (retrive March 1, 2011)
5. Learning Theories Knowledgebase Communities of Practice (Lave and Wenger) at Learning-Theories.com, http://www.learning-theories.com/communities-of-practice-lave-and-wenger.html (retrieved March 10, 2011)
6. Godwin-Jones, B.: Emerging technologies: Blogs and wikis: Environments for on-line collaboration. Language Learning & Technology 7(2), 12–16 (2003)
7. Yang, S.-H.: Using Blogs to Enhance Critical Reflection and Community of Practice. Educational Technology & Society 12(2), 11–21 (2009)
8. Lampe, C., Ellison, N., Steinfield, C.: A Face(book) in the crowd: Social searching vs. social browsing. In: Proceedings of Computer Supported Cooperative Work, pp. 167–170, http://portal.acm.org/citation.cfm?id=1180901 (retrieved March 1, 2011)
9. Arrington, M.: 85% of college students use Facebook. TechCrunch, http://www.techcrunch.com/2005/09/07/85-of-llege-students-use-facebook/ (retrieved on January 30, 2011)
10. Muñoz, Towner; Opening Facebook: How to Use Facebook in the College Classroom, http://www46.homepage.villanova.edu/john.immerwahr/TP101/Facebook.pdf (retrieved January 15, 2009)
11. Lui, A., Tsang, P., Kwan, R., Ng, V., Cheung, Y.H.Y., Choy, S.: An Evaluation Framework of Expertise Presence in Computer Conferences. British Journal of Educational 38(6), 1020–1036 (2007)
12. Lui, A., Tsang, P., Kwan, R., Ng, V., Choy, S.: A Study on Knowledge Contributing Students in Computer Conferences. In: Enhancing Learning through Technology, pp. 136–146. World Scientific, New Jersey (2006)
13. Lui, A., Cheung, N., Kwan, R.: Social Capital Creation and Reciprocity in Online Learning Platforms. In: Proceedings of the 4th International Conference on Web-based Learning (ICWL 2005), pp. 165–174 (2005)
14. Facebook group, http://www.facebook.com/group#/help/?page=414 (retrieved January 15, 2011)
15. Dolan, A.: Video-Conference, a New Facebook Feature Rolling Out. inancialfeed.net (2010), http://www.financialfeed.net/video-conference-a-new-facebook-feature-rolling-out/852389/ (retrieved March 15, 2011)

An Analytic Study and Modeling of Online Asynchronous Instruction via the Notion of Interaction Profiles

Cheng-Huang Yen

Dept. of Management and Information, National Open University
172 Chung-Cheng Road, Lu Chow
24702 New Taipei City, Taiwan, R.O.C
yench@mail.nou.edu.tw

Abstract. Online asynchronous instruction is an important part in hybrid learning. The length of time for reflection is much longer for participants of asynchronous discussion forums compared to that of traditional classroom instruction. However, lack of moderation techniques and control of interaction quality often hamper the confidence of online teachers in pursuit of critical instructional objectives. In this research, the notion of interaction profiles is used to model the interactivity in asynchronous forums. The quantitative data derived from the model reveals the intensity of interaction and thus provides early warning messages or facilitation strategies for moderators. The proposed model can be used to monitor asynchronous discussion forums in real time. Our goal is to embed such functions in learning management systems (LMSs) in order to improve the efficiency and quality of online asynchronous instruction.

Keywords: e-learning, asynchronous discussion forum, transcript analysis, LMS.

1 Introduction

Most online teachers have difficulties achieving instructional objectives through asynchronous discussion forums. In many cases, online moderators choose the ask-and-answer style of interaction to lead online asynchronous discussions. In other words, students post questions and moderators react with replies. Since each discussion forum has a central topic, the content of a post can be reviewed to see if it is relevant and how it contributes to learning. This kind of moderation works fine and sometimes can even be claimed as the best practices. However, there is much space for improvement because the information recorded in learning management systems(LMSs) can be used to help online teachers do better than what they are doing now. In this research, we propose a quantitative evaluation model for online asynchronous instruction. Through this model, we are able to come up with the best time for facilitation along with a series of moderating strategies that establish a solid foundation for quality e-learning.

A discussion forum is composed of posts and threads. A thread is a set of related posts. For example, a post and its replies belong to the same thread. Asynchronous discussion forum plays a major part in an online course. An asynchronous classroom

R. Kwan et al. (Eds.): ICHL 2011, LNCS 6837, pp. 325–335, 2011.

can be defined as a collection of online instructional activities. For example, a discussion forum designed for students to share their thoughts on a topic related to the content of a course. Most online asynchronous activities are centered around a series of discussion forums designed as a part of the entire course plan. To moderate a discussion forum is analogous to giving a lecture in a traditional classroom. The instructor develops the topics to be discussed through instructional design. These topics are scheduled to roll out along with the advancement of the course. The footprint of an e-learning course is partly composed of the footprints of each discussion forum.

1.1 Model and Capture the Interaction Behavior

Forums may have temporal patterns of flow or progress. It is important to see how asynchronous interaction occurs along the timeline. If a post or a discussion thread does have a clear bound of lifetime, what would be the appropriate length of lifetime and how would a moderator take advantage of this characteristic? In other words, the moderators need information to help them decide when to inspire participants to get the best result. Figure 1 shows the interaction among participants through posts and views in an online asynchronous discussion forum. Initially, participant s_1 posts a message p_1. When s_2 logs in, he views p_1. Later when s_4 logs in, he views p_1 and posts p_2.

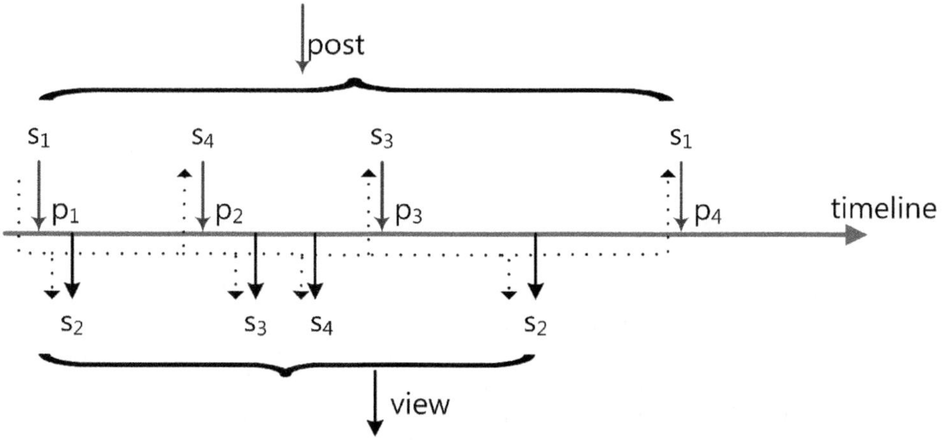

Fig. 1. The interaction among participants through posts and views in an online asynchronous discussion forum

The exchange of messages can be described by interaction diagrams as shown in Figure 2. As can be seen, the interaction diagram expands along the timeline. How the interaction diagram looks depends on how the moderation is done in the forum. In this research, we try to model and capture the time-related interaction behavior that is likely to shed light on the interaction profile of a quality asynchronous instruction.

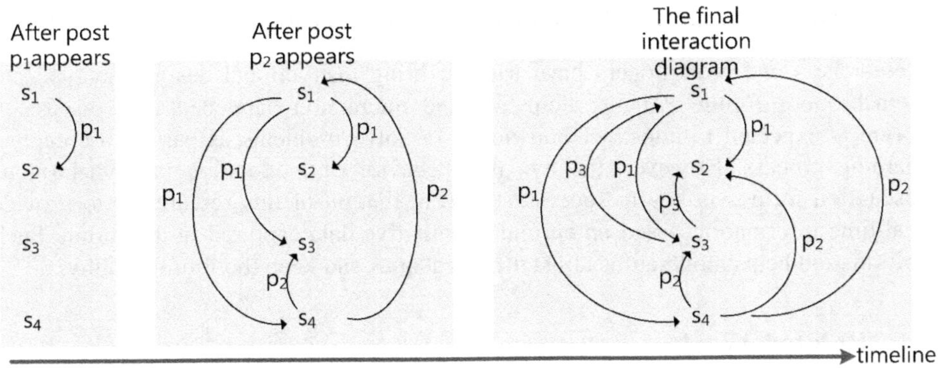

Fig. 2. The interaction diagram evolved along the timeline in an online asynchronous discussion forum

The number of views of a specific post is a changing parameter that indicates the amount of one-way interaction from whomever creates the post to other members of the forum. The replies to a post spawn cross interaction among learners. The chain of messages exchanged forms a discussion thread. Table 1 lists the basic parameters defined in our model. The number of participants who view the post indicates how effective the post attracts learners' attention. Since some participants may click on a post more than once, duplicate views should be discounted. Attendance is an indicator to show the percentage of the community involved in the interaction spawned by the post. The life cycle of a post is an important concept in our model. It represents a period of time when most participants are involved in the interaction triggered by the post. We will explore more on this model in Section 3.

Table 1. Basic parameters defined in the model

$V = \gamma \times (1-\rho)$
V : the number of participants who view the post. γ : the total number of views for a post. ρ : the percentage of duplicate views.
$A = (V/N) \times 100\%$
A : attendance of participants in a forum. N : the total number of participants in a forum.
LC : life cycle of a post.
The period of time between the posting time and the time when the increase in number of views is less than 5% of the number of all participants for three consecutive days.

1.2 Spawn Strategies in the Moderation of Asynchronous Discussion Forums

Researchers and practitioners have tried to bring instructional design theories into asynchronous forums. The participation and interaction happened in a discussion forum is expected to construct knowledge or solve problems as part of a complete learning process. However, the dynamic behavior of moderation in asynchronous discussion forums is key to success. The contribution of this research is to provide real-time information based on current quantitative data captured in the forum. Such information helps moderators adjust their strategies and keep the forum healthy.

2 Related Work

Online teaching differs from traditional face-to-face classroom instruction in its modes of delivery; e.g., synchronous instruction delivered same time and different places[1], asynchronous instruction delivered different time and different places[2], online activities[3], and online collaborative learning via the practice of instructional strategies.

To benefit from e-learning, the quality is a key factor[4]. The standards and the model of evaluation have been an active area of investigation[5].

2.1 Interaction Analysis

Early study of asynchronous forums often focused on participation analysis and interaction analysis[6]. Participation analysis observes the level of participation by forum members, including posts, views and replies. Interaction analysis studies the interaction among forum members, including the relationship between posts and threaded messages.

The methodology for interaction analysis can be further divided into content analysis and quantitative approach. Transcript analysis reviews the content of posts in order to draw conclusions in a qualitative way. Quantitative approach relies on the data collected or computed from LMSs. In our research, quantitative approach is chosen to study the dynamic behavior of asynchronous interaction. However, transcript analysis has also been applied to explain the results and anomalies encountered in quantitative data.

2.2 Importance of Moderation

It has been proposed that online participation is indeed online learning[7]. Therefore, it is important to inspire learners' motivation to participate. Reflection is a critical process in learning and asynchronous discussion is beneficial to learning through reflection[8]. How knowledge is constructed in asynchronous discussion is another issue[9]. Analyzing the content of interaction leads to the understanding of the effectiveness of learning in asynchronous discussion[10].

Whether distance synchronous and asynchronous instruction can contribute to deep learning is discussed in [11]. It was claimed that asynchronous instruction is hard for learners' with less autonomy to achieve effective learning. The result leads to intensive study on moderation in asynchronous instruction. Moderating strategies may be helpful in many situations. For example, peer moderation often reflects more reality[12]. There is much space to accommodate more possibilities in regard to teaching and learning in the moderation of asynchronous discussion forums[13].

Gilly Salmon proposed the so-called five-stage model to describe the process of online moderation[14]. The activities in discussion forums are called e-tivities. Whether the asynchronous discussion forum is focused on topic can be determined through systematic methods[15]. Content analysis methods for posts in forums are summarized in [16]. Posts can be classified according to the content[17]. The topics appeared in discussion forums should be designed in a way that allows online teachers to evaluate the performance of learners[18]. Asynchronous discussion can be seen as a process and posts are the products. Interaction and reflection evolved contributes to learning[19]. The above-mentioned research found that the strategies and techniques of moderation as well as the design of discussion topics and the quality of interaction content are key to successful asynchronous e-learning.

2.3 Temporal Norms

Gibbs proposed the notion of temporal norms[20]. He found that the interaction behavior of asynchronous discussion forums seems to follow certain patterns in different time of day and day of week. Jeong had similar findings[21]. Data mining methods were used to gather information for adjusting moderation strategies[22]. Among the types of data collected, temporal participation indicators are intriguing. The posting time and the reply time are examples of such indicators. This leads to the research on the temporal transitions of discussion forums. The time-related quantitative data were used to determine whether the interaction is intensive or if the thread of discussion has come to an end[23].

The modes of discussion behavior is related to knowledge construction[24]. The data embedded in discussion forums can be used to decide the proper point of time online teachers should intervene[25]. The inter-relationship among posts were investigated in [26]. The quantitative analysis of forum data provides a variety of graphical views that depict the healthiness of the forum[27]. In our research, the number of views is used to analyze both the activeness of a certain post as well as the interaction behavior of the entire forum.

3 The Model and the Practice

The model of interaction profiles is derived from the basic parameters defined in Table 1. We collected data from asynchronous discussion forums in LMSs and computed the various parameters from which to draw conclusions on the interaction behaviors of the forum.

3.1 The Model of Interaction Profiles

Table 2 lists the major parameters computed in the model of interaction profiles. Average attendance (AA) gives a rough estimate of the percentage of participants who view the posts. Average life cycle of posts (ALCP) tells us how long a post attracts participants' attention. The number of active posts (NAP) measures the amount of information that is currently reflected by most participants. The increasing rate in number of views (iNOV) indicates how active participants are in terms of receiving information from the forum. The increasing rate in number of posts (iNOP) indicates how active participants are in terms of sending information to the forum.

Table 2. The model of interaction profiles

parameters	Corresponding data
AA	Average attendance
ALCP	Average life cycle of posts
NAP	Number of active posts
iNOV	The increasing rate in number of views
iNOP	The increasing rate in number of posts

Most parameters listed in both Table 1 and Table 2 change with time. Useful information can be derived from these parameters. For example, the attendance of a certain post can be compared to the average attendance of existing posts to see how well the post attracts participants' interest. As another example, when iNOV is bigger than normal, it implies that participants are actively browsing the content of posts. Higher values of iNOP indicate that forum participants actively express their opinions. When iNOV and iNOP are both high, it tells us that the interaction in the forum is quite intensive. We can certainly make many other observations from these parameters. That is why we name the centerpiece of the model as the interaction profile for an asynchronous discussion forum.

Once the data are collected and computed to obtain the interaction profile of a forum, forum moderators may get an early warning message or a suggestion that help them decide what to do next for the benefit of learners. For example, a cold asynchronous forum needs to be warmed up. A summary post should be prepared when the lifetime of a post nearly reaches the end. Without such information, moderators will do their jobs based on intuition and individual experience.

3.2 A Quantitative Observation of Asynchronous Discussion Forums

Figure 3 depicts the kind of data that can be collected from the asynchronous forum periodically. The analysis of interactive activities happened during the life cycle of a specific post, thread or forum reveals the most active period of asynchronous instruction. The number of views for each post is recorded in Excel sheets for later analysis.

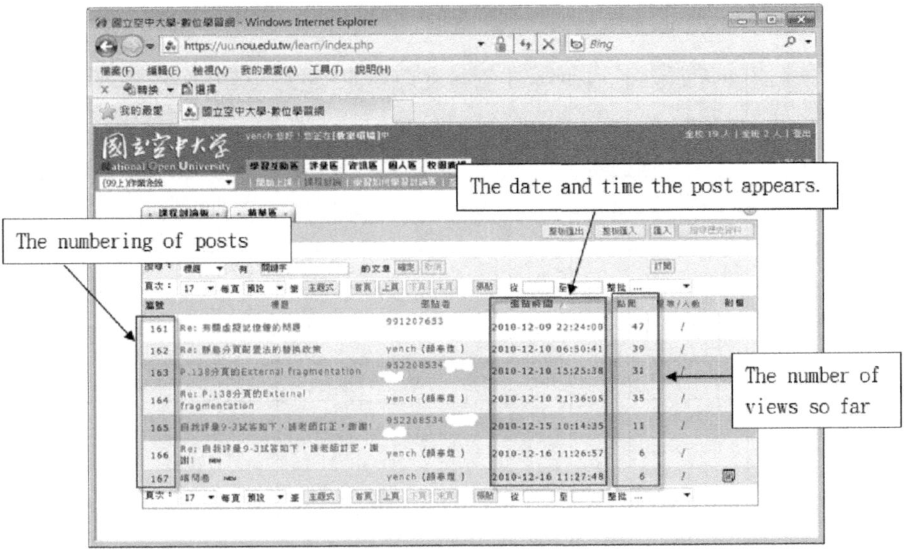

Fig. 3. Online asynchronous discussion forums number the posts, record the date and time the post appears, and update the number of views so far for each post

Table 3 provides a sample of the original data collected from the discussion forum. The data were recorded once a day. For example, post number 3 had been viewed for 15 times till day 5. In day 6, the number of views increased to 21. Each row records the participation level for a post. Each column records the participation level of the forum at a certain instant. The recording can be done more frequently to improve accuracy.

Table 3. A sample of the original data collected from the discussion forum

post	day 1	day 2	day 3	day 4	day 5	day 6	day 7	day 8	day 9	day 10	day 11	day 12	day 13	day 14
1	2	10	15	18	18	19	19	20	21	21	21	21	21	22
2		1	5	6	12	13	17	18	18	19	19	20	22	23
3		5	9	11	15	21	32	34	39	40	41	41	42	42
4				3	8	9	9	10	11	11	11	11	12	12
5					2	11	21	34	38	42	45	49	50	50
6					1	7	14	15	18	19	21	23	24	25

Table 4 provides a sample of data derived from the original data. For example, the number of views for post number 1 is 2 as shown in Table 3. In day 2, the number of views increased to 10. Therefore, we take the result of 10 minus 2, which is 8, as the increase in views, and record in day 2 of post number 1 in Table 4.

Table 4. A sample of data derived from the original data

post	day 1	day 2	day 3	day 4	day 5	day 6	day 7	day 8	day 9	day 10	day 11	day 12	day 13	day 14
1		8	5	3	0	1	0	1	1	0	0	0	0	1
2			4	1	6	1	4	1	0	1	0	1	2	1
3			4	2	4	6	11	2	5	1	1	0	1	0
4					5	1	0	1	1	0	0	0	1	0
5						9	10	13	4	4	3	4	1	0
6						6	7	1	3	1	2	2	1	1
sum		8	13	6	15	24	32	19	14	7	6	7	6	3
total number of posts	0	1	3	3	4	6	6	6	6	6	6	6	6	6
increase in number of posts	0	1	2	0	1	2	0	0	0	0	0	0	0	0

4 Results and Experience

We chose three courses offered in Summer of 2010 and Fall of 2010 to get a glimpse of interaction profiles for asynchronous discussion forums for these courses. The participants of our target group are adult learners. Table 5 lists the data derived from interaction profiles with the percentage of duplicate views $\rho = 5\%$.

Table 5. The data derived from interaction profiles. ($\rho = 5\%$)

Name of course	# of participants	AA	ALCP (days)	NAP(avg)	iNOV(avg)	iNOP(avg)
Multimedia applications	366	9.53%	10.5	12	59	6
Development of Internet Applications	243	6.46%	4.3	6	23	3
Operating Systems	153	7.95%	6.7	7	26	2

The multimedia applications course was a new course with more participants. Its ALCP is higher. The data 10.5 tells us that in average a post in this course is active for less than 11 days. NAP is also higher for this course. This implies that more information is being exchanged. The operating system course was offered a number of times in the past. Although the number of participants is less than the other two courses, the data of its interaction profile sits above average among the three courses.

The data in Table 5 do not tell us much about the intensity of interaction for a discussion forum at any instant of time. The original data, however, do contain such information. A twenty-five percent rule can be used as a quick evaluation tool. Suppose the computed average iNOV so far is 60, then the instantaneous iNOV can be compared against this value. Values larger than 75 are 25% higher than average. It implies that the forum is turning warm. Values larger than 90 are 50% higher than average. The interaction in the forum is quite intensive compared to the past average. On the other hand, values less than 45 are 25% lower than average. The forum is turning cool.

The distribution of views in the lifetime of a post is another interesting phenomena. 83% of the total posts have a right-skew curve in a plot of number of views against the lifetime of a post. This means that most views happened early on in the lifetime of a post. In order to make the best out of the interaction, the result suggests that moderators should keep an eye on a new post as soon as possible.

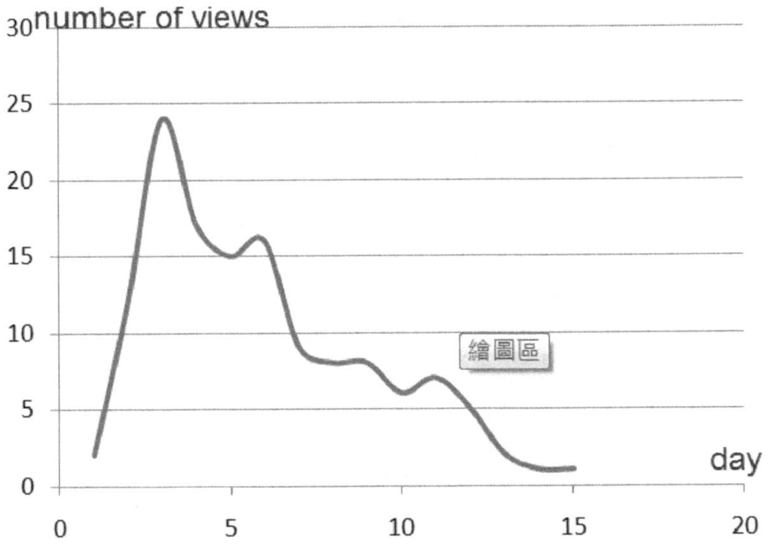

Fig. 4. A typical plot of the number of views against the lifetime of a post is statistically right-skewed

We found that certain data should be trimmed to facilitate the analysis. For example, day of week is a disturbing issue. In most cases, the interaction falls down significantly during weekends and breaks the smooth trend of the data curve. System downtime is another possibility that may be spotted for outliers.

5 Conclusions

The data derived from the model of interaction profiles is dynamic and time-dependent. Useful information can be mined from such data to provide guidance for moderators of asynchronous discussion forums. For a forum of 500 posts running for two months, roughly 15000 numbers need to be recorded. It is a tedious and even infeasible task to keep record of data of this scale. We are looking for possibility to incorporate the recording process in LMSs by programming.

Although it is imperative to know how active the forum participants are in asynchronous discussion, the quality of the content also matters. A healthy discussion forum succeeds with quality posts by active participants. The outliers in collected or computed data can be explained by transcript analysis. The strategies taken by moderators can also be evaluated by observing the corresponding changes in interaction profiles.

References

1. Hofmann, J.: The Synchronous Trainer's Survival Guide. Pfeiffer (2003)
2. Salmon, G.: E-moderating: The Key to Teaching and Learning Online, 2nd edn. Taylor & Francis Books. Ltd., Taylor (2003)
3. Watkins, R.: 75 E-Learning Activities: Making Online Learning Interactive. Pfeiffer (2005)
4. Horton, W.: Evaluating E-learning. ASTD (2001)
5. Kirkpatrick, D.L.: Evaluating Training Programs: The Four Levels. Berrett-Koehler Publishers (2006)
6. Gunawardena, C.N., Anderson, T.: Analysis of a Global Online Debate and the Development of an Interaction Analysis Model for Examining Social Construction of Knowledge in Computer Conferencing. J. of Educational Computing Research 17(4), 397–431 (1997)
7. Hrastinski, S.: A theory of online learning as online participation. Computers & Education 52, 78–82 (2009)
8. Lee-Baldwin, J.: Asynchronous discussion forums: A closer look at the structure, focus and group dynamics that facilitate reflective thinking. Contemporary Issues in Technology and Teacher Education 5(1), 93–115 (2005)
9. Schrire, S.: Knowledge building in asynchronous discussion groups: Going beyond quantitative analysis. Computers & Education 46(1), 49–70 (2006)
10. Saade, R.G., Huang, Q.: Meaningful Learning in Discussion Forums: Towards Discourse Analysis. in Issues Informing Science and Information Technology vol. 6 (2009)
11. Offir, B., Lev, Y., Bezalel, R.: Surface and deep learning processes in distance education:Synchronous versus asynchronous systems. Computers & Education 51, 1172–1183 (2008)
12. Correia, A., Baran, E.: Lessons Learned on Facilitating Asynchronous Discussions for Online Learning. Educação, Formação & Tecnologias 3(1), 59–67 (2010)
13. Wever, D.B., Keer, H.V., Schellens, T., Valcke, M.: Structuring asynchronous discussion groups: the impact of role assignment and self-assessment on students levels of knowledge construction through social negotiation. J. Computer Assisted Learning 25(2), 177–188 (2009)

14. Salmon, G.: E-tivities: The Key to Active Online Learning. Kogan Page, London (2002)
15. Beaudin, B.: Keeping Online Asynchronous Discussions on Topic. J. Asynchronous Learning Networks 3(2) (1999)
16. Wever, B.D., Schellens, T., Valcke, M., Keer, H.V.: Content analysis schemes to analyze transcripts of online asynchronous discussion groups: A review. Computers & Education 46, 6–28 (2006)
17. Murphy, E.: Recognising and promoting collaboration in an online asynchronous discussion. British J. Education Technology 35(4), 421–431 (2004)
18. Liu, S.: Assessing Online Asynchronous Discussion in Online Courses: An Empirical Study. In: 12th Annual TCC Worldwide Online Conference, pp. 24–32 (2007)
19. Black, A.: The use of asynchronous discussion: Creating a text of talk. Contemporary Issues in Technology and Teacher Education 5(1), 5–24 (2005)
20. Gibbs, W., Simpson, L.D., Bernas, R.S.: An Analysis of Temporal Norms in Online Discussions. International J. Instructional Media 35(1), 63–75 (2008)
21. Jeong, A., Frazier, S.: How day of posting affects level of critical discourse in asynchronous discussions and computer-supported collaborative argumentation. British J. Educational Technology 39(5), 875–887 (2008)
22. Dringus, L.P., Ellis, T.: Using data mining as a strategy for assessing asynchronous discussion forums. Computers & Education 45, 141–160 (2005)
23. Dringus, L.P., Ellis, T.: Temporal transitions in participation flow in an asynchronous discussion forum. Computers & Education 54, 340–349 (2010)
24. Hou, H.-T., Chang, K.-E., Sung, Y.-T.: Analysis of Problem-Solving-Based Online Asynchronous Discussion Pattern. Educational Technology & Society 11(1), 17–28 (2008)
25. Hou, H.-T.: Exploring the Behavioral Patterns in Project-Based Learning With Online Discussions: Quantitative Content Analysis and Progressive Sequential Analysis. TOJET:The Turkish J. Educational Technology 9(3) (2010)
26. Chen, G., Chiu, M.M.: Online discussion processes: Effects of earlier messages' evaluations, knowledge content, social cues and personal information on later messages. Computers & Education, 50678–50692 (2008)
27. Bratitsis, T.: Visualized Interaction Analysis Indicators in Asynchronous Discussion learning activities, Research results and trends. In: 8th International Conference on Computer Supported Collaborative Learning: Workshop (2009)

Digital Learning Video Indexing Using Scene Detection

Yuan-Hsun Liao[1], Cheng-Yu Tsai[1], Ming-Hsiang Su[1], Hsiao-Hui Li[2], and Pao-Ta Yu[1]

[1] Dept. of CS&IE, National Chung Cheng University, Chiayi, Taiwan
[2] Dept. of IM, National Chung Cheng University, Chiayi, Taiwan
{lyh96p,tcy97p,sumh,csipty}@cs.ccu.edu.tw

Abstract. The scenes change detection for video indexing is proposed in this paper to improve the capability of learning object retrieval. This indexing technique can be applied to improve the readability of open courseware with web-based format. Besides, the application of technique can include education assistance with the learning objects very important. Hence, our proposed system is integration technology with automatic scenes detection and anchored scenes technology to produce e-learning objects. This system applies automatic detection technology to retrieve key time of the course section. Teachers just have follow the designed process to produce materials, and then reader will be use functions of learning object to search the content for require information.

Finally, we invite scholars' specialized video recording materials using our system to produce new types of learning materials. The materials will be translated into the learning management system to provide students learning.

Keywords: course indexing, interactive learning, scene instruction.

1 Introduction

With the rapid development of the digital learning technique, it allows the production of digital teaching materials to have more tools supporting. e-Learning has become indispensable with every people [1]. Through computer network, learners can get e-Learning content without place or time restriction and then teachers can design content-rich e-Learning courses through various multimedia application softwares [2-4].

The digital technology has focus and research of many researchers to improve teaching objects [5-7]. The production of digital teaching materials include diversified technology to make digital learning which can have several teaching the repetitive learning, reuse of advantages, and maintain the merits of teaching in the classroom.

e-Learning object is general contained video, audio, pictures and other materials, which may be used for learning, education or training [8]. When teachers recorded a video, he/she wants design an e-Learning object to share knowledge with people at network. He/she encountered great difficulties as catching picture from video, loading related data, making indexing for image, and so on. But, there isn't a suitable tool to complete this purpose. Therefore, this paper is to solve those problems through

R. Kwan et al. (Eds.): ICHL 2011, LNCS 6837, pp. 336–344, 2011.

anchored instruction and automatic detection technology and retrieval. Because of the easy-to-use requirement of courseware authoring application, the application can detect the changes of PowerPoint slides and record the corresponding time point in the video. Hence, this can help teachers to make indexing of video and related data. Moreover, the functions of learning object can help students to find their required information.

2 Automatic Detection

Automatic detection technology is to adopt the Sobel mask to process image, and then determine whether two processed images are the same. If the comparison of two processed images is identical, it will indicate that the specific feature of image have no change; otherwise, it indicates that specific feature of image has changed already. Sobel mask is the method which introduces the concept of the first derivative [9]. Since the first derivatives in an image are computed using the gradient, we will introduce the gradient operator in detail.

First-order derivatives of an image are based on various approximations of the 2-D gradient [10]. The image of an image $g(x, y)$ at location (x, y) is denoted by the following vector expression:

$$\nabla g = \begin{bmatrix} G_x \\ G_y \end{bmatrix} = \begin{bmatrix} \frac{\partial g}{\partial x} \\ \frac{\partial g}{\partial y} \end{bmatrix} \tag{1}$$

The quantity in edge detection is the magnitude of this vector ∇g , as shown in (2):

$$\nabla g = mag(\nabla g)\left[G_x^2 + G_y^2\right]^{1/2} \tag{2}$$

To compute the gradient of an image, we have to obtain the partial derivatives $\partial g / \partial x$ and $\partial g / \partial y$ at every pixel location. As shown in Figure 1, one of the simplest ways to implement a first-order derivative at point z_5 is to use the following equations:

$$G_x = (z_7 + 2z_8 + z_9) - (z_1 + 2z_2 + z_3) \tag{3}$$

$$G_y = (z_3 + 2z_6 + z_9) - (z_1 + 2z_4 + z_7) \tag{4}$$

As illustrated in Figure 2, the Sobel mask is the variation for these two equations. We take the right block of Figure 2 for implementation, and the two equations of the Sobel mask are described below (3)(4):

z_1	z_2	z_3
z_4	z_5	z_6
z_7	z_8	z_9

Fig. 1. 3×3 region of an image

-1	0	1
-2	0	2
-1	0	1

-1	-2	-1
0	0	0
1	2	1

Fig. 2. Sobel mask

In the process of calculating the gradient ∇g, there are numerous operators of squares and square roots in an image as shown in (2). In order to reduce the complexity, a method used frequently is to approximate the gradient by absolute values as follows:

$$\nabla g \approx |G_x| + |G_y| \tag{5}$$

After the calculation of the gradient in an image finished, an edge image is produced. However, it is not intelligent to calculate an entire edge image. Since the automatic detection technology only process the specific features of an image, the workload of computer will greatly decrease. Then, two result images are taken to subtract the second image from the first image, and we define the difference as the reference value. For the high quality of images, the reference value which is only greater than zero indicates two different images. For the low quality of images, we need set a threshold as the discriminating value. Similarly, the reference value which is greater than a threshold indicates two different images. Therefore, we provide a comparison algorithm to enhance the automatic detection technology.

3 Methods

Our main contribution in this paper is to propose an automatic scene detection method shown in Figure 3.

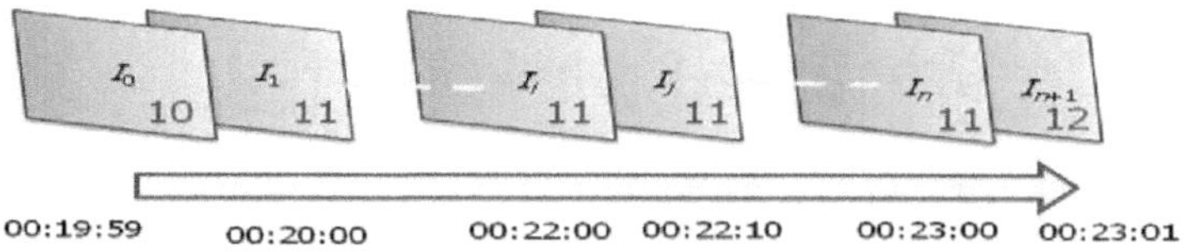

Fig. 3. Automatic Scene Detection Method

The spatial filtering, the edge detection, and the Sobel mask to process the images of instructional video are applied in our method with the binary searching algorithm to find the anchored points. The basic rule is that if the comparison result of the first image I_0 and the last image I_n in an interval is the same, it will reply back that the interval has no target image. On the contrary, the target image exists in the interval. A function is designed to provide a user with the selection of feature area, and they can seek the proper feature area for automatic detection.

3.1 Scene Detection

Our system provides an automatic scene mechanism to detect educational scenes and then give the anchored point corresponding to the detection point. After the whole streaming data is anchored with suitable check points, the system can translate it to an e-Learning content with html-form format based on those anchored information. An illustrated example is shown in Figure 4. Based on snapshots obtained by automatic detection, the lecture streaming data is partitioned into four scenes and the entry time of each scene can be easily found.

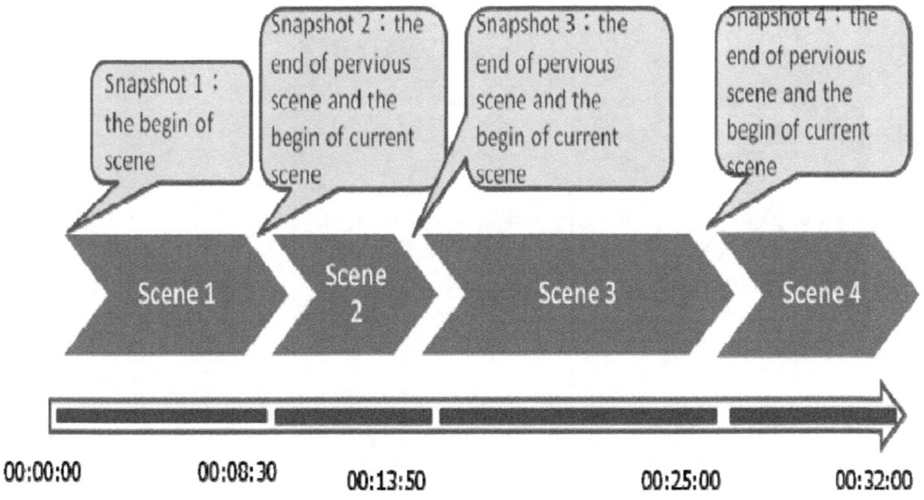

Fig. 4. Scene Concept of Approach

3.2 System Design

The design of the system is to create web-based projects that include streaming video and teaching briefing (PowerPoint) for building materials. It provides an environment for multimedia information integration. The projects can use to learning and gaining knowledge efficiently in online learning object.

This system is divided into two parts: authoring and presentation mode. The authoring mode is described the mode that users are designing an e-Learning object. When the system is in the authoring mode, four system components are available to design. They are the video converter tool, video detection tool, XML generator tool, and the e-Learning object generator. The video converter tool provided a function to help user convert AVI format video to WMV format video.

The video detection tool allows the user to captures pictures from played video, it contains three parts: Feature Area Selector, Automatic Detection, and Manual Catch. The XML generator tool is a tool for matching picture captured from video and briefing data, then output a matching data. It contains two parts: Information Matching, XML Generator. The e-Learning object generator packaged post-processed WMV, XML documents, and raw data to be an e-Learning object. When the system is in presentation mode, it presents the e-Learning content from pre-designed HTML documents that include video, briefing and raw data with matching information.

There are five components in the system. Four components are for authoring the e-Learning object and one component for presenting. Figure 5 shows the component diagram of this system.

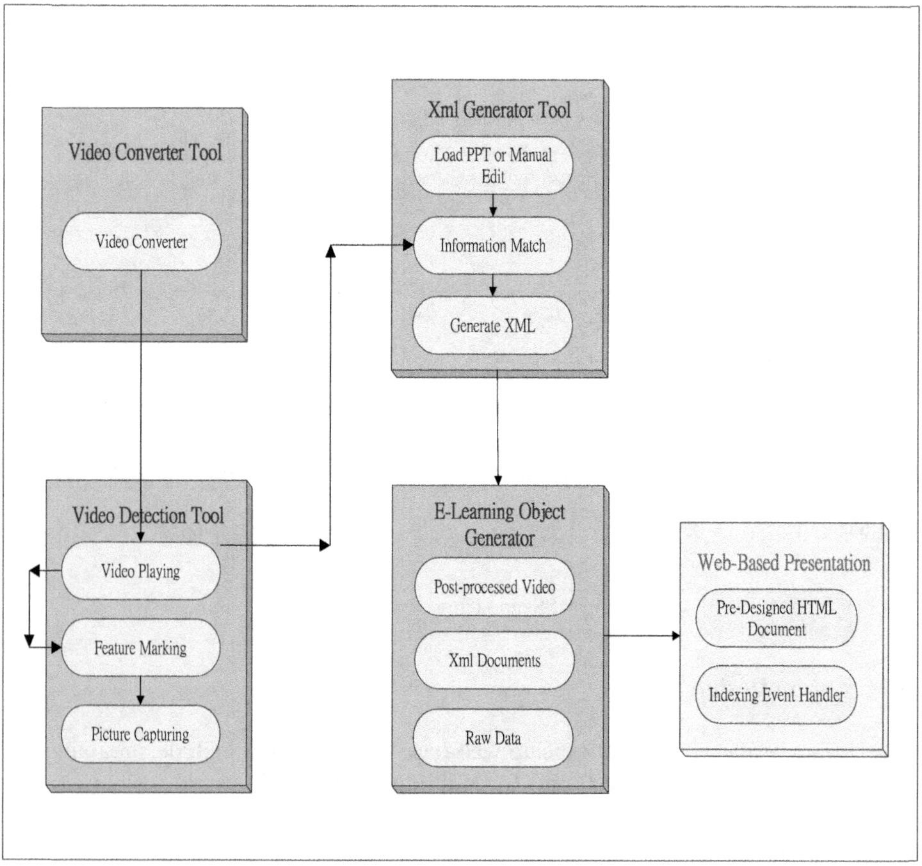

Fig. 5. Component diagram of the system

The system will record the streaming media cataloging retrieval to meet the standards of digital learning materials .The frame is shown as below.

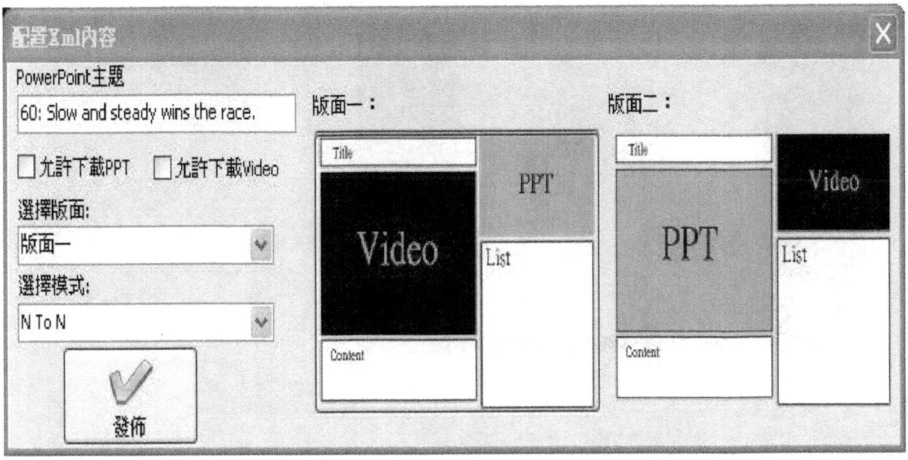

Fig. 6. XML Configuration Frame

Instructional design choice one of these two modes according to the teaching demand and then automatic authoring operations can generate teaching materials for web-based. Directly, learning objects translated into learning platform to provide learners studying and testing.

4 Implementation

Because the video contents are different, we divide into two kinds of way to produce the learning materials. The first way is to use the post-production processing traditional video into learning materials. The second way is to invite experts and scholars to teach the curriculums and use our equipment to record courses.

After recording the courses, we use the authoring techniques to produce e-learning teaching material components for the use of digital learning and we create test questions. After watching the courses, learners can test themself to see how much their understanding of course content.

We invite four experts to teach the curriculums and use our equipment to record courses. Course videos then through our post-production software designed to catalog index learning materials production. These materials can be placed in the network of knowledge sharing, education and training applications.

Figure 7 to 10 are the images are produced using our method. These materials are placed in the network and learners can access through a browser to view the general content of course.

Fig. 7. The result 1 of our method

Fig. 8. The result 2 of our method

Fig. 9. The result 3 of our method

Fig. 10. The result 4 of our method

5 Conclusion

The paper is to design a post-production authoring environment for instruction video. Leaning objects can be completed by using the integration technology. Moreover, teachers can easily build web-based learning objects and then students can operate functions of webpage to learn knowledge from the learning objects.

Our method has conformed to the following advantages:

1. User can build a learning object through some designed steps easily.
2. By using automatic detection technology, user gets the key scene time point which is simple.
3. Learner can learn repetitive and interactive
4. Leaner can enhance effectiveness and convenient operating environment.

In future research, we will add empirical research to substantiate the learning materials produced by the learning. Our research will persist with teaching practice and the learning's effectiveness research.

References

1. Chang, T.W., Yu, P.T., Hsu, J.M.: An Embedded Interactive Information System with Automatic Detection Technology for Instructional Video. In: 2008 Ed-Media International Conference, Vienna (2008)
2. Dashti, A., Kim, S.H., Shahabi, C., Zimmermann, R.: Streaming media server design (IMSC Press Multimedia Series). Prentice Hall PTR, Upper Saddle River (2003)
3. IEEE Standard 1484.12.1.: Draft Standard for Learning Object Metadata - Learning Object Metadata (2002)
4. Snoek, C.G.M., Worring, M.: Multimedia Event-Based Video Indexing Using Time intervals. IEEE Transactions on Multimedia 7, 638–647 (2005)
5. Choudary, C., Liu, T.: Summarization of Visual Content in Instructional Videos. IEEE Transactions on Multimedia 9, 1443–1455 (2007)
6. Li, Y., Dorai, C.: Instructional Video Content Analysis Using Audio Information. IEEE Transactions on Audio, Speech, and Language Processing 14, 2264–2274 (2006)
7. Ngo, C.-W., Wang, F., Pong, T.-C.: Structuring Lecture Videos for Distance Learning Applications. Multimedia Software Engineering, 215–222 (2003)
8. Mittal, A., Krishnan, P.V., Altman, E.: Content classification and context based retrieval system for E-learning. Int. J. Educ. Technol. Soc. 9, 349–358 (2006)
9. Park, M.-H., Lee, J.W., Park, R.-H., Kim, J.-S.: False contour reduction using neural networks and adaptive bi-directional smoothing. IEEE Transactions on Consumer Electronics 56, 870–878 (2010)
10. Gonzalez, R.C., Woods, R.E.: Digital Image Processing, 2nd edn., vol. 76, pp. 116–119, 572-279 (2002)

Data Modeling Technique Made Easy with Hybrid Learning Computer Aided Instruction

Joseph Fong[1], L.F. Kwok[2], and Simon K.S. Cheung[3]

[1,2] City University of Hong Kong, Tat Chee Avenue, Kowloon, Hong Kong
{csjfong,cslfkwok}@cityu.edu.hk
[3] Open University of Hong Kong, Good Shepherd Street, Kowloon, Hong Kong
kscheung@ouhk.edu.hk

Abstract. Although hybrid learning has been adopted in higher education for a decade, it is still a challenge to build a satisfactory Computer Aided Instruction (CAI) on Internet. Not only it is difficult to guide users through the operations of CAI, but also it is hard to measure the learning effectiveness. This paper presents an effective method of using a set of CAI steps to demonstrate hybrid learning on data modeling technique. A constructivist theory is applied for users to go through the CAI steps. The result is a CAI for teaching and learning data modeling techniques. A case study of designing a hospital patient system is used for illustration. Its merit is the effective application of interactivity in teaching and learning data modeling techniques in designing an extended entity relationship model.

Keywords: hybrid learning, constructivist theory, computer aided instruction, data modeling technique.

1 Introduction

A database is a model of an enterprise. It is an interface between people and machine. The design of a database must meet the user requirements and be practical in terms of technology and hardware. A database supports a community of users whose needs partly overlap, partly diverge and partly conflict. All these factors together constitute the complexity and difficulty of database design.

In data modeling, that is, when designing a database, each noun in the requirement statement is a potential entity, and each verb is a potential relationship, Basically, an entity is a uniquely identifiable object, and a relationship between entities identifies the constraints between entities. A constraint means a data requirement or a rule that the database must follow in the usage of the database.

In database modeling, the entity relationship model [1] has been widely used but does not have some shortcomings. It is difficult to represent cases where an entity may have varying attributes dependent upon some property. For this reason, the entity relationship model is usually extended in order to include more semantics such as generalization, categorization and aggregation.

R. Kwan et al. (Eds.): ICHL 2011, LNCS 6837, pp. 345–356, 2011.

The data semantics in database describes the meaning of data and its relationship with other data. For example, cardinality describes the data volume between entities. Weak entity describes the key dependency between weak entity and strong entity. Participation describes the mandatory or optional relationship between entities. Is_a relationship describes the relationship between superclass and subclass entities. The generalization describes the relationship between multiple subclass entities with its superclass entity. The aggregation describes the fact that an aggregation entity must consist of its components in the form of entities and their relationship. A categorization describes the fact that each subclass data must be within one of its superclass entities. N-ary relationship describes that one entity or multiple entities related to each other.

2 Related Work

Constructivism emphasizes real life experienced activities. It assumes that learning should occur in realistic setting [2]. This is an emerging trend in education worldwide and is a movement of the focus from that of teaching to that of learning [3]. Effective university learning are those with high degree of interactivity and engagement and which provide a motivating environment based on well-structured knowledge base [4] These activities and conditions incorporate such tasks as the solution of real world reported to increase student motivation, to develop critical thinking and deepen the understanding of significant content [5]. Classroom training is often characterized by the phrase "sage on the stage" because the instructor must somehow transfer his or her knowledge to the learners [6].

3 CAI Architecture

Due to the fact that data modeling technique has many data interactions between user and engine, a question-and-answer-based approach is not suitable for all cases. CAI was designed to solve this problem. The approach is similar to concepts of ruled-based algorithm and forward chaining. A function (program) is defined. The functions return a value of success or failure (solved or not solved). If it returns with a success value, then the function also returns the sequence of selected steps that solved the problem. It continues to run until getting solved or failed [7].

In general, a knowledge-based system (KBS) is a computer system that provides for solving problems in a given field or application area by drawing inferences from a knowledge base [8]. KBS is sometimes used synonymously referred as expert system, though it is not necessarily restricted to expert knowledge. Some KBS have self-learning capabilities. Knowledge of data modeling will be required to build a KBS. Based on the KBS, an inference engine will be formed by ruled-base system. The user interface will act as an agency to monitor the entire interaction between the inference engine and the user. The inference engine and user interface forms the core of CAI. Figure 1 shows the architecture of CAI.

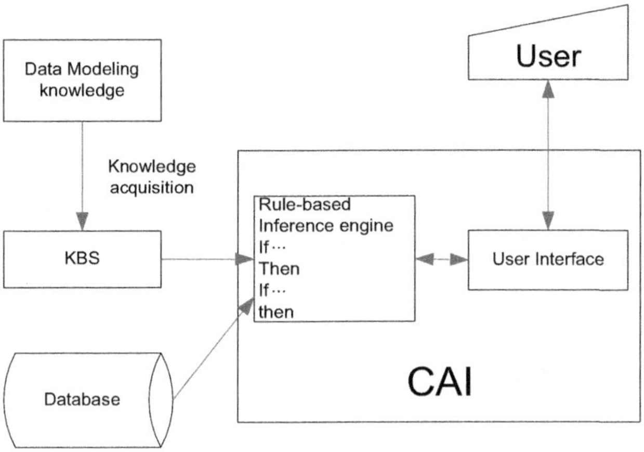

Fig. 1. Architecture of CAI

The main function is to provide step-by-step instruction and examples for users to recognize how to determine each data semantic in an extended entity relationship model and to provide guidance for users to generate the model. Dynamic interaction, graphic user interface, stepwise guidance and multimedia are the system characteristics to attract the users in learning the meaning of each data semantic of database designs. To physically store the database, two major areas are used, namely, model generation and evaluation. User-defined attributes and dependencies are stored in the database of the model generator which contains project table, attribute table, function dependency table multi-valued dependency table, join dependency table, and relational table. The evaluation page provides the evaluation of each data semantic for user to evaluate the usability of this. User can submit their question, comment and feedback electronically.

4 Database Design Using CAI – A Case Study

An important issue of CAI is a good user interface design. The most important part of the guidelines, however, wasn't the catalog of interface widgets and gizmos. It was the list of "design principles" which they believed lay at the heart of any good interface [9]. The following is a list of basic design principles for the user interface development guidelines.

- Consistency: Things that work one way in one part of the system should work the same way in other parts. This allows users to learn something once, then apply that knowledge again and again as they use the computer.
- Aesthetic integrity: A good design is understand and let the user concentrate on the information being presented.
- Perceived stability Even if your program thinks it knows what's best for the user, keep in mind that they're the ones in control, and that no change in their environment should happen without their knowledge and permission.

- See-and-point, not remember-and-type: Instead of making users remember and type this sort of data, the computer should always give them a list of valid possibilities and let them choose from it.
- Direct manipulation: Good graphical interfaces allow their users to feel as if they are directly controlling a little world inside the computer. Instead of abstracting out their work to a set of command words, they can just grab the things they want to work on using the mouse and interact with them directly.
- What You See Is What You Get: Documents on screen should match what they'll look like when they're printed.
- Feedback and dialog: Good programs never keep the user guessing. They react immediately when you perform an action, such as clicking a button.
- Forgiveness: Humans make mistakes. Good programs allow for this by letting them undo their last action, or even revert to a previous version of the document.
- User control : No matter what, the user must be the one in control at all times. Nothing destroys a user's peace of mind faster than having the computer appear to be taking over the action.

We use a case study of a hospital patient system for illustration. It consists of 9 business requirements and 20 data requirements, with description of the entities in the hospital database system, as shown in Figure 2.

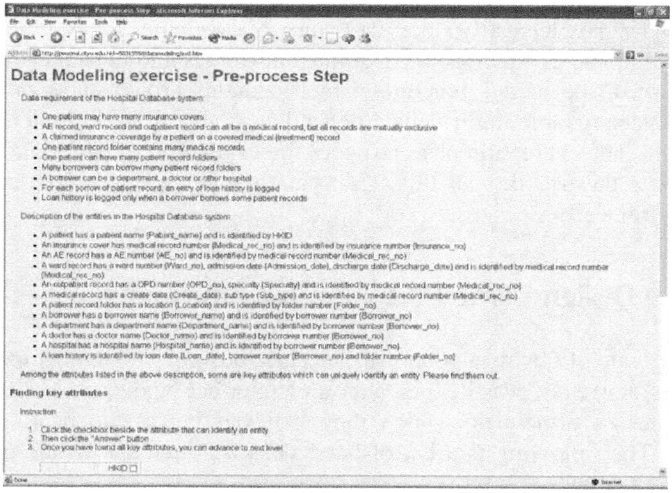

Fig. 2. Business & Data Requirement of a Hospital Patient System

The following is a stepwise of applying a CAI for automating data modeling technique up to the drawing of an extended entity relationship model [10].

Step 1: Find key attributes. A key attribute must be uniquely identifiable. Select the data fields which must have unique value as shown in Figure 3. Since each entity must have an entity key, as a result, each key attribute is an entity key, and each entity key defines an entity.

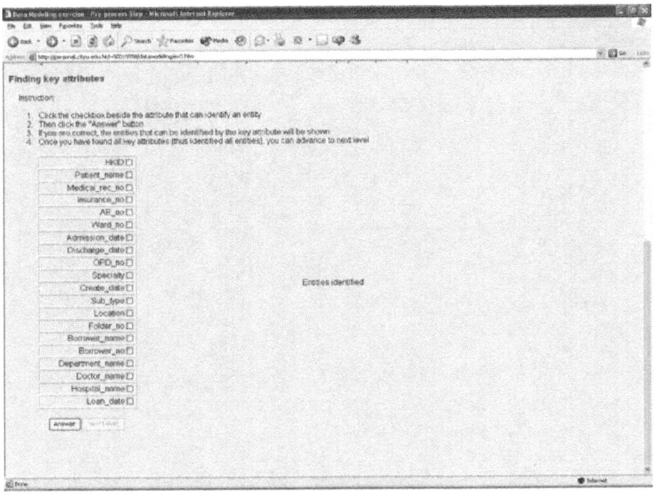

Fig. 3. Select Key Attributes

Step 2: Find is_a relationship. An is_a relationship is a relationship between subclass entity and its superclass entity. All subclass entity data must be in the superclass entity, and they have the same entity key. Select pair of superclass entity key and subclass entity key among the chosen entities keys in step 1, and identify there is_a relationship. For example, A is_a B, which means subclass entity A is in the superclass entity B as shown in Figure 4.

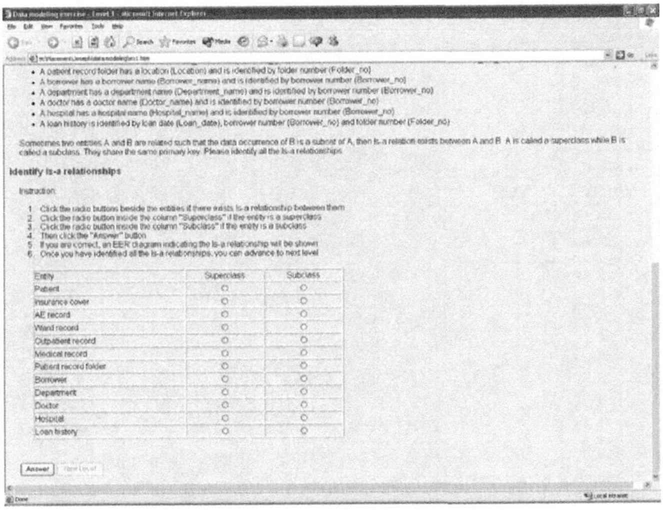

Fig. 4. Identify is_a relationship

Step 3: Find entity attributes. An entity attribute describes the entity properties. Select the attributes among given data fields for each entity as shown in Figure 5.

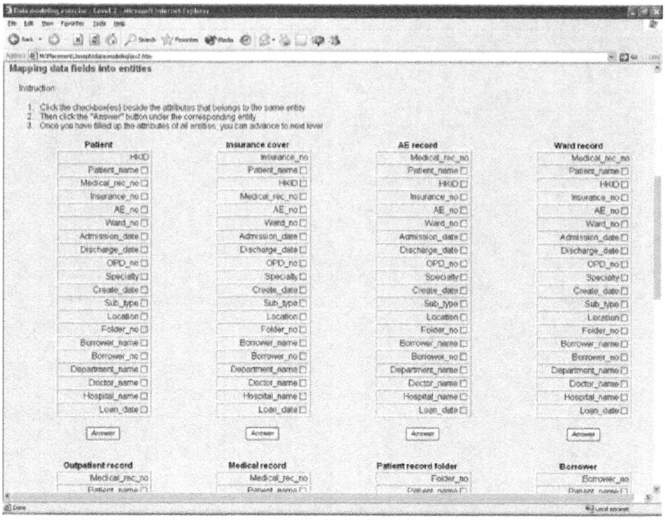

Fig. 5. Identify entity attributes

Step 4: Find relationships between entities. After deriving entities, the user needs to identify their data semantics according to user requirements. Each data semantic must be presented by the relationships among entities as shown in Figure 6.

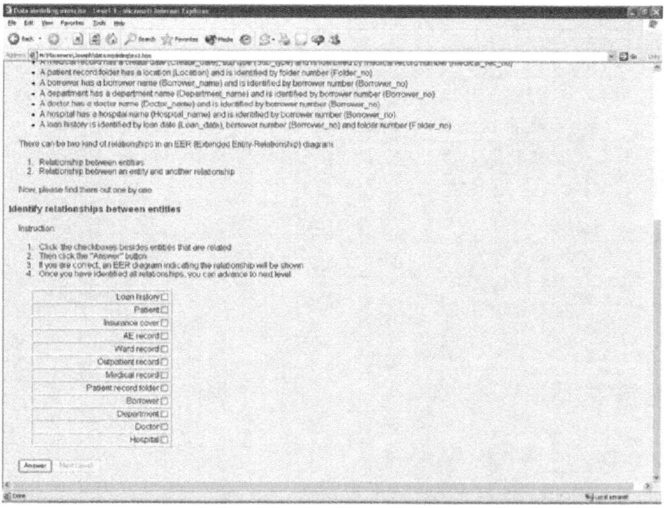

Fig. 6. Identify relationships between entities

Step 5: Find aggregation entity. Aggregation means part of data semantics. When a relationship relates to an entity, we must replace the relationship with an aggregation entity which relates to the entity. As a result, the aggregation consists of components of the relationship and its related entities as shown in Figure 7.

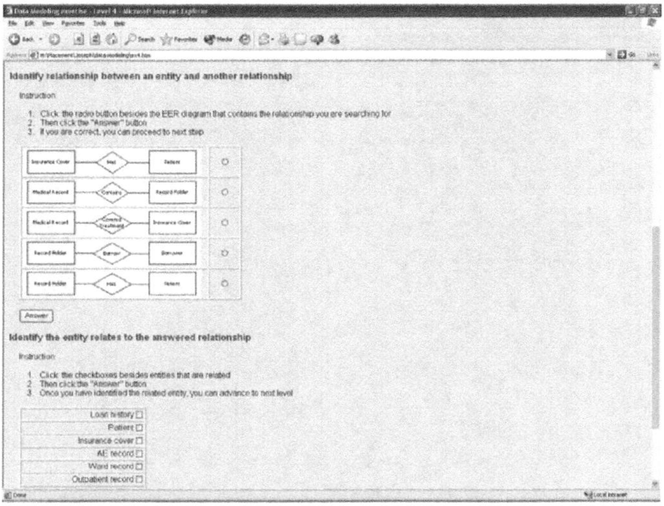

Fig. 7. Replace relationship between an entity and a relationship by aggregation

Step 6: Find cardinality between entities. Cardinality represents data volume relationship between two entities in one-to-one (1:1), one-to-many (1:m) and many-to-many (m:n) relationship. The user can select them among two entities as shown in Figure 8.

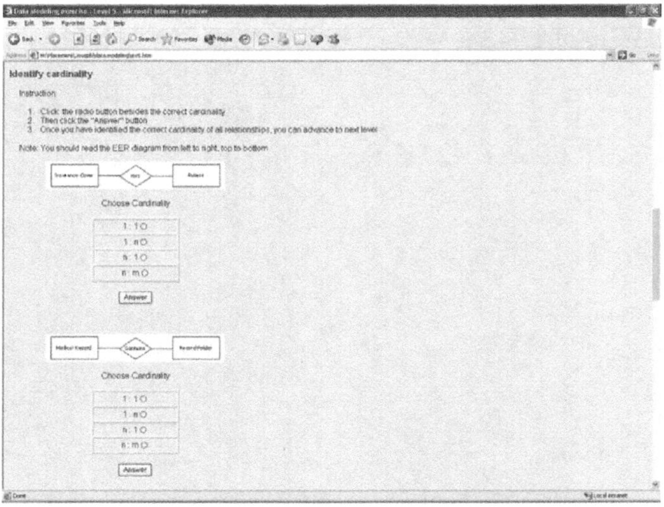

Fig. 8. Select cardinalities among pair of entities

Step 7: Find weak and strong entities. A weak entity key must concatenate its strong entity key in key dependence. The user can select pair of weak entity and strong entity as shown in Figure 9.

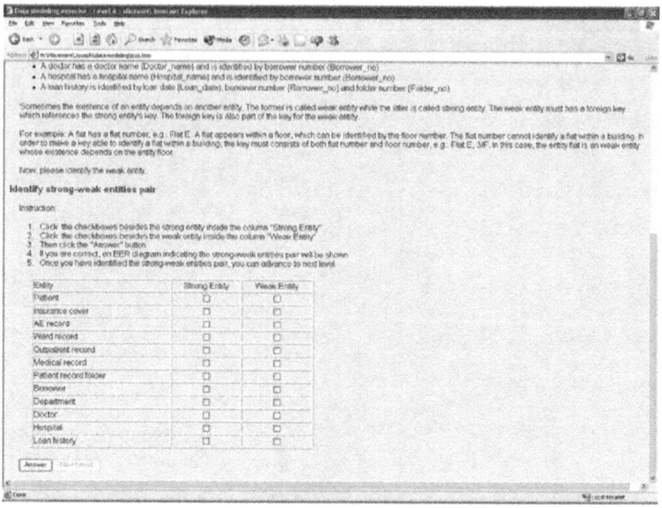

Fig. 9. Select pair of weak and strong entities

Step 8: Find participation among entities. Entity is mandatory related to another entity as total participation, or may not be related to another entity as partial participation. The user can select the mode of participation between two entities as shown in Figure 10.

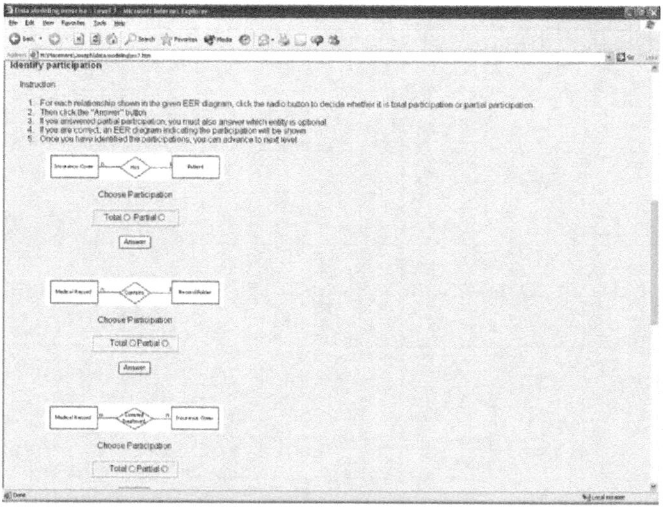

Fig. 10. Select participation mode between two related entities

Step 9: Find generalization among entities. Subclass entities can be generalized into disjoint generalization for mutually exclusive data, or overlap generalization for mutually inclusive data. The user can select them as shown in Figure 11.

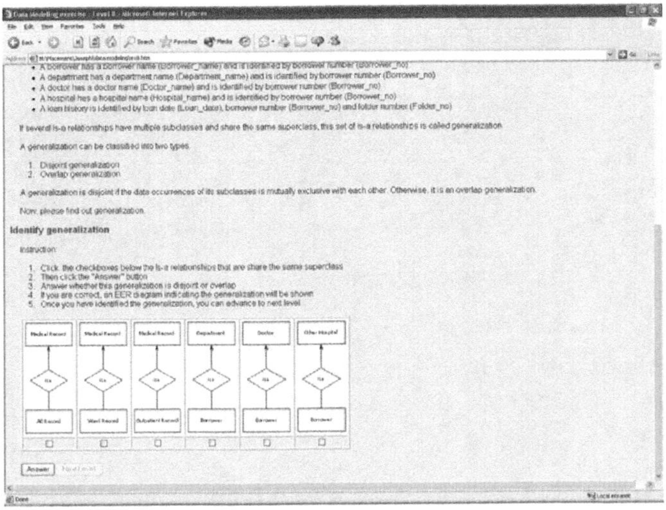

Fig. 11. Identify generalization among entities

Step 10: Find categorization among entities. Superclass entities can be categorized as one superclass entities to a subclass entity in categorization. The user can select the superclass entities and its subclass entity as shown in Figure 12.

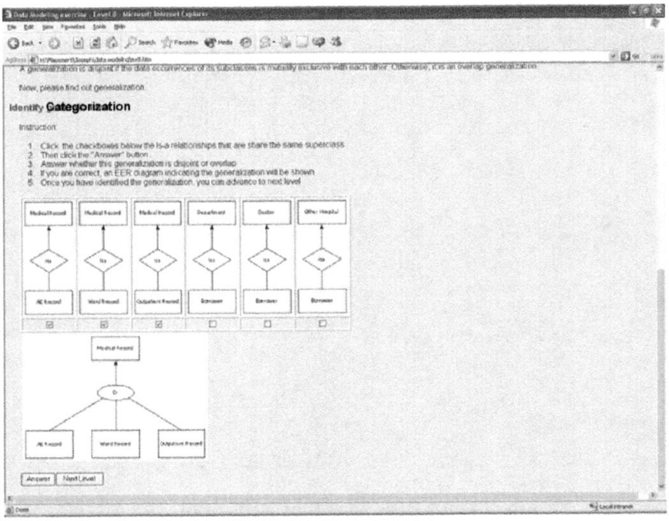

Fig. 12. Select superclass entities and its subclass in categorization

Step 11: Find n-ary relationship. Three entities can be related to each other in n-ary relationship (ternary relationship). The user can select these entities as shown in Figure 13.

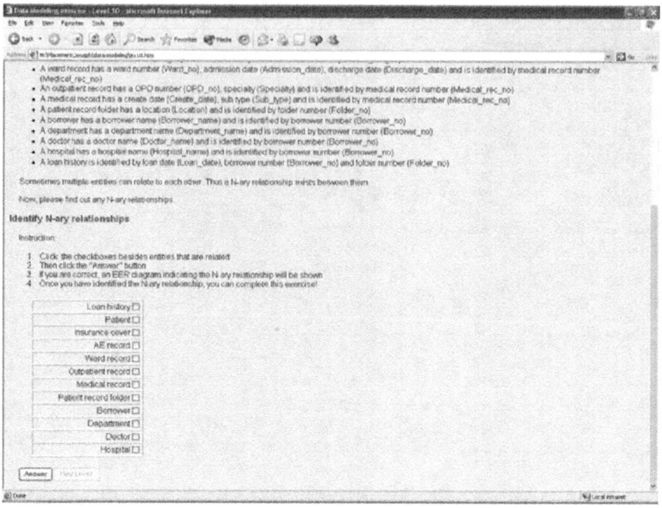

Fig. 13. Select entities for ternary relationship

Step 12: Draw an Extended Entity Relationship Model. Integrate the result of the above steps can be an EER model as shown in Figure 14.

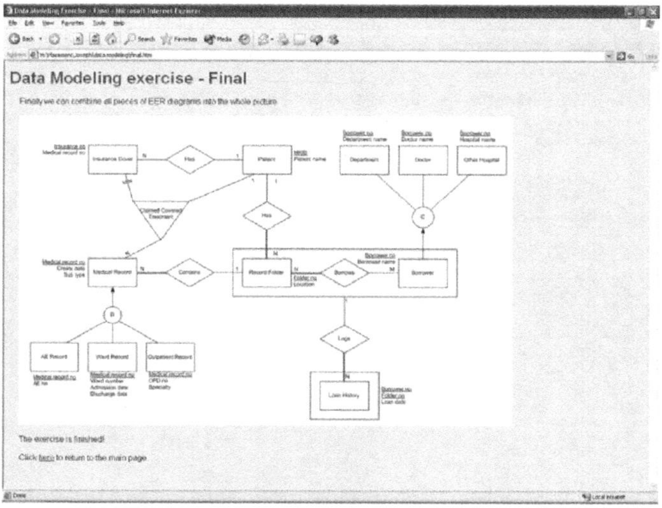

Fig. 14. An EER model as a result of CAI

A survey has been on the above eLearning exercise for a class of 80 with 22 returned forms. This exercise is part of a course on Data Modeling. It aims to use interactivity to guide students to walk through a stepwise procedure of designing a database for their understanding of the data modeling methodology. Students will be guided to follow the methodology step by step until completion.

In our survey, students are asked to rate "1" (totally disagree) to "5" (totally agree) to the following questions:

Q1. Description of "requirements" of data modeling and data normalization
Q2. Description of the "diagrams" of data modeling and data normalization
Q3. Description of the "interactivity" of data modeling and data normalization
Q4. The "usefulness" of eLearning in data modeling and data normalization
Q5. eLearning is better than lectures of data modeling and data normalization
Q6. Overall comments and recommendation of eLearning exercises
Q7. Overall comments and recommendations of cs3462 teaching method

The result is very positive with 3.34 on Q4, and 3.5 on Q5. Written comments for Q6 include:

- "Very good for having a deep understanding of our class. I liked it!"
- "Most of the exercise are easy to understand. However, there are still some that are difficult to understand and find out the answers."
- "Some of the requirements are confused and did not give an explicit explanations that were hard to find answers."
- "Useful to project".
- "good".

5 Conclusion

Computer technology has made a substantial contribution in teaching and learning to higher education during the past few decades. Until recently, as Internet technology promises to become even more pervasive in this arena, there is a paradigm shift from classroom-based teaching to computer-assisted learning, such as CAI. E-learning can be used to supplement classroom teaching as hybrid learning, but not to replace the traditional teaching method. This hybrid learning mode is especially useful for cases, where the teacher and students are geographically wide apart with less chance for human interface.

It is a challenge to build a satisfactory CAI because of the difficulties in guiding users through the CAI operations and the difficulties in measuring the learning effectiveness. In this paper, using the constructivist theory, we presented an effective method of using a set of CAI steps to apply hybrid learning to the study of data modeling technique. The data model of a hospital patent system has been used for illustration. The distinctive advantage is that interactivity can be effectively applied in the teaching and learning process, especially in illustrating the design process of an extended entity relationship model. An simple evaluative survey has been conducted in our study. It is found that the CAI solution taking the hybrid learning approach is welcomed by students.

It is foreseeable that more sophisticated hybrid learning web site, e-Learning Hub and e-Learning Resources Pack would become a trend. These become useful tools to help further enhance the learning effectiveness.

References

1. Chen, P.: The Entity Relationship Model – Toward a unified view of data. ACM Transaction on Database Systems 1(1), 9–36 (1976)
2. Thomas, M.: Constructivism and the Technology of Instruction (a conversation). Lawrence Erlbaum Associates, Hillsdale (1992)
3. Ramsden, P.: Learning to teach in higher education. Routledge, London (1992)
4. Chalmers, D., Fuller, R.: Teaching for learning at university: Theory and practice. Edith Cowan University, Perth (1995)
5. Sage, S., Torp, L.: What does it take to become a teacher of problem-based learning? Journal of Staff Development 18, 32–36 (1997)
6. eLearning.com: http://elearners.com/ (Accessed October 4, 2001)
7. ANSDIT: American National Standard Dictionary of Information Technology (2002), http://www.ncits.org/tc_home/k5htm/Ansdit.htm
8. Gonzalez, A.J., Dankel, D.D.: The Engineering of Knowledge-based Systems: Theory and Practice. Prentice Hall, Englewood Cliffs (1993)
9. Bickford, P.: Interface design: the art of development easy-to-use Software. Academic Press Ltd., London (1997)
10. Elmasri, R., Navathe, S.B.: Fundamentals of Database Systems, 2nd edn. The Benjamin/Cummings Publishing Company, Inc., (1994)

An Audio Instrument Design for Improving Interactive and Cooperative Learning

Cheng-Yu Tsai, Yuan-Hsun Liao, Ming-Hsiang Su, and Pao-Ta Yu

Dept. of CS&IE, National Chung Cheng University, Chiayi, Taiwan,
{tcy97p,lyh96p,sumh,csipty}@cs.ccu.edu.tw

Abstract. An economic approach of self-design instrument for audio devices is proposed to mix the voices of teacher and students such that interactive activities and cooperative learning can be efficiently performed during the lecture hour. For instance, during students running Teams-Games-Tournament (TGT) activity, their voices to response the clear and correct pronunciation about the competitive content are very important. As we know, TGT is one of classroom programs to address the problems of student values, student diversity, and student skills. Therefore, if we can provide a well-design audio environment, we believe that the TGT-related activities can be efficiently handled by the teacher to reach the purpose of TGT. In this self-design approach, two kinds of microphones are considered, one is wired microphone which is suitable for using in steady presentation and the other is wireless microphone which is suitable for using in mobile activities. In this study, we improve the traditional problem of the mixer to provide a low-cost and high scalable audio mixer. "High scalable" means that our system can plug in a variety of audio input devices including Bluetooth wireless microphone. Mainly, we use Bluetooth technology to solve the adaptive problem of multi-branch wireless microphones such that different channels of voices can be accepted in our self-design audio instrument.

Keywords: Cooperative Learning, Teams Games Tournament, Bluetooth.

1 Introduction

For the English teaching with Team Game Tournament (TGT) activity in a small class, the teacher always uses a set of vocabulary cards to guide the game. Especially, the teacher requires the student who joins the game to give the correct pronunciation with respect to the show-up word card in front of the competitive group. During this competitive period, a couple of voices are speaking from students. How to identify who is the winner will highly depend on their pronunciation. Therefore, to mix all the voices from different microphones to let the teacher can adjust the winner is a critical issue to let students feel the fairness about the competition. Consequently, students are willing to continue the learning activity.

Hence, the integration of hardware facilities in classroom especially on the use of sound amplifying systems is an urgent issue nowadays. Basically, a sound amplifying system can mix the sounds from wired and wireless microphones, audio player, and computer. In general, the integration structure of the sound amplifying system inside a classroom can be shown in Fig. 1.

R. Kwan et al. (Eds.): ICHL 2011, LNCS 6837, pp. 357–366, 2011.

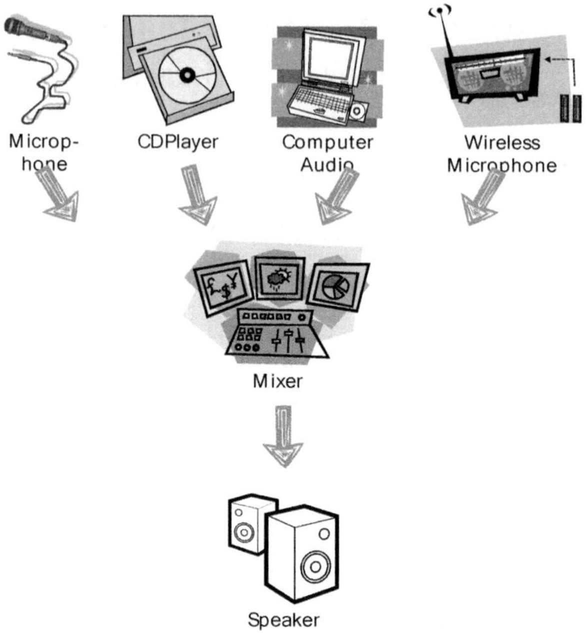

Fig. 1. A possible sound amplifying system used in a classroom

During the competition, the interaction between the teacher and students are quite frequent. In order to give the students having a positive feedback without interruption occurring by unsmooth voice, the better way is to let students hold their own wireless microphones instead of holding wired microphones. However, most of the microphones are already available in their classroom. This motivates us to propose a self-design mixer to integrate those devices together and also possesses a good quality of voices.

The conventional wireless microphone receivers can receive two signals from two different wireless microphones. During the cooperative learning activity, there are at least two teams and each team at least has two members. Therefore, only two microphones are not enough to provide the learning activity. If we use two or three receivers to build the audio environment, this will make the teacher more difficult to handle the devices. Therefore, we need a cheap device to mix more signals instead of an expensive audio mixer with a complicated control panel.

In Section 2, some related studies about cooperative learning are reviewed. In Section 3, the hardware structure of our self-design instrument is proposed. Finally, in Section 4, some conclusions are addressed.

2 Related Studies

Many studies have proven that cooperative learning benefits to students with improving their achievement and learning experience [1-5]. Also, based on mutual cooperation among students, it can enhance students' learning motivation [6]. The five elements of cooperative learning are summarized as follows.

1. Positive Interdependence
   Interdependence is the first element of cooperative learning. Team members can promote positive interdependence via goal setting, resources sharing, role assignment [7, 8].

2. Face-to-Face Promotive Interactions
   A face-to-face promotive interaction is the second element of cooperative learning. Through the guidance of teachers and the arrangements such as experimental groups, group discussions, and group reporting, team members can help each other to exchange information, encourage feedback and progress interaction. Finally, a whole team can be successful in learning and promote to achieve personal goals and group goals [7, 8].

3. Individual Accountability
   Individual accountability is the third element of cooperative learning. In cooperative learning, the group's success is on behalf of each member's success. In the cooperative learning, each member needs to take the responsibility of his/her success to fit the group success. Definitely, this element can reveal the group spirit in contrast to hero-style performance [7, 8].

4. Social Skill
   Social Skill is the fourth element of cooperative learning. During the cooperative activity, each member in a learning group can develop some social skills including effective communication skills, mutual respect and trust.

5. Group Processing
   Group Processing is the fifth element of cooperative learning. During the group processing, students can understand and learn some processing manners with their peer. [8].

Some methods to realize the cooperative learning are summarized as follows [8]:

1. Student's Teams Achievement Division (STAD)
   Slavin developed a cooperative learning model which is suitable for all course contents where students can reply an exact and single answer after they do exercise about those content.

2. Team Game Tournament (TGT)
   Team Game Tournament is very similar with the STAD cooperative learning model. The only different in TGT is a contest with playing a game instead of the examination in STAD.

3. Jigsaws
   Jigsaws were designed by Aronson in 1978. Slavin applied STAD method to improve the dependent structure of Jigsaws in 1980.

4. Learning Together (LT)
   Through the comparison, competition and individual learning effects, Johnson and Johnson developed the Learning Together in 1987. LT stresses on a team goal with emphasizing group tasks and reward.

Therefore, the cooperative learning can enhance the team's solidarity and cohesion. Also, it can increase interaction and enhance each other's feelings to share psychological experience. In this paper, we provide a self-design audio instrument to give a better learning experience such that the concept of cooperative learning mentioned in above can be smoothly achieved. That is, during the cooperative learning activity, the teacher and students can avoid a noisy learning environment.

3 An Audio Instrument Design for Improving Learning Performance

In this section, we propose a design method to overcome the problem occurred in the conventional method. As we know, if we use several wireless microphones from different receivers, the usual problem is the noise interference. Therefore, one of solutions is to increase the scalability of receiver such that only one receiver can receive more wireless microphones. In this system, we also consider Bluetooth microphone is one kind of wireless microphones since we can easily have this device by using a mobile phone.

Before we design each voice module including Bluetooth, we first create a simple mixer system to connect each voice module. The core component of the mixer is the operational amplifier OP-AMP which is mainly used for addition and subtraction. The structure of OP-AMP is shown in Fig. 2 [9].

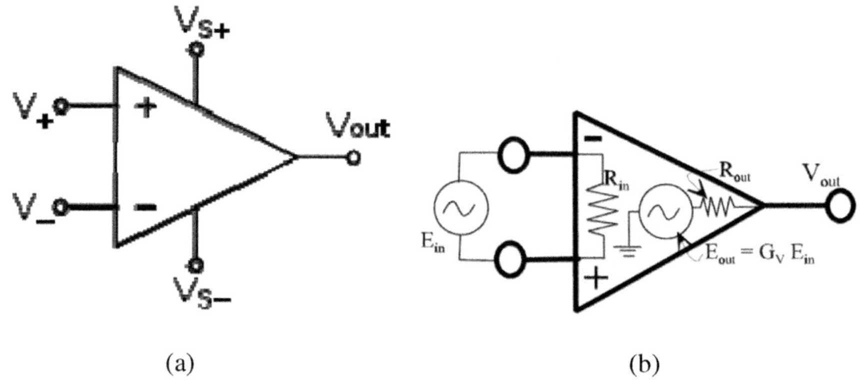

Fig. 2. (a) The circuit symbol of OP AMP (b) The circuit configuration of OP AMP

An ideal operational amplifiers must have the following characteristics [9, 10]:

1. The input resistance R_{IN} would be infinite.
2. The output resistance R_{OUT} would be zero.
3. The voltage gain G_V would be infinite.
4. The bandwidth (how quickly the output will follow the input) would be infinite.
5. If the voltages on the two inputs are equal, then the output voltage is zero (If the output is not zero, it is said to have an offset.)

In order to have three inputs, a revised circuit of summing amplifier is proposed in Fig. 3. The input signal to OP AMP is the addition of three input signals. Those three signals can have different voltages and frequencies to realize the function of mixer.

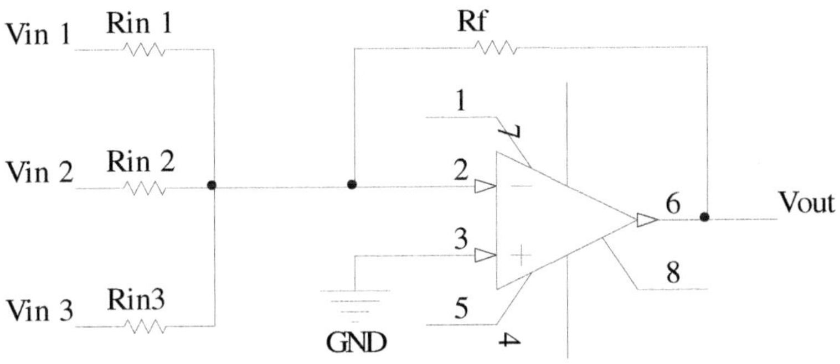

Fig. 3. A summing amplifier: Vout = - (Vin1 + Vin2 + Vin3)

In Fig. 3, the output value is negative. Therefore, a little revise of the circuit is needed to give the positive value. The revised circuit is shown in Fig. 4.

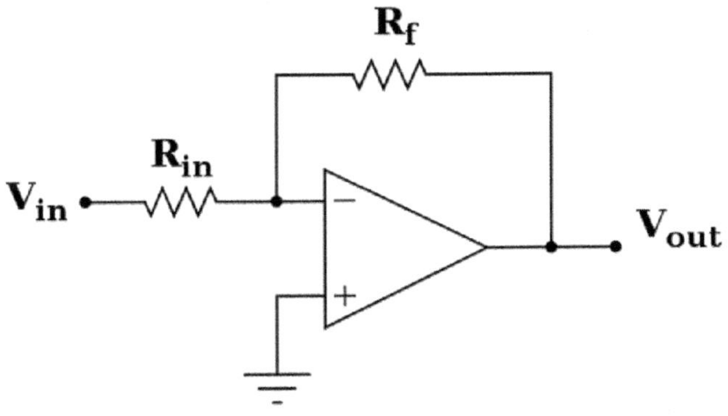

Fig. 4. A unity gain inverting amplifier

As an ideal inverting amplifier operational amplifier, the summation of the current from V_{in} to V- and the current from V- to V_{out} is equal to zero shown in Equation (1).

$$V_{out} = -\frac{R_f}{R_{in}} * V_{in} \tag{1}$$

After we adjust the value of R_f and R_{in}, we can adjust the volume of voice. Therefore, we design two control buttons corresponding to those two values to allow use can control the quality of voice.

In Fig. 5, our design approach is proposed. In this circuit, we try to modulize each amplifier such that we can connect any voice module to form a reasonable self-design instrument. In this figure, we can connect three voice modules, for instance, one wireless microphone, one wire microphone, and one Bluetooth microphone, respectively.

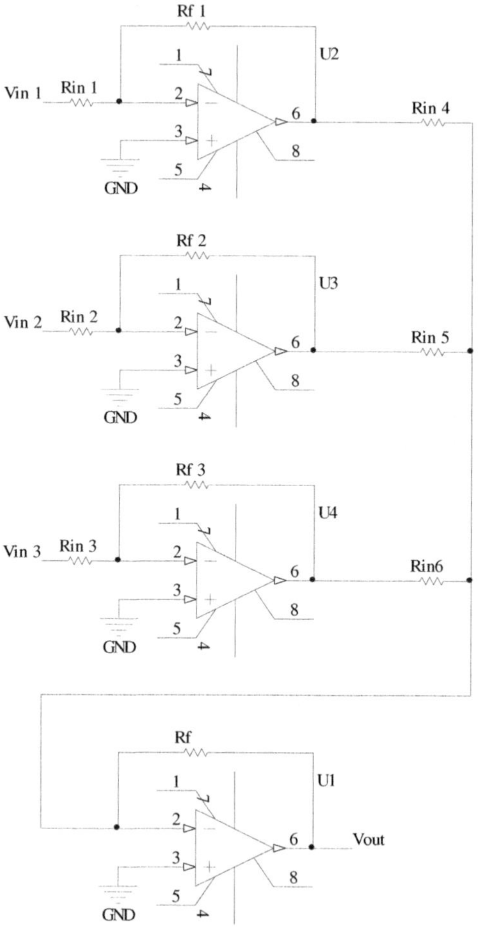

Fig. 5. Our design structure

In this design, we include the Bluetooth voice device which is one of our significant contributions. We take the advantage of the communications technology of Bluetooth to provide users more usability of wireless microphones. Bluetooth possesses a low power (1mW ~ 100mW) and a short distance (10m ~ 100m) communication ability. Bluetooth uses wireless frequencies for the ISM (Industrial, Scientific, and Medical) frequency of 2.402GHz ~ 2.480GHz. ISM band can cut into

79 hopping channels and the width of each channel is 1MHz with hopping 1600 times per second [10, 11]. Therefore, Synchronous Connection-Oriented (SCO) transmission packaged in Bluetooth voice can have more flexible to avoid interference. SCO uses the packet as shown in Table 1[11].

Table 1. SCO packet[11]

Type	Payload Header(Bytes)	User Payload(Bytes)	FEC	CRC	Time Slot Interval
HV1	N/A	10	1/3	No	2
HV2	N/A	20	2/3	No	4
HV3	N/A	30	No	No	6
DV	1 D*	10+(0~9) D*	2/3 D*	Yes D*	V**

Note: * for only the data portion, ** that only voice parts.

Because each SCO channel provides a single point-to-point service, we have to add the same number of Bluetooth modules with the number of Bluetooth microphones. Fig. 6 gives a complete design for realizing our design approach. We can find that this is module design. Users can increase any module as they want.

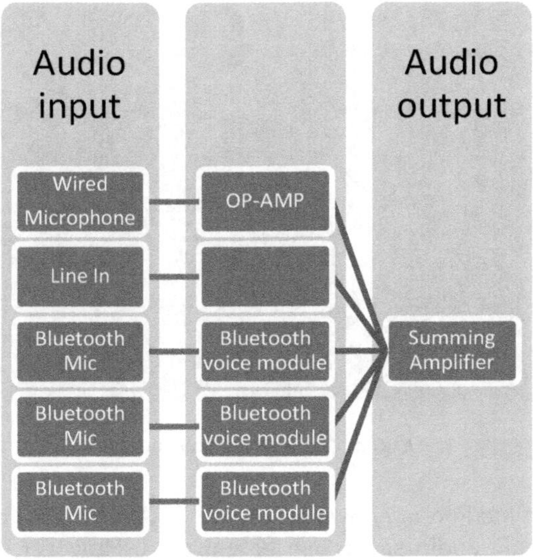

Fig. 6. A complete design structure

The practical design is divided into three modules:

— Mixing module (summing amplifiers) including power supply module.
— Audio amplifier module.
— Bluetooth voice module.

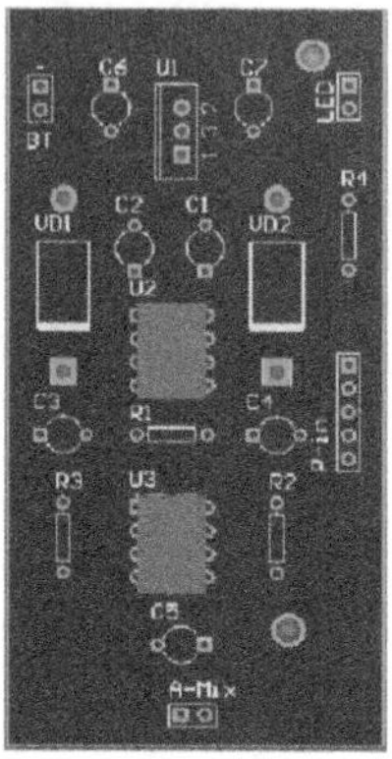

Fig. 7. Mixing module

The mixing module is shown in Fig.7. U1 is a limited voltage protection to avoid excessive DC power input. U2 is the input DC power into the positive and negative DC power output as the supply of the power source for the mixer system. U3 is a summing amplifier via P-in bus to carry the input of audio signal to achieve the operation. Finally, A-Mix can output the mixed audio signal.

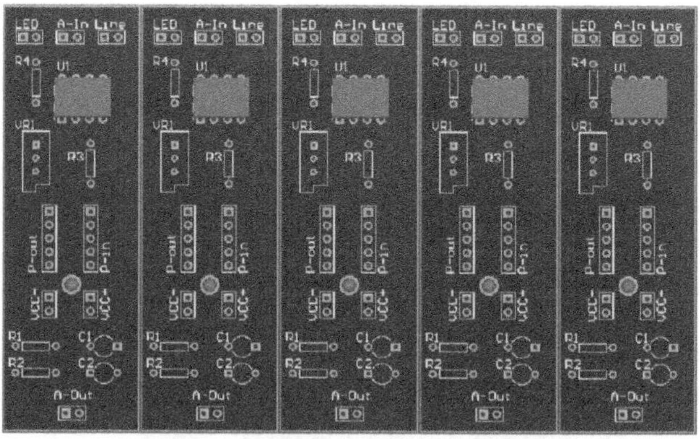

Fig. 8. Audio amplifier module

Audio amplifier module is shown in Figure 8. A-in is the input of audio signal. Through U1, the gain audio signal can be enlarged. However, this function is only workable for the wired microphone. The P-out bus can pass the input signal to the mixer module.

Fig. 9. Bluetooth voice module

Bluetooth voice module is shown in Fig. 9. This module has to connect to DC power input, microphone audio input, audio output cable, and Bluetooth antenna. Finally, the output connects back to the audio amplifier module to complete the structure of voice system.

5 Conclusion

In this paper, we have proposed a self-design approach to integrate an economic instrument for audio environment. This design is not only cheap, but also possesses a reasonable quality of audio for assisting the cooperative learning. In our future research, we will study some appropriate situations using audio instrument to realize the ideal activities of cooperative learning.

References

1. Chiang, L.C.: An Action Research on Integrating Information Technology with Cooperative Learning Strategies into Nature and Life Technology Teaching in Junior High School. Master's degree. National Changhua University (2004)
2. Lee, J.S.: Action research in Science Experiments forCooperative learning to Elementary School. Master's degree. National Hualien Teachers College (2003)
3. Lee, S.J.: Research of the Cooperative Learning Approach in Teaching Introduction to Commerce in the Vocational Senior High School. Master's degree. National Changhua University (2005)
4. Chang, Y.W.: A Study of the Effects of Cooperative Learning on English Learning at Vocational High School. Master's degree. National Changhua University (2003)
5. Williams, K., Harkins, S., Latane, B.: Cooperating Learning and Inclusion. Journal of Personality and Social Psychology 40, 303–311 (1981)
6. Johnson, D.W., Johnson, R.T.: Cooperation in the Classroom. International Book Company., Edina (1990)

7. Hsu, H.C.: Effect of STAD strategy on Motivations, Learning Strategies, and Academic Achievements of Junior High School Students. Master's degree. National Changhua University (2006)
8. Wang, S.C.: Effect of Cooperative Learning Seventh Grader's Motivation and Achievement on the Southern Area in Natural Science. Master's degree. National Changhua University (2007)
9. Jung, W.G.: Op Amp Applications Handbook (2004)
10. The OP AMP, `http://www.physics.arizona.edu/~haar/ADV_LAB/OP_AMP.pdf`
11. Chen, Y.C., Tan, T.H., Wang, H.M., Tsai, W.H.: Performance Evaluation and Analysis of Mandarin Speech Recognition over Bluetooth Communication Environments. In: Proceedings of the 16th Conference on Computational Linguistics and Speech Processing (2004)

Author Index

GPSR Compliance

The European Union's (EU) General Product Safety Regulation (GPSR) is a set of rules that requires consumer products to be safe and our obligations to ensure this.

If you have any concerns about our products, you can contact us on ProductSafety@springernature.com

In case Publisher is established outside the EU, the EU authorized representative is:

Springer Nature Customer Service Center GmbH
Europaplatz 3
69115 Heidelberg, Germany

Batch number: 10844619

Printed by Printforce, the Netherlands